...

THE POWER OF WORDS

A Transformative Language Arts Reader

Social and Personal Transformation Through the Spoken, Written and Sung Word

...

Edited by:
Caryn Mirriam-Goldberg, Ph.D. & Janet Tallman, Ph.D.

Transformative Language Arts Press,
published in cooperation with Mammoth Publications

• • •

Transformative Language Arts Press
P. O. Box 137
Keene, New Hampshire 03431

•

Copyright © 2007 by TLA Press

•

ISBN 0-9761773-5-8

•

expressive arts, creative writing,
storytelling, drama therapy, social change,
poetry therapy, narrative therapy, education

•

Printed in the United States of America

•

Layout by Jeanne Hewell Chambers

•

Cover design by Jennifer Berringer using a
photo of a traditional tribal jingle dress
digitally enhanced by Denise Low.
Photo on back cover by Lucy Winner.

•

Thanks to Irene Borger for her permission to reprint
"Workshop Basics" from *From a Burning House:
The AIDS Project Los Angeles Writers Workshop Collection*,
Washington Square Press, 1996.

•

"Old Goat" in Pat Schneider's essay, "You Are Already a Writer,"
originally appeared in *The North Dakota Quarterly*, Summer,
2006, reprinted here with the permission of the author.

• • •

ACKNOWLEDGMENTS

• • •

This book was a labor of love shared by many people, most notably all the contributors who gave of their time, talent and words: David Abram, Sharon Bray, Irene Borger, Karen Campbell, Mandy Carr, Francis Charet, Patricia Fontaine, Linda Garrett, Jackson Gillman, Greg Greenway, Debbie Harris-Mead, Allison Adelle Hedge Coke, Carol Henderson, Yvette Hyater-Adams, Kelley Hunt, Lana Leonard, Katt Lissard, Perie Longo, Denise Low, Christopher Maier, Shaun McNiff, Deidre McCalla, Nancy Morgan, Caren Neile, Becci Goodall, Rhonda Patzia, Nina Ricker, Pam Roberts, Gail Rosen, Nancy Shapiro, Jim Sparrell, Pat Schneider, Janet Tallman, Katie Towler, Shelley Vermilya, Anna Viadero, and Scott Youmans. These visionary transformative language artists, scholars and activists span three countries, and dozens of communities.

A stellar volunteer team produced and marketed this book: Jeanne Chambers did the spectacular layout for the book; Jennifer Berringer did the gorgeous cover design that inspired us, using a photo created by Denise Low. Bill Beardslee, Pamela Koeppel, and Erin Emerick proof-read and helped sustain us through the project. Scott Youmans helped us set up the new TLA Network website. The TLA Network courageously took on this project as one of its first initiatives. Nehassaiu deGannes and Avery Otto, co-facilitators of the network, helped me keep the faith with their good insights, humor and compassion.

I especially thank my co-editor, Janet Tallman; Janet's deep understanding of the power of words brought to the editing process great clarity and wisdom. Janet's keen sight of where TLA has traveled and her vision of where it can and should go next are also great sources of inspiration and guidance for TLA in general. She also gave me marvelous support, direction and insight during the editing process.

Finally, special thanks to the faculty in Goddard College's Individualized MA program, particularly Margo MacLeod, who first suggested that we create a TLA Reader. Other Goddard faculty and deans who were instrumental in helping TLA develop include Danielle Boutet, Eduardo Aquino, Susan Fleming, Danielle LaFleur-Brooks, Sara Norton, Shelley Vermilya, Suzanne Richman, Jim Sparrell, Francis Charet, Lise Weil, Ellie Epp, Katt Lissard, Tomas Kalmar, Joy Sawyer, Ralph Lutts, Nehassaiu deGannes, and Karen Campbell. Goddard College, in supporting and nurturing TLA development since 2000, served as the container for TLA coming into view.

Apologies to anyone I've forgotten.

-- Caryn Mirriam-Goldberg

Lawrence, Kansas * May, 2007

THE POWER OF WORDS
A TRANSFORMATIVE LANGUAGE ARTS READER
SOCIAL AND PERSONAL TRANSFORMATION THROUGH THE SPOKEN, WRITTEN AND SUNG WORD

• • •

CONTENTS

• • •

WORLDS OF WORDS: REALMS OF
TRANSFORMATIVE LANGUAGE ARTS

•

SNAPSHOTS: A DAY IN THE LIFE OF TRANSFORMATIVE LANGUAGE ARTS

• • •

*Words are intrinsically powerful. They are magical. By means
of words can one bring about physical change in the universe.
By means of words can one quiet the raging weather, bring
forth the harvest, ward off evil, rid the body of sickness and
pain, subdue an enemy, capture the heart of a lover, live
in the proper way, and venture beyond death.*
- N. Scott Momaday

• • •

*Of course, the pen is mightier than the sword.
But the pen must be very sharp.*
- Grace Paley at the 2005 TLA Conference, Goddard College

• • •

Language can do what it can't say.
- William Stafford

• • •

...

INTRODUCTION

...

THE EMERGENCE OF TRANSFORMATIONAL LANGUAGE ARTS

Caryn Mirriam-Goldberg, Ph.D.

• • •

A CALL TO TRANSFORMATIVE LANGUAGE ARTISTS

You tell stories or help others tell stories because you need to, because you know that the story can grow in the listener, and sometimes even the teller, new shoots of understanding, branches of connection, and a canopy of healing. You write because you found that the shortest distance between yourself and where you need to go is across the lines on a page. You do spoken word performance, help others craft community plays, or write and perform songs for the moment you might reach someone. You organize debate for underserved, inner-city youth, conduct anthropological studies of the spoken word, record oral histories for families, or recite poems into the wind because you know there is something that our words hold that can transform the teller and the listener.

This kind of transformation is what a new academic field and emerging profession, Transformative Language Arts, is all about. Transformative Language Arts (TLA) is a meeting ground for those involved in social and personal transformation through the spoken, written and sung word, facilitating storytelling with people in prison, writing workshops for underserved youth, dramatic monologues for elders, or collaborative theatre for community building.

TLA draws perhaps most obviously from literature, creative writing, education, psychology, mythology, and social welfare. TLA looks at the roots of the oral tradition; the pedagogy and psychology involved in effective group facilitation, individual coaching; social change trends and movements related to spoken, written and sung words; and literature and creative writing to create avenues of voice for the voiceless. It also honors the traditions of storytelling, Playback Theatre, poetry therapy, narrative therapy, songwriting for social change, stand-up comedy for diversity, debate and forensics for empowerment, dialogue as a vehicle for drawing diverse voices into civil exchange, healing stories and more.

For those of us who love the spoken and written word, TLA provides a framework to explain what we do without having to shave off what doesn't usually fit into one box or another. By naming this field and calling people together, those of us who facilitate, perform, educate and lead can find each other, and through such a discovery, learn more of who we are and what possibilities exist for our work in the world. By sharing the collective wisdom of storytellers, writers, actors and playwrights, activists, community leaders and healers, we can learn more about recovering and celebrating our selves, forging and keeping connections with others and the earth, finding and naming what gives our lives meaning. Such wisdom encompasses how we create our livings and our lives, including everything from facilitating workshops to grant-writing to the ethics of our work to the art of self-care.

In the classroom or board room, at the clinic or retreat center, TLA also bridges organizations, training programs, and models of workshop and coaching delivery that often evolve without the benefit of cross-pollination. There are many valuable educational and training opportunities such as Goddard College's Transformative Language Arts MA concentration -- the first TLA program of its kind, founded in 2000, or Amherst Writers and Artists training and affiliation; and organizations such as the National Storytelling Network, the National Association for Poetry Therapy, and the Writer-in-the-School Alliance. The newly-created TLA Network, a professional organization for TLA, focuses on networking and right livelihood through TLA. Already, TLA-focused courses and essays – such as the ones here -- are coming into being, very evident at the annual TLA conference – "The Power of Words" – held each fall at Goddard College to gather together storytellers, writers, activists, community leaders, artists, healers, therapists, spoken word artists, actors, and singers. Performing, facilitating, organizing, creating and teaching are all life-long arts with life-long learning curves, and we benefit greatly from each other's company.

This collection -- the first TLA reader -- is a landmark book, gathering questions, ideas, experiences, studies, challenges and possibilities for those who are changing the world, one word, one story, one performance, workshop, or coaching session at a time. In coming together, we also break through the artificial boundaries between the spoken word and the written word as well as between the too-often compartmentalized literary, psychological and political arenas. To paraphrase singer-songwriter Cris Williamson, we each are the changer and the changed, the ones who witness and are witnessed by the stories that change our lives.

Roots and Branches

Every time I tell a story, I am putting out a call to community. A story presumes a community of listeners who will recognize some experience that they have lived or can imagine living in the narrative. It is a call and response (what in Haitian storytelling is known as a Crick-Crack) where the teller tosses out a community-gathering, a community-presuming device, a.k.a. a story, in the hope that the group of listeners will respond by becoming we. To the extent that a "we" responds this means that there is amongst the sea of "I"s sufficient shared assent to the virtual experience of the story that each relaxes the contraction of their I-ness to "we" themselves within the shared world of this story.

\- Christopher Maier

In Christopher Maier's eloquent statement, we see how TLA has its roots, most of all, in the oral tradition of call and response, using stories to put out a call to community. The impulse to draw upon the written, spoken and sung word for community-building and personal development is ancient, mythic and evident in most, if not all, cultures over history from the Australian Aborigine tradition of "song-lines" that connect specific places with specific songs to the evolution of theatre for social change in contemporary American culture.

What makes certain kinds of language endure – such as epic poems like Geoffrey Chaucer's *Canterbury Tales,* the social action songs of Woody Guthrie, the poetry of H.D., or the novels of Toni Morrison – in addition to the quality of the writing – has to do with the mythic dimensions of these works of art. The *Canterbury Tales,* Guthrie's *This Land is Our Land*, Morrison's *Song of Solomon* and H.D.'s epic poetry tell us something vital about who we are, for good and bad, as individuals and as members of communities; and in this way, these works of literature act as agents of mythology. Myth, the building block for any culture because it encapsulates and transmits cultural values and norms, according to Roland Barthes, acts as a "dominant cultural narrative" as well as "a type of speech" (109). TLA often plays out as individuals and communities extending, challenging, subverting or creating anew the "dominant cultural narratives" -- the underlying stories that shape their identity and life choices -- as a way to live with greater clarity, authenticity, and meaning.

These roots feed expansive branching. TLA is evident in many of the obvious places to look for it: storytelling festivals, literary fiction, poetry of protest, spiritual memoirs, theatre for social change. In our culture at large, we can trace deep roots of TLA, even in film, TV, and other media arts when we look for ways in which language is used to catalyze growth for individuals and/or communities. In academia, there are many modalities of TLA easy enough to find in pockets of psychology, social work, literature, creative writing, education and pedagogy, and all manner of the expressive arts courses and veins of study. In music, we can hear in many rap and hip-hop songs as well as traditional folk music and many other forms of music ways in which the sung word helps a people know a bit more about who they are and how they're supposed to live.

This collection of writing draws from wide horizons also, looking for TLA in many likely as well as unlikely places. Katie Towler writes of the Bread and Puppet Theatre Troupe in Vermont, which not only uses some of the most vividly theatrical props and costumes to shed light on social issues but, true to its name, feeds all audience members hearty bread after all shows to give people a taste of everyday sustenance. Christopher Maier and Caren Neile each write about storytelling from various angles when looking at its role in community. Shelley Vermilya explores memoir as a political act in academia. The songwriters interviewed -- Greg Greenway, Kelley Hunt, and Deidre McCalla -- each discuss the role of music in community and cultural change. Allison Hedge Coke shows us how to use TLA in the face of both the beautiful and the horrendous, and David Abram speaks of a rejuvenation of language through awakening our senses.

Throughout this book, we visit many realms in which TLA is present such as in Sharon Bray's writing workshops using the Amherst Writers and Artists model. Yvette Hyater-Adams shows how TLA can inform and shape coaching, and how such an approach can reach those who wouldn't feel as home in writing circles. Denise Low looks at the Native American roots of TLA, and how TLA is still very evident in community ceremony and writing that fosters a greater sense of tradition and greater possibilities for survival of Native peoples. Nancy Morgan writes of TLA in a cancer ward, and how it can reach and help not just patients, but families, chaplains, nurses, doctors. Scott Youmans tells of facilitating a spiritual writing group for incarcerated men.

In all the essays and snapshots in this collection, we see TLA in classrooms and bookstores, on stages and at libraries, out in the field and out on the street, at camps and in urban centers. Taken altogether, this collection also shows us how TLA can be effective with multiple populations: teens, people with serious illness, children, the elderly, women in transition, men in treatment, people with HIV or AIDS, individuals in therapy or coaching, and groups immersed in political action or community-making.

The roots of call and response —-of saying, singing, writing something to reach out and touch someone, to make contact, to make community, and to make, out of this exchange, some meaning -- echo through all the writing in this book. Hopefully, the conversation goes on to another level of call and response between this text and you, the reader.

TLA AND SOCIAL CHANGE

One of my most profound experiences with TLA and social change happened with a group of people whose diversity showed clear down to our shoes: farm boots; pink, high-topped sneakers; tasseled, polished loafers; Birkenstock sandals; hand-beaded moccasins; high heels from Italy; and even some bare feet. We were Republican farmers, Native American activists, environmental agitators, Evangelical career women, angry history buffs, hippie artists, and Jewish writers who found each other to fight a proposed highway route that would devastate farmland and farmers, Native American sacred sites, native prairie and woodlands, historic sites, and many homes.

What happened at our first meeting unified us for many years to come – and it happened simply because everyone stood up to tell his/her story. Farmers stood up and wept. An Evangelical Christian told deeply-moving stories about people killed on the old highway. A Lakota man explained that he knew where the sacred sites were, but he couldn't tell us because of how much it would endanger them to be found. A hippie artist spoke softly about how much she loved the land. A history buff and retired physician told of the covered wagon tracks on his land. A farm wife told of the five generations of her people who farmed that land. The stories catalyzed a group that grew to 300 in membership, and after a four-year struggle, got the highway department to shift its proposed freeway.

This act of exchanging stories was also what Don Adams and Arlene Goldbard would call "community cultural development." As they write in their book, *Community, Culture and Globalization:*

> Community cultural development practice is based on the understanding that culture is a crucible in which human resilience, creativity and autonomy are forged. As everyone knows, an unexamined life is indeed possible: any of us might move through our lives in a trance of passivity, acted upon but never acting as free beings. The root idea of community cultural development is the imperative to fully inhabit our human lives, bringing to consciousness the values and choices that animate our communities and thus equipping ourselves to act -- to paraphrase Paulo Freire -- as subjects in history rather than merely its objects. (15)

TLA can bind together communities, help communities begin to examine their core values, and catalyze communities to action. I once witnessed members of a Latino intergenerational writing group about ten years ago in Kansas City, MO. -- with people ages 8 to 84 participating – spring into action when someone noticed that the stories being shared in this group were not anything like the stories people encountered in American culture at large. Such a realization led to a standing-room-only reading, complete with local Mariachi band, at The Writers Place in Kansas City, a facility usually featuring established regional or national writers. Grandmothers read about leaving Mexico, grandchildren read about learning English, women read letters honoring their ancestors, men read of falling in love. Stories, poems, plays, vignettes -- all vessels of culture -- enable listeners and readers to expand their world, to move beyond the barriers that separate cultures into a clearer kind of seeing.

But what we create with words also can bring a greater sense of purpose and greater power to act and shape the future to the writer too. As Shelley Vermilya writes in her essay, "Writing one's life and then framing it in a social and political context disrupts power dynamics and systems of oppression, individually and institutionally, and places a value on individual experience" (65). In writing, telling, acting out, and generally finding a page or stage to reflect back to us our stories, we see more accurately how we've adopted institutional, cultural, family, or even self-imposed myths that have limited us. We also write or tell or sing our way into challenging or subverting such myths, or writing them anew.

This story is told vividly and musically in Janet Tallman's essay on how the music, poetry, images and words of the 60s not only broke through old myths of how to live, but sustained new and somewhat enduring stories that inform our culture deeply even today.

Other essays in this book investigate from other angles how we dismantle the mythology that chokes us, and replace it with or transform it into more life-living stories that show us how to survive and thrive through what we make on our own and in community out of words. Rhonda Patzia's essay about people with Multiple Sclerosis writing about incontinence illuminates how the written word, and having good witnesses, can transform shame into humor and fellowship. Anna Viadero writes of the importance and necessity of letting those who are often invisible to culture-at-large

-- the elderly -- have their voice heard too. Jim Sparrell's article on narrative therapy shows the political and social impact of changing a story to change a life. The interview with Gail Rosen focuses on how her telling of a Holocaust survivor's story at Auschwitz and other locales brings about greater meaning for all involved in the project.

Our words can also help us connect with the more-than-human world, to coin a phrase from David Abram's book, *The Spell of the Sensuous: Perception and Language in a More-Than-Human World.* In unfolding how our written language has distanced us from the earth, and from our own sensory experience, he calls for us to consider a renewed and renewing way of using our language to re-ignite our relationship with the land, and with our own humanness:

> Our task is that of *taking up* the written word, with all of its potency, and patiently, carefully, writing language back into the land. Our craft is that of releasing the budded, earthly intelligence of our words, freeing them to respond to the speech of the things themselves -- to the green uttering-froth of leaves from the spring branches. (273)

As Denise Low writes in her essay, our words have a profound effect upon how we live as well as how we live on and for the earth: "Through words, humans connect to the realms above, and as intermediaries, they speak for the Earth itself. This is a serious duty. When we use language in healing patterns, we heal ourselves, our communities, and our beautiful planet" (232).

In exploring how we can better live among those in our communities and eco-communities, many of these essays celebrate the connections we make through TLA with our communities. TLA calls us to look at the big picture -- the social conditions that drive so many people into isolation, poverty, mental illness, addiction, hopelessness, and silence -- as well as the deepest truths that transform an individual story from one about an object to one speaking directly to us.

TLA AND PERSONAL DEVELOPMENT

When I first started doing community writing workshops, I thought people would come because they wanted to foster greater craft in their poetry and stories. But when a group of men and women came to sit around a table with me in a vacant downtown loft in Lawrence, Kansas, what I saw were people who came because of what writing could bring to their lives. They were here because they found meaning in what they wrote in late night journals or early morning notebooks, on the backsides of junk mail while waiting in doctor's offices or in small note pads while passing the time on buses or planes.

In the 15 years that I've been facilitating writing workshops for personal growth, there's been an upsurge of these kinds of workshops and a great many fabulous books also on writing for growth and development thanks to the likes of Pat Schneider, Anne Lamott, Natalie Goldberg, Deena Metzger, Susan Woolridge, Nancy Mellon, and dozens of others. Additionally, many scholars, facilitators, therapists, and writers in the fields of narrative therapy, poetry therapy, expressive arts therapies, drama therapy, psychodrama, and many related disciplines have contributed to a rich base of literature and science that shows us why individual expression – aloud and on the page – has something to do with health and healing.

Shaun McNiff, one of the leading writers and scholars on the expressive arts, in his essay on art and the imagination, illustrates the ways in which, "How we express ourselves may have more of an impact than what we say. As with music, the words become agents of transformation, shamanic horses that carry expression and transport people to change" (89).

These shamanic horses, whether traveling by voice or page, in groups or alone, serve those who ride them in many ways. For people who have experienced marginalization because of class, race, sexual orientation, physical difference, religion, ethnicity or other reasons, TLA not only makes visible invisible worlds, but it helps those speaking, writing, singing out loud to hear themselves more clearly, and in doing so, to cultivate and unearth greater meaning in their day to day life.

Yet TLA is also a vital private tool, something people can do on their own to maintain health in body and soul. For those especially facing life-challenging illnesses, such as cancer and chronic mental or physical disease, TLA already is a vital part of helping them navigate their harder moments. Nancy Morgan should know as someone who walks the halls of the Lombardi Cancer Center, handing out journals and facilitating writing sessions and groups. She is someone who found TLA in her own way after losing close family members to cancer, and she now serves patients, doctors, nurses, chaplains, and families. She explains, "Writing is a simple, noninvasive, accessible tool to manage emotions and transcend the psychological and physiological effects of cancer" (257) in her essay on the research behind TLA in this context.

The simple tool is also regularly applied to the deepest losses as a way not to bury, but to witness the "life-long gashes," according to Carol Henderson, who facilitates writing groups for parents who have lost a child and who has written a memoir on the loss of her own child: "Writing helps to shift perspectives, increase understanding, give fresh meaning to what we all know is a life-long struggle, a life-long gash in our hearts" (393).

Francis Charet's important essay on emotional disclosure helps us to be more mindful of our cultural context when it comes to the value of expression and disclosure as a pathway toward healing. Drawing on some of the recent research on TLA, he shows us that how we use TLA varies in different cultures, and that even defining words like "health" and "transformation" is best left to the people telling their stories, reading their poetry, acting out their plays, singing their songs.

Furthermore, we see that TLA is not just about fixing what's broken. There are storytelling, singing, writing, and other TLA-related services and groups for people moving through life transitions from every angle, whether a middle-aged woman is writing about her spiritual awakening or a fifth-grader is creating his first play on the beauty of tree frogs. We can see in these essays examples of TLA for people of all backgrounds, all generations evident in essays on working with teens by Mandy Carr, Nina Ricker, and Rebecca Goodall as well as Jeanne Hewell Chambers's piece of helping elders tell their life stories.

Why it works surely has something to do with where those shamanic horses that take us, through how we use language, beyond literal meanings and into new ways to inhabit our lives more fully; to discover, in the words of Pam Roberts, how "we are more than our stories" and how, to paraphrase Pat Schneider, we are all already writers of our own lives (434 and 387).

As Perie Longo sums up in her essay on poetry as therapy, the effects of such transformative experiences linger long after the experience: "Perhaps that is the main therapeutic benefit of poetry; words remain forever for they are sound waves. Wherever we go, they follow us, from room to room, unconsciousness to consciousness, denial to acceptance, sorrow to joy. And hopefully to health" (62-63).

RIGHT LIVELIHOOD AND TLA

A few years ago, I spent some time at an eco-village in North Carolina where everyone made most things out of what was on hand: trees, dirt, rocks, water. The mountains there were peppered with little round or curvy homes painted in bright colors gardens planted on every level, with about 60 people living off the grid and generating their own electricity and heat. I realized that those of us creating our livelihoods through TLA are living off the mainstream economic grid, building the houses of our work out of the trees, rocks, dirt, water of our experiences, perceptions, knowledge, connections, creating livelihoods that provide shelter and sacred space. We are making our Right Livelihood as we make TLA.

"Right Livelihood" is a Buddhist term that generally connotes working in an ethical way that takes into account the effect of our actions on the world. Marti Beddoe, founder of Right Livelyhoods, gives a definition of Right Livelihood in relation to other steps on the eightfold path that isn't just about enlightenment in the Buddhist sense but speaks to any of us purusing TLA:

> Right Livelihood means to avoid any life that brings shame. It embodies the other seven steps along the eightfold path to enlightenment: Right Thought involves love and devotion through work. Right Mindfulness means consciously choosing your path and your work. Right Understanding evolves from consciously choosing work that is the best of ourselves and having knowledge of our values. Right Speech implies compassion relating to others through our work. Right Concentration means doing work with care and intense awareness and love. Right Action implies doing your work and having no attachment to the results. Right Effort is about choosing work you can do a whole life, keeping yourself in a state of constant learning and beginner's mind. The bottom line is this: work that embodies love, devotion, and service is as much an attitude as the actions we take. (*Conscious Choice*)

The eightfold path resonates with many of the values inherent with TLA (particularly Right Speech) that aim us toward "love, devotion, and service" in treating our life's work as our community service, personal development and livelihood.

When I contemplate what Right Livelihood is in relation to TLA, I see five areas of life-long education, work and play for us:

1. Ethics in Action
2. Engaging Diversity
3. The Art of Self-Care
4. The Art of Facilitation
5. Sustainable Business Practices

Each of these areas spills into the other, and yet all are necessary to pay attention to, continually learn about, question, and through questioning, to quote, Rainer Maria Rilke, "Live your questions now, and perhaps even without knowing it, you will live along some distant day into your answers."

Jim Sparrell's essay on ethics helps us to see the ethical dimensions of doing TLA as inherently community-building and tied to creating a more just world. In understanding ethics, especially in the absence of a codified profession and in the context of community values, Sparrell explains,

> An underlying value implicit in the ethical code for TLA is that TLA is a practice of *connection* and *community*. In this regard, practitioners of TLA seek to remain related to a wider community of those engaged in TLA work to hone their skills, provide support, critique process, evaluate methodology, share techniques and ideas, and to provide consultation on ethical dilemmas that will arise. Community engagement is also evident in the TLA practitioner seeking to know other kinds of therapists, educators, spiritual advisors,

artists, writers, activists, and professionals in their geographical area so that referrals can be made in an informed, supportive way, not just from a phonebook. TLA practice works to resist community fragmentation. (283-284)

I also see ethics as bordering, if not living in the same territory as what we often refer to as a multicultural approach to TLA: to both use TLA to overcome oppression in our communities as well as to engage with diverse communities, letting those we encounter name and claim their own stories rather than posing as the voice for the voiceless. Since TLA is so much about letting and listening to people speak in their own voice, telling their own truths in the language most authentic to them, I don't think it's possible to be a life-long student, facilitator and artist of TLA without also being committed to continually learning about diversity. Such learning and listening create the atmosphere for effective social change as actor Danny Glover explains:

There has to be a level of trust and honesty, and a place where people of color can trust the dominant culture. There has to be a language of respect for the contributions of each other's cultures. It's not in the form of a monoculture; what globalization brings is a monoculture. The strength that we have is understanding, appreciating, and embracing our diversity. Trust begins with celebration and the building of another language. ("Danny Glover")

TLA not only gives us an opportunity to build this language "...or respect for the contributions of each other's cultures," but an ethical imperative to cultivate whatever trust, honesty and open space are necessary to make room for the voices not heard in dominant culture: the voices of people of color, of women, of people with different physical and mental abilities than the mainstream norm, of children and elders, of any community or individual too often making their lives and having their say in cultural margins.

Jeanne Hewell Chambers and Karen Campbell's essay on the ethics of writing on our own and others' experiences raises essential questions. Patricia Fontaine and Karen Campbell's essay on the good ambushes in anti-oppression work gives us essential things to consider as we navigate differences of class, race, appearance, learning styles, ethnicity, religious traditions, sexual orientation, disability and other aspects that challenge all facilitators, consultants, artists and coaches of TLA to deeply and continuously consider how to reach more than just the usual suspects. Lana Leonard's storytelling work for restorative justice introduces us to an effective tool in restoring community as well as justice.

Irene Borger's questions for consideration when facilitating a workshop provide a template for deep contemplation for those who feel called to help others write, tell stories, make theatre, and exchange words aloud or on the page. As she writes, "The workshop that *you* organize (or organize *and* lead) will be a reflection of your particular constellations of beliefs, goals, education, worldview, passions, quirks, limitations, aesthetics, teaching and learning style (as well, of course, as the needs, desires, aesthetics, limitations, etc. of the people with whom you work)" (363). My essay, " 'It Unfolds Before Whoever Walks Along It': Making a Living Through TLA," further speaks to what it takes to do this work as a profession, including the life-long art of facilitation.

Along this life-long art, Right Livelihood also speaks to how we care for ourselves in body and soul, and in balance with our own health and well-being as well as our work in our communities. With a profession emerging like TLA, in which there are few full-time jobs with health benefits and the frequent pressures of making ends meet while meeting obligations, this focus on sustaining us as we help sustain others is integral to Right Livelihood.

All that said, there's still the business side of doing TLA, which, done well, not only puts bread on our table but joy in our heart and life in our communities. Given the bad name that business has in some corners, especially considering the dehumanizing and anti-environmental practices of so many corporations that give investigative journalists ample material to write about -- it's important to also cultivate sustainable practices of doing TLA as a business. Such practices illuminate for us how making a living need not pit us against our own values. It can connect us to our innate sense of what we believe and hold most sacred.

For any of us engaged in TLA -- whether we're storytellers doing gigs at schools and libraries, writers coaching inner-city teens to write their own poems, or consultants advising community groups on developing multicultural theater programs -- we're also artists of facilitation: how to facilitate the language arts in ourselves and in our communities. From being artists, we know that learning how to create is also a life-time endeavor, something that continues beyond any training, education, peer groups or other learning.

A DAY IN THE LIFE: TLA IN PRACTICE

Many of us involved in TLA are here because we learn best through stories: imagery and rhythm help us understand something new and how it relates to our lives. To model what TLA is, we offer up these "snapshots," moments of TLA in action in many settings, with various populations, guided by different approaches. "A Day in the Life," besides being the title of a great Beatles song, is a glimpse into TLA, one moment at a time. These snapshots also provide a diversity of ways to see TLA as it travels through various populations, approaches and modalities – such as writing workshops for care-givers (in Debbie Harris's essay), or performances for school children (in Jackson Gillman's essay).

Nancy Shapiro, in writing about paradox, says, "Yet if we are true to the voices inside us, the heat brings light also, it forces us to see to the other side of things...always with hope ... to sudden realizations of kindness, empathy, the occasional necessity of being singed by flame, the wonder of miracles large and small." In doing so, she writes of how the invisible becomes visible, catalyzing greater capacity for compassion and connection.

This kind of coming together is evident in Anna Viadero's piece about writing with elders. As she explains:

> When elders write it works against the invisibility and isolation that they feel. It helps them find a voice that many have never had. It lets them say what they've never felt brave enough to say. It makes them remember. It helps them leave a legacy. It lets them share in meaningful ways not just with younger audience, but also with their peers. It helps them put their life in perspective at a time when many are hungry to do just that. (440-441)

That hunger to put our lives in perspective through the language arts is something familiar to any of us who have experienced TLA or see it as a river running through our lives on a daily basis. We are writers and artists, lovers of memoir and long-winding novels. Some of us carry folded up poems or letters in our wallets. We are people who know something about how powerful listening is, and being heard. We know it's essential – in the face of the millions of ways the world is on fire and in all the specifics of that suffering that come to us in local newspapers and down the block from where we live -- that we use our words instead of our countries' weapons, that we hold the quiet that heals, and allows those most silenced in our communities to be heard. We know something, even those of us who would never call ourselves Christian, about resurrection through the word; even if we're not Jewish, about praying to be sealed in the book of life; and even if we don't consider ourselves Buddhist, about the courage to sit still and pay attention. With such attention to what comes, we may find – as Linda Garrett did in her essay – the surprise of endings.

This book offers itself as entry into the conversation about how our words and songs, stories and metaphors, symbols and dialogues, jokes and laments bring about real and lasting transformation for those sharing them, and for those listening.

WORKS CITED

Abrahm, David. *The Spell of the Sensuous: Perception and Language in a More-than-Human World*. New York: Vintage, 1997.

Adams Don and Arlene Goldbard. *Community, Culture and Globalization*. New York: Rockefeller Foundation, 2002.

Barthes, Roland. *Mythologies*. Trans. Annette Lavers. New York: Hill and Wang, 1984.

Mirriam-Goldberg, Caryn and Janet Tallman, eds. *The Power of Words: A Transformative Language Arts Reader*. Keene, N.H.: Transformative Language Arts Press, 2007.

Rilke, Rainer-Maria. *Letters to a Young Poet*. Mineola, N.Y.: Dover Publications, 2002.

Stafford, William. *The Answers Are In the Mountains: Meditations on the Writing Life*. Ann Arbor, MI: University of Michigan Press, 2003.

Van Gelder, Sarah. "Danny Glover" *Yes Magazine*. 14 Feb. 2007. <http://www.yesmagazine.org/article.asp?ID=423>.

...

TRANSFORMATIVE LANGUAGE ARTS: A FIELD COMING INTO VIEW

...

THE GATE TO HEAVEN:
STORYTELLING AND SOCIAL CHANGE

Caren S. Neile, MFA, Ph.D.

• • •

What is the difference between heaven and hell? a man asks.
On inspection, hell is a magnificently appointed room with a
table groaning under the weight of fine foods and drink, crystal
and silver. But around the table sit diners thin as corpses, with
chopsticks so long they cannot feed themselves. Heaven, on the
other hand, is the same room and the same table laden with fine
things. The diners, however, are well-fed and rosy-cheeked. They
too have chopsticks that are impossibly long.
But they are using them to feed each other.
- Traditional

Although those who acknowledge the transformative power
of language are apt to be more open to the opportunities created
by storytelling than are others, the idea that an activity as intuitive
as storytelling could serve as an elixir for healing broken lives and
communities may appear idealistic, at best. Nonetheless, tellers and
audiences throughout the world can attest to the changes in attitude
and behavior, be they incremental or life-changing, that result from
storytelling (e. g., the storytelling of O'Halloran, Pearmain, Simms).
It is thus useful to explore some key concepts in Storytelling Studies
in order to fully appreciate the practice of this art form in pursuit of
social change.

The first step in establishing a relationship between
storytelling and social change is to define storytelling. Then, I will
explore certain salient characteristics of storytelling that make it
particularly well-suited to social action. Finally, I will discuss some
means by which storytelling is employed for social action. It should

be noted that because Storytelling Studies is a multidisciplinary field *par excellence*, relevant concepts and insights in support of storytelling as a tool for social change derive from a variety disciplines in the social sciences and humanities, including philosophy, linguistics, anthropology, performance studies, sociology and psychology.

DEFINITIONS

Although the word *storytelling* conjures up images as far-ranging as library storytime and flat-out mendacity, professional storytellers generally adhere to something along the lines of the following definition, according to Sobol, Gentile and Sunwolf:

> … storytelling is *not* …a product that exists authentically within the bounds of any technological extension of the human body and senses—though any media product can employ images and genre markers that have their basis in storytelling. Storytelling *is* a medium in its own right, an artistic process that works with what we may call the technologies of the human mainframe—memory, imagination, *emotion*, intellect, language, gesture, movement, expression (of face and of body) and, most crucially, *relationship in the living moment*— person-to-person or person-to-group. It is a medium that has played a fundamental role in the evolution of these human body/mind-technologies; and it is a medium that continues to carry a fundamental charge for *developing and for maintaining persons and cultures* within their human element. [Italics mine.] (3)

Lipman's five components of storytelling complement the preceding definition. They are: a) language, b) imagination, c) narrative, d) non-verbal behavior, and e) interaction. This is not to suggest that filmmaking or digital storytelling, for example, are not legitimate fields; only that they are not generally understood as storytelling in its most elemental form, wherein the most significant aspects of storytelling, including (1) relationship in the living moment (or, in Lipman's terms, interaction), (2) emotion, (3) developing and maintaining individuals and cultures, and (4) language are employed to their fullest effect. To understand the potential effects of storytelling, it is useful to concentrate on these four characteristics.

STORYTELLING AT WORK

The eldest and richest man in a certain village held a feast for his neighbors. The nine other elders agreed that if he would provide the meal, each of them would contribute a jug of wine. As soon as the words were out of his mouth, however, the youngest of the elders cursed himself for agreeing to part with a precious jug of wine. He decided to bring water instead, figuring that a single jug of water would not spoil so much good wine.

The feast day dawned, and the man put on robes of silk and satin, filled his jug with fresh well water and went on his way. When he reached the party, he added his jug of wine to the great pot in the courtyard.

Soon dinner was served, and the elders approached the head table with great anticipation. The servants filled the guests' cups with the wine, and each of the elders was anxious to taste the fine, refreshing wine.

Yet when they sipped, they tasted not wine, but water. For each one of them had thought that a single jug of water would not harm a great pot of wine. Not willing to admit to their avarice, they drank as if it were the finest wine they had ever tasted. And that day a saying arose among the people of the village: "If you wish to take wine, you must give it also." Traditional, adapted by Elisa Pearmain

For our purposes, perhaps the most salient word in the above definitions of storytelling is (1) *relationship*. That is to say, an act of storytelling creates and/or presupposes a relationship between performer and audience, facilitated in large part by the dissolution of the theatrical fourth wall (e.g., Martin). In other words, the performer appeals directly to the audience, rather than to either an actual (such as a fellow actor) or imagined (as in a monologue) partner. In storytelling, there is generally at least the illusion of authentic communication, although this is sometimes compromised in large festival venues. There is eye contact (most storytellers will not perform onstage with a blinding spotlight). There is an energetic transfer, and, at times, direct dialogue between teller and listener that engenders a collaboration -- for example, a teller who senses a bored listener will fine tune the story to engage her, or a traditional teller might use a call-and-response technique.

With relationship comes responsibility. Put simply, it is more difficult to view a member of one's tribe or family as the Other, an object, or an It rather than a Thou, than it is to view an outsider in these terms. From such empathy emerges an opportunity for dialogue and, thus, tolerance, understanding and change.

(2) The dismissal of *emotion* in serious discourse predates Cartesian dualism. Indeed, the earliest rhetoricians understood the power inherent in emotional appeal. Plato banished the poets (playwrights, storytellers) from his Republic in large part due to the unmanageable release of emotions they engendered, knowing as he did that emotion promotes learning, memory and, above all,

action. In contrast, Aristotle's argument against Plato rested on the heuristic involvement of cognition in emotional response, positing that emotional response is intelligent behavior, open to reasoned persuasion (Fortenbraugh). In addition, Aristotle's rhetorical proof of *pathos* (emotion) promoted *katharsis*. Although this is a vexed term, it is generally understood to mean a salutary physical and emotional cleansing, or purgation. Longinus too encouraged the use of emotional appeal in rhetoric.

(3) Scholars and popular writers alike have noted the socializing influence of folktales, that is, their ability to *develop and maintain human cultures* (e.g., Riesman, Glazer, & Denney; Kilpatrick; Norfolk & Norfolk). When Schirch argues that "world views are shaped by five interacting elements: perception, emotional and sensual cognition, culture, values, and identity" (39), she could be referring to storytelling. Similarly when we think of our own experiences as children or parents with Aesop's fables or Grimms' fairy tales, we can readily understand how, when demonstrated through story, the mores and behaviors of a culture become accessible to young and old alike.

The converse, however, is also true: Stories told of rebels are remembered and celebrated at least as much as -- and, arguably, more than -- those of model citizens, as any devotee of crime movies can attest (e.g., Riesman, Glazer, & Denney). Along these lines, Bruner writes:

> Great fiction proceeds by making the familiar and the ordinary strange again ... by "alienating" the reader from the tyranny of the compellingly familiar. It offers an alternative world that put the actual one in a new light. ... At its best and most powerful, fiction, like the fateful apple in the Garden of Eden, is the end of innocence. (9-10)

Similarly, in his discussion of the Marxist approach to fairy tales, Zipes summarizes the theses of Ernst Bloch and Walter Benjamin:

> The original fairy tales, that is, the oral folk tales in their *Ur-form*, contain elements of political protest and wish-fulfillment that demonstrate the ways through which oppressed peoples can withstand and overcome the power of rich and exploitative rules. It is almost as if they had a messianic mission and illuminated the way to a golden age (239).

Acculturation and protest are more closely related than they may at first appear. Turner noted that when the celebrant of a ritual completes the rite of passage, s/he can either return to the community (integration) or choose not to return (schism). As we will see, the elements of relationship, emotion and acculturation/protest combine with language and imagination to form the transformative ritual that is storytelling.

STORYTELLING, RITUAL, AND SOCIAL CHANGE

Several years ago, I attended a conference in order to learn about the role of storytelling in peace-building. The participants were housed in four-bedroom suites in a college dormitory. The night before the conference began, I lay awake in my dorm room, which shared a wall with the suite's common area. I was suffering from terrible heartburn and could not get to sleep until dawn.

Just as I had started to doze, I heard a loud voice in the common room. I peeked out of my door and politely asked the speaker to lower her voice, explaining that it was 5 a.m. She did so, and I tried, unsuccessfully at first, to fall back asleep.

Two hours later, I was again awakened by the same voice. Again I poked my head out of my door and requested quiet. Again she complied. But my sleep was ruined, and so I dressed and left the room.

All day I felt terrible. That night, I gratefully fell asleep about 10 p.m. Not long afterward, the same voice pulled me awake. Once more I opened my door and requested that the speaker lower her voice. But this time, she lit into me, literally screaming that she had attended the conference to network and that I had no right to silence her. Miserably, I returned to my room. But I could not relax. At last I opened my door and stepped back into the common room. The woman was still there, washing her face. When her eyes met mine, she narrowed them in anger.

I took a breath. "Look," I said. "I just want to explain to you why I need quiet. I have been sick since I've gotten here, and I've hardly been able to sleep."

Before my eyes, the icy features melted. Smiling, the woman came forward and took my hands. "I've been sick too," she said. "Isn't it the worst?"

For the rest of the conference, the woman was quiet in the suite. Every time she saw me, she gave me a hug and asked how I was feeling.

And that is how I learned about the role of storytelling in peace-building.

The three prongs of relationship, emotion, and the development and maintenance (or transformation) of human society that comprise storytelling reach their full expression when viewed in terms of ritual. Indeed, storytelling is a form of ritual in the same way as is theater (see Turner, and Schechner for more on this), leading both story listener and protagonist through the stages of the social drama—breach, crisis, redress and integration -- that are prerequisites for both personal and societal transformation. In other words, through the use of imagination, stories demonstrate that the resolution of conflict is attainable -- through the use of imagination.

Moreover as we have seen with respect to storytelling, there is in ritual both "an element of repetition and an element of newness…" (Schirch 20).

> Transforming rituals … challenge and change the status quo. When a critical number of people in any community desire change, they may use ritual to act as a rite of passage toward a new vision, a new set of values, or new structures in a community … Sometimes peacebuilders can help revive or draw on existing rituals within a culture that can help set the stage for transformational peacebuilding activities and processes. (23)

Examples of transforming rituals abound in Western culture, including rites of passage such as the Bar Mitzvah and first communion, the marriage ceremony, and the funeral service.

Here we return to another element found in the definitions above: *language.* The transformative power of language is highlighted in ritual. The vows taken in marriage and other rites of passage, for example, are, according to Austin's speech act theory, *performatives,* that is, language that transforms rather than describes. Austin's contribution to the philosophy of language overturns the schoolyard response to taunts: *Sticks and stones will break my bones/But words will never harm me.* As anyone defending a client against slander can attest, the saying is in error. Petrey notes:

> Much of the excitement of speech-act theory is its demonstration that entities often taken as incompatible are instead thoroughly interactive. Words and things, speaking and doing are one and the same when language performs. The theory also

brings together the inner self and the outer world, the individual and the communal, but it does so only when we participate perceptibly in communal life. Speech-act theory doesn't have anything to say about the promises we make to ourselves because, not being speech, they aren't acts either. (6)

Petrey further argues that "in practical criticism with a speech-act orientation, pride of place is held by drama" (86). The point is well-taken when one considers that theater occurs in present tense, while storytelling is a description of events distilled through memory. If the words "I now pronounce you husband and wife" are uttered in a drama, the characters are transformed from their liminal state of engagement to marriage. Such a directly performative act does not occur in storytelling.

However, while dramatic action transforms the characters onstage to a degree that storytelling does not, the effect on the *audience*, as noted above, is potentially far more direct in storytelling. If we consider that a storytelling audience is, as noted earlier, a co-creator, sharing ownership of the storytelling event, we see that the audience is an active -- and essential -- participant in the storytelling ritual. Without an audience, a play will go on. But, to paraphrase Petrey, the promises a storyteller makes to herself are neither speech nor acts. A storyteller requires an audience to complete the ritual.

Finally, ritual derives much of its power from *imagination*, another salient characteristic of storytelling noted above. Imagination in ritual is perhaps most evident in Western culture in Mardi Gras festivities or in the transubstantiation of communion, and further examples abound throughout the world (e.g., Carnival in Brazil). When the imagination is exercised through ritual, it is in turn potentially easier to imagine alternatives in one's own life, for everything from dead-end personal relationships to the use of violence. In this way, imagination is related to the transcendence and transformation that accompany social change at its best.

STORYTELLING IN THE SERVICE OF SOCIAL CHANGE

There was once a samurai warrior who set out to visit a monk in search of enlightenment. When he reached his destination, the warrior burst through the door and bellowed, "Monk, tell me! What is the difference between heaven and hell?"

For several seconds, the monk didn't move. Then he looked up from his tatami mat and smirked, "You call yourself a samurai warrior? Why, look at you. You're nothing but a mere slip of a man!"

Furious at this response, the samurai reached for his sword.

"Ha!" said the monk. "You call that a sword? You could not harm a fly with that thing."

The samurai was livid. He drew his sword from its sheath and lifted it to strike off the head of the old monk. At this the monk looked up and said calmly, "That, my son, is the gate to hell." Realizing that the monk had risked his life to teach this lesson, the samurai slowly lowered his sword. He bowed low in gratitude.

"And that, my friend," continued the monk, "that is the gate to heaven." John Porcino

Storytelling is a diverse field, encompassing folk narratives, oral histories, and personal and literary tales. With these tools at their disposal, tellers work toward social change in schools, community centers, theaters, and other venues, bringing a broad array of programs that engage participants in both the telling of and the listening to story. Here is a sampling:

1) In their show *Home to a Place Called Peace*, Nancy Wang and Robert Kikuchi-Yngojo of Eth-noh-tec tell the tale of Takashi Tanemori, a survivor of the atom bomb dropped on Hiroshima.

2) Susan O'Halloran, Antonio Sacre and LaRon Williams share personal stories of racial intolerance and reconciliation in their performance *Tribes and Bridges*, with an opportunity for audience talk-back after the show.

3) Israeli storyteller-actress Noa Baum portrays her mother, herself, a Palestinian woman and that woman's mother in *A Land Twice Promised*, a performance that demonstrates the connections to Jerusalem held by these very different people.

4) Elaine Lawless, Heather Carver and graduate students who participate in their Troubling Violence Performance Project out of the University of Missouri performs stories of victims of domestic abuse, followed by lively audience discussion.

5) In conjunction with Mercy Corps, Laura Simms wrote *Becoming the World*, a collection of folktales and activities for children on the issues of peace, tolerance and community in the wake of 9/11.

6) The organization Seeds of Peace brings together Palestinian and Israel teens to compare and contrast their life stories.

7) Robin Moore, a Vietnam veteran, tells stories of combat wearing full battle gear.

8) Audrey Galex, a Jew, and B. J. Abraham, who is Lebanese, perform *Tapestry*, which combines folktales, songs and personal stories to explore how two women from opposite sides of a conflict can make a separate peace.

9) On its website *www.storytellingcenter.net*, the International Storytelling Center introduces the use of storytelling for peace-building and provides stories and contact information for tellers doing this work.

10) The Colorado School Mediation Project published

Linda Fredericks' collection of folktales and related activities for children, called *Using Stories To Prevent Violence And Promote Cooperation*.

11) This author worked with juvenile offenders in Miami-Dade County on a six-week program to teach tolerance and character education based on hero stories.

12) This author created, in association with Rotary International, a program for middle-school students in Boca Raton, Florida, called Youth Peace Leaders, that uses storytelling for conflict resolution and tolerance.

To date, assessment tools for, and thus research on, this work are rare. (I created a simple pre- and post- assessment tool in the two examples from my own work. In both cases they revealed a small but compelling shift in student attitudes toward storytelling, each other and conflict.) Storytellers generally eschew such attempts at measurement because, they argue, the changes in attitudes and behaviors that their work effects are so difficult to quantify according to Annette Simmons.

Speaking from experience, the tellers may also simply be less than proficient or interested in designing and employing assessment tools. Despite the difficulties, however, further development of methods of assessment is essential if storytelling is to gain further credence with social activists and educators. Like storytelling and social change themselves, the acquisition of wide acceptance of storytelling as a tool for social change is a ritual that appears worth pursuing.

WORKS CITED

Austin, J. L., J. O. Ursom, and Marina Sbisa. *How To Do Things with Words*. Cambridge, MA: Harvard University Press, 1975.

Bruner, Jerome. *Making Stories: Law, Literature, Life.* New York: Farrar, Straus & Giroux, 2002.

Fortenbraugh, W. W. *Aristotle on Emotion: A Contribution to Philosophical Psychology, Rhetoric, Poetics, Politics and Ethics.* London: Duckworth, 1975.

Fredericks, Linda & the Colorado School Mediation Project. *Using Stories to Prevent Violence and Promote Cooperation.* Boulder, CO: Colorado School Mediation Project, 1996.

Galtung, Johan. *Transcend and Transform: An Introduction to Conflict Work.* Boulder, CO: Paradigm, 2004.

Kilpatrick, William. *Why Johnny Can't Tell Right From Wrong and What We Can Do About It.* New York: Simon & Schuster, 1992.

Lipman, Doug. "What is storytelling? The Storytelling Workshop in a Box." *Story Dynamics.* 11 Nov. 2006 <http://www.storydynamics.com/swb>.

Martin, Rafe. "Between Teller and Listener: The Reciprocity of Storytelling." *Who Says? Essays on Pivotal Issues in Contemporary Storytelling.* Ed. Carol Birch. Little Rock, AK: August House, 1996. 141-154.

Neile, Caren. *Stories of America: In Search of American Values in Family Memorate.* Unpublished doctoral dissertation. Florida Atlantic University, 2002.

Norfolk, Bobby & Norfolk, Sherry. *The Moral of the Story*. Little Rock, AK: August House, 1999.

O'Halloran, Susan, Andre Sacre and LaRon Willians. "Tribes and Bridges at the Steppenwolf Theatre." 11 Nov. 2006. <http://www.racebridges.net>.

Pearmain, Elisa Davie. *Doorways to the Soul: 52 Wisdom Tales from Around the World*. Cleveland: Pilgrim Press, 1998.

----. *Once Upon a Time....:Storytelling to Teach Character and Prevent Bullying*. Chapel Hill, NC: Character Development Group, 2006.

Petrey, Sandy. *Speech acts and Literary Theory*. New York and London: Routledge, 1990.

Porcino, John "The Difference Between Heaven and Hell." *Spinning tales, Weaving Hope: Stories of Peace, Justice & the Environment*. Eds. Ed Brody, Jay Goldspinner and Katie Green. Philadelphia, PA: New Society, 1992. 113.

Riesman, David, Nathan Glazer, and Ruth Denney. *The Lonely Crowd*. New Haven, CT: Yale University Press, 1961.

Schechner, Richard, and Victor Witter Turner. *Between Theater and Anthropology*. Philadelphia: University of Philadelphia Press, 1997.

Schirch, Lisa. *Ritual and Symbol in Peace-Building*. Bloomfield, CT: Kumarian, 2005.

Simms, L. *Becoming the World*. New York: Mercy Corps, 2003.

Simmons, Annette. Personal interview. 2001.

Sobol, Joseph, Gentile, J., and Sunwolf. "Once Upon a Time: An Introduction to the Inaugural Issue." *Storytelling, Self, Society: An Interdisciplinary Journal of Storytelling Studies*. 1 (2004): 1-7.

Tribes and Bridges at the Steppenwolf Theatre. O'Halloran, Susan, Andrew Sacre and LaRon Willians. Videotape. HMS Media, Inc.

Turner, Victor. *The Anthropology of Performance*. New York: PAJ Publications, 1988.

Zipes, Jack. "Marxists and the Illumination of Folk and Fairy Tales." *Fairy Tales and Society: Illusion, Allusion, and Paradigm*. Ed. Ruth B. Bottigheimer. Philadelphia: University of Pennsylvania Press, 1986. 237-243.

WRITING, HEALING , AND EMOTIONAL WELL-BEING:
THE THEORY BEHIND THE PRACTICE

Francis X. Charet, Ph.D.

• • •

INTRODUCTION: LOOKING DEEPER AT EXPRESSIVE WRITING

Expressive writing as a way of healing and emotional well-being is increasingly being taken up as a practice and has developed into a growing movement that promotes its use. This essay will briefly look at some of the studies and background that help clarify the healing and other benefits that result from the practice of expressive writing and raise a number of theoretical issues that might be of interest to practitioners and others. What follows is more of an overview than a critical analysis of the existing material or a detailed probing of the issues that have arisen in considering the benefits of expressive writing.

In her widely read *Writing as a Way of Healing*, Louise DeSalvo gives an account of her own experience writing a journal during the time that her mother was dying: "I didn't yet know that though I was journal-writing to try to help myself during this difficult time, my writing -- just describing what I was doing or thinking or dumping my feelings onto the page -- wasn't helping me. It was probably making me feel worse" (18). In other words, she did not experience writing as a way of healing and emotional well-being and she goes on to say why:

> I was still, however, using my writing to fight the feelings I was having, to try to make them go away rather than representing them. I wasn't letting myself feel them deeply, explore them, understand

them, learn their source, and link them to past and present events in my life. I was evading the narrative and emotional truth of my life. So my journal wasn't helping me understand and integrate my feelings during this complex time. I was stopping myself from writing my own life story. I feared I would find it unbearable. (18-19)

This insight about her writing, DeSalvo tells us, was largely the result of encountering one of the pioneering books on expressive writing and healing, James Pennebaker's *Opening Up: The Healing Power of Confiding in Others*. Its contents, she goes on to say, "summarizes ten years of scientific research into the connection between opening up about deeply troubling, emotionally difficult, or extremely traumatic events and positive changes in brain and immune function ...." (19). The key factor that Pennebaker identified was "the relationship between suppressing our stories and illness, on the one hand, and telling our stories and increased health, on the other...." (19). She concludes: "Writing, then, seems to improve physical and mental health. But not just any kind of writing. Only a certain kind of writing will help us heal" (20).

The pioneering study by Pennebaker identifying the kind of writing that DeSalvo refers to, grew out of a research project he conducted with Sandra Beall at Southern Methodist University in Dallas, Texas measuring the effects of writing, and its correlation to medical visits. Two select groups of students were asked to keep a journal, writing for fifteen minutes a day over a four-day period. The first group was asked to write about a trivial subject. The second group was asked to write about their traumatic experiences. This latter group was further divided into three sub groups to test three types of writing about trauma or emotional difficulties: 1) emotional venting; 2) describing without emotion; 3) combining emotion and description. The first group who wrote about a trivial subject showed no marked changes. The second group, made up of the three sub groups, initially showed signs of sadness and dismay with additional minor variations in their reactions. Nevertheless, clear differences surfaced in a four month follow up when the third sub group who combined description and emotion in their writing, reported that they felt they had improved and that this was related to having resolved some emotional issue in their writing. Two months later, medical visits were down in this same sub group by fifty percent, in contrast to the other sub groups (DeSalvo 20-23).

From these results Pennebaker and Beall concluded it was important to learn to initially endure difficult feelings to reap the benefits of emotional well-being and health for those who wrote detailed accounts of traumatic or distressing events. Further studies were undertaken, demonstrating more specific physiological responses that supported the preliminary findings. The upshot of it all led to the theory that "*repressing* thoughts and feelings about traumatic or distressing events might be linked to illness and that *expressing* thoughts and feelings through writing about traumatic or distressing events might prompt significant improvements in health" (DeSalvo 24).

Pennebaker's research and its conclusions attracted attention and produced supporters and skeptics alike. Subsequent studies were undertaken and possible connections between expressive writing, disclosure, and health were explored in more detail, giving birth to what is now a growing literature on the subject. The general conclusions of most of these studies tend to support Pennebaker's findings and consequently have attracted the attention of heath care and counseling professionals (Pennebaker; Lepore and Smyth). The link between expressive writing and emotional and physical well being has implications as well for those engaged in the practice of adjunct and alternative therapies, writers' groups and workshops, TLA practitioners, not to mention the mass market self help industry. It has also raised certain questions and issues.

THE LARGER PSYCHOTHERAPEUTIC CONTEXT

As pioneering as Pennebaker's and his associates' findings are they fit rather neatly into a larger psychotherapeutic context and could be seen as a more recent and essentially self directed form of therapy that was initiated by Freud and others at the end of the late 19th and beginning of the 20th century (discussed fully in Henri F. Ellenberger's classic book, *The Discovery of the Unconscious*). In fact, the emphasis on the repression/expression dynamic and its theoretical underpinnings is central in the method and practice of disclosure and psychological cure in the classical analytic schools, especially psychoanalysis. As Freud once stated: "The theory of repression is the cornerstone on which the whole structure of psycho-analysis rests" (Laplanche & Pontalis 392). The operative assumption is that repression is a psychological mechanism that acts as a defense against events and feelings that the individual is unable to come to terms with. As a result, these events and feelings are resisted by consciousness and transferred to the unconscious where, for the most part, they can be forgotten until psychological or psychosomatic symptoms surface. In the supportive environment of the analytic encounter, the individual is encouraged to find a way to both come to terms with these events and feelings and to integrate them, producing an extension of the personality into greater consciousness and psychological maturity. The key factor in initiating the process leading to integration is to affectively engage the unconscious contents and bring them into the realm of consciousness. The therapeutic consequences are that the symptoms subside or are considerably reduced, and relief in the form of physical and emotional well-being is the usual result. In a nutshell this is the repressive/expressive dynamic in a more clinical or psychotherapeutic context.

This theory of repression, coupled to a psychodynamic process, had enormous influence in the fields of psychiatry and psychotherapy in the 20th century. Its claims and the assumptions they were built on provided the ground for the clinical views of practitioners and were extended to become the unchallenged psychotherapeutic method in the treatment of psychological disorders. Recently, both the theory of repression and the therapeutic dynamic used to address it have come under considerable scrutiny, especially the psychosexual dimensions that are central to the psychoanalytic doctrine (Grunbaum, 1984). This has become entangled with the issue of the scientific legitimacy of psychoanalysis in psychiatry in the light of discoveries in the cognitive and neurosciences, not to mention the field of psychopharmacology (Paris). In other words, the classic analytic idea that repression is at the heart of the psychological disorders and can be treated psychoanalytically is not as persuasive as it once was. And it is no longer given much credence in most psychiatric wards, hospitals, and medical schools where psychiatrists receive their training (Paris).

In some respects, the work of Pennebaker and others has once again raised the issue of the relationship between the *repressive* and the *expressive*, as DeSalvo has put it. At least this is the case when it comes to trauma and emotional difficulties that are within the realm of the non-pathological, which is to say are not related to serious psychiatric illnesses. The distinction between the psychotherapeutic method and the one studied by Pennebaker & company has to do with the medium of expression. Namely in the classical analytic tradition, voice or "the talking cure" is the chief medium, while in the other it is writing. In addition, the various studies on the effects of expressive writing on physical and emotional well-being are evidence of the efficacy of an easily learned method of disclosure and self expression outside of a clinical or therapeutic setting dominated by mental heath professionals. On the other hand, both the expressive writing method and the outcome is currently so replete with therapeutic language and goals, that this has created some boundary issues with non-clinical practitioners who are sometime at risk of confusing their role with that of certified therapists.

CURRENT THEORIES ON EXPRESSIVE WRITING AND WELL-BEING

While the repressive/expressive theory, uncoupled from a psychoanalytical superstructure, still maintains a status in the psychotherapeutic tradition, it has had to vie with alternate theories that attempt to explain why expressive writing seems to work in the majority of the studies that have been conducted (Sloan & Marx 122-125). These alternative theories include the model of cognitive adaptation and exposure/emotional processing (122-125). The former is a structural model of human behavior that focuses on cognitive processes and the need to adapt established patterns of learning to traumatic and emotionally difficult events and feelings; the latter is rooted in the behavioral treatment of anxiety disorders and consists of positive and negative reinforcement as a way to induce adjustment and adaptation. A recent evaluation of 27 studies of expressive writing and its benefits has yielded certain indications about the validity of these three theories (122-125).

The repressive/expressive theory, otherwise termed emotional inhibition, has a degree of support but also faces a number of difficulties such as "there is no evidence to support the notion that decreases in inhibition (referring to the repressive/expressive theory) mediates the relationship between writing about stressful/ traumatic events and improved health" (Sloan & Marx 125). Moreover, it fails to account for the fact that some studies indicate writing about "imaginary traumas produces the same effects as writing about deep emotions related to experienced traumas" (125). The conclusion is fairly clear: "Overall, the emotional inhibition theory has not received much support as an underlying mechanism of the written disclosure paradigm, and this has led researchers to shift their attention away from the emotional inhibition theory and towards other theories" (125).

The next theory, cognitive adaptation, has also had its difficulties, only in this instance these have to do with testing the theory empirically. The common use of linguistic indices, namely the number and type of words that surface in expressive writing, such as those determined to be insight-related, emotionally toned, causation-related etc., is the usual method to measure cognitive changes. To date, the results lack cogency because linguistic indices don't seem to be able to capture accurately the more nuanced cognitive restructuring that appears relevant to an understanding of positive change. To summarize: "In general, there has not been consistent support for a cognitive model of the written disclosure paradigm" (Sloan and Marx 126). The last of the theories under consideration, emotional processing/exposure, has faced more difficulties than the other two in that insufficient data has been collected to adequately test this theory. What studies there are indicate: "The findings obtained, thus far, have not provided consistent support for the exposure hypothesis...." (129-30).

From the detailed survey conducted by Sloan and Marx, it has become clear that there are indications that expressive writing can bring about benefits in physical and emotional well being, though the latter has not received adequate attention so far. What seems to be equally clear is that there is no single theory to date than can sufficiently account for these benefits by isolating and identifying the mechanism(s) involved. Given this, the authors are also prepared to consider: "One possibility that has not yet been entertained fully is that a single theory may not fully account for the effects of written emotional disclosure. Instead, it may be the case that a combination of these previously theorized mechanisms underlies the beneficial effects observed" (130).

Presumably, wishing to err on the side of caution, Sloan and Marx, though hopeful about the potential use of expressive writing in clinical practice, nevertheless conclude "there is insufficient evidence to support the use of the writing paradigm as a therapeutic modality at this time" (134). Instead, they call for further research: "What is needed now is attention towards understanding the mechanism(s) underlying the paradigm. In focusing on this question, we would better understand the crucial components of the paradigm as well as the types of individuals who would be best served by its use" (134).

Pennebaker, while initially subscribing to the theory of repressive/expressive, otherwise known as the theory of emotional inhibition, has come to regard the matter as considerably more complex (122-23). In a commentary on the comprehensive article by Sloan and Marx, he concurs that no single theory has, to date, adequately accounted for the observed effects of expressive writing and that it might well require a number of different theories to do so (122-23). As for its psychotherapeutic possibilities, he is more optimistic and pragmatically suggests that, in addition to the research agenda to determine the precise mechanism(s) involved, there needs to be a parallel agenda. As he puts it: "In the real world, a large number of people need inexpensive, fast, and effective treatments in their dealing with traumas, emotional upheavals, and daily stressors. Why expressive writing works is certainly an interesting and important question. But for the general populace, we also need to know when and how well it works" (141).

SOME ADDITIONAL ISSUES

In the research and evaluation of the various studies that have been undertaken, there seem to be a few matters that have not received sufficient attention, and I would like to raise a few of them. First, the fact is that not enough research has focused on the subject of emotional well-being and the method(s) used to measure this. To date, most of the research has been more concerned with the physical benefits, presumably because they are easier to measure. Another limited feature of the studies is the selected populations: 17 of the 27 studies examined by Sloan and Marx consisted of students, and at least 14 of these at the college level (123-24). More data on the populations involved and a wider range of selection, both in the U.S. and elsewhere, to include different socioeconomic, cultural groups and so on, would potentially add to the accumulated data important elements. Preliminary indications suggest that social and cultural factors are of some importance for both the application of the model of expressive writing, its efficacy, and any generalizations that might emerge with a claim to general and cross cultural validity. This is of current significance less for global considerations than for the potential of bringing into relief the specific social and cultural features of the self, healing, and well-being.

It seems fairly clear that Western culture has, for some time, developed a preoccupation with constructing a notion of the private self, along with and in contrast to, a public or social self. In fact, the preoccupation with disclosure as a means of acquiring individualized self-knowledge goes back to the classical Greek philosophical traditions and its sustained practice is evident among the Stoics of the first few centuries of our era (Georges 13). Reinforced by the rise and establishment of Christianity, it took the form of the practice of confession, declared obligatory from the 13th century, and subsequently secularized in modern psychotherapeutic practice (13-14). The development from the more traditional to the modern notion of the self has been the subject of much discussion, and arguments pro and con in favor of the uniqueness of this in the West invite discussion. Nevertheless, what seems to characterize modern Western identity is inwardness that produces a sense of a private self, the affirmation of ordinary life that arises from this, and the notion of nature as an inner moral source (Taylor). In the end, it would be difficult to underestimate the degree to which the Western conception of the self is implicated in the measurable effects of expressive writing on the well-being of body and mind.

DISCLOSURE AND WELL-BEING IN NON-WESTERN CULTURES

In a brief analysis of the Toraja, an Indonesian tribal group, Wellenkamp, a psychocultural anthropologist, has found some evidence of the similarity with Western conceptions of disclosure and healing, though she makes it clear "that private forms of disclosure would not be effective for at least some Toraja individuals" (308). In addition, the author cautions her readers about generalizing: "Although I believe that it is noteworthy that there are cultural groups that hold beliefs that parallel the research findings linking emotions to health, I should make clear that there are other traditional, non-Western cultural groups that do not hold such beliefs" (305).

Similarly, Eugenia Georges, a medical anthropologist, drawing on the work of Hallowell on the Ojibwa and Turner on the African Ndembu, notes "a clear and positive association between the disclosure of personal events and the restoration of health" (17). Yet, here again, the emphasis is on public disclosure and not private. She offers the following summary, contrasting these tribal groups with Western behavior and practice:

> Whereas Western practice of disclosure is dyadic and private, occurring between an individual and a confessor, who may be only symbolically present, confession for the Ojibwa and the Ndembu is public and embedded within, and oriented toward, the social group (the family and larger community). While for Westerners the goal of disclosure is enlightenment through the process of self-reflection or alleviation from the 'work' or 'burden' of containing negative emotion, for the Ojibwa and Ndembu the goal of therapy is collective: to restore social relations to a harmonious keel. (18)

Georges offers two additional examples of fieldwork among the Balinese and the Chinese that clearly indicate disclosure of negative emotions is considered unacceptable and members of these societies are socially conditioned to integrate this value system. In fact, among the Balinese, disclosure of personal feelings is thought to put an individual at jeopardy because of the widespread belief in witchcraft. In short, disclosure would potentially have malevolent effects. In China, even the efficacy of psychiatric treatment is held to be related to:

> an understanding of the self that is more sociocentric, more attuned and resonant with relational and situational contexts than to inner, private states. ... It is the existence of these commonalities between lay and professional understandings and, more specifically, of congruent expectations regarding the clinical encounter, that is the requisite for the credibility and efficacy of specific therapies. (21)

It seems quite clear in these cases that the social self is far more important than the private self, even in the instance of psychiatric treatment. These brief examples indicate that expressive writing and its benefits are probably more tied to social and cultural constructions of the private self and the attendant values system of Western culture. In other words, the various studies of the experiences arising out of the practice of expressive writing may not have universal applications or validity and theoretically this might be extended to sub groups or minority cultures within Western culture where the social self is more prominent. At the very least this is an area that invites investigation.

Summary and Conclusion

The practice of expressive writing clearly has measurable benefits, especially in terms of physical health and well-being, though no single theory has emerged to adequately account for why this is the case. It can be engaged in without long term clinical or specialized training and with the likelihood, in a practicing or client population of mainstream members of Western society, of a beneficial outcome. Whether it is possible to consider it a potentially therapeutic modality of use to clinical practitioners in a more psychologically fragile population is less clear. So, too, this practice may not apply to non-Western cultural groups or minorities in Western culture who place greater emphasis on socially centered conceptions of self and identity. In other words, expressive writing can claim to be a legitimate personal means to attain some measurable degree of physical and emotional well-being in the majority of the population in this country. With a recognition of its benefits as well as its limitations, training in its method and appropriate use in practice is something that will likely find a key place in emerging fields as it has already at Goddard College.

WORKS CITED

DeSalvo, Louise. *Writing As a Way of Healing*. Boston: Beacon, 2000.

Ellenberger, Henri F. *The Discovery of the Unconscious: The History and Evolution of Dynamic Psychiatry*. New York: Basic Books, 1970.

Georges. Eugena. "A Cultural and Historical Perspective on Confession." *Emotion, Disclosure and Health*. Ed. James W. Pennebaker. Washington, DC: American Psychological Association, 1995. 11-22.

Grunbaum, Adolf. *The Foundations of Psychoanalysis: A Philosophical Critique*. Los Angeles: University of California Press, 1984.

Laplanche, Jean, J. B. Pontalis, and Donald Nicholson-Smith. *The Language of Psychoanalysis*. London: Karnac Books, 1988.

Lepore, Stephen J. and Joshua M. Smyth, eds. *The Writing Cure: How Expressive Writing Promotes Health and Emotional Well-Being*. Washington, DC: American Psychological Association, 2002.

Paris, Joel. *The Fall of an Icon: Psychoanalysis and Academic Psychiatry*. Toronto: University of Toronto Press, 2005.

Pennebaker, James W. *Opening Up: The Healing Power of Confiding in Others*. New York: Morrow, 1990.

---. *Emotion, Disclosure & Health*, ed. Washington, DC: American Psychological Association, 1995.

--- "Theories, Therapies, and Taxpayers: On Complexities of the Expressive Writing Paradigm." *Clinical Psychology: Science and Practice* 11 (2004): 138-142.

Sloan, D. M. and Marx, B. P. "Taking Pen to Hand: Evaluating

Theories Underlying the Written Disclosure Paradigm." *Clinical Psychology: Science and Practice* 11 (2004): 121-137.

Taylor, Charles. *Sources of the Self: The Making of Modern Identity.* Cambridge: Cambridge University Press, 1989.

Wellenkamp, Jane. "Cultural Similarities and Differences Regarding Emotional Disclosure: Some Examples from Indonesia and the Pacific." *Emotions, Disclosure and Health.* Ed. James W. Pennebaker. Washington, DC: American Psychological Association, 1995. 293-311.

POETRY AS THERAPY

Perie J. Longo, Ph.D., PTR (Registered Poetry Therapist)

• • •

It is difficult
to get the news from poems,
yet men die miserably every day
for lack of what is found there.
- William Carlos Williams

Since 1991, I have been conducting group poetry reading and writing sessions at Sanctuary Psychiatric Centers. My interest in this field began as far back as I can remember, before I ever knew there was such a thing as poetry therapy. As a child I remember sitting in school daydreaming. My mind would wander out the window, and as it did, my feet would begin to tap a rhythm. The more I would fall into the rhythm, the more complex it would become, and then words and images would swim to mind. Before I could write them down, however, the teacher would call me back to the classroom, where shame would quickly replace ecstasy, having lost one focus for another.

Only years later would I understand that entering the space of rhythm was the place where poetry dwelt, and that place resisted the mind of everyone but the individual, the creative Self, the "I." In the years that I have been writing poetry with many different groups, I have come to respect more and more the indefinable place from which the poem comes (which I like to call "The Secret Place"), the ability of each individual to travel to that source of creativity easily and naturally; and how much the poem has to teach us about ourselves and the world, as form and sound give rise to silence.

One of the benefits of poetry reading and writing is not only that it helps define the "I", but it strengthens it. This is necessary if we are to be a part of the world. The process attaches us to the greater part of ourselves, to all that is whole and good and beautiful. And when we feel ourselves as not alone in the world, but a part of and integrated with all that exists, self-esteem grows. The good news is we discover we are the same heroes and heroines of the old mythology, and in writing ourselves we extend it into the present, and forward, creating new stories to mark us.

Some of the members of the poetry groups at Sanctuary Psychiatric Centers have been coming for two to three years. Each week their poems are typed and added to a notebook. Some of them have several volumes. It seemed important to me to fasten their poems down, so that when they moved from place to place, they could take their poems with them to provide some continuity. When this activity first started I asked a group how it felt to have their creations in this form. One young man, who dictated all his words, clutching his book to his heart said, "I feel like I am somebody, finally."

It is important to mention here that the focus of poetry for healing is self-expression and growth of the individual, whereas the focus of poetry as art is the poem itself. But both use the same tools and techniques; language, rhythm, metaphor, sound, and image, to name a few. In the end, the result often is the same. The word therapy, after all, comes from the Greek word *therapeia* meaning to nurse or cure through dance, song, poem and drama, that is the expressive arts. The Greeks have told us that Asclepius, the god of healing, was the son of Apollo, god of poetry, medicine and the arts historically entwined.

HISTORY OF POETRY THERAPY

Though poetry as therapy is a relatively new development in the expressive arts, it is as old as the first chants sung around the tribal fires of primitive peoples. The chant/ song/poem is what heals the heart and soul. Even the word psychology suggests that: psyche meaning soul and logos speech or word. In mythology Oceanus told Prometheus, "Words are the physician of the mind diseased." Though it was recorded that there was a Roman physician named Soranus in the first century A.D. who prescribed poetry and drama for his patients, the link between poetry and medicine has not been well documented. It is interesting to note, however, that the first hospital in the American colonies to care for the mentally ill, Pennsylvania Hospital founded in 1751 by Benjamin Franklin, employed several ancillary treatments for the patients including reading, writing and the publishing of their writings in a newspaper they titled, "The Illuminator." The term "bibliotherapy" is a more common term than poetry therapy, which became popular in the 1960's and 1970's, which literally means the use of literature to serve or help. Freud once wrote, "Not I, but the poet discovered the unconscious." Another time he said, "The mind is a poetry-making organ." Later on, many other theoreticians such as Adler, Jung, Arieti and Reik wrote of how much science had to gain from the study of poets. In the 1950s, Eli Greifer, a poet, pharmacist and lawyer began a "poemtherapy" group at Creedmore State Hospital in New York City and in 1959 at Cumberland Hospital in Brooklyn, facilitated by psychiatrists Dr. Jack J. Leedy and Dr. Sam Spector.

Dr. Leedy published the first definitive book on poetry therapy in 1969, *Poetry Therapy*, which includes essays by many of the early pioneers in the field. About this time more and more people in the helping professions began to use poetry integrated with group process. Among them was Arthur Lerner, Ph.D. of Los Angeles, who founded the Poetry Therapy Institute in the 1970s on the West Coast and in 1976 authored *Poetry in the Therapeutic Experience*. Finally, in 1980, a meeting was called to bring together those active in the field working all over the country to formulate guidelines for training and certification in poetry therapy and form what is now called the National Association for Poetry Therapy (*NAPT Guide to Training*). For more information on this organization you may visit their website at http://www.poetrytherapy.org.

HEALING COMPONENTS OF POETRY THERAPY

> Poetry is the response of our innermost being to the ecstasy, the agony and the all-embracing mystery of life. It is a song, or a sigh, or a cry, often all of them together. - Charles Angoff (Lerner xi)

> Poetry humanizes because it links the individual by its distilled experience, its rhythms, its words to another in a way which no other form of communication can. Poetry also helps to ease the aloneness which we all share in common. - Myra Cohn Livingston (Lerner xi)

> I believe that a poem is an emotional-intellectual-physical construct that is meant to touch the heart of the reader, that it is meant to be reexperienced by the reader. I believe that a poem is a window that hangs between two or more human beings who otherwise live in darkened rooms. I also believe that a poem is a noise and that noise is shaped. - Stephen Dobyns (Dobyns xii)

The above quotations encompass some of the therapeutic aspects of poetry mentioned in the opening of this article. Often those in a therapy group have never written a poem, or if they have, it was unsuccessful and they feel they are "no good" at writing and want to leave the group. It is important to explain they do not have to write, they need only join in the discussion when they are ready.

It is also important to mention that this is not a class as in school and there are no grades, and no editing unless they want to do so on their own. This is a space not for criticism, but self-expression and exploration. And then we begin. Each session, a poem is presented. Selection of material is based on the "isoprinciple" also effective in music therapy. This means that the emotion of the poem is one that hopefully captures the mood of the group. If depression is a dominant mood, then a poem about depression is helpful, as long as there are lines that reflect hope and optimism. This principle is very comforting, because it allows the participants to realize they are not the only ones who suffer, that someone understands them because they have experienced it and written about it. They can share in their despair (Leedy 82).

The facilitator can present a reason for the poem choice for that day, or wait until someone reads it, and let the group members decide if it has anything to do with them. Often the poem is read twice by one or two of the members so that the rhythm, the music of the poem will enter their minds to help focus, replacing the chaos of thought. Usually there will be a silence after the reading, as members survey the field of words as if it were a lake or meadow or scene to absorb. The silence gives way to a breeze, as members begin to discuss lines that appeal to them, or images. Maybe only a word will call to them. Or maybe they won't like it at all.

The mystery of the poem is discussed. They love to ask "what does it mean" and we try to respond, not for the correct answer, for there never is one, but for the possibilities that can exist. And the possibility becomes an avenue for seeing things in a new way, even a predicament they can be experiencing. Whatever they have to say, or not say, is heard and accepted, never judged.

A poem does not have to rhyme, but it must have rhythm, and does. I find when people speak from their heart, there is usually a rhythm, subtle though it may be. Rhythm comes in many forms in a poem and often carries with it repressed feelings integrating chaotic inner and outer events into one's own experience according to Joseph Meerloo (Merloo 15). A change in rhythm can often help move participants from one place to another, or help them be aware of the feelings that are causing pain or fatigue or withdrawal. Often rhythm will release the tension in the beginning of a group. The rhythm is carried in the beat of the words, the repetition of certain sounds. And it is that repetition that has its hypnotic quality that helps create "the secret place," the bridge to the unconscious, from which the poem springs.

As participants respond to the gentle suggestions of what they see in the poem, they see more and begin to speak to each other. Isolation is broken. The poem brings them not only in touch with their own music, but with each other's.

Poet Donald Hall describes the primitive pleasures of rhythm in poetry as "Goatfoot, Milktongue, and Twinbird," saying they are the ancestors, the psychic origins of poetic form. The infant kicks rhythmically, without thought; experiments with sound, babbling vowels and consonants; plays with its hands and seeks nourishment from the mother, bonding in repetitive motions. There is the pleasure of appearance-disappearance as in the peek-a-boo play, words appearing and disappearing again (Hall 26-36).

The ability to be poetic is natural in our system of survival, and it is the facilitator's task to ease participants into this birthright to catch their thoughts and write them down, or have someone write them down, in a form that unlocks the mind. Form is an important component of the therapeutic value of poetry. Sometimes, if the issue at hand is too frightening, we can actually draw a box in the middle of the page and limit words to that space. Emotion will not run amok in this way, but be protected in the frame natural to the order of poetry.

In free verse, the constraints of couplets and quatrains no longer exist, with rhyme removed, but still we know poetry has shape and form, and we can impose that naturally with the workings of our mind and the natural rhythms and images that come forth. "Form makes arrangement out of derangement, harmony out of disharmony, and order out of chaos" (Heninger 57). When strong emotions can be expressed in an acceptable, safe manner, these feelings can subside. There is great release, and enjoyment in sharing with others, who identify. Balance is restored. Shapes can also be invented as in concrete poetry. Children often love dancing the words on the page in circles and spirals, drawing arrows where one word leads to another in a sort of map. There is great feeling and release in that playfulness.

Poetry does not have to be the serious business we were once taught. Rules can fly out the window and we can make up our own as we go along. Often I will take a phrase from a poem and repeat it for each group member to orally fill in their thoughts, before they write their own poem. One day I began with such a phrase, "I have the right." As we went around the circle seated in the living room, most touching lines were being spoken: I have the right to get a cup of milk in the middle of the night; I have the right to breathe; I have the right to play my guitar; I have the right to comb my hair, etc. Suddenly one young man who was suicidal said, "I have the right to get a gun to shoot myself." A woman, who had sat quite silently lost in herself each time she came to group, which was not often, spoke up. Turning to him she said softly but firmly, "And I have the right to take it from you." In that moment the silence was stunning. Everyone felt the impact of these simple words: certainly a poem. A sound and shape that still resonates with all of us.

The sounds of words themselves are healing not only in and of themselves but in conjunction and juxtaposition with each other. Constantine Stanislavski, founder of the Method School of Acting once wrote "Vowels are the rivers of the soul and consonants are the banks." Poetry is language and language is what humans do with air. How we define words, defines us. How we use them also defines us and when we realize they are notes like drops of rain we can have a little storm or a big one, make a composition of our interior life. As we speak our emotion, sadness may roll out in long *o* sounds as in "The Negro Speaks of Rivers" by Langston Hughes: "I've known rivers ancient as the world and older than/the flow of human blood in human veins./My soul has grown deep like the rivers" (4). In the same poem, the line "I built my hut near the Congo and it lulled me to sleep" uses sharper sounds (4). These allow the soul to flow. They also give tension to the sound, conveying stress, anger, struggle. And so a woman can write of losing her baby in a poem expressing her pain and grief through the sound of vowels, and her anger through the firmness of consonants.

Poetry has the ability to carry many emotions at once, and hold them intact. Often that is exactly what is needed in the therapeutic environment. One of the most often quoted poems in American literature in conjunction with literary genius and word sounds is Robert Frost's "Stopping by Woods on a Snowy Evening" (Oliver 24). It is also used often in poetry for healing, focusing on the intent to keep going with the journey, no matter how rough it gets, how cold the weather, or how enticing the moment of wanting to linger in the woods, "lovely, dark and deep." Mary Oliver in her Poetry Handbook discusses the beauty and repetition of the sounds of the poem, the repetition of *w's* and *th's*, the double *ll's* (24). The sounds set the quietness of the tone in the first stanza ("Whose woods these are I think I know./His house is in the village though"). In the second and third stanza the horse is the focus of the poem: "He gives his harness bells a shake/To ask if there is some mistake." The *k* sounds give the snap, the tension, carrying the conflict of hesitation (24). This is how sound works in writing, but often it is subconscious.

In an essay "Sing It Rough" poet Tess Gallagher says in writing poetry, nothing is more important than the heart, for there is the passion and the struggle. Often this comes about by hitting the "wrong notes", not just making pretty music. She quotes a poem by Cahil McConnel:

You can sing sweet

and get the song sung
but to get to the third
dimension you have to sing it
rough, hurt the tune a little. Put
enough strength to it
that the notes slip. Then
something else happens. The song
gets large. (Gallagher 88)

Each time I come away from poetry groups for healing, I carry the immense songs sung by the members, spoken or written, with what has happened. They have the courage that Gallagher describes, maybe because the focus is on the emotion rather than craft, and artifice is never stressed. There is a natural drive to survive and the language, the sounds of the words help achieve that.

A client I had a few years ago in private practice started coming to me because she had things to say and wanted me to help her get them down. She loved poetry, and wanted to participate more freely in it. For five months we saw each other almost on a weekly basis. As a child of seven, she had contracted equine encephalitis in Mexico from mosquito bites and gone into a coma for six weeks after complete cardiac arrest following wild convulsions. That she recovered was a miracle. That she could talk and walk again took years of work. When I started seeing her, she was almost 30, though her brain had suffered severe damage so that her thought processes were still as a young child's. Because she could barely write, her right arm and hand limited in motion, I would write down what she spoke. One day she had a massive convulsion and left without warning. But she left a legacy of poems that portray how words can lift someone from despair to hope. One of her poems, engraved on her grave site reads: "I cry not/For if I die, I go as one/The body, spirit, mind and soul/Connected now/Set free" (Longo 65). Perhaps that is the main therapeutic benefit of poetry; words remain forever for they are sound waves. Wherever we go, they follow us, from room to room, unconsciousness to consciousness, denial to acceptance, sorrow to joy. And hopefully to health.

WORKS CITED

Dobyns, Stephen. *Best Words, Best Order: Essays on Poetry.* New York: St. Martins Griffin, 1997.

Gallager, Tess. *A Concert of Tenses: Essays on Poetry.* Ann Arbor: The University of Michigan Press, 1986.

Hall, Donald. "Goatfoot, Milktongue, Twinbird: the Psychic Origins of Poetic Form." *A Field Guide to Contemporary Poetry and Poetics.* Eds. Stuart Friebert and David Young. New York: Longman, 1980. 26-36.

Heninger, Owen E. "Poetry Therapy in Private Practice: An Odyssey into the Healing Power of Poetry. *Poetry in the Therapeutic Experience, 2nd edition.* Ed. Arthur Lerner. St. Louis: MMB Music, Inc., 1994. 57.

Leedy, Jack J., ed. *Poetry As Healer: Mending the Troubled Mind.* New York: Vanguard Press, 1985.

Lerner, Arthur, ed. *Poetry in the Therapeutic Experience, 2nd edition.* St. Louis: MMB Music, Inc., 1994.

Longo, Perie J. "If I Had My Life to Live Over – Stephanie's Story: A Case Study." *Journal of Poetry Therapy* 10 (1996): 55-67.

Longo, Perie. "Poetry As Therapy." *Sanctuary Psychiatric Centers.* 1996. 2 Feb. 2007. <http://www.spcsb.org>.

Meerloo, Joost. "The Universal Language of Rhythm." *Poetry As Healer: Mending the Troubled Mind.* Ed. Jack J. Leedy. New York: Vanguard Press, 1985: 15.

Oliver, Mary. *A Poetry Handbook: A Prose Guide to Understanding and Writing Poetry.* New York: A Harvest Original, 1994.

The National Association for Poetry Therapy Guide to Training. New York: NAPT, 1997.

MEMOIR: AN ACADEMIC, DEMOCRATIC, POLITICAL AND LIBERATING FRAMEWORK

Shelley Vermilya, Ed.D.

• • •

There's an idea that there's this great mainstream,
which may be wide but is shallow and slow-moving.
It's the tributaries that have the energy.
- Grace Paley

My work on the faculty of Goddard College with non-traditional age students at the graduate and undergraduate levels has, for seventeen years, involved students in the writing of their lives. In this work, I have insisted that they intentionally locate their experiences in the larger social, political and/or religious story that has made them who they are. Robert J. Nash's work at the University of Vermont, as described in *Liberating Scholarly Writing: The Power of Personal Narrative*, offers one lens through which to view the integration of personal narrative and scholarly discipline. I would like to add to Nash's conversation, to explore the variety of lenses, and other optical devises if you will, with which to consider memoir as a foundation for research and scholarly application.

Writing one's life and then framing it in a social and political context disrupts power dynamics and systems of oppression, individually and institutionally, and places a value on individual experience. This self-reflective writing claims uneasy territory on the edges of academe. My experience suggests that this work can be life saving or can offer life-saving forces for individual writers as well as readers, because understanding their role in systematic oppression, as well as how such oppression for both dominant and marginalized people liberates internalized oppression. This liberation may or may not be intentional, nor is it in any way predictable, although there are developmental and identity theories that offer potential guidelines in such change which I explain in other writings.

Before exploring the path of the student-writer on an academic memoir journey, I'd like to answer some of the questions frequently asked about the language we use: What do the terms "memoir," "autobiography," "autoethnography," and "scholarly personal narrative" mean? How are they, or are they, distinct from one another? Are the differences between these genres important? Are these forms scholarly? What might "scholarly" writing look like when focused upon or springing from the experience of the writer? The answers to these questions rest at least in part in the foundations of the work I do with students, and in my own research and personal writing.

In my research, I found some working definitions for memoir from Judith Barrington and William Zinsser which allowed me to name just a little more precisely the power and responsibility of such writing. As Barrington writes,

> To write honestly about our lives requires that we work at and refine our artistic skills so that our memoirs can effectively communicate the hard-won, deep layers of truth that are rarely part of conventional social discourse. (14)

Zinsser revised his 1987 publication in 1998 to include the voices of women and African Americans. He claims that, " ... the new memoir at its best, ... is written with love" and "A good memoir requires two elements -- one of art, the other of craft. The first is integrity of intention ... The other element is carpentry. Good memoirs are a careful act of construction" (6).

Both Barrington and Zinsser agree that memoir is a portion of a life, a theme developed, refined, endured and surpassed, even transcended. Autobiography, according to Zinsser, "moves in a dutiful line from birth to fame" while Barrington says it "is the story of a life: the name implies that the writer will somehow attempt to capture all the essential elements of that life" (22).

THE COMPLEXITY OF OUR LIVES

My research and writing emerge from my experiences and my positionality in race, class, gender, sexual orientation, adoption, and transracial families in Vermont, USA. My research and writing also include the voices of other authors, those whose stories line library and bookstore shelves, and those resting in thesis binders in the Goddard College library. These writers have taught me, and become part of me through their craft and search for meaning. In company with these stories, I want to illuminate the complexity of the social, academic and personal issues that make up a life (a memoir) from the very beginning; bring them to voice. No, let me be more emphatic. I want to bring a chorus to my readers of beauty, tragedy, forgiveness, and alarm that we have changed our ways so little in the face of such beauty, tragedy, and relentless forgiveness by those who have been harmed by prejudice and injustice. I want to write my heart and mind and soul and love for the dangerous dialogues -- the discourse the academy and society as a whole just don't want to hear. I want to write of the dangerous naiveté (lack of awareness due to privilege) and for justice and peace and hope and love and faith and finally, forgiveness. This is praxis for the complexity of our lives; this is the praxis of a passionate pedagogy. Education philosopher Maxine Greene writes:

> A new pedagogy is obviously required, one that
> will free persons to understand the ways in which

each of them reaches out from his or her location to constitute a common continent, a common world. It might well be called a democratic pedagogy, since, in several respects, the object is to empower persons to enact democracy. (70)

To demonstrate this praxis, which Greene defines as "a type of radical and participant knowing oriented to transforming the world" (13), I offer my own autobiographical writing as example. A guiding purpose in my life and in my writing is witnessing -- out loud -- reluctance and resistance to social change when the exquisite consequences of tolerance and acceptance are so apparent. I am writing on the theme of recognizing how race and heterosexual normativity were constructed for me as an American child and teen, and my adult attempts to deconstruct those paradigms. The complexities in the stories I hold are from the context of a white female child of heterosexuals who evolves to become a teacher, a lesbian, an adoptive mother of two African American siblings and race traitor. The (r)evolution of thought necessary to survive and nurture non-traditionality provides the emerging paradigm and informs my dream of an epistemology of liberation.

VELVET (OR DENIM) EXILES IN THE ACADEMY

To tell the truth of our lives requires that we break silences and taboos that have been used to coerce and condemn, belittle and sabotage the full possibility of our lives. The cost of true expression may be tumultuous. Lives change; victims become survivors and agents of change. In working with students I have had to be willing to get out of the way, to provide a space for the student to be the 'expert' rather than insisting on that role myself, as students find their voices. I have had to stand by a student who comes to discover silences and the betrayal in such silence, to accept raw outrage, humility, shame and guilt as part of a discovery process and to know that with good facilitation that energy may evolve into pure poetry and potent activism.

I am a student writing to teachers. I am a teacher writing what she has been teaching. This border land of teacher and student offers me the opportunity to express my concerns about the expectations teachers bring to this work, the new lens teachers need to critically appreciate this work, the guiding principles teachers can share with students in order to enhance the work (Collins 35-39). Teachers have not been trained to work with students in this methodology. My students taught me that there was in fact a methodology to be declared and they also taught me valuable lessons for "teaching" or guiding a student. I have come to understand that there are phases and stages of identity development, liberation or anti-oppression recognition that a student moves through as the writing unfolds. It is helpful to consider these questions as teachers or facilitators of this work: How does a writer evolve from believing she has nothing to say or no authentic way to say it to believing in her own voice and the importance of what she has to communicate? How do we bridge the personal with the collective, and the individual identity with the societal context?

Autobiography/memoir/autoethnography/scholarly personal narrative resist a clear formula for interpretation or evaluation. These (for now let me call them) self-referential studies inspire an epistemology that is disobedient to the power relations of traditional pedagogy. That is to say, these genres, anthropologies of witness, blur lines between disciplines, frazzle expectations for compartmentalization or firm rubric declarations. For these reasons, and more, students and teachers engaged in this work are met with skepticism, dismissal, and distrust.

"We've all at some time been made to feel alien in the academy and consider it a principle of our work that our writing will not be a tool for the alienation of others," Ruth Behar writes in the introduction to *Autobiographical Writing Across the Disciplines* (xvi). Self-referential work -- variously defined and named autoethnography (See the work of Carolyn Ellis & Art Bochner), scholarly personal narrative (such as explored by Robert Nash), and the power of memoir (in my own writing) remain on the margins in the academy. Behar speaks for many of us working in these margins:

> We think it is totally possible to do rigorous scholarship and be personal and personable in our work. We deplore stuffiness and choose to write concretely in the everyday poetry of our speaking voices ... We've studied hard and been rewarded for our efforts, but we're not totally satisfied. We are the velvet exiles of the academy, able to comfortably do the work expected of us but choosing instead the more difficult position, that of the outsider within. (xvii-xviii)

I am an exile (more denim than velvet) of the academy. My work belongs on the precipice of acceptability, for that is my location in this society and it is where quintessential creative energy resides, just as Grace Paley illustrates in the quote that began this essay. Memoirs are literal searches for meaning. The voices of marginalized individuals are dangerous to the Western Canon because they erode the very foundation of manifest destiny; they challenge the arrogance of dominance and unquestioned authority. They offer lives, ideals, and visions that reach beyond conquest and the image of history as a calendar of wars won and lost. The voices of people, both dominant cultured in experience or marginalized, challenging hate, violence and abuse, and surviving to turn their lives around from victims to active participants are voices that are truly dangerous to a culture based on submission, aggression, and power as defined as "over" another. [2] I love memoir work for these very reasons.

TENACLES OF PATRIARCHY AND DRAG QUEENS

First World and First Nation Peoples, oral traditions, pre-printing press mythmakers and storytellers were probably the true originators of this form. However, for me it was feminist writers and my undergraduate advisors at Goddard College (albeit feminists working in a pedagogy based on the work of John Dewey) who showed me the value of seeing the personal is political, writing from the heart, consciousness raising, uncovering the hidden designs of power and the "tentacles of patriarchy" (Hartsock 157). The message I took to the page was: write, write, write.

My childhood and teen years were bolstered by the civil rights era of the 60s, the Vietnam Protests of the 70s and the Second Wave of feminism washing in the Gay Liberation movement of these same years. The drag queens at the Stonewall Inn in New York City erupted in protest one June night in 1969 against police harassment. These acts of indignation at injustice, these demands for civil rights and social justice made my coming out in the early 70s a possibility. My academic work in the late 70s examined the feminist writings of the day and the emerging gay and lesbian history. It was all so fresh, and daunting, but I was too young to realize I was political; little did I know I was the embodiment of the feminist and critical theories of change.

There were new voices being published during the 70s, voices that called out to those of us searching for the meaning of feminism, the meaning of lesbian, the meaning of everything we had managed to turn inside out. Adrienne Rich was one such voice. She had dutifully raised three sons and then declared her lesbian identity as well as her identity as poet, essayist, and activist. This section from "Transcendental Etude" speaks to the challenge before women: to examine life and take it as seriously as science or music. This was a new concept, especially for women who lived without reflection on their experience.

> No one ever told us we had
> to study our lives,
> Make of our lives a study, as if
> learning natural history or music,
> That we should begin with the simple
> exercises first and slowly go on
> trying the hard ones,
> Practicing till strength and
> accuracy become one with
> the daring to leap into
> transcendence.
> And in fact we can't live like that.
> We take on everything at once before
> we've even begun to read or mark time,
> we're forced to begin in the midst
> of the hardest movement,
> The one already sounding as
> we are born. (72-77)

"No one ever told us we had to study our lives/Make of our lives a study ... Practicing till strength and accuracy become one with the daring to leap into transcendence ... ". Study our lives to leap into transcendence: that is precisely what the authors of memoir/ autobiography/ autoethnography/SPN can accomplish, if they dare. Certainly, not all do, transcendence being an adamantly individual assessment that is difficult to define.

I wrote "Writing for Our Lives: The Power of Memoir for Marginalized Students" after only six years of work with students at Goddard College. Students taught me this form. I did not have the language of "autoethnography" or "scholarly personal narrative." I had students writing their lives; students exposing the core of harm done to them in a society where children, women, people of color, people of different sexual persuasions, or white men who did not fit a macho profile were all condemned as different and suffered the consequences. In a country where misfits landed at Plymouth Rock, a country made up by immigrants and exiles from different continents, religions, and colors it is beyond ironic that there is so little tolerance, celebration and respect for difference. The voices of my students started out quietly and became stronger and stronger as each individual found some new recognition through his or her writing.

As I worked with students in the early and mid-90s at Goddard College it became apparent that I had to assume some expectations and standards for academic quality. My guiding principle was to acknowledge the growth of the individual as indicated by writing quality, power of voice in the writing and even the stature of the individual. Sometimes literal transformations occurred in the physical body of the student between semesters. I had no rubric, but I had evidence in eloquent, written final products and heart-pounding presentations. I had the evidence of graduating students standing taller and prouder for finding their truth in the context of great social injustices and inequities.

A More Empowered State of Selfhood

Despite all the research in recent years on the workings, value and ethics of memoir, particularly through writers and researchers in the emerging field of autoethnography, which calls on us to articulate the cultural as well as the personal layers of how we know what we know, questions still abound. Some of my colleagues have remained unconvinced and remain skeptical about how memoir serves students. They ask, "Why is this work academic? Where's the line, do you think, between self-indulgence and transformation in this work? Is it in intention? Or in result? Is it through the application of art, the development of craft? What are the differences between memoir, autobiography, autoethnography?" And from the most resistant among us, "Why don't they just go to therapy?"

How do we put academic value upon self-referential, personal narrative? Can we insist on transformation? How can we assess individual stories? My guiding principles have led me to the contextualization of the individual, as stated earlier, in a social and political context. In such a context, memoir can serve as its own methodology.

My students write memoir. The themes are either clear from the very beginning or emerge during the semester: grief; incest, rape and physical abuse survival; gender transformation; drug and alcohol addiction; eating disorders; gay and lesbian coming out stories; African American male and female experiences in white America; gang membership; Vietnam veteran survival. While it seems that most of the episodes students started out writing about entail violence and violation of either mind, body or spirit, all arrive from the experience of this writing at a more empowered state of selfhood.

Doing this work is not a panacea. Students do return to the troubles that haunted them and continue to wrestle with their demons. This is a potentially damaging discourse, which must be undertaken in respect, honor, deep care and nurturing. As a teacher, I tell individuals that they will need a support system of their own because I am not a therapist nor their parent. My role is to be an ally in change: Listen, respond, honor, and insist on clarity, truth and context, knowing that truth sometimes requires revision over a lifetime. I also tell them that they are fully responsible for how far they go with this work. I share with them some of my own experiences as a writer and frequently recommend authors and the work of former students that may coincide with what they are thinking about.

Memoir is a form of literary research for the writer, the

research into the past to illuminate the present. Interestingly, tragedy or despair is not a requirement for this work but it seems to be a catalyst, a motivating force. Discomfort prompts, injustice drives. And there is also the delight of desire or joy. Writing, as literary research, involves building a relationship with the narrative of our lives.

NOTES

[1] Laurie Finke writes, "What is perceived as marginal at any given time depends on the position one occupies ... In other words, you have to see centrality and marginality, oppression, oppressor, and oppressed as relational concepts. And so what you have to do is keep the whole thing moving ... keep seeing it as relational, keep seeing it as position. See F. A. Maher and M.K.T. Tetreault's *The Feminist Classroom: Dynamics of Gender, Race, and Privilege*. Lanham, MD: Rowman & Littlefield, 2002. 22.

[2] To synthesize Starhawk's three points about power: "Power-over" is in every institution, every school, every workplace, court and medical office. Resources we need are controlled: money, food, medicine, information, and approval, even love. "Power-from-within" is the mastery we feel in our accomplishments, arises from a sense of connection, bonding with people or the environment. It sustains our lives. "Power-with" or influence, is power not to command but to suggest and listen, begin to see what happens. a.k.a.: respect for each unique person. Starhawk. *Truth or Dare: Encounters with Power, Authority, and Mystery*. San Francisco: Harper & Row, 1987.

WORKS CITED

Barrington, Judith. *Writing the Memoir: From Art to Truth*. Portland, OR: Eighth Mountain Press, 1997.

Behar, Ruth. *The Vulnerable Observer: Anthropology That Breaks Your Heart*. Boston: Beacon Press, 1996.

Bochner, Art and Carolyn Ellis, eds. *Ethnographically Speaking: Autoethnography, Literature, and Aesthetics*. Walnut Creek, CA: Altamira Press, 2002.

Collins, Patricia Hill. "Learning from the Outsider Within: The Sociological Significance of Black Feminist Thought." *Beyond Methodology: Feminist Scholarship as Lived Research*. Eds. Mary Margaret Fonow and Judith A. Cook, Bloomington, IN: Indiana University Press, 1991. 35-39.

Ellis, Carolyn. *The Ethnographic I: A Methodological Novel about Autoethnography*. Walnut Creek, CA: Altamira Press, 2004.

Freedman, Diane & Olivia Frey. *Autobiographical Writing Across the Disciplines: A Reader*. Durham, NC: Duke University Press, 2003.

Greene, Maxine. *Landscapes of Learning*. New York: Teachers College Press, 1978.

Hartsock, Nancy. "The Feminist Standpoint: Developing the Ground for a Specifically Feminist Historical Materialism." *Feminism and Methodology*. Ed. Sandra Harding. Bloomington, IN: Indiana University Press, 1987.

Maher, Frances A. & M.K.T. Tetreault. *The Feminist Classroom: Dynamics of Gender, Race, and Privilege*. Lanham, MD: Rowman & Littlefield, 2001.

Nash, Robert J. *Liberating Scholarly Writing: The Power of Personal Narrative*. New York: Teachers College Press, 2004.

Rich, Adrienne. *The Dream of a Common Language: Poems 1974-1977*. New York: W.W. Norton, 1979.

Starhawk. *Truth or Dare: Encounters with Power, Authority, and Mystery*. San Francisco: Harper & Row, 1987.

Sparks, Andrew C. "Autoethnography: Self-Indulgence or Something More?" *Ethnographically speaking: Autoethnography, Literature, and Aesthetics*. Eds. Art Bochner & Carolyn Ellis. Walnut Creek, CA: Altamira Press, 2002.

Vermilya, Shelley. "Writing for Our Lives: The Power of Memoir for Marginalized Students." *Higher Education for Democracy: Experiments in Progressive Pedagogy at Goddard College*. Ed. Steve A. Shapiro. New York: Peter Lang Publishing, 1999.

Zinsser, William, editor. *Inventing the Truth: The Art and Craft in Memoir*. Boston: Houghton Mifflin, 1998.

--- *Writing About Your Life: A Journey Into Your Past*. New York: Marlowe & Company, 2004.

GIVING VOICE TO ART AND IMAGINATION: A METHOD OF TRANSFORMATIONAL INQUIRY

Shaun McNiff, Ph.D.

• • •

THE PURPOSE OF SPEAKING FROM THE IMAGINATION

When I lecture and teach, I am often greeted with a curiosity about the process of dialoguing with images as described in my book *Art as Medicine: Creating a Therapy of the Imagination.* I became immersed in the process of imagal dialogue during a period in the 1980s when I was working with James Hillman and it fit naturally with my emphasis on responding to art with creative expressions and mixing poetry and imaginative language with the other arts in therapy.

I was having a conversation with Hillman about a painting of a male figure and in keeping with the Jungian tradition's method of personifying images he said that perhaps the man had a very different sense of himself than what we were saying about him. Hillman suggested that maybe we were "laying a trip on him" with our descriptions rather than looking even closer at how he was presenting himself and then allowing him to do the talking.

We began to speak from the perspective of the artwork, giving it a voice. The figure turned the tables on our interpretations and helped us to look at its expression in a completely different way. Our stories, as Hillman says, needed "doctoring" and more imagination (17).

As we encouraged the image to speak through us, I was struck by the accuracy of the statements and how they cut through the intellectualizing that often characterizes conversations about art. I could distinctly feel the shift from conventional talking to a poetic and dramatic mode of speaking that felt more visceral, insightful, and in sync with the painting's expression. The process of imaginal dialogue brought the painting to life.

Graduate students in art therapy increasingly study imaginal dialogue as one of the core ways of relating to artworks, and over the years I have directed them to *Invisible Guests: The Development of Imaginal Dialogues* by Mary Watkins, which gives a wonderful over-view of this process. The students sense the value and importance of this way of relating to pictures, objects, and dream images and they see how it creates opportunities for a discourse that simply cannot happen when we speak in more conventional narratives. I repeatedly discover how something very different happens in human communication when we personify artistic expressions, give them voice, and then do our best to listen to what they have to say about themselves. The conversation invariably shifts its emphasis from the head to the heart.

The speaker becomes much more vulnerable, sensitive, and uncertain when conversation no longer happens from the habitual ego perspective of the first person singular. New dimensions of communication are opened when images speak.

For many it feels weird, difficult, and even crazy to talk to and with images, to let them speak through us as agents of their expression. "You are increasing madness," I have been told. I reply, perhaps yes, but it is a poetic madness, a way of speaking that has existed for millennia. Poets talk to rocks and trees and these figures speak to poets, and to one another. And this process of personifying the physical world and figures of the imagination clearly differs from psychosis in that imaginal dialogue is pursued as a way of integrating and healing the deepest and often opposing strains of our inner lives.

Shakespeare shows us all how to personify. I love the passage in *The Winter's Tale* when Leontes says, "Does not the stone rebuke me for being more stone than it?" And there is also the wonderful dialogue that Pyramus and Thisbe have with the wall in *A Midsummer Night's Dream*: "Thou wall, O wall, thou sweet and lovely wall" and later "O wicked wall through which I see no bliss! Curs'd be thy stones for thus deceiving me!"

If the immortal writers are so effective in speaking to objects and having them talk back, why not use their example as a model for our therapeutic methods? Giving voice to psychic and poetic images can open us to a wider spectrum of information and insight. The process takes us beyond the limits of the linear, ego-based, and descriptive narratives that actually offer a very limited view into the larger complex of our lives and emotions.

Fiction is not necessarily false or unreal. Freed from the need to present literal facts, a fictive narrative follows the truths and inclinations of emotions. Our imaginal dialogues might voice the positions of fanciful or disturbing characters and other conditions that we deny, fear, disregard, and simply overlook. Besides furthering emotional expression, the depth and range of cognitive knowing is enhanced through this augmented discourse.

Within the discipline of art therapy there is an especially keen interest in imaginal dialogue. I believe that this results from artists realizing that the diagnostic reduction of artworks to psychological categories is a seriously flawed process with no scientific validity. Yet art therapists and the people making art in therapy want to get closer to their expressions, find ways to further their communication, and interact with them through verbal language. Imaginal dialogue offers a more intimate way of achieving these objectives, and we have even found that it can be far more psychologically insightful than conventional clinical explanations.

The moment art therapists begin to encourage this kind of conversation with art objects, they have entered the realm of poetry and creative language therapies, an expansion that affirms my longstanding insistence that the different expressive arts therapies need one another and cannot avoid the blurring of media boundaries that accompany free and imaginative artistic expressions. Poetry therapy, art therapy, and other disciplines are integrated whenever the creative process is free to imagine itself further and move from one expression to another.

JUNG'S CONTRIBUTIONS

C. G. Jung's practice of active imagination was characterized by this integration of different art modalities and the process of personifying images was a foundation of his practice. I keep trying to remind the expressive arts therapy discipline that in the early 20th century Jung anticipated just about everything we do today and his essays on active imagination are still among the best materials ever written about the arts in therapy.

Jung gave voice to personified figures of the imagination and emphasized how they "said things that I had not consciously thought" (Chodorow 30). His declaration suggests, and I have written about this in my earlier work, that creative examinations of experience through the arts have something important to offer us when we seek understanding and new knowledge in all forms of disciplined inquiry from therapy to research.

When describing this method of engaging images, Jung encouraged a contemplative process of "looking psychologically" and suspending the normal ways of thinking rationally about what we see. This deep and attentive looking animates images and breathes life into them.

In his classic letters written to Mr. O. in May of 1947, Jung encouraged the selection of a detail or feature of an expression as a focus for concentration. "Start with any image" he said, adding, "Hold fast to the one image you have chosen and wait until it changes by itself" (164).

He asked Mr. O. to personify a figure from a dream-- "Treat her as a person...as something that does exist...you must talk to this person in order to see what she is about and to learn what her thoughts and character are" (165). This method invites images to tell us about themselves and it assumes that these communications will convey information that lies outside our current frames of reference. Jung also emphasized how the process of imaginal dialogue would have an energizing effect on the person.

Well before the discipline of expressive arts therapy was consciously created Jung encouraged people to move from one medium to another, such as amplifying a painting with a dramatic dance or story. He cultivated an environment in which one could, "let things happen in the psyche" (74) and where one expression emerged from another in a way that was unique to the individual person's expressive inclinations.

From my years of experience in working with the arts and healing, I feel that the most essential and defining aspect of the discipline involves letting go, trusting that the creative process will always take us where we need to be. And as Jung said, if we can stay focused on an image, "it changes by itself."

There is a true discipline involved with relaxing the ego, lightening our grip on the controls, and permitting situations to transform themselves. People seeking change, as well as the therapists and guides who try to help them, can find it difficult to step aside and patiently allow a conflict, state of confusion, or a longing for expression to find its own way to completion. As the psychoanalyst D. W. Winnicott stressed, we all too often ruin a therapeutic and creative process with our interventions, clever interpretations, and needs to fix things for others. When we inject ourselves into these situations we can obstruct a deeper and more influential course of change that grows organically within the intelligence of the creative process.

I see this same need to allow change to happen organically within organizational life. Jung's descriptions of the self-regulating system of personal change can be amplified to what occurs within social institutions and communities. Leadership becomes a process of cultivating a creative environment that has the resources and intelligence to transform itself spontaneously. All too often leaders, in keeping with Winnicott's observation, obstruct a more creative process of change with their needs to direct the dialogue and strategically resolve problems.

The trust that a complex situation will change by itself when we apply focused creative energy and attention can be likened to the process of dialogue. The conversation among different participants is a form of thinking, often more complete than what can happen through solitary and passive reflection. We discover what we think about situations by talking about them, responding to the statements of others, and expressing ourselves. I have learned through my conversations how fundamental the active element of shaping a statement is to my thought. When engaged with others, new ideas invariably spring from the discourse.

The same applies to the more solitary process of writing or painting. Even when I am creating alone, I work together with the emerging text or canvas in an active process of forming expressions and thoughts. Nothing happens unless there is movement of some kind, with my ideas and insights being sharpened through interaction with something other than myself.

Jung described how his work with images involves a circumambulation of psyche, a circular movement that keeps returning to an object of contemplation from different vantage points. Each expression makes its contribution to a whole that integrates the varied efforts and insights. The process of dialogue, whether alone or with others, can be viewed as holding this multiplicity of viewpoints and encouraging the greater depth and imagination that result from their integration.

THE CHALLENGE OF IMAGINAL EXPRESSION

My training groups with artists and therapists consistently affirm how imaginal dialogue introduces ways of viewing experience that are strikingly different and important. But I have also discovered that although some find imaginal dialogue liberating and transformative, others resist it and cannot get past their usual ways of interacting with the world. The process can be difficult because it involves changing our most ingrained ways of viewing reality and speaking. It requires letting go of control, opening to what comes to us from outside existing frameworks of understanding, and taking on a completely different persona, often giving voice to more than one new character.

I liken this process to drama and children's play. Adults and teenagers who are able to let go and play like young children tend to dialogue effortlessly and greatly benefit from the opportunity to express themselves in this playful way, which can become very serious and discerning. The process is spontaneous and improvisational, which can also be challenging for so many people who do not speak until they know in their minds beforehand what they are going to say. With creative expression we do not necessarily know where we are going when we begin to speak or move with an artistic gesture. The process unfolds through the creative action.

In my training studios for professional art therapists, I consistently see how simple exercises, such as speaking as a figure or gesture in a painting, meet with feelings of resistance, fear, and ineptitude.

The process requires that we relax the fixity of our egos and move those egos off to the side so that imagination can express itself according to its own wisdom. People tend to find it easier to make lists of words, phrases, or even poetic passages in response to their images and resist taking the more engaging step into dialogue which does not have to involve anything more than simple, heartfelt statements as I will describe later.

When people do try to dialogue, I observe how they often open with questions – Who are you? What are you doing here? What are you trying to tell me? This way of beginning puts the image on the defensive and the whole context starts to feel like an interrogation. One of my students remarked that this way of speaking "puts the artistic expression in a corner."

We can make use of everything we do and ask ourselves why we go about interacting with our expressions in this way. I sense that it has something to do with control and not knowing how to proceed. I liken this discomfort to being in the presence of someone new and unknown. Is this how we would like to be treated if we were strangers in a new place? It may be more effective to engage images as guests, with kindness, hospitality, and an open curiosity about what they might have to say to us. I have found in both my relations with others and in the process of dialoguing with images that a person's attitude will have a large impact on the quality and depth of communication.

One of the most effective moves that we can make to get beyond these blocks is to compassionately ask an image what it needs from us. We might be surprised by its response.

"Lighten up," the image might say. "Don't try so hard to say something important. Do your best to sit with me and look deeply at what I would like to give to you."

Or the image might say, "You are caught up in yourself and unable to see me for what I am and what I bring to you."

I have found that people tend to respond relatively well and with a greater degree of openness and spontaneity when I suggest that the artwork may have a story to tell about itself. My college age students have surprised me with how the storytelling response to a painting ignites their imaginations.

Perhaps the making of a story is a more natural fit with imaginal speech than dialogue which can be tied to more literal habits of conversation. I try to keep the storytelling process embedded in imagination by asking people to do their best to speak from the perspective of something other than themselves. "Feel free," I say, "to let any aspect of the image, whatever catches your fancy, tell a story."

Language structures tend to reinforce self-centered fixations even though this does not necessarily reflect the nature of reality. In English, the painting is an "it," inanimate, neuter, and without gender or personhood. If I am speaking, it is always as myself in the first person, and to do otherwise might suggest that I have lost my hold on what is real and unreal. Syntax thus becomes a major inhibitor of imaginal speech which like poetry needs to encourage the lifting of restrictions and rules about verbal expression.

I do my best to anticipate the various obstacles to imaginative dialogue. I tell people that it is easier to begin talking to an image as ourselves, simply looking at the picture or object as a living thing and then telling it what we see in it. If you can personify the artwork, I say, and see it as a living being, you have entered the realm of imagination.

As we begin to look into the expression and tell it what we see, it becomes natural for the object of our dialogue to respond, perhaps telling us how it feels about what we said. We take on the dual role of both speaking and listening to what the other says about itself. If I am not working with another person who can witness and record my statements, I tend to write as I speak to an image or tape the conversation so I can return to it again.

People constantly affirm that the presence of another person as a witness helps the dialogue to unfold in ways that may not be possible when they are working alone.

Experience has also shown me that people may feel reluctant to express feelings or statements within an imaginal dialogue that will reflect negatively upon them. Therapists are especially aware of how spontaneous and free expressions will project uncensored utterances and they know how diagnostic systems latch onto anything unusual or unsavory as a manifestation of psychopathology.

I try to embrace the resistance as a learning moment to reveal the simplistic literalism of these diagnostic practices. As in literature, the voice of the character in a story, play, poem, dialogue, or dream is not necessarily the literal voice of the writer/speaker. In art, therapy, and imaginal dialogue we may benefit by adopting an amoral or shadowy vantage point in order to more completely understand a situation or establish empathy with a troublesome urge that exists within ourselves. If we can step out of our self-referential thinking and imagine our expressions as autonomous beings, with important things to say to us, we might also be able to apply these approaches to some of the more vexing social problems of the world.

KEEPING THE DIALOGUE SIMPLE

When people begin to dialogue with images, my principle suggestion is to keep the process simple. "The simpler the deeper," I say. "Deep down is here-now; depth is on the surface. You do not have to write pages of dialogue in response to an image. The most important exchanges might involve only a few words that carry considerable thought and emotion. Or if free writing comes easy to you, write automatically for five to ten minutes and then go through all of the lines that you wrote and select a passage or two upon which you would like to concentrate your attention."

This approach to simplicity provides a "can't fail" method and it relaxes inhibitions and the restraints of expectations and the tendency to plan what we want to say in advance. I will even encourage people to engage whatever happens to manifest itself in consciousness as a starting point for dialogue.

If there are too many words and passages in a person's expression, it can be difficult to focus, digest, and practice the methods described in this chapter. I stress the importance of selecting key statements and words and then repeating them many times, changing their relationships to one another and so forth. This approach also liberates the voice and sets the stage for a wider range of vocal improvisations and expressions that involve the whole body and its movements.

"Let the words come up through the ground and your whole body," I say. "Focus on how it feels to say them and then vary your tone and cadence. Let one expression build upon the other. Give as much attention to the rhythm of your speech as to the content of the statements and invariably this complete immersion in the expressive process will take you to a different place."

Often the sustained application of creative energy generates a change that emanates organically and with little fanfare from the dialogue. The change might be nothing but a transformed feeling toward a problem, an altered attitude rather than a conceptual resolution.

We can achieve major changes in completely unforeseen and uncomplicated ways. For example, the circular movement might be nothing more than the release of tension, fears, and inhibiting expectations. The sustained rhythm and pulse of a dialogue, the soulful tone, rather than the content of the words, might be the force of transformation. I encourage people to work with whatever words and statements occur rather than thinking too much about what they want to say. Even complete nonsense words and the process of uttering them can take us to new and transformed places. Any word or collection of words can become a healing charm and carry transformative magic when spoken with conviction and creative energy.

How we express ourselves may have more of an impact than what we say. As with music, the words become agents of transformation, shamanic horses that carry expression and transport people to change. Interestingly enough, I have found that the authenticity and aesthetic power of people's statements are constantly enhanced by this simple play with words, voice, rhythm, and emotion. Expressive energy and deep connections to personal experience tend to emerge more consistently from this type of experience than from more direct attempts to sit down and write something significant.

Gertrude Stein in her classic way described an instance of how she kept writing, restating, and slightly altering a simple observation that she made of "big fat pigeons in the yellow grass" and how she "kept on writing" and playing with these words and images until she drained herself of emotion. (Personal interview cited in Bowers 139) Dialogue and expression can be nothing but a creative exercise, a play of imagination for its own sake that fills us with feelings of vitality or perhaps does the reverse in purging our emotional systems in times of need.

When working creatively with words and language as ways of responding to art objects I emphasize how these are simply methods of interpretation that translate expressions in one medium into another. The goal is to get closer to our expressions – seeing, feeling, and knowing them more completely. My over-riding goal is the infusion of creative energy into our lives and I have found that this is how art heals. I emphasize how artistic expressions in painting, movement, and voice are not necessarily narratives and our goal is not a reduction of their expression to this verbal modality. Narrative is one of the many ways of creatively responding to an expression and it is a work of art in its own right. Often the process of dialoguing and using words in a creative way will serve the purpose of activating rhythmic or vocal energies that transcend the scope of a narrative.

In my studios we play with words in the way suggested by Gertrude Stein. For example, a person makes a painting of many intersecting and swirling lines. When contemplating the image, the following statement emerges: "Join me," the picture says. "Dance with me. Move like me"

As the artist moves into the center of our group circle with her painting, she is encouraged to say the words that she recorded and repeat them, restate them, and change their relationship to one another. The work with the group augments the power of imagination as we all live the experience vicariously. We each have our individual relationships with the expressions.

In this situation and others I see how the process of creation is everywhere and always capable of being accessed if we can just open to the moments of expression and let go. But no matter how reliable this experience is and how simple I try to make the invitation to create, the tension is always present. The persistence of this reluctance to express oneself creatively is actually quite remarkable to me. I probably have stayed with this work for so long because it has always been the most challenging thing that I do. It is never easy because people tend to fear self-expression so much.

Returning to the dialogue above, I can say that the entirety of the work that I do with the creative process can be encapsulated in the invitation from the image: "Join me. Dance with me. Move like me."

It is as simple as getting up from our seats, both literally and metaphorically, and entering the space of creative imagination where we can move and dance like the forces that exist everywhere around us in nature and within ourselves unrecognized. There is no beginning and no end to the movement. It can start anywhere and continue as we forget ourselves, let go of our plans and judgments, and just begin to move, to join what is already present and unacknowledged. We can move anywhere we are and in any direction if we just begin. "Move like me," the image says. "Join me."

I see year after year that the success of this work with creative expression depends upon the ability simply to open to what is always with us wherever we go. As Henry Miller said, artists know how to "hook up to the currents which are in the atmosphere...we are only intermediaries" (Strickland 156).

Everything significant is always present but it needs to be "given voice." The job of imaginal dialogue is one of bringing forth and transmitting what exists within us but which we do not know.

WORKS CITED

Hillman, James. *Healing Fiction*. Barrytown, NY: Station Hill Press, 1983.

McNiff, Shaun. *Art as Medicine: Creating a Therapy of the Imagination*. Boston: Shambhala, 1992.

--- "Letting pictures tell their stories." *Sacred Stories: Healing in the Imaginative Realm,* Eds. Charles Simpkinson and Anne Simpkinson. San Francisco: Harper Collins, 1993.

--- *Art-Based Research*. London: Jessica Kingsley Publisher, 1998.

--- *Trust the Process: An Artist's Guide to Letting Go*. Boston: Shambhala, 1998.

--- *Art heals: How Creativity Cures the Soul*. Boston: Shambhala, 2004.

Strickland, Bill, ed. *On Being a Writer*. Cincinnati, OH: Writer's Digest, 1989.

Watkins, Mary M. *Invisible Guests: The Development of Imaginal Dialogues*. Hillsdale, NJ: Analytic Press, 1986.

Winokur, Jon, Editor. *Writers on Writing*. Philadelphia: Running Press, 1990.

CREATING COMMUNITY THROUGH STORYTELLING

Christopher Maier, M.A.

• • •

People are starving for something that was meant
to pass between them but is not presently passing.
Call it a vibration, if you like, or attention, or love.
- Jacob Needleman

I was in a university theater, and a man on a bare stage was telling stories. I was weeping quietly as I listened. For years, decades actually, I couldn't really explain to myself why. The stories were not sad. Often I laughed as well and even then, the tears flowed. I did discover that a similar response would happen at other events called "storytelling," so I went to such events (wearing sunglasses) and continued to wonder at the depth of my response. My language offered me the phrase "my heart is being touched" as its attempt at an explanation. But why? How did it happen? Why did it feel so essential and nurturing even as tears flowed down my cheeks?

There is so little we know for certain. I'm tempted to trumpet out a proud declaration that storytelling is The One Best Way to the Water of Communal Life -- that water of which merely a drop on the lips will awaken each and all to a consciousness of the I-That-Is-We. I would love to know that storytelling will be the Way that will salve the fear and isolation rife in the epidemic of lone individualism from which my country suffers. When I was younger, I allowed myself such messianic certainty. But now I am older. And I have examined the evidence and found contradictions and complications in that heady experience which continues to occur, both at large storytelling festivals and in tiny circles of story sharing, of *communitas*, (ethnographer Victor Turner's term for a deep renewal of a sense of community amongst people as noted by Joseph Sobol). I feel obliged to integrate these qualifications into my song of praise, even as I draw daily upon the continuing resonance of that core experience to motivate and hearten me to do the work of crafting, telling, and healing stories.

Every time I tell a story, I am putting out a call to community. A story presumes a community of listeners who will recognize some experience that they have lived or can imagine living in the narrative. It is a call and response (what in Haitian storytelling is known as a Crick-Crack) where the teller tosses out a community-gathering, a community-presuming device, a.k.a. a story, in the hope that the group of listeners will respond by becoming "we." To the extent that a "we" responds this means that there is amongst the sea of "I"s sufficient shared assent to the virtual experience of the story that each relaxes the contraction of I-ness to "we" themselves within the shared world of this story.

So yes, storytelling builds community, or at least helps the process when the conditions are right over time. No one can guarantee exactly what will be the effect with any one telling of any one story by any particular teller with any particular listener. But yes, storytelling is an essential activity by which community grows.

Perhaps one reason I feel so compelled to qualify my conviction is that there is so little we can strap down and photograph regarding that which flows amongst us in a moment of joint beholding of story, so little we can measure and verify. And yet we still need each other, and thirst for that sense of belonging as we approach the Other across a vast high plain with low shrubs, an expansive opening between us which we attempt to navigate with plot lines. Storytelling is a process of meaning-making that takes apparently meandering pathways to get directly to the heart of the act: the approach to an Other. "Yes:" writes Wittgenstein in one of his pithy remarks about the philosophy of language, "Meaning something is like going up to someone" (135). Wittgenstein offers not a noun in which to contain the mystery of meaning but a verb, a verb blurred by simile: Meaning is like the action of approaching someone, one who is not oneself, an Other (what I want to stress by capitalizing the term). Meaning is not contained within words like gold within old Spanish coins, but meaning arises in the approach of one person to an Other -- a person, a landscape, a stray cat. Meaning is an emergent property of the intersection of systems. Like sweetness arising in the systemic coming together of carbon, hydrogen and oxygen molecules to form simple sucrose ($C_6H_{12}O_6$), meaning arises in a triadic coming together of teller, listener, and tale. (And it is more complex than that simple triangular model suggests; but that will come later.) Each can be seen as meaningful unto itself, dissimilar from carbon, hydrogen, and oxygen, none of which contains the quality of sweetness within itself. Still, it is in the act of approaching an Other that meaning is made new. Each of us mimics this act of approach in our inner ruminations: we tell ourselves stories by playing out games of otherness within ourselves. Yet it is when I am approaching that which is truly beyond me, in the sacred realm that Martin Buber called "The Between," that meaning is most clearly created anew (Friedman 121).

Let me specify what I mean by storytelling, by community, and, to begin with, the key issues I believe we need to consider in examining how the two intersect. The issues can be classified as theoretical, ethical, and pragmatic, though none of these areas are discrete. We need to have a theoretical map of the process by which storytelling builds community sufficiently precise so that we can guide our practice, correcting our course when we are missing the intended destination. One way we can go astray is by ethical insensitivity. The very power that makes storytelling a potent cultural tool opens the possibility of abuse of this power. In a storytelling performance aimed at creating community, lines of connection are attempted among a variety of cultural worlds:

the cultural homes of the story, of the teller, and of the variety of listeners one is attempting to gather into a comprehending "we." Cultural appropriation, exaggeration of or denial of differences amongst these worlds, are some of the missteps one can unwittingly make in one's enthusiasm for fomenting unity via storytelling (Conquergood 5). Beyond the ethical issues, there are the many pragmatic challenges faced by one attempting to apply storytelling to projects of community building. To at least survey these challenges, I will offer some guidance derived from the field experience of myself and other applied storytellers.

THE HEART OF CONNECTION

While every cultural expression from cave painting to video games can be considered beneath the conceptual lens of "storytelling," here I am focusing the term on the unmediated sharing of narratives from articulators-to-listeners. (I would say "speakers-to-listeners" except that I have witnessed powerful storytelling done without a vocalized word by "tellers" using mime, gesture, and sign language). By unmediated I mean with nothing (at least nothing material) between the bodies that meet in this activity, not even a podium with notes or an open book. There is something about that directness of contact that is key to the power of stories to build community. By community I am referring here to an experience of belonging to a collective in which I find identity even as it extends beyond my individual personhood. Not as a concept but as a lived experience.

While I certainly don't want to devalue the transformative power of live reading of stories (or poetry, as for this discussion I don't see the need to distinguish the genres), there seems to be an inverse relationship between the amount of attention that a teller gives to a fixed text and the depth of contact that is experienced by listeners. While this is most apparent in cases where the "teller" is entirely focused on a printed text (and so becomes a "reader"), it is more subtly apparent when tellers give a predominant share of their attention to an inner, memorized text, such that listeners can tell that the irises vaguely pointed in their direction are not really available to make contact. Somehow we listeners can tell when our own presence has diminished in importance to the teller; we have been upstaged, as it were, by the "teller's" commitment to the text. Conversely, I have heard "readers" (William Stafford and Robert Bly quickly come to mind) whose readings felt more like tellings, in that most of the attention of the "reader" was focused on his/her relationship to the listener. So while I have defined a focus for the term "storytelling" -- the paradigm of unmediated contact, an approach of self to other via the story -- I have deliberately not defined an outer, exclusive boundary to delimit what should not be included.

The fact that such subtle "reading" of another's eye-contact is possible strikes me as amazing testimony to how critical true emotional contact is to the vitality and full-actualization of our species. To comprehend this claim, I need to offer a brief synopsis of the triune brain theory developed by Dr. Paul MacLean, which showed that functionally and structurally it is useful to understand the human brain as actually three brains, the later two wrapping around, augmenting and modifying an earlier developed brain structure. The innermost brain stem is referred to as the reptilian brain (as it consists of those brain structures that are similar to those found in reptiles) which is surrounded by the mid- or limbic brain which is what is shared with all other mammals. Our beloved neo-cortex (structures we share with the great apes and some marine mammals), while allowing all the intricate symbolic processing needed to read this essay, is still intricately linked and dependent upon the earlier two brains.

It is the mid- or limbic brain that does the lion's share of relational and emotional processing. It is that brain that is dominant in the crucial processes of attachment between dependent infant and primary caregivers, according to Daniel Siegel in his book, *The Developing Mind*. When the regular needy cries (for food, touch, movement, and later, acceptance, affection, admiration) are not regularly responded to, the child (that survives) develops the rest of its psychological capacities on top of a shaky foundation riddled with defensive patterns that attempt to contract away from feeling the pain of an untrustworthy world. It is also within the limbic brain that the shared ground of empathy is founded. By means of limbic matching, limbic regulation, and limbic revision, the "talking cure" of psychotherapy is possible, as discussed in Thomas Lewis, Fari Amini and Richard Lannon's *A General Theory of Love*. The mid-brain of the client connects with the mid-brain of the psychotherapist to regulate itself and ultimately to revise its core schemas about what rules will govern the individual's relations with self, with others, and with life itself.

What led me to realize the centrality of relational skills to storytelling was my self-directed apprenticeship in storytelling. It was after I had achieved some facility with the many craftual issues of writing and performing that I realized there was still another, more subtle level of craft I needed to develop. This insight came when I noticed how much change there was between the story that was shaped on my word-processor (the written story), the story that was formed by me when I rehearsed it aloud on my feet (the oral story), and the story that developed after performing it repeatedly for and with audiences. That last we might call the relational story, because it consisted of the knowledge of creating and modifying three relationships such that they are kept vital and honest. The first two relations I had suspected and even had occasionally heard tellers mention: the relationship of teller to listener, and the relation of teller to story. The third relation was the surprise -- the relationship of the persona of the storyteller to the multiple truths of the storyteller's being. Only by keeping all three of these relationships vital and honest am I able to do truthful storytelling.

When I have told stories to children and adolescents in a psychiatric ward, I have most tangibly experienced the linking between their mid-brain and my own. I feel their tentative trying on of a different set of relationships with an Other (me), themselves, and the world. They link to my set of relations with an Other (them), myself, and the world, and they do so through taking in my tones of voice and my facial expressions. They are eyeing me to see if I am a reliable caregiver to whom to attach. As evidence, they note not only how I relate to them, but also how I relate to the characters and the world of the story and how I relate to my selves. Yes, it's plural because there are so many selves beyond my public storytelling persona that I relate to when I am telling. When I take on the perspective of a frightened youth or a harsh adult in a story, how truthfully do I do so? The truthfulness comes when I have discovered how to own each character as belonging to some possibility within me. I feel my listeners watching and listening for subtle signs of inauthenticity, and for all the nuanced indications of relational posturing. When what they find feels authentic, they take the risky leap of tentatively and momentarily trying on a different set of relational lenses through which to make meaning of their experience.

Experiences such as those, supported by my study of the recent research on the neurological basis of attachment and emotional intelligence (as investigated in *A General Theory of Love*, and also in Daniel Siegel's *The Developing Mind*), have led me to enrich and expand the model I use to comprehend how storytelling builds community. I used to think it was the story alone which was the common meeting ground upon which strangers – listeners and tellers -- made contact. But that model was inadequate to explain the actual skills it took to make such contact occur and to make sense of the subtle gradations of contact that are significant in comprehending how and why storytelling can build community. I have modified the basic triadic model of storyteller, story, and listener which is conceived within a two-dimensional plane of meeting.

However, before turning to my new model, I want to point out something I had long overlooked in the old model. While the "standard" triangular diagram directs us to see storyteller and listener meeting via the story, we should not overlook the "direct route" (from teller to listener) without the "stop" in story. That line of connections suggests the importance of interpersonal contact above, below, and beyond the meeting in the story, through the shared presence of teller and listener in the living space of storytelling. It also can remind us how the current paradigm of contact as represented by professional platform storytellers is exceptional in the scarcity of contact listeners have with them beyond the time of telling. While the storyteller in some sense only has a story to the extent that she is a stranger to us, and so has stories we haven't already heard (though that may be because we are the ones "new to town"), even with the itinerant storyteller there traditionally would be a series of social exchanges -- e.g. trading with a peddler, sharing of a meal or participating in a shared task -- prior to and building anticipation for the hoped for sharing of a tale.

This extra-textual relationship between teller and listener goes on as well during the actual telling. Tellers quickly learn that they need to tend at least as much to the time of the telling as to the time of the told. It is by their attending to the present shared with listeners that some of the more memorable and delightful moments of storytelling emerge. An unexpected event occurs -- a "listener" speaks up, a camera flashes, an announcement comes over the P. A. system in the school auditorium in the midst of a story performance. Or even a somewhat expected though distracting event occurs -- the train whistle blows listeners' hair back in a tent during the National Storytelling Festival. It is the teller's fresh response to the present event, the absurd and yet possible inclusion of it in the time and the world of the told, that grabs listeners' attention and their appreciation disproportionately. Sixty minutes of storytelling, and yet the moments I have seen most relished by listeners and shared with friends in the post-performance savoring are often those moments which only happened that time, the time that we were there. Such moments capture the rare joy of knowing that our presence mattered. And so we marvel even more at the capacity of those tellers who never abandon us even as they are able to take us away to another world.

REVISING THE WORLD: A WIDER VIEW OF WHAT THE TELLER AND LISTENER BRING

I became conscious of the need for an expanded view of what the teller and the listener bring to the event of storytelling through my intimate tellings to small groups in a psychiatric day-treatment program for children and adolescents. I've since realized this more expanded view -- one that asks us to widen and deepen our understanding of what happens in the telling and listening of a story -- happens in any communication event that addresses the heart. Both teller and listener bring with them their relations with self, other, and world. In the meeting site of the story telling, these two triangles of relations approach and, as it were, sniff each other, twisting and adjusting to see how they can clasp each other. It is in that dynamic dance of finding a way of clasping another's set of relational postures that I imagine the work of community-building is effected. To the extent that the clasping occurs, a shared world is enacted that projects its pattern down upon the lived world that the two imagine they share. Thus the world can be revised so that teller and listener can leave with more of a shared world than the ones they arrived within.

I have simplified the relations to those three -- self, other, and world -- in part because even that is tricky to convey. But each of these three sets of relation can certainly be examined more closely to reveal all sorts of further possible divisions and augmentations.

I will offer but one example of how this model can be augmented from first the teller's and then the listener's set of relations. A teller relates to the world of the story by bringing to it his relations to the consensual world he assumes is shared with listeners. The world he projects into the story is established on his relations to the extra-textual world. That extra-textual world includes how the teller relates to the cultural home(s) of the story. Naturally the more a teller knows of the culture within which the tale has been living (as also the cultural world in which his listeners have been living), the more he can bring that knowledge to inform his telling of the tale.

But all knowledge has limits, and the more we find ourselves Hermes-like carrying tales between cultural worlds the more our telling must include not only our knowledge but our ignorance. By no means is this a call to limit our tales to what we know. A primary task of mythos is to stretch our quest for meaning out beyond the known. How else do new worlds begin to be conceived? However, this is done with integrity by acknowledging where our dreams claim no ground in consensual knowledge. The teller's respect for both a tale's cultural past, as well as the courage he musters in venturing the tale into the present as a proposal for the future, shape the ethical relations that are manifested to the sensitive listener.

I also see the listener arriving to the meeting with tale and teller with her various sets of relations to self, other, and world. What constitutes a listener's relations to self certainly includes all her self-concepts and her self-judgments about her own inner cast of characters -- both those imaginable and those cast out of imagination. But beyond those relations to herself as first-person singular are the relations a listener has to herself as a "we" -- her self-concept as first person plural. How does she relate to her various collective identities, which is a significant part of the delight in being a member of a storytelling audience?

INSIDE AND OUTSIDE COMMUNITY AND STORY

Much of what is significant in what transpires in a storytelling event seems beyond the reach of measurement. In any particular combination of tale, teller, and listener, there are so many variables that influence the experience that a particular outcome seems impossible to predict. Using this model, we can articulate a bit more definitively what factors make each listener's experience so idiosyncratic. Each listener's set of what psychotherapists call "object relations" will govern whether a particular combination of tale-teller-listener can make an affective connection, and further, whether that connection stands a chance of revising that listener's relational map of the world.

I need to add a further issue that troubles any project of community building, no matter what the means one is using, and will name that the paradox of inclusion-exclusion. One of the ways it seems our species has evolved its capacity for collective bonding is by defining inclusiveness in terms of who is excluded. There is hardly any ethnic or other group identity that does not have a name for the Others, those that are not us (pagans, barbarians, goyim, gaje, etc.). This is so deeply entrenched that one wonders if we as a species are yet capable of building a sense of community without simultaneously creating or strengthening a sense of distance from those excluded.

I have found myself puzzling over this general question when I attempted to comprehend some hostile feelings that have paradoxically come along with experiencing great waves of communitas. Often at times such as described at the very opening of this essay, when I felt my heart was most touched by a shared story, I also would notice myself bristling with hostile judgments at those who didn't appear to be sharing my response. I noticed that with the deepening of my affective response often came a corresponding heightened sensitivity to the separateness of my responsiveness. How ironic it seemed to find that my experience of deep human connectedness made me feel more separate from those boors in the next row chatting afterwards about lunch possibilities! From my Buddhist training, I clearly could see how attached I was to those emotional experiences, and so I took them less seriously. Recently this paradoxical experience has troubled me less, perhaps just because I have developed greater acceptance of the paradoxical nature of truth. Still, I couldn't honestly leave these hesitations out of my portrait of this topic.

BEGIN FEEDING THE MOUTHS, THEN THE EARS AND THE HEART WILL RESPOND

Community building always looks toward the inclusive, and continually learning how to make connections. Every step of the journey involves discovering, sharing, co-creating and revising stories – from the grant proposals you write, the interviews you give, the conversations you have with city employees whom you need to grant you a permit, to the chats with people after the event about how it all went. Making community events as welcoming as possible -- particularly through offering food to feed the body as well as stories to feed the heart -- brings people to the most ancient ground for gathering: sharing food as well as tales are primordial needs of our being. I know of no better adage than the F.E.A.S.T. events (Friends Eating and Storytelling Together) put on in Santa Fe, New Mexico by storytellers and community-builders Bob Kanegis and Liz Mangual. Bringing people together to eat and visit can open the doors to the lifetimes of stories within the group.

There is so little reference that people have for sharing their experience with each other, that we must give away free tastes of that experience so that they will remember their yearning for this contact. What helps one to continue to give away free tastes is that in the giving one also always receives. One realizes that one's own hunger for community is fed both by the giving and the receiving of stories.

WORKS CITED

Benjamin, Walter. *Illuminations*. New York: Schocken Books, 1969.

Conquergood, Dwight. "Performing as a Moral Act: Ethical Dimensions of the Ethnography of performance." *Literature in Performance:* 5 (1985): 1-13.

Friedman, Maurice. *The Healing Dialogue in Psychotherapy*. New York: Jacob Aronson, 1985.

Lewis, Thomas, Fari Amini, and Richard Lannon. *A General Theory of Love*. New York: Random House, 2000.

Siegel, Daniel. *The Developing Mind: Toward a Neurobiology of Interpersonal Experience*. New York: The Guilford Press, 1999.

Sobol, Joseph. *The Storytellers' Journey: An American Revival*. Chicago: University of Illinois, 1999.

Wittgenstein, Ludwig. *Philosophical Investigations: The English Text of the Third Edition*. G. E. M. Anscombe, Trans. New York: Macmillian Publishing, 1968.

"TLA IS A GREAT BRIDGE AND MORE THAN A BRIDGE": AN INTERVIEW WITH ALLISON ADELLE HEDGE COKE

Caryn Mirriam-Goldberg, Ph.D.

• • •

Allison Adelle Hedge Coke begins her powerful memoir, *Rock, Ghost, Willow, Deer: A Story of Survival*, by telling who she comes from, and how song and story relate to those origins:

> I descended from mobile and village peoples, interracial, ingenious, adventurous, and bold. None famous, none of any more than humble means, though in this great ancestral river thoroughly bloodstreamed true, I am born from those so devoted to their beliefs and way of living they would eagerly choose to be memorialized through songs or stories of honorable doings, or maybe through sharing a bit of tobacco on special occasions, rather than by accumulating material legacies in life.
>
> Before me and around me were warriors, fighters, hunters, fishers, gatherers, growers, traders, midwives, runners, avid horse people, weavers, seamstresses, artists, craftspeople, musicians, storytellers, singers, linguists, dreamers, philosophers; they were Huron, Tsa la gi (Cherokee), Muscogee, French-Canadian, Portuguese, English, Alsace-Lorraine, Irish, Welsh; and there was the insane.
>
> I understood this by the age of three....We

prayed to greet each morning and to protect us through the night. We sang whenever the feeling moved us.

And my father raised us with attention to story as a simple daily ritual, as regular as changing clothes or brushing hair. (1, 12)

As a writer, storyteller, singer, actress, community organizer, professor, mentor and poet (and author or editor of close to a dozen books of poetry and prose), Hedge Coke migrates around the country -- and the world -- giving talks, readings, workshops and seminars; she also teaches at the University of Nebraska. Simultaneously, she's an accomplished artist who has shown her work at galleries and shows around the country. Much of what she focuses on has to do with the power of words -- aloud and on the page -- to serve individuals and communities, tribes and cultures.

Caryn Mirriam-Goldberg: One of the workshops you give is called "Coupling the Beautiful and the Horrendous." You also bring the historic into these workshops. How do these three things come together for you as a writer, teacher and facilitator?

Allison Adelle Hedge Coke: I found that coupling the three threads -- the beautiful, horrendous and the historical element -- really replicates human experience. We experience the good, the bad, and learn to transcend by dealing with one or another appropriately. The experience offered us is also a deeper revelation than just understanding the experience we have in our own life time. The great thing about this type of workshop -- whether it's master classes in New York City with well published writers and songwriters, or with kids in a high school program, or in a juvenile detention facility -- is that there's not been a time yet that you couldn't have a collective piece out of it even though everyone in the workshop was dealing with different sets of experiences, images, histories. I've never presented it where you couldn't call on students around the room like a conductor of a symphony, and say, "Give me a line of glory, give me a historical element," and it wouldn't fit together; it's really amazing.

CMG: You're a writer, storyteller, poet, actress, playwright, songwriter, and you've taught in schools, colleges, community centers and all around. In your wide experience, what's the common thread you see in using language transformationally?

AAHC: In all of the ways in which we present, portray, deliver, make available to whatever audience we're working with, the common thread is really about communicating, processing as humans, reaching into and delivering, presenting, reaching out to the people we need to be in touch with at present. Any opportunity to do this -- on stage, in a classroom, even alone in a room playing guitar -- culminates in being in the right place for transformational work to occur. It's often times said that whoever's at a meeting or gathering are the ones who should be there. I look at the different mediums and genres I work with -- including sculpture, writing, artwork -- as the choice of the day that sometimes comes to me by nature, by inspiration or muse, but whatever that choice is, that vessel is conducive to the environment that it's meant to serve. The real thread is availability and presence.

CMG: Could you say more about presence, and how presence relates to being a transformative language artist?

AAHC: First, I'll speak from the perspective of teaching using transformative language arts. Often times, particular students, artists, writers, people who come forward for a workshop and to work in this area have a voice that is available to them at the present time that they're ignorant of, or that they've never had privilege of. Unlocking that device of dignity and presence is the force that actually helps the real work to occur. The bottom line is that a lot of people never had the opportunity to learn to be real, to be present, to be in the moment, and let go of any other engagement they carry around with them continually. As a teacher, my task is to assist them in unlocking themselves, causing (me to work from) that state of presence at a higher level and at a more humble level. As a presenter, performer and artist, I know that presence is essential to every opportunity to deliver the message … It's important for me to stay within presence each and every time I create … It's a continual conversation to move ahead toward whatever we need to be in this transformation.

CMG: You obviously grew up in between borders of language, culture, countries, and regions. How does border crossing relate to TLA?

AAHC: A lot of the borders I embraced and was then suppressed by seem to me to be unnecessary constructs …. However, there are lessons to be learned from all of those borders because it's the border that keys us into where problems and issues lie with whoever imposes borders. So I like to look at the border as sort of a mystery puzzle of strategic imbalance that needs to be addressed and remediated. TLA work helps to do all those things because TLA is a great bridge, and more than a bridge. It's sort of something that can decompose borders that are placed upon us for a variety of reasons. One is that central parameters of TLA comes from that inspiration to connect, and then things become more fluid. With that fluidity, it's a lot easier to transcend borders and make crossings.

CMG: You also speak of our role today as "narrativising" consciousness. What does that term mean to you?

AAHC: When I'm speaking of this, it comes from my background in oratory and the oral tradition, and working with people in a very contemporary world. As humans, we are a narrativising culture. When someone begins telling a story of framing a photo and then someone else talks about using scrapbooks to preserve memories, we begin doing this, and before you know it, people will break into metaphor and simile as they need to communicate what they want each other to understand. A speaker will use particular images to bring people to a particular perspective. That's where language beings. We're all connected that way. Sign, symbol, speech, written word, pictures, paintings -- all have narrative in them. There's a huge conversation going on at all times, and that conversation can be punctuated by new paintings, sculptures, books. We're constantly punctuating, and that punctuation changes and transcends culture just as culture created the punctuations in the first place. The effect on culture and creations of culture come back and motivate culture in new directions as well.

CMG: This relates to what you've written about eco-ethics as a way to punctuate what's currently going on in the world. Could you speak about this in relation to paying attention?

AAHC: We have to pay attention. We can no longer ignore things at this time. Culture effects story, and story effects culture. Traditional society and Indigenous societies around the planet still hold traditional laws that come from cultural stories about the environment as a relation. So they tended to the environment accordingly, nurture to nurture. If you take something, you have to give back; there's a balance system. Any time you deviate from that, there are repercussions, and in today's world, we are facing them now. In today's conversation, the punctuations that are necessary are the ones which restore that balance.

CMG: What is the transformative language artist's role in this?

AAHC: There is a cultural duty, a socially conscious duty, a personal individual duty to be part of the conversation for the greater good, the greater understanding, and within that, to find ways to motivate and move audiences to a level of understanding where things can transpire. It has to do with recanting traditional beliefs and philosophies that kept the world in balance, and with bringing that conversation into contemporary times so that [the world] can be restored effectively.

CMG: What is the role of poetry in helping us to tune into the need to find that balance?

AAHC: Poetry is an effective language vessel in that it literally encompasses the greatest devices in oftentimes the most concentrated amount of space one could utilize to present something, and I would venture to say that it works as an incantation, further inspiring the audience to consider, to dwell, to muse, to ponder. In my last collection of poetry, *Blood Run,* I wrote a verse play which deals with an Indigenous mound at a site that's been totally ignored and yet also harbors some of the species that have been eliminated elsewhere. Doing the work about this mound site and presenting it as a verse play became necessary -- to write it as a play and as singular poems in monologues -- to give voice to landscape and beings there today and in the past. [This work is about] starting a new conversation, punctuating it with what needs to be said ... That's what's essential and important especially when dealing with things from a distance.

CMG: Your work is also very sensory, using images to help us connect with our senses. Could you say more about this?

AAHC: I think there's really 32 senses if you count magnetism, and sense of direction and others. I like to think of all these things as being senses that are key to us. Our sensibility in the world is inherently important to us because it's what we have to help us maneuver, to orchestrate our lives. It's a learning tool, and given that we're here to learn and move on, this is how we have to do this. Magnetism is one of the strongest senses because it brings us back to balance in the world. If we have our sense of bearing, we have our balance; if we know what direction we're going, we have the balance; if we have our intuitive sense, we can protect ourselves from getting into dangerous circumstances and into problems we probably shouldn't have to endure and then we can enjoy the world more as well as maneuver through it. If we're not paying attention to what our senses are bringing in, we don't give our mind the opportunity to protect our body.

CMG: How would you relate this to TLA?

AAHC: The language arts are the ultimate expresser, the ultimate medium in which to engage and provide remedy for and information for whatever need is occurring in society, in our individual lives, within our family networks, within our community, within our social groups. First and foremost, language is the primary way we receive and give information beyond our own primary and intuitive senses.

WAKING OUR SENSES:
LANGUAGE AND THE ECOLOGY OF
SENSORY EXPERIENCE

David Abram, Ph.D.

• • •

I'm beginning these thoughts during the winter solstice, the dark of the year, during a night so long that even the trees and the rocks are falling asleep. Moon has glanced at us through the thick blanket of clouds once or twice, but mostly left us to dream and drift through the shadowed night. Those of us who hunger for the light are beginning to taste the wild darkness, and to swallow it -- taking the night, quietly, into our bodies.

According to a tale told in various ways by diverse indigenous peoples, the fiery sun is held, at this moment, inside the body of the earth. Each evening, at sunset, the sun slips down into the ground; during the night it journeys through the density underfoot, and in the morning we watch it, far to the east, rise up out of the ground and climb into the sky. But during the long nights of winter, and especially during the solstice, the sun lingers longer in the ground, feeding the dark earth with its fire, impregnating the depths with the diverse life that will soon, after several moons of gestation, blossom forth upon the earth's surface.

It is a tale born of a way of thinking very different from the ways most of us think today. A story that has, we might say, very little to do with "the facts" of the matter. And yet the tale of the sun's journey within the earth has a curious resonance for many of us who hear it, despite our awareness that the events that it describes are not literally true. For the story brings us close to our senses, and to our direct, bodily awareness of the world around us.

Our spontaneous, sensory experience of the sun is indeed of

a fiery presence that rises and sets. Despite all that we have learned about the stability of the sun relative to the earth, no matter how thoroughly we have convinced our intellects that it is the earth that is really moving while the sun basically holds its place, our unaided animal senses still experience the sun as rising up from the distant earth every morning, and sinking beneath the ground every evening. Whether we are scientists or slackers, we all speak of the "rising" and the "setting" of the sun, for this remains our primary experience of the matter. Which is why I am pausing, at this moment, to feel the sun's fire nourishing the deep earth far below my feet.

*

Going to grade school in the 60s and 70s, I was repeatedly taught not to trust my senses -- the senses, I was told again and again, are deceptive. This was a common theme in the science classes, at a time when all the sciences seemed to aspire to the pure precision of physics -- we learned that truth is never in the appearances but elsewhere, whether in a mysterious, submicroscopic realm which we could reach only by means of complex instruments, or in an apparently disembodied domain of numbers and abstract equations. The world to which our senses gave us direct access came to seem a kind of illusory, derivative dimension, less essential than that truer realm hidden behind the appearances.

In my first year at college I had a rather inane physics professor who would periodically try to shock the class by exclaiming, wild-eyed, that the chair on which he was sitting was not really solid at all, but was constituted almost entirely of empty space. "Why, then, don't you fall on your ass?," I would think. And I began to wonder whether we didn't have it all backwards. I began to wonder if by our continual put-down of the senses, and of the sensuous world -- by our endless dissing of the world of direct experience -- we were not disparaging the truest world of all, the only world we could really count on, the primary realm that secretly supports all those other "realities," subatomic or otherwise.

*

The sensory world, to be sure, is ambiguous, open-ended, filled with uncertainty. There are good reasons to be cautious in this enigmatic realm, and so to look always more closely, to listen more attentively, trying to sense things more deeply. Nothing here is ever completely certain or fixed -- the cloud-shadows darkening the large boulder across the field turn out, when I step closer, to be crinkly black lichens radiating across the rock's surface; the discarded tire half buried in the beach suddenly transforms into a dosing seal that barks at our approach and gallumphs into the water. The world we experience with our unaided senses is fluid and animate, shifting and transforming in response to our own shifts of position and of mood. A memory from a hike on the south coast of Java: it is a sweltering hot day, yet a strong wind is clearly stirring the branches and leaves of some trees across the field. As I step toward those trees in order to taste the moving air, the wind rustling the leaves abruptly metamorphoses into a bunch of monkeys foraging for food among the branches. Such encounters, and the lack of certainty that they induce, may indeed lead us to reject sensory experience entirely, and to quest for "truth" in some other, less ambiguous, dimension. Alternatively, these experiences might lead us to assume that truth, itself, is a kind of trickster -- shapeshifting and coyote-like -- and that the senses are our finest guides to its approach.

It seems to me that those of us who work to preserve wild nature must work as well for a return to our senses, and for a renewed respect for sensorial modes of knowing. For the senses are our most immediate access to the more-than-human natural world. The eyes, the ears, the nostrils catching faint whiffs of sea-salt on the breeze, the fingertips grazing the smooth bark of a madrone, this porous skin rippling with chills at the felt presence of another animal -- our bodily senses bring us into relation with the breathing earth at every moment. If humankind seems to have forgotten its thorough dependence upon the earthly community of beings, it can only be because we've forgotten (or dismissed as irrelevant) the sensory dimension of our lives. The senses are what is most wild in us -- capacities that we share, in some manner, not only with other primates but with most other entities in the living landscape, from earthworms to eagles. Flowers responding to sunlight, tree roots extending rootlets in search of water, even the chemotaxis of a simple bacterium -- here, too, are sensation and sensitivity, distant variants of our own sentience. Apart from breathing and eating, the senses are our most intimate link with the living land, the primary way that the earth has of influencing our moods and of guiding our actions.

Think of a honey bee drawn by vision and a kind of olfaction into the heart of a wildflower -- sensory perception thus effecting the intimate coupling between this organism and its local world. Our own senses, too, have co-evolved with the sensuous earth that enfolds us. The human eyes have evolved in subtle interaction with the oceans and the air, formed and informed by the shifting patterns of the visible world. Our ears are now tuned, by their very structure, to the howling of wolves and the honking of geese. Sensory experience, we might say, is the way our body binds its life to the other lives that surround it, the way the earth couples itself to our thoughts and our dreams. Sensory perception is the glue that binds our separate nervous systems into the larger, encompassing ecosystem. As the bee's compound eye draws it in to the wildflower, as a salmon dreams its way through gradients of scent toward its home stream, so our own senses have long tuned our awareness to particular aspects and shifts in the land, inducing particular moods, insights, and even actions that we mistakenly attribute solely to ourselves. If we ignore or devalue sensory experience, we lose our primary source of alignment with the larger ecology, imperilling both ourselves and the earth in the process.

I'm not saying that we should renounce abstract reason and simply abandon ourselves to our senses, or that we should halt our scientific questioning and the patient, careful analysis of evidence. Not at all: I'm saying that as thinkers and as scientists we should strive to let our insights be informed by our direct, sensory experience of the world around us; and further, that we should strive to express our experimental conclusions in a language accessible to direct experience, and so to gradually bring our science into accord with the animal intelligence of our breathing bodies. (I think of an article I read by a conservation biologist some years ago, on how a research agenda that lacks any felt or visceral connection with that which it studies will necessarily yield poor results. He's right! For such science denies the scientist's own embeddedness in the very world that he seeks to study. Such science is not really Darwinian enough -- it pretends that we humans, by virtue of our capacity for cool reason, can somehow spring ourselves free from our co-evolved, carnal embedment in a more-than-human web of influences). Sensory experience, when honored, renews the bond between our bodies and the breathing earth. Only a culture that disdains and dismisses the senses could neglect the living land as thoroughly as our culture neglects the land.

*

Many factors have precipitated our current estrangement from the sensuous surroundings, and many more factors prolong and perpetuate this estrangement. One of the most potent of these powers is also one of the least recognized: our everyday language, our ways of speaking. What we say has such a profound influence upon what we see, and hear, and taste of the world! To be sure, there are ways of speaking that keep us close to our senses, ways of speaking that encourage and enhance the sensory reciprocity between our bodies and the body of the earth. But there are also ways of wielding words that simply deaden our senses, rendering us oblivious to the sensuous surroundings and hence impervious to the voice of the land. Perhaps the most pervasive of these is the habit of endlessly objectifying the natural world around us, writing and speaking of every entity (moss, mantis, or mountain) as though it were a determinate, quantifiable object without its own sensations and desires -- as though in order to describe another being with any precision we first had to strip it of its living otherness, or had to envision it as a set of passive mechanisms with no spontaneity, no subjectivity, no active agency of its own. As though a toad or a cottonwood was a fixed and finished entity waiting to be figured out by us, rather than an enigmatic presence with whom we have been drawn into relationship.

Actually, when we are really awake to the life of our senses -- when we are really watching with our animal eyes and listening with our animal ears -- we discover that nothing in the world around us is directly experienced as a passive or inanimate object. Each thing, each entity meets our gaze with its own secrets, and if we lend it our attention we are drawn into a dynamic interaction wherein we are taught and sometimes transformed by this other being. In the realm of direct sensory experience, everything is animate, everything moves (although, to be sure, some things move much slower than other things -- like the rocks and the hills). If while walking along the river I find myself suddenly moved, deeply, by the sheer wall of granite above the opposite bank, how, then, can I claim that the rock does not move? It moves me every time that I encounter it! Shall I claim that this movement is entirely subjective, a purely mental experience that has nothing to do with that actual rock? Or shall I admit that it is a physical, bodily experience induced by the powerful presence of this other being, that indeed my body is palpably moved by this other body -- and hence that I and the rock are not related as a mental "subject" to a material "object" but rather as one kind of dynamism to another kind of dynamism, as two different ways of being animate, two very different ways of being earth?

If we speak of matter as essentially inanimate, or inert, we establish the need for a graded hierarchy of beings: stones have no agency or experience whatsoever; bacteria have a minimal degree of life; plants have a bit more life, with a rudimentary degree of sensitivity; "lower" animals are more sentient, yet still stuck in their instincts; "higher" animals are more aware; while humans alone are really awake and intelligent. In this manner we continually isolate human awareness above, and apart from, the sensuous world. If, however, we assume that matter is animate (or "self-organizing") from the start, then hierarchies vanish, and we are left with a diversely differentiated field of animate beings, each of which has its gifts relative to the others. And we find ourselves not above, but in the very midst of this living web, our own sentience part and parcel of the sensuous landscape.

If we continue to speak of other animals as less mysterious than ourselves, if we speak of the forests as insentient systems, and of rivers and winds as basically passive elements, then we deny our direct, visceral experience of those forces. And so we close down our senses, and come to live more and more in our heads. We seal our intelligence in on itself, and begin look out at the world only as spectators -- never as participants.

If, on the other hand, we wish to recall what it is like to feel fully a part of this wild earth -- if, that is, we wish to reclaim our place as plain members of the biotic community -- then we shall have to start speaking somewhat differently. It will be a difficult change, given the intransigence of old habits, and will probably take decades of careful attention and experimentation before we begin to get it right. But it will also be curiously simple, and strangely familiar, something our children can help us remember. If we really wish to awaken our senses, and so to renew the solidarity between ourselves and the rest of the earth, then we must acknowledge that the myriad things around us have their own active agency, their own active influence upon our lives and our thoughts (and also, of course, upon one another). We must begin to speak of the sensuous surroundings in the way that our breathing bodies really experience them -- as active, as animate, as alive.[1]

NOTES

1. The social-construction scholars are no doubt right to claim that our ideas about the world are social constructions, that even our most taken-for-granted notions about nature are inevitably influenced by our particular culture with its specific habits of exchange and interaction. Post-modern theorists rightly recognize that the phenomena we take for granted are not fixed, not objective in the positivist sense -- that we are not passive receivers of sensory information from a so-called objective world, but rather active organizers and interpreters of all that reaches us, that our experience is always already structured by the multiple social forces, polarizations, distributions and dissimulations of power in which we are culturally situated. Many deconstructive critiques stress the extent to which our experience of other-than-human phenomena is already structured by human culture -- to the extant that "nature," itself, may be said to be a cultural construction. And I am largely in agreement with these analyses. Yet I wish to supplement the warranted assertion that our experience of non-human nature is largely constructed by human culture, with an acknowledgement that human culture is itself structured and informed, in diverse ways, by the wider-than-human matrix of powers in which it is embedded. While our notions of the world may be structured by our particular culture, cultures are themselves structured by the interplay of gravity, winds, waters, and sunlight, by the migratory movements of various animals and the nutritional and medicinal powers of particular plants. Human culture, that is itself influenced, organized and mediated by many agencies that are not human or of human artifice.

It is this that those who consider themselves "post-moderns," along with most moderns, all too often miss: the way whole civilizations draw their style from the lands that support them, the way human societies are secretly sustained by the bacteria that break down fallen leaves and the worms that churn the soils, and the manifold others -- wolves, salmon, ravens, thunderstorms, buffalo, bumblebees -- that draw us humans into interaction with them, and so induce us to speak, to dance, to create stories and to weave images, to create culture. Our ideas of nature and the wild are profoundly influenced by our culture, yes, but culture itself is under the influence of a much more-than-human field of forces.

In the absence of such a recognition, social construction analyses risk perpetuating, in post-modern guise, the most spurious of all modern presumptions -- the presumption that humankind is the sole creative (or constructive) agency in the earthly world. Such analyses all too easily become merely a new justification for the exploitation and destruction of other-than-human realities for purely human purposes. They risk being taken up, for instance, by those who wish to justify the biogenetic engineering of other-than-human organisms for purely human benefit: since nature is largely a social construction, then why not continue to construct the rest of nature as we see fit?

Constructionists are right to assert that the "reality" we so easily allude to is not a fixed and determinable realm, but they are wrong to attribute this indeterminacy only to the shifting contestations of power within human society. The more-than-human terrain in which human societies are situated is not a static, mechanical order but is itself a fluid, ever-shifting webwork, a dynamic field of alliances, affiliations and contestations between diverse shapeshifting collectives and nodal agencies. It is not only humankind that constructs our experience of things; the things themselves play with us and among themselves -- attracting, hiding, displaying, fusing, multiplying and metamorphosing, actively participating in the ongoing emergence of "the real."

Gravity, sunlight, air, soil, rain, bear, magpie, cedar, granite — in one sense these are human words with particular social and scientific histories; yet these words are also provoked by our bodily encounter with various wild and shapeshifting powers, animate forces that lend their palpable influence to all our endeavors, to our communities and our economies, so much so that, without ever pretending to completely fathom these powers, we can justly acknowledge them as active agents in the "construction" of our societies and our identities.

By acknowledging the direct, material influence of these

agencies, we do not pin human reality to a static or determinate order of essences. For by affirming the canyons, the wind, the moon, and the forest as actors, as animate agents like ourselves, we simultaneously acknowledge their formative influence and their otherness (their wild indeterminacy, their existence not as fathomable objects but as inscrutable entities with whom we stand in a living relation).

Of course the world we experience is not an objective and determinate reality -- there is no doubt that it is a social creation! But the "society" that constructs this indeterminate world is much vaster than any merely human society -- it includes spiders and swallows and subterranean seepages along with us two-leggeds. Surely it is time to outgrow this most tenacious of modernist presumptions: for all our craftiness and creative ferment, we humans are by no means the sole, or even the primary, agents of the world's construction.

...

WORLDS OF WORDS: REALMS OF TRANSFORMATIVE LANGUAGE ARTS

...

EDUCATION OF THE HEART: TRANSFORMATIVE LANGUAGE, AMERICAN CULTURE AND THE 60s

Janet Tallman, Ph.D., M.L.I.S.

• • •

INTRODUCTION

> *High culture and common culture can be acquired only by initiation. Neither can be learned by sociological study or historical analysis. You are inducted into a culture, and this process of induction is also an education of the heart.*
>
> - Roger Scruton

> *I saw the best minds of my generation destroyed by madness, starving hysterical naked, ...*
> - Allen Ginsberg

Language gives us everything -- our thoughts, our identity, and our social place. It also has the power to transform us, individually and as members of the wider culture. I watched the transformations of language in a special time and place -- America, especially Berkeley, in the 1960s, while I myself was coming of age.

What I experienced in the 60s was fresh, unexpected, the concomitant experience of hundreds of thousands of people, mostly my age, pushing against the status quo and defining new ways of being and thinking. The hope that Kennedy and King brought to us was not yet tainted by the shock of their assassinations. Our revolutionary music and slogans had not yet been incorporated into Muzak and advertising. Women and people of color had not yet been suppressed once again by backlash. We did not know that stopping one war was no guarantee that we could stop all the rest of them.

I want to explore here the language artists who helped to transform me and my time during that period when I was shaping my identity and vision of the world. I also want to look at America in the 60s, and name some of the language artists who carried me and many progressive and radical members of my generation into a new way of looking at the world.

First, let me contextualize this in terms of cultural changes. Cultures change constantly, and this change happens through the hearts and minds of the members of that culture. In modern Western European culture, that change often comes through language -- through the books we read, the words of the music we listen to, the scripts of the movies and videos that are presented to us constantly. The stories we tell, our arguments and conversations, are the externalized manifestations of our inner life. They transform us, advance our thinking, and help us to shape our identities.

Almost all of us use language, and we are part of culture that, sometimes slowly, sometimes quickly, evolves. We are also all part of age groups that go through similar stages of development, from the dependent periods of childhood through the self discovery of adolescence, from our absorption into the social and political world around us to an understanding of deeper levels of meaning, however we might define them. Language constantly mediates these changes, through our personal and social language use and through our experience of the more public language that reaches us through education and the media.

A few among us, let us call them language artists, use language in a special, skillful, poetic and charismatic way, to help us shape our time and culture, to move us forward. We experience these artists through their writing -- through books, newspapers, and magazines; on the internet, on television, in movies, and in songs; and through speeches, slogans, and storytelling. Most of these language artists reach us where we ordinarily live, perhaps opening our minds a bit, perhaps helping us to support what we already know. A few of them go beyond where we are, and move us further. Of that number, a tiny handful puts into words the thoughts of our times we didn't even know we were thinking, or they give us a vision that speaks to a longing that we didn't even know we had.

I want to draw circles around what I include and leave out of this essay. I will wander without distinction between high and low culture, drawing on popular literature, music, oratory, statements of liberation and poetry as well as works considered high art, naming various sources that led to changes in consciousness that came about not only in my own life, but in my culture. The education of my own heart that happened during the 60s came from established poets, anonymous freedom fighters, unknown musicians, great civil rights leaders, French philosophers, and marginalized wordsmiths who came from the edges to define and lead a new generation. Sometimes these sources were unique to me; most of the time I was one of many they reached.

For many practitioners, the transformative language arts have both a healing aspect and a self awareness component. Through both the practice and the teaching of transformative language arts, transformative language artists bring others, often marginalized Others, into self awareness, through journal writing, poetry writing, memoir, songwriting, theater or storytelling. In some cases this self awareness moves the transformed individuals further into social action; in others, the transformation of Others is considered to be social action in itself.

In this essay, the dyadic or group related transformation through language, with a language artist changing another or Others, is not my focus. I treat myself alone (but as a typical example of many like me) as the one transformed, and the artists who have transformed me are my own private guides. In many instances the language artists who were transforming me were also catalysts for changes that transformed hundreds, thousands and hundreds of thousands during my time and later. Often they were conscious of their use of language as a tool of social change, but sometimes they were not. Thus this is both a very private, and at times a very public, examination of the power of language artists to transform us, individually and collectively.

I am tempted to argue that all of us could trace our coming of age in any time and place, noting the role of language artists in our development and education; and that we could all discover the interplay of public and private, status quo and revolution. However, I also feel that that place and time, America in the 60s, and my position in it, are unique. More specifically, I believe that the shifts in consciousness which occurred in the 60s were more intense, transformative, and creative than those that happened in the 40s and 50s, the 70s, 80s and 90s, up to today. In addition, I believe that these speeded up periods of transformation reoccur on a regular basis, and draw from the revolutionary periods that preceded them while helping to shape the periods of change that will come.

During the 60s, as we were experiencing our cultural revolution and watching the changes in South and Central America, Europe and China, we were also drawing on the Socialist Worker's movement from the turn of the Twentieth century, earlier pacifism in many generations, the Communist Revolution, Russian and early American anarchism, the ex-patriots and Bohemians of the Twenties, the suffragette and abolitionist movements of the Nineteenth century, and such visionaries as William Blake, Karl Marx, Mao Tse-tung, Walt Whitman and Sigmund Freud. These movements and thinkers all came from other periods of strong revolutionary change, in which language artists and transformative language art were central to the movements and visions.

Born in 1941, I saw the wave of change begin that was to engulf the Baby Boomers arriving in 1945 and later. Born Canadian and raised American, I had a slight distance from the culture that surrounded me, the slightly different focus of someone who did not automatically take the culture for granted. Born disabled, with dislocated hips, I had long hospital stays through my childhood, held rigid by half-body casts, isolated from my family; I grew up bookish, and found so much of my learning coming through a study of history and language artists. Finally, from my position in the Midwest, I could look somewhat dispassionately at both the West Coast and the East Coast, from where so many of the changes were coming.

I came into the world as a heterosexual, white female, was raised in the semi-rural suburbs outside Minneapolis, and had all the benefits and tensions of an upper middle class Republican, Episcopalian upbringing. All of these existential qualities impacted my experience of the 60s. Looking back forty years later, I understand that my experience of this time, except tangentially, excluded people of other classes, ages and race, sexual preferences, and those with less privilege. The boundaries of my class, race, and gender are apparent in this catalogue of what and who transformed me.

Like so many potential intellectuals in the Midwest, I knew by the time I was 16 I couldn't stay where I was. I went to San Francisco for a summer in 1960 and moved there in 1962. I entered UC-Berkeley in January of 1965 and left America for two years in 1969 to do fieldwork in Yugoslavia. When I returned in 1971 the social movement that I had known was passing for me, although for many it was just getting started. I write briefly about the periods before the 60s and after, but my main focus is on the 60s.

In this writing I examine the transformation of American culture, focusing on works of a few of the language artists who, for me, caused a shift of consciousness, a new way of looking at my time and culture. Their words, visions, and ideas, their fresh points of view, angry critiques, and charismatic renaming of our experiences still shape my understanding of the world. I have chosen works which shifted not only my awareness but also the awareness of people around me, and ultimately the culture. Many other language artists opened my mind in literature and linguistic anthropology, my fields of study, but unless they also changed the minds of those around me or anticipated the changes that were to come, I have not included them.

COMING OF AGE, ALIENATION AND PROTEST

One good of poetry is that it gives us a closer approximation of the sorts of consciousness that live in and animate a single person, a culture area, or even a historical period.

\- Paul Freiderich

...dragging themselves through the negro streets at dawn looking for an angry fix,...

\- Allen Ginsberg

Although the Midwest is devalued in American mythology, I consider myself lucky to have grown up there when I did. However, I felt early the longing for something more than the comfort and safety of a middle class, Midwestern, suburban life. When I was 15, I experienced the adolescent hysteria brought on by Elvis, and the rock-and-roll that was beginning to emerge through Bill Haley and the Comets seemed to promise a sexual freedom very different from the virgin-until-you-are-married mindset that constricted me and my classmates. Slowly, alternatives began to seep in to awareness, sometimes from progressive teachers in high school, more often through my peers.

At 16 I read J.D. Salinger's *The Catcher in the Rye*. Holden Caufield's alienation, his cynicism, his disdain for the phoniness of his time and culture, and his implicit longing for something more authentic became a mirror for me to hold up to the unexpressed, perhaps even unconscious, distresses I felt in my parents and their contemporaries. The martinis and the cocktail parties, the men's long hours of work away from home, the women's boredom and the social realities of a church life that blotted out anything spiritual spoke to the emptiness of The Good Life.

Holden Caufield was someone who had it all -- private schools, a posh apartment in Manhattan, easy money, a certain amount of sexual freedom as practiced among his preppy peers, and all the high culture he could possibly want at his fingertips. He, however, wanted no part of it. He hated the coarseness of his classmates' sexual encounters, but the sincerity of an intimate, sexual encounter eluded him. He found the members of his social circle empty headed, opportunistic and with little inner life. His peers were cruel in their hazing and exclusion of socially awkward contemporaries. He could find no relief in alcohol, and therapists didn't reach through his cynicism. His education and social training were meant to prepare him for a professional life that did not interest him. His father's profession as a lawyer lacked all idealism and instead was built on social ambition and political compromise. Only his younger sister's innocence and loyalty gave him the sense of righteousness he craved.

I felt that Holden Caufield had looked right into my life, noticed my father's absence as he created his career, noticed the despair my intelligent mother felt as she was tied down to the house, the demands of four children, and the inane social life of the suburbs. I saw that he knew, also, how my love for my younger brother was the only thing that made sense to me in the hidden tensions of our family and the social world around us.

For those of us coming of age in the middle and upper middle class, in the process of being trained in some scaled down version to participate in the life that Caufield rejected, his disgust and alienation rang true. His story was in a sense tragic, stating the problem but leaving us with no solution. At the end we don't know what happened to him. He was defined as "sick," e.g. mentally ill. Those of us who were captured by his story had a sense that the culture, the morally compromised work, the social expectations, the exploitative sexuality, the easy alcoholic escape were what was really sick. Like him, we were reluctant to leave our adolescence to join that bleak adult world.

As an undergraduate, I discovered T. S. Eliot, his early writing and especially his poem, "The Wasteland," which took Salinger's implied critique of 50s American middle class culture and broadened the problem to encompass all of the twentieth century and Europe as well as North America. I read, studied and wrote about Eliot, and about "The Wasteland" in particular, day and night for a year. As I moved into adulthood, inarticulate and yet suffering from the contradictions, shallowness and escape into alcohol that marked my parents and my older contemporaries, I found in Eliot's depiction of an emotional , intellectual and spiritual wasteland a metaphor for my dis-ease.

My attraction to Eliot was a move back to the existential crises of the Twenties rather than an anticipation of the 60s, but at the same time it helped define the hollow spirituality, fragmentation and emptiness of the Twentieth Century which had produced and preoccupied Salinger and Holden Caufield. The loveless coupling of the typist home at tea time and the small house agent's clerk (Eliot 38-39), the superficiality of the women who come and go talking of Michelangelo (3-4), and the crowd of the dead flowing over London Bridge (31) could all have come straight from Caufield's world. My study of Eliot led me back to the white American ex-patriots of the 20s and from there to the Beat writers and poets of the 50s. By this route, I discovered the voice of the American shadow and underbelly.

Eliot's despair was echoed by the writers of the Beat Generation, though Kerouac went a step further and gave us a plan of action. Holden Caufield had only imagined giving it all up and hitting the road, going west to a cabin in the woods. Jack Kerouac did it. Although many years later I was repelled by the misogyny and self-destructive themes in his writing, in 1960 Jack Kerouac showed me and many of my contemporaries the True Way in *On the Road*. Freedom, mobility, altered states of consciousness, and the Bohemian way of life became for me the only honest response to the materialism, hypocrisy, secular Christianity, and middle class smugness of white America. He went on in *Dharma Bums*, through the figure of a fictionalized Gary Snyder, to turn many of my generation toward Eastern religion. He led a number of my contemporaries to join the Forest Service to spend lonely, meditative summers in the fire stations of the west. His visions of San Francisco, therapy, drugs and the creative life compelled young people from around the country to leave home, heading for that city of freedom.

While many of us were creating a critique of the 50s' military-industrial mindset and its shortcomings, others were turning to grassroots politics to speak to issues of social rights. I began to feel a sense of the social unrest that was to culminate in the social movements of the 60s. Kennedy had just been elected, and freshness, hope, change, youth and meaning all seemed possible. In 1961, in Minneapolis, under the influence of Quaker friends, I got my first peace button, joined a Ban the Bomb protest, and at hootenannies began to learn the peace songs and labor movement history of the Thirties.

In the last months of my undergraduate years, in 1962, I knew, along with the intellectuals of my time and place, I had to go find the Real Life. As soon as I graduated, I went west, looking for Jack Kerouac and Joe Hill. I was to spend a few years following Jack Kerouac, absorbed in the hallucinogenic world of the flower children. Only later did I find the organized social protest, which in many manifestations was the reemergence of the labor and worker movements of the generation before us, transposed to the young of the middle classes.

On the Road, Freedom and Fellow Travelers

Come writers and critics
who prophesize with your pen
and keep your eyes wide
the chance won't come again
and don't speak too soon
for the wheel's still in spin
and there's no tellin' who
that it's naming
for the loser now
will be later to win
for the times they are a'changin'
- Bob Dylan

...angelheaded hipsters burning for the ancient heavenly
connection to the starry dynamo in the machinery of night...
- Allen Ginsberg

I arrived in San Francisco in that unnamed period of time after the Beats and before the hippies. I had come too late for Allen Ginsberg's North Beach reading of "Howl." The Summer of Love was yet to come. I became witness to the changes that were arising, and watched the transformation unfold. Musicians, poets and writers led us in the changes, and experiments with mind altering drugs and sexual freedom preoccupied us.

My first act upon arriving in San Francisco was to go to City Lights Bookstore in North Beach and sit among the local intellectuals, idols of my imagination, and read "Howl." Ginsberg knew and spoke my truth, and confirmed my awareness that the best and most sensitive and creative minds around me were going mad. People I knew were committing suicide, drugging themselves with alcohol, becoming paralyzed by depression, and acting out an angry and yet impotent rejection of the anti-sensual, middle class, military-industrial straight world that was America. I read "Howl" as a definition and a description, and only later understood it as prophesy. Ginsberg gave me the words to describe the undercurrent of despair around me, and lessened my sense of isolation, of feeling that I was the only one that realized that America was in pain.

In San Francisco in August of 1963 I found a place in a quiet neighborhood called the Haight, and became friends with people in two communal houses nearby, houses that eventually became the center for the whole transformation of Haight-Ashbury. Into those houses flowed marijuana and hallucinogens; out of those houses flowed social activists. Sexual freedom was taken for granted. Living in that house was the son of the *San Francisco Chronicle* journalist Donovan Bess; he told his father about these experiments in communal living, and a series of newspaper articles starting in January 1964 made the neighborhood famous.

I met my first lover in one of those houses, and together we moved to Berkeley, where with two other housemates we formed our own communal house. In early 1963 Janis Joplin, on her first train trip from Texas to the Bay Area, crashed in our Berkeley house for a couple of weeks. She would wake up late each morning hung over from her visits to the coffee houses and late night music venues, then drink more coffee and sing her gravelly voiced songs in our run down Berkeley kitchen.

In the spring we moved back to Haight Ashbury, and we experimented and played with mind expanding drugs. We could still get peyote buttons legally from Laredo, Texas, and LSD from Sandoz. Two years before this time Richard Alpert (who later would change his name to Ram Dass) had announced to his psychology class that he had just taken a drug that would change his life, (LSD), and with Timothy Leary he started the International Foundation for Internal Freedom. At that same time a new folk singer named Joan

Baez was singing in Harvard Square, and my friends were being hosed down the stairs outside the HUAC hearings in San Francisco. The Cuban missile crisis gave rise to rallies in support of Castro's experiment in Cuba.

Right after moving back to the Haight, I heard people talk about a certain song and a singer-songwriter. I remember the first time I heard Bob Dylan's "The Times They Are A'Changing," and soon after, I heard his "Blowing in the Wind." The words were mysterious, and I didn't quite know what they meant, but I knew that something was shifting, that I was part of it, and that I would never be the same. Everything hinted at in those songs came to pass, quickly, and with powerful consequences. Suddenly everyone seemed to be hearing these words of our own prophet-poet.

For two years from 1965-1967, I remained at the center of this cultural shift, watching young people from all over the country pour into San Francisco "wearing flowers in their hair." Drugs were benevolent, sex was safe, and the music of the Beatles and the Rolling Stones, The Grateful Dead, Jefferson Airplane and Big Brother and the Holding Company, brought us together in great outdoor concerts and in wild dancing at the Fillmore into the late hours.

On the edges of this period of sensual exploration and consciousness expansion we were aware that major events were taking place. Our pro-Cuba and anti-HUAC protests evolved into rallies and marches in support of the civil rights movements. In August of 1963 Martin Luther King, Jr. transfixed a nation and gave voice to the African American place in this culture with his speech "I Have a Dream" and his March on Washington for Jobs and Freedom. Slowly the conditions of African-American existence, civil rights and non-violent disobedience began to penetrate my white consciousness.

In November of 1963, John F. Kennedy was assassinated. Suddenly many of us sobered up. Hedonistic self-exploration seemed trivial after the power and tragedy of that event. I began a five month period on the road, traveling to different parts of the country to see how widespread were the changes I knew in San Francisco. Certainly in the big cities of the East, among the young and educated, the times were changing. I stayed seven months at my parent's home in Minneapolis preparing to enter graduate school at Berkeley.

In the first day of summer 1964, three civil rights workers, James Chaney, Andrew Goodman and Michael Schwerner, were killed. The anguish I felt at their deaths, experienced in the indifferent Republican atmosphere of my Minneapolis home, showed me that I had to pay attention to the political processes of our country and to work toward social change. These three men, students, intellectuals, and fighters for social justice, had given their lives for others. I identified with them, wanted to be like them, and had found the antidote to the meaninglessness and hypocrisy of the life I had experienced until then. Soon I was to learn that I was not alone in these desires to act out my social criticism and anger.

SOCIAL MOVEMENTS, SOCIAL PROTEST AND THE WAR

There is a time when the operation of the machine becomes so odious, makes you so sick at heart, that you can't take part; you can't even passively take part, and you've got to put your bodies upon the gears and upon the wheels, upon the levers, upon all the apparatus, and you've got to make it stop. And you've got to indicate to the people who run it, to the people who own it, that unless you're free, the machine will be prevented from working at all.

- Mario Savio

...who passed through universities with radiant cool eyes hallucinating Arkansas and Blake-light tragedy

among the scholars of war
who were expelled from the academies for crazy &
    publishing obscene odes on the windows of the
    skull, ...
- Allen Ginsberg

In the first part of the 60s I had been among young college drop-outs experimenting with alternative lifestyles, expanded consciousness, experimental sexuality and underground ways of making money. In the second half, I was among the university people who were leading the movement for social change.

Although I came to the document itself later, at Berkeley I could feel the effects of the Port Huron Statement, created in 1962 by Tom Hayden and other founders of the Students for a Democratic Society (SDS). This statement created the vision, and members of SDS created the leadership, for a grassroots movement that ultimately challenged every aspect of the American status quo. The statement put into words what so many had been feeling: "We are people of this generation, bred at least in modern comfort, housed now in universities, looking uncomfortably to the world we inherit." (Gosse 65-66). It went on to highlight racism and the Cold War as the two major issues of the day, and called for participatory democracy which would bring back to individuals control of the social order to which they belonged.

The Port Huron Statement represented for me one more very concrete articulation of how we, my generation, might be in the world. Caufield and Eliot had helped me to name the problems, Ginsberg had given me a voice for my anger, Kerouac had offered one solution, and the deaths of the civil rights workers had shown the need for another. The Port Huron Statement was a manifesto for those of us, perhaps the best minds of our generation, at Berkeley, Columbia and other universities around the country, and it showed us the steps to take, and the reasons behind those steps, for social action and change. It gave me meaning and purpose.

Following the lead of SDS, campuses across the nation began to organize around issues that were more relevant to students than corporate profit and military domination. Students, primarily graduate students in the more prestigious colleges and universities, created a network of social activism and protest. I arrived in Berkeley one month after Mario Savio gave his cry to challenge the universities in their complicity with the Department of Defense and major corporations. At Berkeley students were demanding, through rallies, speeches, pamphlets and civil disobedience, the right to disseminate information about radical social action, especially the civil rights movement, and they called for the right to free speech. All over the campus -- in teach-ins, study groups, large gatherings, and discussions over coffee -- we learned about these issues. These learning experiences were much more meaningful than our classes.

The war in Vietnam began to escalate in 1965, and student leaders shifted the focus of the discussion away from free speech and the civil rights movement and toward protests against the war. Teach-ins on Vietnam took the place of classes for many of the students and some faculty, and out of the universities came the March against the War in Washington DC. Through the SDS network information on actions, reports of frequency and size of protests, and plans for organized protest sped from campus to campus.

During this period, although a few people had taken leadership of the movement, no one language artist predominated and no one document shaped the changes that were occurring so quickly. The most powerful focus of the anti-war movement was not a document, transformative language, but rather a picture posted in the newspapers of a Buddhist monk who set himself on fire in protest against the war. Language was transforming us, but it was ephemeral. Speeches came from anyone who had the ideas and the courage to address huge rallies and marches. Pamphlets, newsletters, newspapers and leaflets were put out by committees. Such works, words, slogans, lyrics, and chants, as well as being anonymous, were transpersonal, finding each of us in our individuality, and transforming us into a collective united by language. Walking down the street with tens of thousands of others shouting "Hell, no, we won't go!" united us in our ideas, intentions and actions.

I often go back in my memory to those years we spent on the street. Why were they so powerful? For me answer is twofold -- they helped me break through the sense of isolation I had felt that no one else cared about the social problems I saw. Also, they gave us the experience of action beyond community. We were not paralyzed. We could change the world, and we saw ourselves doing so. Much of what we were learning came from ephemeral writing, a paper version of the Internet, writing with a life span of a week or at best a month. Here is an example of one of the leaflets that came out during and from those who called themselves the Free Speech Movement. In it, the unnamed writers are conscious of their task, their political context and their educational purpose.

> *Throughout the semester, the FSM has been producing leaflets and pamphlets at a furious pace. We have been patient, repetitious, sometimes boring, we have tried to explain what we're doing and who we are. As we look back at our written communications of the semester, we discover that to some extent we have failed. Each day was an emergency, a crisis, so that although we said important things, issues arose which were not of the moment -- important issues which we have not adequately discussed. We take this opportunity to more fully discuss our movement, the university, and our education. ("We Want a University")*

I would read this and think, "Yes, this is what I know, what I have experienced, what is relevant to me right now!"

The writers, probably some of the leaders of the movement, then go on to define the purpose of the movement, the place of the multiversity in America, and the importance of resisting the university status quo. Through such leaflets we could constantly define who and where we were and what we were trying to do.

A few well known prophets, critics, poets and songwriters were present and part of the movement. Noam Chomsky came from MIT and spent some months at Berkeley. During the day he discussed his revolutionary transformational grammar with that small group of us studying linguistics. When he switched from linguist to anarchist philosopher and political critic, he electrified large crowds of us with his highly informed speeches about Vietnam, the war, American corporate culture and government non-accountability. Allen Ginsberg showed up at the marches from time to time, chanting. The night before one march aimed at the draft board in Oakland, rumor had it that he dissuaded the Hell's Angels from disrupting the march by dropping acid with them. At one anti-war march in San Francisco, to my delight, I found myself walking next to Pete Seeger, who played his banjo and led us in anti-war songs. Here was a man who embodied not just the present struggle but the earlier struggles that were teaching us, feeding us -- the workers' struggle for rights, communism and socialism and the resistance to the American anti-communist movement, and I was shoulder to shoulder with him. I was part of history.

One song, simple and powerful, adopted from gospels and the African-American labor movement, brought up through Pete Seeger and the civil rights movement, became the anthem of the anti-war movement, "We Shall Overcome." This was our hymn, our prayer, our hope, and our announcement.

As the 60s progressed, the anti-war movement began to escalate its tactics. The civil rights movement was evolving into a movement of more militant Black leaders. Malcolm X's assassination, the Watts rebellions and uprisings by radical and poor black people all over the country led to the creation in Oakland of The Black Panther Party, at one level an organization of self defense, led by armed men, and later a social program which brought food the young children and social services to the community.

At Berkeley the anti-war leaders and the leaders of the Black Panther party shared the podium at marches and rallies. Huey Newton, Eldridge Cleaver, Kathleen Cleaver, Angela Davis and Bobby Seale became familiar on campus and in the marches and rallies on the streets, and one time I even showed Eldridge Cleaver a poem I had written about Huey. As non-violent civil disobedience was giving way to rebellion and the destruction of property by both Black and white militants, the energy began to change. Blacks began to self-organize in Oakland and San Francisco, and then throughout the country. The Ten Point Program which defined the goals of the Party, was a powerful document calling for an end to Black oppression. It ended with the Declaration of Independence, giving us a poignant rereading with new meaning. (Black Panther Party for Self Defense 1966). Reading this, I rethought both independence and the meaning of who was American.

The recognition of the racist underpinnings of the draft, the realization that a disproportionately larger number of men of color were fighting in Vietnam against other oppressed people of color, the obvious influence of class privilege on the draft gave way to a frustration and rage that began to shape the movements. African-Americans retaliated by arming themselves. I remember once studying in a coffee shop in Berkeley while at the table next to me, three white men opened a suitcase to show a collection of guns to several African-Americans dressed in the militant uniforms of the time, and the negotiations began.

In 1968 the assassinations of Martin Luther King and Robert Kennedy spread waves of violent rebellion throughout the country.

The members of the Black Panther Party were hunted down and arrested by police, and the FBI used assassination and destruction of centers to break the movement. Several leaders went into exile or underground. The SDS split, part of it becoming the Weathermen, a group committed to violent action to bring about social change. Broadly in France, Germany and Czechoslovakia and to a smaller scale in other European countries, students and workers formed alliances that never solidified in America, where the police and army went armed to suppress the activists.

In Berkeley activity had shifted from peaceful though angry and intense rallies to encounters with the police. One protestor had been killed during one of the protests, and police violence was escalating. We gave each other training in how to protect ourselves against tear gas. The day before my doctoral orals the campus was tear gassed from above by a police helicopter. For the first time in my professors' memories my orals had to be held in a private home; we were afraid to come to campus. I could not go out to celebrate my successful completion afterwards, because we had a curfew and police patrolled the city. At the time, my orals and the lack of celebration felt very natural, at one with the wider events. Even the curfew had come to seem normal. Later, looking back, I realized how odd this must have been for my professors, who had lived most of their academic lives in peaceful settings. I remember this lack of celebration when reading about people in war, unwilling to celebrate important personal events with bombs landing on their cities.

In the summer of 1969 I left America to begin two years of fieldwork in Serbia, Yugoslavia. I wrote in my journal just before I left, "For a year and a half I leave America—the war, the cities, Blacks, police, student politics, pollution, Easy Rider and all it stands for. I end my thinking about these, learn a new set of worries and cares of a people not my own."

When I returned in the summer of 1971, the public movement

against the war had abated, the Vietnam War was ending, and the leaders of the various movements were dead, in jail, or had moved on in their professional and personal lives. Altamont in December 1969 ended the innocence of the hippy movement. Kent State in May 1970 had shown how far the government was prepared to go in silencing students. Still, the ideas and visions of the movement began to permeate all aspects of American life. Those of us who had been so deeply transformed by that time took our understanding and strategies into our work, our teaching, our writing, and we began to spread the word. For me this meant that I could not teach in traditional universities and I have made my career at the edges of academe, in experimenting and alternative colleges and universities; and, in my teaching and writing, I must look behind events, look for the contradictions, and apply critical thinking to everything.

Other movements also blossomed as the main movement dissolved, first on the West and East Coasts, and then permeating the country. For me the women's movement was foremost among these, and I will return to that, but also the gay liberation movement was emerging after Stonewall in 1969, as were movements for identity and political rights among Latinos, Asian Americans, Native Americans, the elderly, the mentally ill and the disabled. Each of these had its own leaders, its writers, its manifestos, and its struggles.

I will step back in time again to the mid-60s, to look at one of the movements that was beginning to emerge from under the umbrella of the major public movements. As men struggled with the help of women to change and perhaps overthrow the current social order, women struggled to understand their relationship to men, and to themselves.

WOMEN, VOICE, POWER, AND SEXUALITY

If what Proust says is true, that happiness
is the absence of fever, then I will never know

happiness. For I am possessed by a fever for
knowledge, experience and creation.

> *I think I have an immediate awareness in*
living which is far more terrible and more painful.
There is no time lapse, no distance, between me and
the present. Instantaneous awareness. But it is also
true that when I write afterwards, I see much more, I
understand better, I develop and enrich.
>
> - Anais Nin

> *...who talked continuously seventy hours from park to*
> *pad to bar to Bellevue to museum to the*
> *Brooklyn Bridge, ...*
>
> - Allen Ginsberg

The movements of the 60s were largely run by men, reflected male strategies and male privilege, and flourished and floundered on the battles of men's egos. Conventional wisdom has it that the force for women's liberation came from the women who were relegated to the backroom tasks in the anti-war and Black liberation movements. Men took the lead, because, after all, it was men who were drafted and dying in Vietnam and on the streets of America through police brutality. The movement's women petitioned for their own rights to speak and act in the movement, and then, gathering with each other, they started a grassroots movement to improve women's position publicly, at work and at home.

My shifting understanding of the role, identity and potential of women came from a rather different, much more private source, was almost wholly founded in books rather than action, and was more French than American. Because I was upper middle class from an elite university, unfettered by husband and children, able to get by on my intelligence, I was *almost* accepted as an equal by my male teachers and colleagues. I did not existentially feel the need to struggle for my political and economic rights.

I was much more interested in the psychological oppression that led us as women to doubt and question everything we did, that culminated in our suppressed rage and depression, and that branded us with silence. I turned to women writers, especially three writers rooted in France, who had struggled with these questions, and quietly, privately, I began the long road of changing my consciousness.

At this point I am not talking about a song, a manifesto, a poem or a book that accompanied personal and social transformation. I am talking about large bodies of work written in lifetimes, by three writers: Anais Nin, Colette, and Simone deBeauvoir. Anais Nin, through her journals and experimental fiction, gave me a path through writing to my interior life and to my voice. Colette gave me a model for my social independence and sexuality. DeBeauvoir showed me the life of a fully manifested and independent intellectual, who had a powerful awareness of social forces and consciousness.

I came to Anais Nin in 1966 through a friend, who had found and read Volume 1 of Nin's Diary when it first appeared. Through Nin, through her diaries and experimental fiction, I received permission to explore every aspect of life -- artistic ideas, political attitudes and worries, the nature of the spiritual life, and above all, the power and vagaries of love. The delicacy and beauty of her writing, her emotional risks, the intimacy of her subjects, her honesty to herself inspired me as a writer. I also idolized her life style. Reading about Nin's romantic nights in the Thirties on her houseboat, her wandering through Paris to hear Gypsy music, gave me a lifestyle to emulate, and took me one step further away from the suburban Midwestern life I had shed.

More than writing style, freshness of subjects and life style, Nin gave me permission to think and write like a woman. She made me understand that the fluctuations of the heart, the sea changes of emotional life, and the interior reflection on everything that passed by her were suitable topics for literature. She also gave me permission to explore the use of the diary, so female, so undervalued in male literary life, and to treat it as an art form as well as an emotional release. Forty years later, I have a bookcase full of my journals, and a much richer life because of my reflection on that life through writing. I write every day, recording and analyzing, creating a memory and personal history and also bringing into consciousness the contradictions and uneasiness of my daily actions. My journals have kept me honest.

Through my exploration of my own thoughts and voice, following Nin's lead, I also began to externalize that experience. I became much more fully aware of how women's voices, ways of thinking and ways of experiencing the world, our expertise on relationships and emotions, our concern for interior development, were dismissed and denigrated by the male world of thought and literature. In the 60s, when I was in graduate school, only one in seven women finished their doctoral programs. I knew that my voice was not heard in seminars, that my ideas were absorbed by my male classmates and passed off as their own, and that only my ability to write got me through my courses and garnered me some respect for my intellectual ability. Only later did I realize that my sojourn in this male world had damaged me. For ten years I could not write with fluency, and I doubted my voice. Slowly, with the help of other women, I re-learned how to make my voice heard.

In graduate school I felt constantly alienated from the topics and conversations and concerns of my teachers and peers. As I read Nin, I found a voice, a style, topics and issues that were mine, and then discovered other women writers who spoke and thought like me. My journals, enriched and inspired by Nin, sustained me in my emotional life, and gave me a place to formulate and work out my ideas. I came to the realization that I would succeed in graduate school only if I learned to talk and write as though I thought like a man. I wrote analytically, critically, effacing myself, while privately holding onto and developing my voice as a woman. I became one of the few women of my age group who succeeded in finishing graduate school.

The second writer who transformed my life and consciousness was Colette, a French woman of letters in the first half of the Twentieth Century (Colette). Like Nin, she wrote of the interior life, of love, of her relationship to her mother and of the importance of nature to her life. I loved her writing, its delicacy and humor, its slyness and passion. Perhaps more than that, I loved her relationship to life. She was a woman who had it all -- she married young, a rather open and wild marriage, and ultimately she rejected her husband's attempts to shape and dominate her, especially as an artist. Later she married more happily, and had a daughter. She lived in the racy world of the theater, and she was an early cross dresser in the Twenties, performing in men's clothing. She explored relationships with women, and in intimacy, crossed age barriers herself and through the lovers in her novels. Something about her French-ness, which allowed her to accept and revel in her own erotic nature, allowed me in the midst of American Puritanism to revel in my own. She was a fully liberated woman of the 20s and 30s, beautiful, a prolific and creative writer, and a very successful artist. She gave me a model of a strong, feminine, creative and joyful woman.

In the mid-70s I began a serious study of Simone de Beauvoir, and she helped me to understand the nature and social position of women. In *The Second Sex*, using history and literature, socialist and existential theory, the findings of psychoanalysis and her outstanding intelligence, Simone de Beauvoir accomplished three things. First, she acknowledged that women held positions in society inferior to men's. Second, she explained how that had come to be. Third, she showed a way out through the empowering of women through economic, legal, intellectual and social independence. Being French, she was more accepting than were Americans of women's sexuality and our freedom to own and live our sexuality independently. As an intellectual, working equally with Sartre as they changed French intellectual thought, she gave us a model of how to be a fully manifested thinker.

In the American women's movement de Beauvoir's themes were reflected in the ground breaking scholarship of the 70s. Feminists explored women and madness, sexual liberation, the reclamation of women's accomplishments from history, the ways of knowing and writing used by men that excluded or devalued women, and women in political and academic life. We were empowered to take over responsibility for our own bodies, and we developed our own voice.

This manifested itself in my own teaching. One of the first classes I taught was an exploration of rape, in which we read about the prevalence of violence in American culture, and of men toward women. In addition, using women's ways of thinking, we also explored our own experiences of rape, and used those experiences to critique the denial in American culture of the extent to which men abused women. The women's movement also manifested itself in my scholarship. I was an anthropologist who could study the place of women around the world, and I could also study the ways women spoke in conversations as I developed my linguistic anthropological work in conversation analysis. Not only did I not have to teach and study the received wisdom of men, I could expand and critique that received knowledge in my own research and study.

In the 70s, not only did women come into their own, but many other groups flourished as well under the influence of the movements of the 60s. My own activity focused on women and was manifested through teaching. I studied and taught about the writings and life of action of Emma Goldman, the Russian-American immigrant activist, an earlier generation's fighter for women's liberation (Goldman). Her grounding of women's position in the political and economic framework of capitalism, and her belief in the power of anarchism to dissolve difference of race class and gender, sustained me. She had anticipated many of the ideas that were re-invented in Berkeley in the 60s. Teaching her ideas of free love, equality of men and women, the fallibility of the government, the importance of struggle for human rights, and the problems of intolerance, I could share those ideas, made safer by being bound in an historical framework, with my students and colleagues, and to bring to a rather conservative, small New England town the open-mindedness I had found in the 60s at Berkeley.

I followed the development of Latinos, Native Americans, Asian Americans, and especially African Americans as they struggled for political, legal, social and creative freedom. When I moved back to the Bay Area in the 80s, Gay Liberation was the defining movement of my time and place, and once again we were in the streets asking for justice. In Berkeley, the Center for Independent Living raised our awareness of the invisibility of the disabled and it created changes in our environment to make normal participation in ordinary life possible for the visually and hearing impaired, people in wheel chairs, and others with disabilities. The subtleties of those movements, the defining events, people, and documents, are other people's stories to tell. Instead, I will conclude with a short look at the time period since the 60s, briefly mention the transformations which have persisted and moved more fully into American culture, and contemplate the role of transformative language artists today.

AFTERMATH AND CONCLUSIONS

> *It was as if all the arts and sciences in the 1960s had been given a rocket boost of creative shakti that paralleled the titanic technological, social and political explosions of the decade—a creative power capable of hurling human beings around the Earth and into space, within and without.*

- Richard Tarnas

...who scribbled all night rocking and rolling over lofty incantations which in the yellow morning were stanzas of gibberish, ...

- Allen Ginsberg

In 1984 I was back at Berkeley getting a degree in library science when people gathered on campus to celebrate the twentieth anniversary of the start of the Free Speech Movement. Two decades seemed to drop away as I saw the familiar faces and heard the familiar voices of the former leaders of that movement. Many of the leaders had gone on to write books, gain political office, and become active in education. I stood at the rally with tears flowing, passionately asking the question: "Have we been true to the ideals of the movement?" The answer that came back was "Yes!" Sometimes I have to look hard. America has a way of eating up its memories, and the government has a way of suppressing the stories it does not want told. But I find evidence that the influences of the 60s still survive, and that people young today are looking back forty years for guidance and inspiration.

I see the manifestations of the 60s, our transformations, in the alternative life style movement, in our relationship to America's militarism, and in civil rights. With regard to lifestyle, the "natural" and "back to the land" ideas of the 60s have manifested in widespread access to organic foods and healthy foods in general, and to respect for the environment in food, shelter and transportation. Ginsberg's looking toward the East for spirituality manifested in many practices and practitioners of Buddhism, meditation, and alternative medicines. Women have revived Paganism and women's understanding of medicine. Open sexuality is much more accessible to the young and to those who are not monogamous heterosexuals. Alternative education, an outgrowth of the teach-ins and Free

Universities of the 60s, and an answer to the multiversities we critiqued endlessly, is available to those who want something more progressive than public schools.

Student protests made it impossible for the United States government to continue the war in Vietnam. Resistance to the draft gave way to a volunteer army. However, in this arena the gains of the 60s have resulted in an increased sophistication on the part of military leaders in methods for suppressing protest, privatizing war, and withholding and distorting information about military decisions and actions. People continue to protest the wars, military actions and invasions that have occurred since Vietnam, but the media is much more highly controlled and news of these protests is suppressed. At the same time the government has pursued its policies regardless of the resistance or disagreement of a majority of Americans.

The civil rights advances of the 60s and its aftermath have been extensive, but these too have been under attack in this time of repression. Women and people of color, those marginalized by sexual preference, disability, religious views or something else, have found more room in mainstream America, and have expanded their civil rights. The rights of children are much more widely respected. However, backlash in all these areas is strong and effective. Gays and lesbians are denied the legal rights of married heterosexual couples, women have made only small gains in the higher levels of leadership of the country, and people of color are imprisoned in much higher rates proportionally than white people. The poor are losing many of the gains from a century of struggle, around food, medicine, education, and shelter, as the gap between rich and poor widens.

New issues have emerged which we couldn't have begun to imagine in the 60s, including globalization of economies and the exploitation of the global poor; global and imperial warfare from the United States; climate change and global warming; and the expansion of the number of political and environmental refugees and their immigration to the industrialized nations. In the 60s we could not have predicted the collapse of the Soviet Union and the turning of that country and of China toward a mixture of communism and capitalism; nor did we imagine the unification of Europe. We had not foreseen the power of AIDS to call into question all of the liberation we felt in the movement toward free love. We did not realize that the American government would use prisons for the poor, and repressive psychology and drugs for the middle class, to eliminate the voices of protest and resistance. We could not have imagined how fully the press would be harnessed toward the policies of a handful of governmental right wing Christians and war merchants. We had no glimpse that something like the Internet and cell phones would allow us to be virtually present at Tiananmen Square and in the bodies of the planes hijacked by terrorists on September 11, 2001. As we struggled to find our voices as women, we did not know that domestic violence was killing and imprisoning so many women and children in American culture and around the world.

These are now all issues at the forefront of our thinking. Transformative language artists still have power to shape and change our thinking about such issues. Our change agents are many -- word artists who come from the underbelly; leaders of world government; or our personal guides, therapists, students and teachers. They open us to new ways of knowing, new ways of naming the world, new ways of thinking about ourselves and the social situations in which we find ourselves. We live within words -- spoken, sung and written; they sink into our minds, give us stories, name what we cannot name alone.

I remember sitting in my car on December 7, 1988, before taking the train to work, and hearing Gorbachev address the United Nations General Assembly. He talked about how the Soviet Union would demilitarize and democratize, and take part in global cooperation, concluding: "One would like to believe that our joint efforts to put an end to the era of wars, confrontation and regional conflicts, aggression against nature, the terror of hunger and poverty, as well as political terrorism, will be comparable with our hopes. This is our common goal, and only by acting together may we attain it." His hopes were not realized because of America's military expansion and isolationism, but in that moment of history, Gorbachev's words ended for me my adulthood fear of the Cold War and the American government's excuse of the threat of communism to suppress our freedom.

Sometimes I wonder if the power to transform through the language arts is diminishing, and perhaps passing away. True, the generations after me have expressed and created social transformation through the words of rap and hip hop, which have become global and are adopted by people of any color in America. My middle class progressive friends followed passionately the writing of Aaron Sorkin during the years of "The West Wing," when our political desires and fantasies became real in a fictionalized way. People are still out in the streets protesting the war in Iraq, suppression of civil rights, the WTO, and they are making speeches, singing songs, chanting slogans.

Yet the potential transformative language artists and carriers of social justice and social change are more frequently at ease with the ordinary everyday speech of websites and blogs, the instantaneous information of the Internet, and the individualized musical repertoires of iPods. We don't seem to share language collectively any more in social action and social change. MoveOn.org, by naming political issues and actions is creating social transformation, but not in an artistic way.

I may also be speaking as an older person, at this age outside the flow of language that calls for transformation and cultural shift. Perhaps the people now in their twenties have their equivalents of my Mario Savios, Jack Kerouacs, Allen Ginsburgs, Holden Caufields, and Simone de Beauvoirs, and I simply have lost touch. Perhaps it is the case that the oral tradition is the locus of social change. We have an upsurge of interest in oral history and storytelling. People are creating their own stories as a means of transforming themselves and re-evaluating their experience, or using stories as teaching tales to help others grope toward understanding, knowledge and wisdom. Perhaps their changes are coming through non-verbal media -- MTV, films, home videos, and concert artists. Perhaps even more radically they are coming as acts of resistance, violence and terrorism.

Finally, I have to consider that there may not be much social change happening at this point in history, that this is a time when the status quo has such a grip on the thinking of Americans that the voices, the literary works, the poetry and prophesies have been still born, and do not have an impact on the wider social order. However, I don't believe that. It is American nature to grope toward freedom of expression, to resist the attempts to take away our rights to participate in the decision-making processes of the government. In spite of censorship, anger suppressing drugs and prisons, we raise our voices and call for change, or spend our days and nights reading, writing and thinking about how best to make sense of our own experience, to transform ourselves and thus transform the world.

Even if the language arts are diminishing in power, they are still very strong. I return to what I said at the beginning: language is at the center of everything we do, the ways we think, and how we perceive the world. Language allows us to name most of the world around us, and in so naming, we bestow meaning. Through this meaning we can be transformed, allowing ourselves new forms of consciousness to develop.

I look at my own life, the ways that language has helped me to name the sickness that I see in American culture, the loneliness and alienation, and at the same time language and language artists have led me out of despair and into action and hope. I found the voices that spoke to me -- Salinger, Kerouac and Ginsberg, who named my world; de Beauvoir, Nin, Goldman and Colette, who named my identity; and the others who gave me political direction and aesthetic standards, the Kennedys, King, Dylan and Joplin.

When I think about the future of the transformative language arts, I realize that I cannot predict where this discipline is moving. I would love to see other people take their own coming of age stories, their social movements and their chosen decades of change, and look at them through the lenses of the transformative language arts, identifying the works that have transformed them. The transformative language arts, although they may be playing a shrinking role in the consciousness of the young, are irrepressible. The pen is mightier than the sword, the dollar and perhaps even the power of love. As humans we create and share our creations, changing ourselves and others in the process. If we understand in the following song that "singing" means to put into words and learn from words our own understanding and identity, our urge for social justice and wisdom, then Pete Seeger, in his variation on a theme, sings it well in this old hymn shaped to leftist consciousness:

My life flows on in endless song
Above earth's lamentations,
I hear the real, though far-off hymn
That hails a new creation.

Through all the tumult and the strife
I hear its music ringing,
It sounds an echo in my soul.
How can I keep from singing?
...
When tyrants tremble sick with fear
And hear their death knell ringing,
When friends rejoice both far and near
How can I keep from singing?

In prison cell and dungeon vile
Our thoughts to them are winging,
When friends by shame are undefiled
How can I keep from singing?

WORKS CITED

Black Panther Party for Self Defense. "The Ten Point Program: What We Want/What We Believe, October 1966." 16 Nov. 2006. <http://www3.iath.virginia.edu/60s/HTML_docs/Resources/Primary/Manifestos/Panther_platform.html>.

Colette. 22 Nov. 2006. <http://en.wikipedia.org/wiki/Colette>.

De Beauvoir, Simone. *The Second Sex*. 1953. Parshley, H. M., trans. New York: Knopf, 1957.

Dylan, Bob. "The Times They Are A'Changin'." 16 Nov. 2006. <http://www.bobdylan.com/songs/times.html>.

Eliot, T. S. *The Wasteland and Other Poems*. 1930. New York: Harvest Books, 1958.

Free Speech Movement. "We Want a University." December 1964-January 1965. 15 Nov. 2006. <http://www.fsm-a.org/leaflets/WeWantUniversity.html>.

Freiderich, Paul. "Culture in Poetry and Poetry in Culture." *Culture/Contexture: Explorations in Anthropology and Literary Studies*. Ed. E. Valentino Daniel and Jeffrey M. Peck. Berkeley: University of California, 1996. Pp. 35-57.

Ginsberg, Allen. *Howl and other Poems*. 1956. San Francisco: City Lights, 1959.

Goldman, Emma. 8 Nov. 2006. <http://en.wikipedia.org/wiki/Emma_Goldman>.

Gorbachev, Mihail. 20 Nov. 2006. <http://www.cnn.com/SPECIALS/cold.war/episodes/232/documents/gorbachev/>.

Hayden, Tom and Students for a Democratic Society. "The Port Huron Statement." 1962. *The Movements of the New Left 1950-1975: A Brief History with Documents*. Ed. Van Gosse. Boston: Bedford/St. Martin's, 2006. 65-67.

Kerouac, Jack. *The Dharma Bums.* New York: Harcourt Brace, 1958.

---. *On the Road.* New York: Viking, 1957.

King, Martin Luther, Jr. "I Have A Dream." 14 Dec. 2006. <http://americanrhetoric.com/speeches/mlkihaveadream/htm>.

Nin, Anais. *The Diary of Anais Nin 1931-1934.* New York: Swallow, 1966.

Salinger, J. D. *Catcher in the Rye.* Boston: Little Brown, 1951.

Savio, Mario. "Mario Savio: Sproul Hall Steps, December 2, 1964." <http://www.lib.berkeley.edu/MRC/saviotranscript.html>.

Scrouton, Roger. *An Intelligent Person's Guide to Modern Culture.* South Bend, Indiana: St. Augustine's Press, 2000.

Seeger, Pete. 22 Nov. 2006. <http://www.peteseeger.net/howcanikeepfromsinging.htm>.

Tarnas, Richard. *Cosmos and Psyche: Intimations of a New World View.* New York: Viking, 2006.

"We Shall Overcome" 21 Nov. 2006. <http://www.en.wikipedia.org/wiki/We_Shall_Overcome>.

SHAMANS OF SONG: INTERVIEWS WITH DEIDRE MCCALLA, KELLEY HUNT & GREG GREENWAY

Caryn Mirriam-Goldberg, Ph.D.

• • •

The following interviews all examined the role of the singer-songwriter, and his/her music, in social and personal transformation. All three of these singer-songwriters interviews -- Deidre McCalla, Greg Greenway, and Kelley Hunt -- embody diverse musical genres, and social and personal transformation through their songs. All have been on the road for more than two decades each, making a living through performance, workshops and commissions. In their words, we hear some of what it means to mediate between worlds and bring forth the music that tells us more about who we are and how we live.

Deidre McCalla

Deidre McCalla is an award-winning singer-songwriter, modern-day troubadour and pre-eminent performer in both folk and women's music circles, having performed with notables such as Tracy Chapman, Suzanne Vega, Odetta, Cris Williamson, and Sweet Honey In the Rock. An African-American lesbian feminist with five albums to her credit, Deidre's words and music traverse the inner and outer landscapes of our lives, chronicling our strengths and weaknesses and celebrating the power and diversity of the human spirit. Her CDs include Everyday Heroes and Heroines, Don't Doubt It, With a Little Luck, *and her latest,* Playing for Keeps.

After Deidre McCalla's excellent performance at The Power of Words conference at Goddard College in August of 2005, where she was a keynoter, I arranged for a phone interview with her. This conversation took place in early September of 2005.

Caryn Mirriam-Goldberg: Many of your songs speak both from experience and hunger for justice. What motivates you to write?

Deidre McCalla: I usually need to write when I'm trying to make sense of the world around me. For any person with a creative outlet -- that could be something in the arts or an automobile mechanic -- however one expresses oneself creatively is one way of ordering what's around you, making sense of it. This could be something personal I'm going through, something interpersonal I'm going through, something I'm observing around me.

CMG: For songs like "God Only Knows" ….

DM: "If God Only Knew"

CMG: Sorry, I mixed you up with the Beach Boys. Bet that doesn't happen often. Anyway, what triggered that song?

DM: That was triggered by what I saw, felt happening in this country in the aftermath of Sept. 11, 2001. What struck me was how easily, how often, the word "god" was being invoked in every corner, everyone claiming to know what god wanted in this situation no matter who their god was. A lot of music, particularly some country music, invoked…an American sense of god, a European sense of god, saying what we should be doing on god's behalf, which is very presumptuous.

CMG: What about a song that seems to come from a very different direction, and one I find immensely moving no matter how often I hear it – "Mama Loves Me" (a children's song that celebrates lesbian, gay, single-parent and multi-race families)?

DM: I've only gotten positive response to that song. I don't do it every show -- it has to be a show where I'm connecting with the audience. But any audience that draws the song out of me really takes it in. It's a simple song. I actually found in my career that my simple songs, written in a solo, off-hand easy fashion as opposed to the ones that I ridiculously labor over each and every word, really connect the strongest with audiences. Particularly with (gay, lesbian, transgender community) families, there's so little music that speaks directly to our lives. There's a real hunger for it. Our children need songs that celebrate our lives, empower our lives. I did that song at a Quaker conference that I performed at in July. A woman with the dearest of intentions stopped me and asked if I considered adding a verse for heterosexual families to see themselves in that song. I said to her was that there are so many other songs for children of heterosexual families to find themselves in. I don't want to provide that kind of balance in that song. What I hope is that as people take that song into their families and groups, other verses can be added about other families … add or subtract verses that're applicable to their community.

CMG: Where does the writing in you come from?

DM: You know, Caryn, if I knew, I would tap into it on a more sustained basis. I don't know where it comes or why it comes. I sure wish it would come more often and more consistently. I was reading a book on songwriting, something I do often, and one of the things … is that there's the creative muse writer, and then there's the editor. My challenge is that I have a much stronger editor -- if she would just shut up and let me write, just go away! Even before the creative muse can get out the gate, the editor goes, "Well, that sucks, that's trite, that's bad." I can only regard it (the muse) as a gift.

CMG: Even if you have a very strong editor, you must have a very strong muse. Are song-writing part of your spiritual path? Or is it a political act for you? Or all of the above?

DM: I do believe singing and writing are what I was meant to do. One of the things that intrigued me about the TLA conference was the whole concept of right livelihood, which is a concept that I stumbled upon about 15 years ago, and I hadn't heard anyone else really talk about since then. When I discovered it, I thought, yeah, this is what everyone should have in their life. At the time, I was doing music about five years, and I realized this was the path I was on, this is the work I was meant to be doing. Whether it's going to keep a roof over my head ultimately, I don't know, but one of my ways to judge the rightness of it all is when people tell me what the songs have meant to their lives, and realizing that what I have created resonates in other people's lives in the same way that Joni Mitchell's music resonates for me, or Paul Simon's. I know what a treasure that is to actually feel in kinship with or understood by another artist. Everyone has one singer-songwriter who sings their lives, and for me, that was Joni Mitchell. And for me, to have someone having the same reaction to my music means something's ringing true.

CMG: I love Joni Mitchell too, but you know, here you are, an African-American lesbian singer-songwriter living in the south raising your child on your own, and Joni is a white, heterosexual Canadian who gave up her child for adoption. What an amazing connection!

DM: It's about illumination. The specifics of some people's work, Joni Mitchell's work, -- like when you know she's talking about James Taylor or you just have too much personal information -- don't matter as much when the songs are cast in such a way that they illuminate an essential tradition. Then that light can light through a multitude of lives. Even though her work might be very personal to her, its expression to me just radiates beyond the specifics of whatever incident sparks it in her life.

CMG: What's a song that means a lot to you?

DM: There's Sandy Denny's "Who Knows Where the Time Goes" – great illumination, great imagery, great poignancy in that song.

CMG: And yet deceptively simple.

DM: But it's larger than its simplicity.

CMG: You sing with such energy that really pulls the audience in vividly. Your performance doesn't feel so much as a performance as something that's happening between us.

DM: I majored in theater in college, and performance was my whole entry. For the longest time I wanted to be the next Jane Fonda. At a period in her life. I thought she was just exquisite, but music took a stronger tack for me, and it was all on a continuum. (Theater) is a craft I put a lot of energy into, thinking about what is a show, in terms of pacing, and all the technical stuff like that. If I couldn't perform, I wouldn't do it. Maybe I'd still write, but to me, it is a performance … the connection with the audience is the point. In my everyday life, I'm quite a shy person but for some reason I'm much more comfortable up on stage in front of a room full of people than at a party at someone's house. It's really manipulation, and even as an audience member I know that the audience wants to be manipulated -- in a good way -- taken somewhere, safely on a journey. That's what my shows are, come ride with me for a while, let's do this together, let's explore it together.

CMG: Are you surprised often when you're up on stage?

DM: Am I surprised?

CMG: By what happens or what you decide to do?

DM: I have to be honest and say, sometimes I am, but for the most part, I really do look upon it as a play and so I've kind of basically sketched out how to get from A to B. If for some reason a song doesn't work with a room, then I have to scramble, but that's not surprise as much as fear, "Oh man, I messed that up."

CMG: You home-school your son, and he travels with you too. How does this work with being a singer-songwriter for you?

DM: Anne Lamott said in a piece she wrote that she's had to learn to write on the margins of the rest of her life because being a parent is so consuming that the time that's left for the artistic part is on the margins of the paper. I do wish I knew where the muse came from so I could tap her more regularly. The fact is, I'm exhausted, and I daily struggle with trying to clear enough time to listen for the music. Fortunately and unfortunately, a lot of my creative energy has gone into my son, having to relearn algebra, and (being a single parent), wearing all the hats ... He's starting 7th grade, starting to work a bit more independently too, so we'll see how it goes.

CMG: What's the role of community for you?

DM: I think I would have a very different career if it wasn't for the women's music movement and gay and lesbian community because that really is, for the longest time, where the work was and where the need was. There were so few strong, confident women in music and definitely no lesbians, and now we live in an age with Melissa

Ethridge and Katie Lang, and Brittany and Madonna kissing like they are, and so we did our job so well that there's no hunger for that as much. Community has given me a strong enough base to continue doing what I do, even on my level, which wasn't as popular as Cris Williamson but I'm still able to survive. I'm still very grateful that when I'm getting ready to do my album that I can raise money from fundraising ... I must be doing something right because every time people come through -- they give me money, they buy albums ahead of time, sometimes it's outright, "I really want to support what you're doing, please keep doing it." Things like that give me a great sense of belonging and that I am doing what I'm supposed to do.

CMG: What's the role of courage in this kind of life for you?

DM: (laughter) I don't know if it's courage or stupidity. I think you gotta be a little daft to do this because there's so many out there saying you're crazy to do this and on a very practical level, when I sit down and write the pros and cons of continuing with this lifestyle, there's a lot more cons -- there's the health insurance con and no retirement con, and I-don't-know-three-months-from-now-where-the-money-is-coming-from con. It's very similar to the list of when I was deciding whether to raise a child. All that was on the pro side outweighed a million cons. I'm not quite sure it's courage as much as belief, and putting one foot in front of another, and taking care of all the ducks in the world that it makes sense to take care of, and there's some you can't line up. I'm very grateful that I have a couple of people in my life who came through when times were dark, saw me trying like a ram (to get through a wall), and said, "Here's an extra step ladder, use mine" as opposed to many people I know in my life, who when they come to a wall, sit down and say, "It's a wall, and I can't get through."

CMG: It sounds like you're the vessel for something that's got to come through at times. And that surely enters into your performances. How do you prepare yourself for getting out on stage?

DM: Most performers have their little rituals, and one of the things I say to myself is that I'm not here to sing but to be sung to.

Kelley Hunt

Kelley Hunt is a rhythm and blues singer who has three CDs to her credit, including the recent award-winning New Shade of Blue. *Her previous CDs include* Kelley Hunt, *and* Inspiration. *She regularly tours the U.S. and Canada with her band, performing at blues and jazz festivals, on television and radio shows, in movies, and at concerts in a variety of venues. She has been featured many times on National Public Radio's "Prairie Home Companion" as well as on "Austin City Limits." She also regularly leads workshops on jazz piano, songwriting, and singing. She also composes for film and various projects.*

Hunt is also known as someone who collaborates extensively: She regularly composes with many long-time songwriters as well as emerging ones, including me (we also run a small business together, Brave Voice, offering writing and singing workshops). This interview took place in my home office, the purple piano we co-write on behind us and my laptop in front of us.

CMG: Have you always known that you needed to make music?

KH: I can't remember a time when I didn't know that. My first memories of myself as a child involved music, either hearing my mother or my father, or hearing music in the house when I was just a tiny little kid. I never questioned it and the people in my family never questioned it.

CMG: More than anyone I know, you play in many genres at once.

What gives?

KH: I think a common thread runs through all of them that has to do with my development as a person. It also has to do with what I was exposed to as a child and what I chose to surround myself with that gave me comfort when I was growing up. So instead of trying to put some kind of censor on myself and think, I'll just do this style or that, a few years ago, I made a conscious decision to not be conscious of the style and simply let happen what was going to happen, knowing it was going to be unique to me, and also fully understanding it would be incorporate a lot of things. And that's when my music and creativity opened up, when I took the fences off from the different styles and quit separating them.

CMG: One of the styles that you do, gospel, speaks to a spiritual center and yet I hear that in so many of your songs. Is singing and writing songs part of your own spirtitual practice?

KH: Yes, I think it's the major part. It's also a reflection of things that fed me as a young child and as a young woman. My grandma sang gospel and spiritual music, my mother and father, and especially my mother sang in church so when I was very, very young, like two, I had a memory of watching my mother be the entire choir in the little church I was in. It wasn't so much about saving souls but about the music she was doing, and the style was gospel. As a little kid, I thought that's what you do, it's the no bullshit approach, it's celebratory because she absolutely exposed herself, tears coming down her face, smiling and very unguarded in her music. I found that endearing.

CMG: Who wouldn't? Where else did you learn about music and community?

KH: I also saw my mother in different settings sing different styles of music, and I would observe the people that were observing her, and see how moved they were, and seeing what she put out that moved them somehow that wasn't about the music but what she did. Even as a young child, I realized how moving that was for other people, like a direct line to somebody's soul.

CMG: Kelley, you grew up in Emporia, Kansas which is what we might call a medium-sized town in a small town state.

KH: I think it was 18,000 people when I grew up there.

CMG: What was the role of music in both community and identity when you were growing up?

KH: Well, I'd say, interestingly enough, it had a very strong role in the school system that I was in. There was a lot of singing, dancing, music from other cultures that was brought in (like part of learning Spanish), but I had exceptional teachers in junior high and especially in high school in singing. I was bored a lot -- there wasn't a whole lot going on in my world, or anyone else's -- so I tended to get involved in singing in school choir, church choir, rocket adult choir. And in my home, it was music all the time, mom singing, my parents' friends coming over and playing music -- they all played music. My older sister sang and wrote songs, my brother was singing in a choir in junior high, and there were records and radio always. I woke up in the morning and my Mom would be downstairs with the radio going on, playing the hits of the day, and when I came home from school, she always had music playing in the house. It was something for me to do with my time, a way for me to be unique. In a lot of ways I didn't fit in -- I wasn't the blue eyed, blond hair Kansas girl. But when, although I was really shy about it for a long time, the cat was out of the bag, and I played in a talent show with a guitar and singing, I realized I was the only one doing this. Music allowed me to be myself.

CMG: It seems like music also allowed you to convey where you come from, such as in songs like "Rose's," which is about the corner grocery store in your town, and "Queen of the 88s," famously about the woman who taught you to boogie-woogie. You've used your songwriting to keep some of that life going on.

KH: I hadn't thought about that, but it's so meaningful to me and helped me make some choices in my life and helped form who I am. There's something very dear and limiting about growing up in a small town. My choice was to leave that town, but I think I've written about the things that meant the most to me in one form or another.

CMG: I've also noticed that a lot of your songs celebrate the essence of being alive. What's happening between you and the page and piano when you write?

KH: I lose my sense of time when I'm writing. I get very energized, I get really focused and excited, and three hours can go by and it feels like ten minutes. There are days when ten minutes go by and feels like three hours but more often than not, I'm very energized by it. Sometimes I have to work on songs a long time, and sometimes I finish them quickly, and sometimes I go back to them a year later. But when I really feel like a song in done, and I have some investment in that song, often I immediately take it to a performance setting just to see how it flies. When I take (a song) to an audience, I have a preliminary experience of taking it to a band and fleshing out the arrangement, which can be real exciting or put a big damper on the song if it isn't working. My intention is when I'm writing to write something well, and if not, let it go.

CMG: One thing that I find particularly unique about your process is that you write songs with so many people. You collaborate constantly. Why?

KH: I didn't do that for most of my adult life. I only recently started co-writing in the last four years, three years. I used to be very adverse to it; in fact, I turned down an incredible songwriter -- I turned him down for seven years, the head of the gospel songwriting division at Universal. When I really took a hard look at why I was turning down these opportunities, I realized it was about fear, fear about being unequal, fear of sounding silly. I was just afraid. I wasn't ready, so it was good I didn't do it until I was ready. I was scared to death and now when I do it (co-writing), I realize it's not going to work with everybody, but I'm going to grow from the experience in one way or another.

CMG: One other thing I wanted to ask is how you sustain yourself when keeping yourself employed full-time as a performer, and keeping a whole band employed and being on the road so much under so much pressure with all those guys.

KH: That's been a real process for me over the years, always surrounded by men in my work with occasional women writers or performers. I have to really work at it. I need time by myself to be quiet, I try to eat healthy food, I drink an ocean of water, and I do a lot of reading that is positive, uplifting, interesting. We call our tour bus the book mobile because I always show up with five to six books, books that inspire me, that feed my emotional/spiritual female self. I feel like I have to work keeping my attention and thought process in a healthy place. It's easy to get discouraged when physically fatigued, easy to go to that bitter place of "why am I not wealthy and debt free when working as hard as many people?" It's a conscious focus to take care of myself, also keep in touch with women friends and family … and find pockets of time alone.

CMG: It takes a lot of courage to do what you do, to live the dream without any holding back.

KH: (laughter) Well, I think there's some courage involved, there's strong will involved, there's some audacity involved, and there's just some insanity involved. There's a big price, or has been, almost as if I'm driven to it and have to do it. It's a blessing and curse but more often it's a blessing, it's my choice, but then again, I can't see doing anything else.

CMG: I've found your concerts to be deep exchanges, soul to soul. What's happening for you when you perform that you can give so much, so vibrantly to the audience?

KH: I feel as though I'm in my element, it's my joy, it's what energizes me, and if I'm lucky -- and although this doesn't happen all the time -- my day has been spent preparing for that burst of energy. I've been quiet, I've been restful in whatever ways I can on the road. Sometimes I'm out there when I'm sick, sometimes when I've just had an upsetting incident when walking out, but generally what happens is that once I've began the process of playing and performing, it lifts me up. It has a lot to do with the audience. I feel very part of the audience -- I don't feel separate from them -- and we're all participating in this event. I just feel like I'm in my element. I know how to prepare, to be present and do that job. That's what I'm here for.

CMG: If you were talking to yourself 20 years ago, what advice would you share?

KH: I'd say, listen to your intuition more. I'd say, don't take yourself so seriously. Enjoy your gifts and spread them around.

CMG: And one more question -- especially considering the very political songs you've been writing of late -- what's the role of music and social change for you?

KH: A lot has to do with personal growth. When you're aware of what's happening, and it becomes important to you, and you're ready to say something about it in public, then it's time to do that. Many times -- in all of our history in music and politics -- music has played an important role. When commentary needed to be had, it could be out in the song and out in the world, like in the work of Woody Guthrie. A lot of my songs tell a story, but it's not necessarily a conscious decision to say, "Here's a political song," yet because of something that's been on my mind, it comes out in my work. It can take a bit of courage to do that out in the world -- it won't always be well-received. A good song doesn't necessarily need to beat you over the head, but a good political song will last forever.

GREG GREENWAY

Greg Greenway has performed throughout the U.S., including at Carnegie Hall in the New York Singer/Songwriter Festival which was rebroadcast on NPR's World Cafe, an appearance on nationally syndicated Mountain Stage, and a show at the Rock and Roll Hall of Fame honoring Phil Ochs. In August of 2000, Greenway was seen world wide on CNN's World Beat in a segment on socially conscious artists. He was filmed at the Clearwater Hudson River Revival Festival performing along with Folk legend Pete Seeger and others. Greenway was recently featured on the weekend edition of NPR's All Things Considered. *Greenway now has five critically acclaimed solo releases:* A Road Worth Walking Down *(nominated for two Boston Music Awards),* Singing For the Landlord *(top five CDs for 1995 on the Internet Folk DJ list),* Mussolini's Head *(1998),*

Something Worth Doing *(2001),* Greg Greenway: Live *(2003), and* Weightless *(2006).*

My first interview with Greg Greenway took place back in 2001 over the phone for an article for the National Association for Poetry Therapy newsletter. We had a follow-up interview in person, at a small coffee shop in Lawrence, Kansas, in the spring of 2006 before his performance that evening.

CMG: What do you see as your role in calling for justice and your connection to poetry?

GG: The first thing that overrides everything is that I do what inspires me. I think that has as much to do with my view of what an artist does in the world, and it also has an equal portion to do with where I grew up (the south). I grew up in a situation where literally when Martin Luther King, Jr. was assassinated, somebody walked by me and said he was nothing but a troublemaker. That critical time was when music entered my life, and it was the natural thing for me to gravitate toward social things ... and toward poetry. I remember a line from "Easter 1916" by (William Butler) Yeats: "A terrible beauty was born." That was the first time I realized how real worlds could be, and how much you could say in a small place. Poetry is astounding because it's metaphorical, and therefore, it's loaded. In one way, it makes me more inaccessible to the general public than other (song) writers. But people into poetry and words love metaphor, and to me, it's language times ten. If I listen to music that literal and not into language, I feel like I'm only listening with one cylinder.

CMG: What's the creative process like for you?

GG: The single most important thing about creating anything is will, the will of the writer because you can write about absolutely anything -- it really is about finding a point of you that reveals something because if you think of it, any kind of dramatic art falls upon the same thing. David Wilcox said at a songwriting workshop that the anatomy of a song is the anatomy of a joke: You have to get from point A to Point B, and what makes it funny is that Point C is somewhat askew but true. The job of a writer is to take you on a little twist. When I first walked into the building that houses the statue of David, I saw it's a 20 foot high statue, but what is revealed when you walk around that statue is that three dimensional view that shows you the statue in a way you've never seen it before. What makes a great song is when you hear the first verse, and guess what? You don't know where the artist is going with it, but you appreciate the fact that the artist has considered you in the journey, and that little communication right there is art.

CMG: Exactly. Say more about how you compose songs.

GG: You're always testing it [composing] against a feeling that you have a sense, an indefinite sense because music is a gift to people, it's a magical thing. It has emotion to it, it has space to it. Words and phrase, you sing it and it has a music in it, and the biggest thing to me is finding that bridge. I noodle in this all the time. The thing that makes it possible is what you're conveying, saying. What really bears this out is when you convince the listener that when you're most emotional, you can be most simple. I work backwards, start with the crescendo, and then try to figure out how to get there, like "In the Name of Love." I started with lines from U2's "In the name of love" -- it says everything, contained the emotion of it, the stress of it, the pathos of it. But how to do you go backwards from it? One day I was in Grace Norton Rogers school in Hightstown, New Jersey, and I was in the hallway, and I was just messing around. I played in a weird tuning, and I asked, what if I put a third on this, then what's available around that note? That little piece of logic, a little math, allowed me to get to "In the name of love." Then the heart part is how to bring people from 0 to the chorus in three verses and telescope it very personally with some metaphor that's very concrete, and how do you get there from Gandhi and Martin Luther King, Jr.? Well, you make it a parable, you don't say Gandhi or Martin Luther King, Jr. but "There was a little man." You put yourself in it: "when I get tired/get dropped into the sea/swim your whole life ..." It has physical sensation of being in water and muscle memory of being tired in the water, swimming against the tide, and then the whole idea of swimming across something and having someone there to be at the other side. The other thing that occurred was I was driving through the south – Birmingham, Atlanta, other points -- while listening to Martin Luther King Jr. speeches, and I heard him say to "Make a way out of no way," and later I thought of Bono's line, "They took your life but they could not take your pride."

CMG: You also have some powerful songs about finding voice and meaning, such as "Needles and Fairy Tales, in which you ask, "Once my voice would not work/ It would not recognize my songs. It wandered off and lost its faith/ What went wrong?" And this song also speaks about a relative of yours caught in drug addiction and how that relates to voice.

GG: The whole idea of "then I sang a voiceless song" was a very big learning process for me. That song, and the song, "On my way to find out" on that record (*Mussolini's Head*) ask "who are you" because that "Who are you?" is about how my self-worth is only important in how it relates to yours. Both of those songs are admonitions to myself to always know that my importance is in harmony with the importance of those around me. I think that's a big step of healing because we have to realize that we don't make it through this world by ourselves.

CMG: What has this to do with risk-taking and spirit for you?

GG: Risk-taking is crucial. My whole life has been a risk in terms of becoming a songwriter and a singer. It's often been said that every great performance requires risk. If you're not putting yourself on the edge, if you're not testing your views and outlooks all the time, then you get stagnant. Some people find that a safe place to be, but I find that anti-life.

CMG: What is the role of the artist as a singer-songwriter?

GG: Earlier in my career, I had only the moment I stood on stage, and more recently, people have asked me to teach what I do, and that's required me to get more precise about what I do, so when I'm old and have no teeth and they have to wheel me onto the stage, hopefully the ideas will be more important than what I sing and how I perform. I have the opportunity to go to schools and places where people are really interested in this kind of thinking, being a part of this great flow. In a way it's shamanism -- we're the shamans of our culture, we're the pressure valves. It's our job to hold the practical people up to the impracticality of our dream.

CMG: Which brings me to your performances which have, according to many critics and my own experience, a kind of evangelical quality, but not in terms of pushing any particular religion, of course. You just seem to come alive in a way that wakes people up.

GG: I just find tremendous empowerment from being able to express myself and being able to address that side in other people. I get to start the conversation, and very often, through my music, I can address a side of people I find really affirming. That's why I write songs about people who cross boundaries, who get you to see what you couldn't see. It's all toward a certain kind of enlightenment. I am a conduit instead of a "look-at-me" kind of performer.

CMG: You focus so much in your concerts on really bringing the audience into songs -- through the stories you tell, the opportunities to sing along or even sing about not wanting to sing along. Obviously, you don't see yourself as someone just delivering a product, but someone involved much more in a process of making music with the audience.

GG: I love to include other people's energy. Performance is like a blind date, and you really need to get to the places you want to get to, and begin this relationship. You need to talk about things really important to you. You know, I had this defining dream a long time ago about people taking turns conducting a class as if they were conducting a symphony. One guy, a schlumpy guy, when he got into it, would transport everyone. When this guy would do this, a radar station would receive a 19-second blip on the screen. At the end of the dream, this translucent golden horse came flying through the air, and the horse leaned his head over to me and said, "I only do this for 19 seconds." When I woke up, the thing that came to me was the magic of music, the physical dance of it all, when all those human experiences came together in a moment of truth, then that's when the horse flies.

CMG: So where do you see yourself being led?

GG: I'm being led musically to a greater understanding of what I do. I have learned music is infinite, and the more I learn about it, the more it changes how I hear. It's a metaphor for life – the more I learn about life, the more I can utterly see the world differently. There's also the theme of blindness. Growing up in the South teaches you how to see and how not to see. To make a journey across that blindness was critical. And once you escape one blindness, you ask, "What else am I blind to?"

A Road Worth Walking Down

I have seen my brother stumble
I have seen my father fall
Like shadows from behind me
Reaching out so far that I always have wondered
My feet are so blinded
If ever they'll find their ground
 On a road worth walking down.

Sometimes it rises up inside you
Sometimes I feel that I may drown
Vanish without ever saying
This is my life, this is my ground
And I wonder, my mind is so blinded
I won't know it when I've found
 A road worth walking down

I have seen my mother's courage
You give them life, you let them go
And I have chosen my own direction
So far away, so far away from it all
That I wonder, my heart is so blinded
I won't know it when I've found
 A road worth walking down.
- Greg Greenway

Interviewer's Note: In even singing about what blindness he finds in himself, Greenway – as well as Hunt and McCalla and many other singer-songwriters of our days and nights – makes visible the places within and around us ripe for transformation. Through the channel of the song, something in the listener can resound with something in the words and music, the rhythms and tones. As Plato said, "Music and rhythm find their way into the secret part of the soul."

In this way, singer-songwriters can function as what shaman John Perkins calls "an agent of change," sparking that ability within us to recognize our own abilities in this time. As Perkins explains, "The role of the industrial shaman is the same role as it always has been. It's shapeshifting. It's leading the people into the next shape. It's helping the culture as a whole to visualize the next dream and to apply the energy that is necessary to have that dream manifest" (Webb 23).

WORKS CITED

Deidre McCalla. 10 Feb. 2007. <http://www.deidremccalla.com>.

Greg Greenway. 10 Feb. 2007. <http://www.greggreenway.com>.

Kelley Hunt. 10 Feb. 2007. <http://www.kelleyhunt.com>.

"John Perkins" (Interview). Ed. Hillary S. Webb (Hillary Smith). *Traveling Between the Worlds: Conversations with Contemporary Shamans.* Charlottesville, VA: Hampton Roads Publishing Company, Inc., 2004.

THE POWER OF WRITING TO HEAL: THE AMHERST WRITERS AND ARTISTS METHOD

Sharon Bray, Ed.D.

• • •

DISCOVERING THE AWA METHOD

"We are all artists," Pat Schneider, founder of Amherst Writers and Artists (AWA), told the 14 other adults and me one summer day six years ago. We sat in a circle, clutching our notebooks. We were enrolled in Pat's weeklong writing workshop at the Pacific School of Religion in Berkeley. "We are all writers," she continued.

"Sure," I said quietly under my breath. I had my doubts. It was just weeks after I'd completed treatment for an early stage breast cancer and resigned as the CEO of a dying non-profit organization. I had been swinging on an emotional trapeze, moving between an overwhelming feeling of professional failure and the numbing realization I had joined the ranks of "cancer survivor." I had reason to be cynical.

Yet I loved to write, and my notebooks had become my only refuge in the weeks of decision-making and treatment. Alone each day, I filled page after page with a deluge of emotions and unanswered questions. I reexamined the events leading up to my diagnosis and resignation, not sure which of the two was more painful. Old hurts from the past re-ignited and tumbled onto the page. In isolation, I replayed each one, becoming the valiant martyr. I wrote in circles. I wrote backwards, looking for a clue, an answer: why me? I tried writing poetry, but my internal critic trounced on every pallid attempt.

For the first time in my life, I was without purpose, without direction. One night, I cried into the telephone to a long-time friend, a faculty member at PSR. "Why don't you take Pat Schneider's workshop this summer?" She asked, adding, "I think you have more creations in you than you know."

A few weeks later, I sat quietly in the circle of men and women, feeling a wave of panic. I watched as Pat pulled a large bag to the middle of the floor and began laying out objects on a white cloth: a ring of ancient keys, a crucifix, a wooden spoon, a man's shaving brush, an empty whiskey bottle. "The world comes to us through our senses," she said. "Choose an object that speaks to you and write about it."

We stared at the assortment of objects, uncertain what we could write about. Pat smiled encouragingly. "Start with what's there and just go. Don't worry about the form; it will take care of itself. Writing is about telling the truth, not manipulating the material," she said. "Just let the words come." People began moving toward the objects. "We'll write for 20 minutes," she added. The pressure was on.

I leaned forward, scanning the array of objects; certain none of them had anything to say to me. I fingered a ring of keys and wondered if anyone would take the crucifix. That's when I saw it: a half empty pack of Camel cigarettes. I smelled the stale tobacco as my fingers traced the camel pictured on the cover. I picked up my pen and began writing rapidly. Memories of my father spilled onto the page: the ever-present bulge in his shirt pocket, the first spark of a lit match, riding together in his old Chevrolet pickup on narrow mountain roads, and his stories, one after the other, told to the enraptured child at his side. I heard the echo of his easy chuckle and remembered the heartache when he died of lung cancer just a few years earlier. "Damn it, Dad," I wrote as I came to the end of the writing exercise, "I never got to say goodbye."

When the time was up, I was breathless. My heart was pounding. "Would anyone like to read aloud?" Pat asked the group.

I tentatively raised my hand.

As my words were released from the page and into the room, I heard my voice gain strength. The lump in my throat intermingled with the sheer excitement of sharing my words aloud. I imagined my father smiling as I shared my work. I was honoring his legacy of storytelling.

I finished reading and sat in silence as Pat invited the group to respond. "What did you like?" She asked. "What stays with you?" As I heard the group acknowledge the strength of my writing, I felt every nerve ending in my body come to life: I was on fire. I'd been catapulted into a new realm of creative self-expression and discovery. I could re-live and re-frame my life. I could reclaim and tell my stories. Through writing and telling my stories, I could make sense of my life: integrate pain, loss and suffering into all that it meant to me.

Since that first experience with the AWA method and becoming trained in the method, I have gone on to use it in writing groups with cancer patients, people dealing with grief and loss, at-risk youth, and senior citizens. Each summer I now train helping professionals and clergy in the AWA method at Pacific School of Religion in Berkeley, so that they might use writing for transformation and healing in their ministries. I have witnessed its power to help individuals from all walks of life reclaim their voices, heal their wounded spirits, and deepen insight. In every group, no matter the circumstances that join them in a shared experience, the joy of writing and reading their words aloud together is testimony to the fundamental human need for creativity and self-expression. "Simply telling the truth," Naomi Rachel Remen said, "heals" (Fox xiii).

THE BEST PRACTICES OF THE AWA METHOD

What makes the AWA method such a transformative process for creative writing groups? One only has to view the award winning documentary film, *Tell Me Something I Can't Forget: Low Income Women Write About Their Lives*, to witness the power of the AWA group method in action. The film tells the story of a group of women living in public housing, previously silenced by poverty and circumstance, who came together to write with Pat Schneider and share their stories and poems aloud. Not only did they discover the power and beauty of their words, but they grew in confidence and self esteem. Many of them returned to school and opened up new opportunities for themselves and their families. Several of the original members now lead writing groups for other women and youth in low-income communities.

As someone schooled and trained in psychology and learning, I returned from my first workshop experience wanting to understand more about the AWA method. In recent years, I have also explored other group approaches to creative or transformative writing. In those that seem to work best -- those that inspired and motivated my participants to write most deeply and beautifully -- I found some common, if not always clearly stated, elements. Prime among them was the provision of safety to explore whatever was in participants' hearts and minds and to listen deeply and non-judgmentally. To write deeply and honestly demands risk-taking, even courage, and that requires safety and acceptance.

I now incorporate many different approaches and techniques in my writing groups, but the AWA method provides the foundation for what I do. What I like most about it is that its assumptions and basic practices are clearly articulated, able to be taught and used consistently by other individuals, who, while driven by a love of writing and a commitment to outreach, may not have strong backgrounds in group facilitation.

In her book, *Writing Alone and With Others*, Schneider outlined the basic assumptions and practices that form the foundation for the Amherst Writers and Artists method. The assumptions underline the belief that writing is an art form available to everyone. I have excerpted the assumptions and practices from Schneider's book (186-187).

ESSENTIAL AFFIRMATIONS OF THE AWA METHOD

- Everyone is born with creative genius.
- Writing, as art form, belongs to all people, regardless of economic class or educational level.
- Craft can be taught without damage to a writer's original voice or artistic self-esteem.
- A writer (as William Stafford said) is someone who writes.

Accompanying the essential affirmations are the basic practices that define and ensure a safe and supportive environment in which to write.

THE FIVE ESSENTIAL PRACTICES

- A non-hierarchical spirit is maintained at all times.
- Confidentiality about what is written is maintained and the writer's privacy protected. Everything is treated as fiction unless the writer asks that it be treated as autobiography. No one is ever required to read aloud.
- No criticism, suggestions, or questions are directed in response to the writing done together in real time. Critique is offered only when a writer asks for it and distributes work in manuscript form. Critique is always balanced between affirmation and suggestions for change.
- Teaching craft is a serious part of the workshop format and is conducted through exercises that invite experimentation and growth.
- The leader writes along with the group and reads aloud at least once each writing session. This helps to build mutual trust and equality of risk-taking.

WHEN WRITING IS HEALING:
MARRYING THE METHOD TO RESEARCH

It was only a few weeks after my first workshop that a colleague, knowing of my interests, placed an article from *MAMM Magazine* (a journal focused on breast and ovarian cancer survivors) on my desk. In it, the pioneering work of psychologist James Pennebaker was described (Mayer 27-28), work that correlated well with the AWA method. Both the AWA method and Pennebaker's research stress confidentiality; the absence of corrections or criticism; free-writing about emotions and thoughts in a regular timed routine; and an environment of safety to write freely. Pennebaker also outlines the necessary conditions for writing to truly enhance the health and healing of the writers: emotional processing, a coherent story, post-writing processing, and a trustworthy setting (Lepore and Smyth 283-284). The AWA method also encourages these key conditions.

EMOTIONAL PROCESSING

We need the freedom to invoke our feelings when writing about an emotional topic whether our words are positive and negative. Writing in a safe and supportive environment gives greater freedom for honest emotional expression. The writing prompts have no conditions other than to simply evoke images or memories, acting as triggers for writing. We honor wherever the writer is, letting him or her focus on whatever needs to written at that moment. In timed writing, the emphasis is to keep the pen moving, and then our internal critics don't have room to interfere! Whatever reveals itself in words is accepted without judgment.

A COHERENT STORY

Pennebaker also found that the greatest health benefits occur when people write a "coherent" story, one that involves structure, causal explanation, repetition of themes, awareness and appreciation of a listener's perspective (1249). We all have a natural tendency to create story, whether in the form of a poem or a personal narrative. Using a variety of writing prompts triggers the memories so critical to story formation. Knowing that we may share our words aloud, even if we elect to pass, foists the presence of an audience into the writing experience. To keep our listeners with us, we implicitly create what is natural among humans: story. We also tend toward writing toward coherent stories because such a tendency allows us to put the pieces of our lives, or at least of a particular issue at a particular moment, in order.

POST-WRITING PROCESSING

After writing, we continue to think about what we've written; the words may linger in our minds for days afterward. Participants in my writing groups will often return the following week saying, "I couldn't stop thinking about it ..." or "I kept working on that piece I started in class." Writing gets feelings and experiences outside of us, available for viewing, for reflection, and thus, helps to promote self-understanding and greater perspective. "The beauty of a narrative," Pennebaker stated, "is that it allows us to tie all the changes in our life into a broad comprehensive story ... it helps us bring structure and meaning to our lives" (1250).

A TRUSTWORTHY SETTING

The safety and confidentiality of the setting in which writing occurs must be protected in order for people to write true. Ensuring the safety and support for participants to find their voices is at the core of the AWA methodology. The basic practices and presence of a supportive leader are instrumental to ensuring that trustworthiness and confidentiality is preserved for every writer.

I've found that one of the most powerful of the practices in the AWA method that builds trustworthiness is having the leader write with the group. Just as we are asking those who write with us to be vulnerable and authentic in their writing, so must the leader be willing to take the same risks. In one writing session with a group of homeless teen-age girls, I used Raymond Carver's poem, "Fear" as a prompt, inviting the girls to write about their own fears (60). One girl, I'll call her Maria, wrote about her conflicted feelings about never seeing her mother again, who was in prison for heroin use and other crimes. "I fear my mommy *never* coming home," she wrote at the beginning of her poem. Then, in the very last line, she wrote, "And did I tell you, I *fear* my mommy coming home?" As she finished reading aloud, she began to weep quietly.

I also wrote about my own fears that day, which were then focused on my youngest daughter, who was suffering from depression after a miscarriage. I read aloud to the group and, as I finished, asked for responses to the writing. Maria raised her hand. "I like," she said quietly, "how you are still a mother. Your daughter is all grown up, and you are still a mother to her. I really like that." I thanked her and didn't bother to remind her that we treat everything as fiction.

Priscilla, another member of the group, nodded approvingly, then looked at me and said, "and I like that you are so honest with us."

"Thank you," I replied, adding that I had to be as honest with them as I was asking them to be with me.

An ear to ear grin spread across Priscilla's face. She turned to the other girls and shouted, "I love this woman!" I drove home feeling as if I'd gotten the equivalent of a Pulitzer Prize!

As Pennebaker noted, an essential ingredient for writing to be healing is an environment in which participants feel their writing is treated confidentially, taken seriously, and will not have any adverse social effects (Lepore and Smyth 284). By writing about my own fear and sharing it aloud, I was also building trust and a sense of security with the writing group members.

WRITING IN THE PRESENCE OF OTHERS

While the important research done by Pennebaker and his colleagues on healing and writing shows us why these best practices work, those of us who regularly facilitate writing groups for various populations have a great deal to add about the value of writing in community.

The importance of writing in the presence of other people, just as speaking about our experiences in the presence of someone else, even if that person is not a therapist, helps us to heal from painful life events. Judy, a member of one of my breast cancer groups, told me "writing together provides a supportive environment that is important to my healing process. Sharing our experiences with this life threatening illness has changed us. It is marvelous" (personal communication).

It is certainly helpful to put our thoughts and feelings on paper, to write about our lives and express ourselves in prose and poems. But as I have led my writing groups over the years, I have come to believe that it is even more astonishing to hear our words as we read aloud and share them with others. In some ways, it's as if we truly "hear" ourselves for the first time. In reading aloud what we have written, we bear witness to the life we have lived, and in turn, others are witnessing our lives. Reading aloud and sharing our work seems to strengthen the power of words to transform and heal. It binds us together in the intimate sharing of human experience. We become a strong and vibrant community, joined in the sharing of story.

Jean, who died of metastatic colon cancer just last fall, wrote about her writing group experience just months before her death.

> {Writing together} helped me find my long hidden
> voice and ... to sing again. Without {the writing

group}, I would have buried my sorrow, my pain. I would be dead by now. The encouragement and love that enfolds me each week and in-between sessions, the warmth and kindness, the gifts that are given me, brought out of the darkness of a surely terminal diagnosis, have made me believe that I will survive this, and much more. (Bray 131-132)

CONCLUSION

It is difficult to imagine what my life was like before my experience with cancer and my exposure to the AWA method. My own world was rearranged in those many months, and I knew firsthand about the power of writing to heal and transform our lives. Since I've been leading my own writing groups, I have never looked back. Now, it is hard to imagine a life without the extraordinary gifts I witness each time my writing groups convene, hard to imagine a week that passes where I am not reminded of just how precious life is.

It is the community formed in the groups I lead for cancer patients, adults dealing with loss, at risk teens or adults in the winter of their lives where I feel most grounded and reaffirmed that my work has meaning. It is through writing together and sharing the stories of our lives, that I, too, am remind of our common humanity and connectedness to a world much larger than ourselves.

Not only have I observed how the men and women in my writing groups open their voices and self-understanding, but I have found that my own life has been enriched in ways I did not know possible. The joy that I experience and the gratitude I feel for the opportunity to do this work is boundless.

WORKS CITED

Bray, Sharon. *A Healing Journey: Writing Together Through Breast Cancer.* Amherst: Amherst Writers and Artists Press, 2004.

----. *When Words Heal: Writing Through Cancer.* Berkeley: North Atlantic Books/Frog Ltd., 2006.

Carver Raymond. *All of Us: The Collected Poems.* New York: Vintage Contemporary Press, 2000.

Fox, John. *Poetic Medicine.* New York: Jeremy P. Tarcher-Putnam, 1997.

Lepore, Stephen J. and Joshua M. Smyth, eds. *The Writing Cure: How Expressive Writing Promotes Health and Emotional Well-Being.* Washington D.C.: American Psychological Association, 2002.

Mayer, Musa. "Scribbling My Way to Spiritual Well-Being." *MAMM Magazine* April (2000): 26-29.

Pennebaker, James W. "Confronting a Traumatic Event: Toward an Understanding of Inhibition and Disease." *Journal of Abnormal Psychology* 95.3 (1986): 274 - 281.

----. *Opening Up: The Healing Power of Expressing Emotions.* New York: The Guilford Press, 1997.

----. "Writing About Emotional Experience as a Therapeutic Process." *Psychological Science* 8.3 (1997): 162-166.

Pennebaker, James W. and Segal, Jane D. "Forming a Story: The Health Benefits of Narrative." *Journal of Clinical Psychology* 55.10 (1999): 1243-1254.

Schneider, Pat. *Writing Alone and With Others.* New York: Oxford University Press, 2003.

Tell Me Something I Can't Forget: Low Income Women Write About

Their Lives Prod. Diane Garey and Larry Hott. Perf. Pat Schnieder. DVD. Florentine Films, 1993.

TLA AS A COACHING PROCESS

Yvette A. Hyater-Adams, MA-TLA

• • •

INTRODUCTION

How I came to appreciate TLA was to combine my lived passions as a poet, musician, and photographer with my business career in systems change, diversity and leadership development. Blending these disciplines helped me create a transformative language arts practice I call *Renaissance Muse®*, business and life coaching service using the written, spoken and visual word as a foundation.

It took several years for me to "get" why I write. As a little girl, I used a two-octave tabletop organ to put music to my lyrics. My songs had much to do with boy crushes, heartaches, rebellion, and independence, and soon my sung stories evolved into writing short fiction, then plays for my junior high school English class to perform. Along the way, writing became both a great release from adolescent pressures as well as an artistic endeavor.

After several years of start-stops with my writing, I reached my late 20s and participated in a professional development program where I reluctantly kept a journal on my feelings. It proved to be so useful an experience that I stayed with the habit until it developed into something more than a diary. Seeing my feelings on the page pushed me to explore, work through and make sense out of them. I mapped out "what if" situations (e.g. should I go back to college for employment law or paralegal school? Write a story about where each would take me.) I figured out my options and planned out next steps (e.g. list the people I know who are lawyers and paralegals … interview them and learn about their lives in their profession). I made a collage of potential obstacles (e.g. as I approach the end of my 20s, married and childless, what would it mean to be a mother and changing professions -- conflict or complement?)

I found that answers came to me in affirmations, poems, lists, collages, photographs and narratives. I re-structured recording daily events into reflection and inquiry, used re-framing techniques found in coaching to see new possibilities, and allowed the answers to emerge through various art forms, charts, and stories. I learned that this form of expression promoted an inner dialogue that profoundly shifted my perspective. A shift in perspective can be the impetus for being different, resulting in a personal transformation. This realization, and the tools I developed along the way to overcome barriers within myself – when combined with what I was learning as a professional coach and business consultant -- became the foundation for Renaissance Muse.

A STARTING GROUND IN COACHING

My own starting ground in coaching came from working as a business consult, coaching clients toward the changes they wished to make in their companies. From there, I began working with clients in personal coaching, a movement that evolved out of the personal development and self-improvement markets that gained momentum in the mid-1980s drawing from philosophy, spiritual, psychology, management, and the arts.

In general according to the International Coach Federation (ICF), coaching assumes that individuals have the wisdom and desire to change their circumstances. The role of a coach is to act as a facilitator or guide who is skilled at asking good questions that lead individuals to discover their own best solutions. Partnering with a client to help them define goals and identify realistic steps to enhance personal and work performance, coaches walk alongside the individual offering encouragement and support for personal change. An effective coach is thought to be someone who has been there, seen it, lived it and been a practitioner ("International Coach Federation").

Prior to the boom in life coaching over the last few decades, coaching was primarily associated with improving job or career performance. Executives and managers in corporations use coaching as an advantage to increase personal value within the organization. In the mid to late 1990s, coaching left the boardroom with the popularity of self-improvement gurus such as Stephen Covey and Tony Robbins, particularly after corporate executives and entertainers praised their effectiveness. Combining spiritual, psychological, and management concepts became the trend. For example, Covey credits the influences in his work to Mormon religious beliefs as well as principles espoused by Viktor Frankl, founder of logotherapy (therapy based on acceptance of self), existential analysis, and author of the powerful book about surviving the Holocaust, *Man's Search of Meaning* (Covey 69).

The term "life coach" was coined and credited to coaching pioneers such as Thomas Leonard (Coachville), formerly an accountant and financial planner, who connected with many people who were "emotionally well-adjusted" who wanted and needed advice on how to move their lives forward. In the last decade, many people have turned to coaches to help figure out relationships, transition from an employee to an entrepreneur, better work/life balance, and enhance self-esteem.

According to the ICF, what distinguishes coaching from psychotherapy is that coaching is about improving performance and learning in a way that improves the quality of life for the client. Psychotherapy focuses on treating emotional disorders or psychological pain. Emotional healing is not the focus of coaching, although through the coaching process, a person might experience an emotional release and healing. ("International Coach Federation")

Coaching is a self-regulated field, with ethical guidelines and training standards set by the ICF as well as other professional associations that also offer referrals to coaching schools deemed competent and ethical. Many coaches are concerned with credentialing to ensure that people who call themselves a "coach" have the proper training and skills to help those who come to them.

Transformative Language Arts is similarly situated. TLA is a new and emerging profession that straddles the written, spoken, visual and sung language arts as well as psychology, social change, and education. While TLA promises to have individuals partake in an "experience" that could elicit change, it also does not profess being therapy or being in the business of treating emotional disorders.

I believe the key to using TLA in the coaching process lies in opening up avenues of creativity, self-expression, and self-awareness as part of the coaching process and as a valuable tool for behavioral change, organizing and planning, manifesting and achieving goals. In this way, TLA offers the world of coaching essential and enduring language tools that enhance coaching as a profession.

TLA AND COACHING: THEORETICAL FRAMEWORK

As TLA evolves as a profession, those of us who do TLA in the world do well to keep track of whose research and ideology influences our thinking, opinions, and developing work. In building a TLA coaching practice, my theoretical framework derives from the applied behavioral sciences, creative writing and writing approaches used in narrative, journal and poetry therapies. Since most of my professional life has centered around organizational development, social justice, teaching, and as an artist, my interest has been to integrate these elements into a model for personal change.

Here are the writers and scholars who have influenced me the most, or helped explain to me what I was witnessing in my work and in myself when it comes to TLA and coaching:

- Change theories from Kurt Lewin and William Bridges, which primarily focus on helping people manage change and transition within organizations, are a major influence on how I think about the transitional steps individuals must take to shift from one level of being to another.
- Abraham Maslow's self actualization and Carl Roger's client centered therapies offer a humanistic psychological perspective in my work, supporting my belief that people have the capacity to reach peak performances in a way that they navigate their own journey.
- David Kolb's adult learning cycle demonstrates how individuals learn through experimentation, application and reflection, all of which informs how I see my role in TLA and coaching.
- Writers such as Pat Schneider, Natalie Goldberg, and Louise DeSalvo apply creative and expressive writing as a way to empower lives in naming, mending, and healing silences by putting "self" on the page.
- Facilitators of narrative therapy such as Michael White, David Epston and their colleagues from the Dulwich Centre in Australia use the concept of "re-storying" as a means to help shift the mindset and internal landscape for personal change.
- Most importantly, James Pennebaker, Stephen LePore, Joshua Smythe, Fiona Sampson and Celia Hunt's research and application of writing in therapeutic and personal growth processes shape many of my ideas about how structuring an intentional writing practice can improve both emotional and physical wellness.

Drawing from these many sources over the years, I have found ways to contextualize much of the theory behind the Renaissance Muse model, which I elaborated upon in far more detail in my master's thesis. Yet for this article, I feel it's important to pay tribute to some of the overall thinkers who have informed my own way of seeing TLA and coaching, and how to bring together all these disciplines into an effective tool for change.

TLA AND MANAGEMENT COACHING TOOLS

TLA-as-coaching stems from the combination of several new and older traditions including journal writing, poetry therapy techniques, narrative therapy techniques, creative writing methods, career development, and management skill building such as scenario planning, strategic planning, visioning, and project management.

Creative writing -- drawing on techniques of poetry, fiction, creative non-fiction and drama -- helps sharpen a person's skill with language and expand the imagination while also building confidence. Techniques and literary forms, such as character development or writing sonnets, can help clients discover more of what they have to say to themselves through metaphors and similes as well as through dialogue, plot, themes and other literary tools.

Journaling, perhaps more familiar to many within mainstream culture than even creative writing, is a reflective and "remembering" process that extracts and examines forgotten or hidden aspects of self. For example, Henriette Anne Klauser, author of *Write It Down, Make it Happen*, encourages her readers to write down their dreams and desires, contending that writing down these things becomes the first step in making them real. Her message is to use positive thinking *and* writing out goals as a catalyst for the personal change process to begin (79). According to the *Adult, Career, Vocational Education Practical Application Briefing*, journaling is a means of processing and integrating raw experiences with existing knowledge for self-exploration and personal growth (Kerka 1). Writing down past, present and future selves on the page can help unpack what is typically complex, look at patterns of choices and decisions, and imagine new or "preferred stories" that reflect an authenticity where true aspirations and real goals can be developed.

Telling real or imagined stories can unleash a "hidden knowing" in the unconscious self, thereby tapping into unknown and untapped material. It also promotes exploring dreams and fantasies that make up potential doable visions. Additionally, storytelling can help clients learn more about the stories currently playing out in their own lives, and how they can take more charge of scripting the story that they want.

Narrative therapy practices, like writing and storytelling, offer a form to tell and make sense of one's story. In narrative therapy, problems are identified as evolving out of troubled stories authored by individuals, their families and the cultures in which they have to live and operate (Dulwich Centre). Narrative therapists work with the client in developing new or preferred stories as a way to move forward. While coaches -- as stated earlier -- do not work as therapists, some of the approaches and exercises used by narrative therapists can be adapted -- as can creative writing, journaling, and storytelling approaches and exercises -- to enhance coaching.

I also draw exercises and approaches from the relatively new field of poetry therapy, which is focused on the poetic power of words for individual growth and development. Poetry therapists, and non-clinical practitioners called Applied Poetry Therapy Facilitators often use poems (with a hopeful outcome) as writing prompts to help clients recover and express emotions, explore life options, or address and transform trauma (Hynes and Hynes-Berry 14).

There are also management tools useful in the TLA-as-coaching process. Scenario planning is a change management technique used by companies such as Royal Dutch/Shell in the 1970s as a disciplined method for imagining possible futures for the company on a range of business issues (Paul Schoemaker). Scenario planning structures a series "what if" situations that create possible futures. This process is a vehicle for putting forth all types of ideas, from the mundane to the outrageous. Ideas for developing scenarios take into account the scope, major stakeholders, trends, and uncertainties, and from these, develop a series of themes, both positive and negative. From the themes, there is more idea generation, drawing out possible stories as outcomes (not unlike some of the outcomes in narrative therapy, journaling, storytelling or creative writing).

Visioning, strategic planning, and project management are common coaching and life tools for implementing and tracking progress. Visioning helps form a mental picture of the ultimate outcome or desire. From vision, a purpose or mission can develop where the broad idea shifts into to an action oriented focus. In strategic planning, the mission is supported by three or four goals, followed by a few objectives that break down into specific tasks. Project management methods help put tasks into "chewable" daily, weekly, or monthly steps that keep things moving forward. Borrowing these management tools offers a disciplined and organized approach to keep individuals focused on what they say is most important to them in their lives.

I use all of these tools in my TLA coaching practice, drawing on the breadth of my own life and work experiences. As a poet, writer, group facilitator and business adviser, I've found the connections between TLA and executive development to dovetail in ways that can help individuals write their way toward their dreams and goals effectively, and enhance their lives.

THE RENAISSANCE MUSE COACHING TLA MODEL

After years exploring and researching personal transformation models in spirituality, social justice, and expressive arts, I wanted to find creative ways to help navigate clients through the paradox of living in a fear-based yet prosperous culture. It was important for me to build a model where I could honor my own history as a writer and change agent, and where I could use creativity, reasoning, and holistic development as an approach that lead to personal change. From years of coaching and performance management for executives, entrepreneurs, and men and women in transition, I have uncovered the benefits of creating a model for coaching that slows the pace and mindset through establishing a writing practice as the focal point to support personal change. Renaissance Muse, represents this for me. The words Renaissance Muse literally means *the revival of our creative genius.*

The writing process can help release the energy that blocks clear thinking. Establishing a writing practice is both a creative and integrative process for self-discovery, thinking, and moving to action. The intentional use of the written and/or spoken word establishes a stronger sense of identity unpacking the personal myths we live by. It also helps us re-story our myths into workable action steps that break old ways of thinking.

People's lives contain multiple stories. Some stories carry successes and joyous times; other stories carry hurts and disappointments. All stories carry our choices and the resulting outcomes. While these stories can vary from person to person, they can also vary from population to population.

The populations that I work with are women, ages 35-60, typically professional women, looking for a creative way to do professional development and personal growth work. I also outreach to communities of color (in particular African American communities) where some people are reluctant to use mainstream coaches or seek help from mental health workers. Some people of color justifiably wonder if coaches are equipped to understand systemic racism or sexism and how it plays out their lives. These are real and not imagined barriers.

I have collected many stories from women of color who desire forums to talk about feelings, struggles with racism and sexism, and learn productive ways to move through these barriers in our work and home lives. The Renaissance Muse model, while offering mainstream populations a TLA-based coaching experience, also offers people of color a model where they can be heard, understood without being discounted as too sensitive or having a chip on their shoulder. Part of my motivation in developing this model was specifically to address the void of resources to support people of color in mending their broken lives in a creative, expressive and organized process.

STARTING UP: THE COACHING AND WRITING ENTRY PROCESS

When starting with a new client, I begin by holding a contracting session. During this contracting session, we talk about why the client is choosing to work with a coach, his/her goals, and expectations. We also talk about the commitment to do writing and expressive work. For most of my clients, writing is not a big deal. For those who have trouble with the idea of writing down their thoughts because it feels intimidating and strange, I have them instead start with mindmaps (brainstorming non-linear items, concerns, desires, etc. to see what's on our minds) and lists that become the basis for verbal storytelling. We eventually work our way toward more full and explicit writing over time.

I typically write a letter to the client after our first meeting. The letter sets the tone for how writing as a coaching process typically works. I capture the essence of what I heard from the client, at our contracting meeting and in his/her own words. I'll cover items such as the number of sessions contracted, fees, what we'll cover at the next session, and materials needed. I require clients to select some sort of journal or notebook to use as we work together, even if they choose to do most of their writing on a computer. Sometimes I'll ask a client to draw images or put together a collage, so a paper notebook is useful for these types of exercises.

PARTIAL SAMPLE LETTER

Dear Sharon,

This letter is to confirm our business and life coaching arrangement through the Renaissance Muse TLA writing process as we discussed last week. I am looking forward to assisting you with meeting your personal and professional goals.

The following paragraphs will give you a feel for how we can work together. After understanding how this type of process typically works, we can dialogue on how to make it work best for you.

How I like to work with you is to immediately create an environment where we are slowing the life pace down. In our busy world around us, we often complain about not having enough time to "think." The paradigm we will create in our work together is one that slows us down and is nurturing.

As I listened to your concerns and goals, you wanted to focus on:

1. *Doing more creative work,*
2. *Spending more time with friends and family,*
3. *Figuring out your next career move, and*
4. *Finding a romantic relationship.*

Your goals fit comfortably within a TLA coaching relationship. As such we have four major objectives in working together:

- *to establish a safe and supportive relationship*
- *to reflect and identify your patterns of thoughts, choices, and behaviors*
- *to create an overall personal vision and life mission, then strategies and steps to achieve your goals*
- *to use creative and expressive means to discover, name, and imagine avenues that lead to personal transformation.*

This process requires that you use a journal as a way to reflect, think through, and plan your work. You will be given writing exercises -- and assignments that may include drawing, collage, storytelling, letters, and other forms of expression.

Taking the time to write a welcoming letter sets the tone for what to expect out of a TLA coaching process that features writing as a tool.

Since laptop computers have become more affordable and compact, along with the fact that each person has a different learning style, I also recommend three software products that are useful thinking and reflecting tools:

- *LifeJournal for Writers* at www.lifejournal.com for Windows users
- MacJournal, Journaling and Blogging Software at www.marinersoftware.com for Mac users
- *NovaMind Mind-mapping Software* at nova-mind.com for Mac and Windows users

Prior to the first session or most certainly during the first meeting, it is important that the client understand the difference between coaching and therapy. Here are a couple of distinguishing factors:

TLA COACHING PRACTICE	THERAPY
Works with written and verbal narratives, songs, visual images, and storytelling as a non-clinical approach to personal development.	Often deals with healing pain and internal conflict stemming from diagnosing the past that interferes with emotional functioning.
Focuses on the present and ways to move forward, is action oriented and accountability driven	Focuses on improved psychological functioning

In my TLA coaching practice, a typical engagement lasts

six months to a year, with 12 to 20 visits. We meet twice a month, usually 60 minutes in person or occasionally by phone. It is important to keep the time between sessions 7 to 14 days so that the coach can keep things moving along. Clients usually want to be accountable to someone as a way to help them meet their goals. Too much time between sessions can result in diminishing results.

I try not to work with a client longer than 12 months on the same goals. If after a year, I find that the client frequently misses agreements, repeatedly avoids or "forgets" the goal, and if after several rounds at finding ways to meet the goal, there is no moving forward, this could be indication of a deeper problem that's left to a therapist and the client to explore. For example, I had a client where one of her goals was to have an improved relationship with her live-in mate. Once we unpacked what "improved" meant (e.g., creating more time together, sharing in chores, including each other in individual interests), and the relationship continued to dwindle, I recommended that she and her partner attend couples therapy. A TLA coach must be skilled in recognizing when the coaching relationship must end to make way for a therapeutic relationship. In some cases, a client can work with a coach and a therapist. In such cases, I highly recommend that the TLA coach establish clear boundaries to differentiate the personal development work to ensure the client a healthy experience.

After setting the ground and being clear about my boundaries, I begin using the four-step Renaissance Muse model, which is illustrated on the next page.

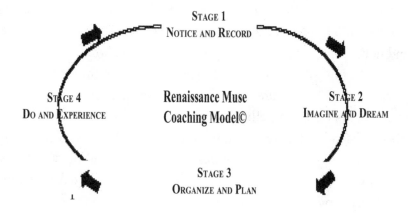

STAGE 1
NOTICE AND RECORD

STAGE 4
DO AND EXPERIENCE

Renaissance Muse
Coaching Model©

STAGE 2
IMAGINE AND DREAM

STAGE 3
ORGANIZE AND PLAN

There are four stages to making the TLA coaching process come alive in my Renaissance Muse practice: 1) Notice and Record, 2) Imagine and Dream, 3) Organization and Plan, 4) Do and Experience. This cycle spirals and repeats itself as the client takes steps toward personal change.

STAGE ONE: NOTICE AND RECORD

In my diversity work, we practice a skill called tracking. To track is to notice the pattern in behavior, attitudes and action of self or others; how values and assumptions are attached with these observations; what decisions and choices are made as a result of the experience. There can be both positive and negative patterns and outcomes. In a coaching process, there is a pattern of experience through past choices that unfold and provide useful information.

I like to begin the coaching process with clients noticing and recording their habits, past and present. I want them to explore the results of their decisions and choices along their life path. I ask them to tell me their most significant lived stories of what has worked well -- and what happened to make it work? On the flipside, I ask what challenges have they faced. Why didn't it work well? What did they want to have happen?

I typically ask clients to put together a picture collage (cutting or tearing images from magazines) that responds to these questions. After building the collage, I ask clients to write about what they see and notice in their pictorial response to the questions.

Using the collage exercise, I work with spoken word storytelling. The collage picture and the journal reflection hold the components of a compelling story. I invite the client to tell her/his story. I listen hard. I pay attention to words used and body language. I ask genuine questions of interest and clarity, making sure to use their words and not reframe with my own words. I ask questions about anything that feels missing based on information collected in our contracting meeting.

When put in the situation of looking at their lives over time and the choices and decisions made, many clients begin to track a pattern of experience that they may not have noticed before. It's often obvious how attached people are to their stories, filled with assumptions, attitudes and limiting beliefs without question. I once had a client who noticed how when she and her partner struggled in their relationship, she found herself changing jobs, letting go of treasured friendships, and stopping activities that interest her. She planned her free time around her partner's activities and hobbies. Convinced that she loved car racing as much as he did, it was easy for her to use all of her vacation time following NASCAR events with him. Even though they spent lots of time together, she felt alone and isolated. When she tried to talk with her partner about including more of what she wanted to do in their time together, the results were usually her making a change in jobs, friends, or any of her interests.

Writing her story unveiled her pattern. She had not linked her job and life changes with the uneasiness felt in her relationship. In narrative therapy, a client's "problem" is externalized and talked about as being separate from the person (Morgan 18).

To use the case of my client, the "problem" would take

on the name "Overly Accommodate." Every time she found herself adjusting her desires she could say something like "Overly Accommodate" wanted to move the weekend plans but I insisted that we attend the art exhibit. Taking one's story from the subconscious to verbalizing it on the page can give a different view to explore more deeply.

The Noticing and Recording stage can take a couple of coaching rounds to paint a full picture. Sometimes after unpacking the story and pattern, we need to go back and adjust the client's goals because of learning something as a result of the self-disclosure and self-awareness exercises. Yet it's also important to look at the story and pattern in a larger context.

When working with people of color, I recognize the distress that living and navigating through racial inequities can trigger. Therefore, exploring the cultural context for problems or issues is important to understand. In working with a black woman, I might frame a question such as, how might African American traditions and ways you may have to adjust within the mainstream culture be supporting this problem? Acknowledging that everyone doesn't have the same experience is validating.

STAGE TWO: IMAGINE AND DREAM

When working with clients to envision the future, I look for their big "bodacious" dream or fantasy. How I work with visioning is to come up with a "larger than life" goal that may or may not be achievable. A vision is like a beacon of inspiration. I also look for the "what if" stories. What if I chose to pursue the life of an artist rather than the life of a teacher? Where would this take me? Identifying the "what ifs" leads to lots of ideas and possibilities for change. "What if" stories come out of my work with organizations and groups using scenario planning (Ogivy and Schwartz 10) where a continuum of possibilities told in narrative form are derived from current cultural climate and trends. It was an easy translation to use this same approach when looking at an individual.

Robert Frost's poem, "The Road Not Taken" is typically a good poem to share with a client when working with visioning and scenario planning.

> Two roads diverge in a yellow wood,
> And sorry I could not travel both
> And be one traveler, long I stood
> And looked down one as far as I could
> To where it bent in the undergrowth...
> (Pinsky and Dietz 92)

This poem puts on the page the proverbial "fork in the road" many clients name as their place of confusion or anxiety. Their written work is to brainstorm all of what feels like missed opportunities, delayed dreams, or forgotten hopes. From this list, we can build themes and begin to "play out" scenarios that could happen or feel outrageous, but possible. Giving detail to each scenario is important.

When I was working with one client, she realized how she continuously compromised herself by taking jobs that were not quite what she wanted. She quickly ended up feeling miserable within months of starting the job. She then found herself looking for a new job within a year. When working together in developing scenarios, it turns out that her true love was in doing textile art, which was far from her financial services career. We began to build scenarios that explored what constitutes textile art and what was possible in terms of working in this field and making a living. Borrowing from scenario planning, we brainstormed ideas and shaped them into narratives where there were characters, plots, beginnings, middles and ends. Because we were dealing with a range of conditions that were uncertain, it helped the client to "see" possibilities that were within her reach. Much like when I've used scenario planning with business groups, a nexus emerges where the client can begin to make clear and informed choices.

This is where the coach can be of great help. The client might fall into old stories and patterns of thinking. The coach can push back and challenge old thinking as well as introduce some alternative ideas, helping the client come up with new stories to pursue. In the case of one client, she wanted to "stop chasing time." As a busy executive, her calendar was filled with board meetings, business travel, fundraising, and networking, running from meeting to meeting until she collapsed in complete exhaustion when she got home. Although her husband understood and was supportive, she knew that continuing this dynamic would inevitably be a strain in her marriage.

One of her barriers was an old story that the boss arrives before employees and stays late into the evening. Using writing and other tools, we first worked to unpack the story she held about work and time, which she learned from her father about work and time in his small business where he worked side by side with his employees, and then added long hours taking care of management responsibilities. My client never saw her dad when she was growing up because of how much time he put on the job.

We worked to "re-script" what "putting time in" meant for her as an executive woman. By finding a more life-supporting story about working, my client was able to find greater balance in her life and marriage. Like many of us, she had some stories that ran deep. In this situation, I was able to help her explore the root of the story through TLA tools and approaches.

STAGE THREE: ORGANIZE AND PLAN

At this stage of the coaching process, the client is ready to select a scenario or two as a point of focus. Here the client feels a little scared because we are done with thinking in the clouds and it is now time to put some real stepping-stones into place. At the organizing and planning stage, I ask my clients to list all of their daily, weekly, and monthly activities. Clients tend to pile their coaching assignments onto an already heavy load of work. Assisting clients requires steering them to choices and decisions about how they spend their time.

Process questions during this stage include:
- Where am I overcommitted in my life?
- What of my routine am I willing to change?
- What rituals are important for me to create?
- Where will I have to watch out for sabotage?

A coach also helps the client focus on small steps. Sometimes, I have to start with the basics like helping my client work with a calendar or planning tool. There are lots of paper based and electronic planners that work well. I tend to help my clients customize a planning and calendar tool that is work-friendly in their lives. I like the organizing tips covered in Stephen Covey's books, *Seven Habits of Highly Effective People* (Covey 147) and *First Things First* (Covey, Merrill & Merrill 91) as resources. For my creative and right brain clients, I use *Time Management for the Creative Person* (Silber 142) and *Organizing for the Creative Person* (Lehmkuhl & Lamping 51).

Keeping track of goals and progress is an action that tracks change as it happens. I give clients a one-page chart for them to keep in their day planners or to pin up on the wall. The client writes in the chart her accomplished tasks that support the goal. The diagram on the next page is an example of what I use.

GOALS

Easy Ways to Move my Body for Exercise	Make My Home a Sanctuary	Be Awake and Reflective as a Practice	My Next Career Move
5/14 – Walked around block 2 times	5/14 – Bought candles for coffee table	5/17 – wrote in journal for 20 minutes	5/14 – Talked to Donald about owning a bookstore
5/27 – Frisbee with dog	5/25 – cleaned up front porch	5/21 – Fully present while attending photography exhibit	5/20 – Called Donald's referral

NUMBER OF SESSIONS

SAMPLE CHART

Key to this stage is for the client to shift from stories that "didn't work" and look for the "can do" choices. "Can do" choices are small, doable, tasks that move a client closer to her goals. Lucille Clifton's poem "It was a Dream" -- which I often use with clients – gives a vivid image of excuses and choices:

what,
i pleaded with her, could i do,
oh what could i have done?
and she twisted her wild hair
and sparked her wild eyes
and screamed as long as
i could hear her
This. This. This. (29)

A good writing piece here would be for the client to write a story how s/he imagines getting up everyday and making these new changes work daily, weekly, and monthly. Having a detailed crafted story can create an image of success.

STAGE FOUR: DO AND EXPERIENCE

The *Do and Experience* part of the model is when the client implements choices or starts living a new story. This stage of the coaching model is where the client takes the lead in implementing her story. The client reports back her experience at the next scheduled session. Many times, I open up the coaching session with a 10-minute write on *the story of experiencing my journey, week 1* (or whatever week session) or *write about how it felt to make your home a sanctuary* (or whatever the specific goal.) As the coach, I encourage celebrating successes, no matter how small, and to give great details. On commitments not kept, we take a deep look at them to make adjustments or accommodate some life realities. This may require the client to loop back to stages one, two or three to get "unstuck."

I find it helpful to work with the client in creating affirmations or inspirational writings. I absolutely love the poem, "Finding Her Here," by Jane Relaford Brown which I sometimes use as a motivational piece when coaching women.

> I am becoming the woman I've wanted,
> grey at the temples,
> soft body, delighted,
> cracked up by life,
> with a laugh that's known bitter
> but, past it, got better,
> knows she's a survivor—
> that whatever comes,
> she can outlast it. (Halderman Martz 1)

I also point clients toward other affirmations -- whether through the work of metaphysical healer Louise Hay, or even the Buddha:

> The thought manifests as the word;
> The word manifests as the deed;
> The deed develops into habit;
> And habit hardens into character.
> So watch the thought and its ways with care,
> And let it spring from love
> Born out of concern for all beings.
> ---The Buddha (International Federation of Library
> Associates and Institutions)

Reading and writing affirmations encourages and builds confidence and is an act of self-love. That is what this work is all about -- the courage and commitment to love and nurture self to be of service to others.

What I've Learned For Now: A Convergence of Coaching and TLA

TLA as a coaching process does not work for everyone. Those who benefit most from the experience tend to be open to writing. With that said, in most cases the people I work with fear writing. They hang on to "old stories" told to them by teachers or bosses from the past who may have negatively judged their words. Some have shared that putting their words on the page is a painful way of seeing what is real. What is masked can stay in place if one chooses not to write down the truth.

Needless to say, I spend the early stages of the coaching relationship getting my clients not to fear their words. These fears transcend race, socioeconomic class, and education. When asked to write, many women I have worked with report that writing shuts them down, and they don't have anything important to say, they go blank or freeze when asked to write what they know, think or feel. For those who brave through it, they often find it's their most powerful and liberating experience ever. I've learned to ease the client into writing by starting with making lists, adding descriptions to each item listed, and then shaping them into poems or stories.

I also believe that as a TLA practitioner, I need to engage in a continuous personal growth process. I maintain my own writing practice as well as attend TLA related conferences and seminars annually. I need to connect with my own community of writers, facilitators, healers, and coaches. In doing so, I learn two things: 1) different ways to build and expand my practice to reach a deeper and broader audience; 2) increase my own skills and competencies in this evolving profession.

Along with participating in a learning environment, I write about TLA, its uses, and share what I know with colleagues, newcomers, and people on a path to personal growth. I feel it important for TLA practitioners to keep writing about the work and what they're doing, sharing what works and what doesn't contribute towards developing this field of practice. Moving from anecdotal experiences to more scientific and measurable outcomes will aid in professionalizing what we do. As TLA evolves, each voice can make a major contribution in shaping something wonderful for the world to experience. How about holding this as a vision for change?

WORKS CITED

Clifton, Lucille. *Book of Light*. Port Townsend, WA: Copper Press Canyon, 1993.

"Coachville." Thomas Leonard. 13 Nov. 2005. <http://www.cycommunity.com/Public/Secondary/AboutCV/index.cfm>.

Covey, Stephen R. *The Seven Habits of Highly Effective People*. New York: Simon and Schuster, 1989.

Covey, Stephen R., A. Merrill, and Rebecca R. Merrill. *First Things First*. New York: Fireside, 1994.

Dulwich Centre. 11 Feb. 2007. <http://www.dulwichcentre.com.au/questions.html>.

Frankl, Viktor. *Man's Search of Meaning*. Boston: Beacon Press, 1959.

Goddard College. 28 Oct. 2005. <http://www.goddard.edu>.

Hay, Louise. *You Can Heal Your Life*. Carlsbad, CA.: Hay House, 1999.

Hynes, Arleen McCarty and Mary Hynes-Berry. *Biblo/Poetry Therapy: The Interactive Process: A Handbook*. St. Paul: North Star Press, 1994.

"What is a Coach?" *International Coach Federation*. 10 Nov. 2005. <http://www.coachfederation.org>.

International Federation of Library Associates and Institutions. 10 Feb. 2007. <http://www.ifla.org/faife/litter/origin/b.htm>.

Klauser, Henriette Anne. *Write It Down, Make It Happen*. New York: Fireside, 2000.

Lehmkuhl, Dorothy and Dolores Cotter Lamping. *Organizing for the Creative Person*. New York: Three Rivers Press, 1993.

Martz, Sandra Haldeman. *I am Becoming the Woman I've Wanted.* Watsonville, CA.: Papier-Mache Press, 1994.

Ogilvy, Jay and Peter Schwartz. "Plotting Your Scenarios." *Global Business Network.* 2004.

Oliver, Mary. *Dreamwork.* New York: Atlantic Monthly Press, 1996.

Pinsky, Robert and Maggie Dietz. *Americans' Favorite Poems.* New York: W.W. Norton, 2000.

Schoemaker, Paul. "Scenario Planning: A Tool for Strategic Thinking." *MIT Sloan Management Review* 36.2 (1995).

"Paul Schoemaker" 11 Feb. 2007. <http://paulschoemaker.com>.

Silber, Lee. *Time Management for the Creative Person.* New York: Three Rivers Press: 1998.

White, Cheryl and David Denborough. *Introducing Narrative Therapy.* Adelaide, South Australia: Dulwich Centre, 1998.

HEALING STORIES, HEALING SONGS: NATIVE AMERICAN TRADITIONS

Denise Low, Ph.D.

• • •

In Native traditions, words have the power to heal. A commonly used word for personal power among Native peoples is "medicine." "Making medicine" is a phrase representing an array of activities that may include herbal medications and also word compositions such as prayers, songs, ceremonies, and spells. In this worldview, words have power to rearrange physical and other dimensions. Spoken and sung verses also may link an individual to cycles of sacred stories, as Christmas carols reference the life of Jesus. This aligns individuals with essential narratives of the cultures -- and the entire cosmology. Words, carried by breath or "wind" (among *Diné* or Navajo) people, link an individual to the human and natural communities. Words have significance, are weighed carefully, are selected and spoken with forethought, and voice participation in the ongoing creation of reality. Words are central to human powers.

Indeed, some traditions hold that words sustain all earthly existence. In the Mayan creation account, the *Popul Vuh,* the gods' first three creations fail because human-like beings cannot pray -- or articulate a relationship with the gods of creation. Mud-people, wooden people, and then monkey-people do not have language, and so they cannot sing or praise. The final creation, the Mayan fourth world, includes flesh human beings who have the power of speech. For Mayans, regular ceremonial prayers are required of all people, to sustain creation (Tedlock 75). Words hold the world in its course, and words hold people in their proper balance.

This importance of word composition among indigenous Americans contrasts to mainstream society's values:

In the Euro-American tradition, we tend to think of literature, indeed all the arts, as something associated with marginal misfits and the discontented. These are associations to leave aside in approaching native literatures. In native communities stories and songs count, they make a difference, and those who make and perform them are among the most valued members of the community. (Even and Pavitch 57)

The roles of the storytellers and the singers are central to the well being of a Native community, and the Anglo American observers go on to note how they "remind the people of who and what they are, why they are in this particular place, and how they should continue to live here" (Even and Pavitch 57). This attitude about the sacredness of the word underlines all Native practice of verbal arts that I have encountered.

I have learned and experienced Native literary expression in twenty-plus years of studying and teaching American Indian literature at Haskell Indian Nations University, an all-Native inter-tribal college. I have some Native heritage from both my parents, along with German and British ancestry -- a mix typical in Appalachian settlers like my ancestors who moved into central Kansas grasslands after the Civil War. I learned from Native neighbors in my home community, and at Haskell, I have experienced songs, prayers, powwows, ceremonies, Veterans Day observances, drama, film, poetry readings, political speeches, lectures, humor, and many other Native modes of spoken word. In each, a common thread is the critical role of language in survival. Words sustain the cultures, and words sustain individuals.

A healing aspect of words is self-empowerment, I believe, accomplished by sincerity. Formal religious formulas can be empty husks, or a worshiper can invest them with feeling. The choice to become open to healing words is a merging of self with the reality represented by those words. For example, symmetrical forms can calm the mind: if I think of a nautilus shell, I can imitate the spiral chambers in my imagination and create more regular brain waves. I re-create order and calm, so the act of imagination is also an act of creation. The physical nautilus and the one I picture are both real. I can choose to create this image in my mind, and so I can empower my own vision of reality. Being a successful patient is to be active in the healing process, beginning with self-willed creation of images and words.

A patient who creates a positive verbal environment for herself, through affirmations for example, takes an active role in healing. This act of creation also has a counterpoint: the patient learns to listen to the inner voice of intuition -- an inner verbal dialogue. This voice informs personal power, and this is the voice Native spiritual healers follow. Native medicine practices are not all rote. Some healing ceremonies depend on adaptation of traditional knowledge to the immediate situation. After that adjustment, then, the patient's will is an important factor. A healer can perform ceremonies for an ill person, but the patient must affirm that ceremony in his or her own consciousness. The spiritual healer is an important intermediary, but a person must agree to his or her own healing. Part of this process is trusting intuitions and dreams, which are the ways healing energy sometimes dialogues with conscious awareness. When I was a teenager, an older woman taught me to pass my hands over fruits and vegetables to sense which ones would "feel" healthful. This also taught me to trust my own inner direction.

Leslie Marmon Silko's novel *Ceremony* shows this participatory process. The war veteran hero Tayo goes through four healing ceremonies throughout the book, and the final one is when he himself learns the plants, completes a pilgrimage, observes real stars from a dream, and finds sincere prayers coming to his lips. In this process he heals himself, and he gains the knowledge of the process so that he can heal others. The final stage of his healing is when he takes his story to the Pueblo elders, and they validate his experience for the community. Tayo's most inward explorations ultimately lead outward to group healing. His individual story -- with a Laguna Pueblo Yellow Woman figure, a Mountain Lion Man, Bear, and witches -- connects to essential creation stories of his people. No individual exists in isolation from community, and a single person healed affects everyone. A shaman does not seek healing or ecstatic experience for one person, but rather healing for his or her entire social network.

N. Scott Momaday, the first American Indian writer to win a national prize for literature, writes extensively throughout his long academic career of the importance of words and the Native oral tradition. For some of his poetry he borrows structure from the *Diné* Beautyway Ceremony and other ceremonies. He is familiar with these because he lived on a *Diné* reservation as a child and learned some of their language and ways. In "The Delight Song of Tsoai-Talee" Momaday uses the repetitive, parallel formula of *Diné* prayers. He opens the poem with an assertion of unity with the natural cosmos:

> I am a feather on the bright sky
> I am the blue horse that runs in the plain
> I am the fish that rolls, shining, in the water
> I am the shadow that follows a child
> I am the evening light, the lustre of meadows
> I am an eagle playing with the wind
> I am a cluster of bright beads
> I am the farthest star
> I am the cold of the dawn
> I am the roaring of the rain
> I am the glitter on the crust of the snow
> I am the long track of the moon in a lake

I am a flame of four colors ... . (*Gourd* 27)

He ends with a reference to directions of the physical world:

> You see, I am alive, I am alive
> I stand in good relation to the Gods
> I stand in good relation to the earth
> I stand in good relation to everything that is beautiful...
> You see, I am alive, I am alive. (*Gourd* 27)

Repetition is central to Momaday's own Kiowa lyrical tradition: "Ideally, a song should be sung through at least four times" (Lassiter 114). *Diné* people also repeat songs to acknowledge the four sacred mountains of their country, with emphasis of harmony in each direction of the world around them. Besides a similar poetic form, Momaday uses the *Diné* concept of *hozho*, which is a word that he translates as "in good relation" or according to other translations beautiful, harmonious, balanced, and/or serene. This is the state created by the poem's ceremonial words. The parallel structure of words is analogous to patterned chambers of a nautilus shell or rows of corn kernels on an ear or the arc of a rainbow. When Momaday weights his poem with this ceremonial ending prayer, he invokes the idea of continuous healing.

For comparison, here is a *Diné* walking song presented in a video by Andrew Natonabah. This is a secular song for travelling purposes, and it may be shared with outsiders, unlike the sacred healing songs, dances, sand paintings, and ceremonies of the *Diné* people. However, even this apparently secular song has the intent of healing. When traveling outside the four mountains of the Dine people or even outside the home community, a person may encounter danger, and this song's spell protects the man from bodily harm.

This song has the same parallel structure as Momaday's

"Delight Song," yet it also has a more pronounced repetitious effect that suppresses logical thought and enhances a state of mind conducive to healing:

> I am House God.
> By this song I walk.
> By means of pollen, my feet
> By this song I walk.
> By means of pollen, my leg.
> By this song I walk.
> By means of pollen, my body.
> By this song I walk.
> By means of pollen, my face.
> By this song I walk.
> By means of pollen, my voice.
> By this song I walk.
> By means of pollen, my feather.
> By this song I walk.
> By It Beauty before me.
> By this song I walk.
> By It Beauty behind me. (Natonabah)

For brevity I have omitted three rounds of this long poem that complete the four sections that correspond to the four directions. In this excerpt, the walking man asserts his role in the world around him, through ritual use of pollen and feather. Every part of the singer's physical body connects to the world and to its beauty. *Hozho* here is translated as "Beauty," and the speaker affirms beautiful details of this world.

Momaday also is an essayist, and he consciously writes about the critical importance of words to southern plains Kiowa and other Southwest Indigenous Americans. He writes, "at once the names of things and the things named" (*Man* 15). In an interview, he explained the second reality of named things:

> Words are intrinsically powerful. They are magical.
> By means of words can one bring about physical
> change in the universe. By means of words can one
> quiet the raging weather, bring forth the harvest,
> ward off evil, rid the body of sickness and pain,
> subdue an enemy, capture the heart of a lover, live in
> the proper way, and venture beyond death.
> (*Man* 16)

In addition to magical and healing powers, Momaday specifies how words create an entire syntax of reality. The crucial elements for wellness -- health, safety, love, and faith -- are within the realm of language. Momaday's parents were teachers for *Diné* and Pueblo communities, so his work reflects Southwestern cultural experiences. In an interview, he explains the parallel reality of named things:

> I think there is inherent in the Native American
> worldview the idea that naming is coincidental
> with creation; that, when you bestow a name upon
> someone or something you at the same time invest
> it with being. It's not an idea, by the way, that's
> peculiar to Native American experience; it's a
> worldwide kind of idea, but it is certainly important
> in American Indian society. And I think, yes, this is
> where things begin -- naming. (*Winged* 92)

The articulation of a reality, such as "diabetes" or "grief," is the point where healing can begin. In twelve-step programs, also, the naming of the addiction is the beginning of healing.

Healing songs often are accompanied by dance-steps and

music. In the contemporary intertribal powwow tradition, which dates from the 19th century, particularly the jingle dress dance is a healing dance. Women dancers make their own dresses of cloth, with 365 "jingles" made of tobacco can lids bent into a cone. The women who make these dresses pray each day for a year and then each day sew on jingles until they circle the entire dress. With each dance step, the jingles create melodious sounds. A former jingle dress dancer explains: "One of the most profound elements of Jingle Dress dancing is its spiritual power, which originates as an energy generated from the sound of the cones that sing out to the spirits when dancers lift their feet in time with the drum" (Browner 53). In a Lakota version, the jingles sound like "leaves on your sister the tree" (Norma Rendon, quoted in Browner, 55). The dance is requested by those who need healing: "Often spectators, musicians, and other dancers will make gifts of tobacco to a dancer and request that she pray for an ill family member while she dances" (Browner 53). During the dance, all dancers and spectators are aware of how this dance is an embodied prayer; often the emcee will emphasize the sacred intent of the dance to help focus people's attention.

Several versions of this oral tradition dance exist. Browner describes its origin in Whitefish Bay, Ontario, among *Anishinaabeg* (Chippewa or Ojibwa people) (53). Another version places the dance's origin among *Anishinaabeg* in Mille Lacs, Minnesota, with emphasis on the transformative power of the dance:

> In a Holy Man's dream, four women wearing jingle dresses appeared before him. They showed him how to make the dress, what types of songs went with them and how the dance was performed. The dresses made a pretty sound to him. Upon awakening, he and his wife made four of the dresses, called the four women who in his dream wore them, dressed them in the dresses, brought them forth at a dance and

told the people about the dream, and that this is the way the medicine women were to dress and dance. ("Jingle Dress")

In other versions, the dreamer's own granddaughter is ill. She is dressed in the jingle or "prayer" dress, and carried around the dance circle. By her fourth transit, she is dancing on her own and is healed. Jingle dress dancers often carry eagle fans, but in the older style, the dancer raises her bare hands, not a fan, for healing when the drummers beat the loud "honor" beats of the song (Gathering of Nations). In addition to dancing to heal themselves and spectators of their illnesses, jingle dancers may also dance for the healing of the Earth itself (Gathering of Nations). In this dance, as in other powwow dances, the participants bring serious commitment to maintaining prayerful, positive thoughts throughout the powwow. Words in the songs, and the story suggested by those words, are integrated into a multimedia ceremonial context. They become even more memorable and powerful.

Other healing dances based on narrative accounts and performed with repeated verses of songs include the *Gaan* or Crown Dance of the White Mountain Apaches. I have seen this dance a number of times at Haskell, and each time the emcee introduces it with cautionary words about its power and healing nature. Photographs are not allowed, to protect the sacred context. In addition to the singing and drumming that accompany the dance, one dancer will use a bull-roarer to make the sound of mountain winds. The bull-roarer is a disk of slotted wood attached to a cord and swung sharply in a circle, like a lasso, to create an eerie sound that seems to penetrate dimensions. The dance originates, according to Apache storyteller Rudolph Kane, with the story of a hunter who went too far North and got lost among the *Gaan,* or Mountain Spirits. When the community went to the base of the mountains to dance for the hunter, they found he had transformed into a *Gaan* himself, and he was among them. He could not return, but he reassured the people, " 'Wherever you go pray, I will pray for you too' " (Kane 3). Today, the dance calls the Mountain Spirits to a gathering, and the dance heals the listeners.

Another healing cycle of dances is the *Helushka* of the Ponca people in Oklahoma. Jim Charles, who danced as a young man, quotes a Ponca *Helushka* singer and drummer about the healing powers of the ceremonial songs: "The old Indians say that when you are sick, you want to get the rhythm of the drum. You forget all your pains and aches. You forget about the sickness and you are just around there having a whale of a time, enjoying yourself" (2). I have heard singers and drummers from other traditions, including Kiowa and Cheyenne, also affirm the healing power of singing and drumming. The music, the dance, the singing, the scents of sweetgrass or sage, and the visual harmony of the regalia all combine to affect the sensibilities of participants and onlookers as well.

Words have a tangible reality among Native peoples. Language theorists like J. L. Austin address this reality in terms of "performativity": "A performative is a semiotic gesture that is a being as well as a doing. Or, more accurately, it is a doing that constitutes a being, an activity that creates what it describes" (Hedges). When a person says "I wed you" in a marriage ceremony, the word "wed" performs the action the moment it is spoken. The valence of words to enact vows and other realities also exists in the Native view. Musical instruments, dance, visually beautiful beadwork and dress, aromas of herbs, and other sensory experiences can heighten the impact of healing word arrangements. Finally, though, the trigger-points of healing are the words in healing songs and the healing stories. Words have real power.

Ultimately, literature is a sacred activity. People ingest plant and animal substances from the earth; then they breathe out words that connect them to the heavens. Native people often use visible sage or tobacco smoke to assist their prayers in reaching the sky. Through words, humans connect to the realms above, and as intermediaries, they speak for the Earth itself. This is a serious duty. When we use language in healing patterns, we heal ourselves, our communities, and our beautiful planet.

WORKS CITED

Browner, Tara. *Heartbeat of the People: Music and Dance of the Northern Pow-wow.* Urbana: University of Illinois Press, 2002.

Charles, Jim. "Songs of the Ponca: Helushka." *Wicazo Sa Review* 5.2 (Fall 1989): 2-15.

Even, Larry and Paul Pavich. "Native Oral Traditions." *A Literary History of the American West.* Tucson: University of Arizona Press, 1987.

Hedges, Warren. "Performance Theory." *Southern Oregon University.* 3 Nov. 2005. <http://www.sou.edu/English/IDTC/Terms/terms.htm#anchor42031>.

Kane, Rudolph. "The Origin of the Crown Dance: An Apache Narrative." *Words & Place: Native Literature from the American Southwest.* Nov. 3, 2005. <http://parentseyes.arizona.edu/wordsandplace/kane.html>.

"The Jingle Dress Dance." American Indian Education Committee of the Minnesota State Board of Education. <http://www.spiritconnectionstore.com/ARTjingledressdance.htm>.

"The Jingle Dress Dance." *Gathering of Nations.* <www.gatheringofnations.com>.

Lassiter, Luke E. *The Power of Kiowa Song.* Tucson: University of Arizona Press, 1998.

Momaday, N. Scott. *The Gourd Dancer: Poems.* New York: Harper & Row, 1976.

-----. *The Man Made of Words: Essays, Stories, Passages.* New York: St. Martin's Griffin, 1997.

-----. *Winged Words: American Indian Writers Speak.* Ed. Laura Coltelli. Lincoln: University of Nebraska Press, 1992. 92.

Natonabah, Andrew. "By This Song I Walk: Navajo Song." *Words & Place: Native Literature from the American Southwest.* 2 Jan. 2007. <http://wordsandplace.arizona.edu/bythissongiwalk.html>.

Silko, Leslie Marmon. *Ceremony.* New York: Viking, 1977.

Tedlock, Dennis. *Popol Vuh : The Definitive Edition Of The Mayan Book Of The Dawn Of Life.* 1986. New York: Touchstone, 1996.

DO YOU WANT TO HEAR WHAT I HEARD? THEATRE AS A TOOL TO ADDRESS GOSSIP, SILENCE, AND THE HIV/AIDS PANDEMIC IN LESOTHO

Katt Lissard, MFA

•••

SKELETONS IN THE CLOSET?

It was a simple exercise, but it changed everything. When I asked my students at the National University of Lesotho in southern Africa to write a monologue starting with the phrase, "I have a skeleton in my closet," I had no idea what might emerge from that hidden place. Not only was I giving them permission to put down on paper the most egregious examples of gossip-worthy behavior they'd ever witnessed, heard about, or been victims of, but I was also giving them permission to pretend that whatever they wrote had nothing whatsoever to do with them. One young woman began her monologue like this:

I Have a Skeleton in my Closet ...

It haunts me every hour of my life. When this skeleton shrieks, I shrink – and the echoes of shame churn in my mind. Who am I going to turn to? I can't tell my husband, he will kill or desert me. I can't tell my mother or my sisters because I know what they will do. They will laugh and laugh, and then spread what I have told them all over the village ...

I was in Lesotho on a Fulbright. In January of 2005 I travelled from my home in New York City to the small mountainous country of 2 million people inside South Africa, where I would

A village in the Malealea Valley
Photo by Katt Lissard

spend eight months teaching, researching and creating theatre with students at the National University of Lesotho (NUL) in the Roma valley. Geographically, Lesotho is both stunningly foreign and oddly familiar, like a heightened vista from the American Southwest, with foothills of colorful stratified rock and higher, more rugged mountains rising just beyond those foothills. This stark beauty is contrasted by images of unrelenting poverty. The valleys, plateaus and arable mountainsides are covered with small subsistence farms, where the majority of the Basotho (1) people still live, carving a barebones existence from the increasingly drought ridden, dusty red earth. Circular thatched-roof dwellings, called rondavels, and elaborately piled rock enclosures for corralling sheep and goats, present a deceptively vivid, organic texture to the scarcity of everyday life. But, Lesotho, like much of the developing world, is a country in transition, where the old traditional ways are clashing with the influences of globalization's onslaught, and the agricultural base which has served as the cultural backbone of the nation is crumbling, no longer able to bear the weight of the growing schism.

Mpho Nthunya & granddaughter, the Roma Valley
Photo by Katt Lissard

I'd chosen Lesotho because of an interest in the history of Theatre for Development (TfD) (2) there and because of the country's astonishing HIV infection rate, which is often cited as the third highest in the world. If Westerners have heard of Lesotho at all, it's because Bill Gates, Bill Clinton, Prince Harry and Angelina Jolie have all visited recently, their celebrity appearances prompted by the tiny, obscure nation's huge infection rate. The Global Policy Network currently estimates that 35% of the total population is HIV positive, with the rate among pregnant women 25-29 at just under 40% (*Global Policy Network Report*). I wanted to see where, if at all, theatrical expression and the alarming pandemic were intersecting and what might be happening at the juncture where they met.

TWO PIECES OF THE PUZZLE

Recognizing that I was limited by time and resources, I

chose to focus my research on two pieces of the larger puzzle of what was feeding the engorged, ever-accelerating pandemic. I hoped by examining these smaller, particular parts I might be able to grasp something more of the whole. Being a theatre practitioner as opposed to a scientist or sociologist I was interested in looking at elements that might translate theatrically into dramatic weapons in the battle against HIV. One of these pieces was the fact that in sub-Saharan Africa, the virus is primarily infecting women, young women between the ages of 18-24 ("Global Coalition on Women and AIDS Report"). The other was the fact that despite decade-long campaigns by a wide array of groups and agencies, with messages about safe sex and information about how the virus is spread on display throughout sub-Saharan Africa, behavior wasn't changing; instead, the numbers of infected and dying were growing exponentially.

In her remarkable book, *Letting Them Die: Why HIV/AIDS Prevention Programmes Fail*, Catherine Campbell examines the question of behavior in relation to HIV by looking at miners, sex workers and young people in a South African community she refers to pseudonymously as Summertown. While her work was based in adjacent South Africa, Campbell's observations are deeply resonant to Basotho culture. Even though the number of men from Lesotho employed as miners in South Africa has been decreasing steadily over the last decade due to mechanization, a large percentage of Basotho men who still have a job of any kind (adult male unemployment is about 60%) work in the mines of South Africa. And of those men, a significant percentage have unprotected sex with prostitutes -- high-risk behavior that most miners have been made aware of through HIV programs sponsored either by the mining companies or by NGOs. The men then bring the virus home with them on their annual or bi-annual visits back to their families in Lesotho, one of the principal avenues by which the virus has traveled into the country.

It is this kind of high risk, unprotected behavior, even when individuals have full knowledge of the dangers of the epidemic, that baffles health officials and NGOs, but which Campbell explores by reframing the investigation as one that must be socially and communally contextualized: "The forces shaping sexual behavior and sexual health are far more complex than individual rational decisions based on simple factual knowledge about health risks, and the availability of medical services" (7). You have to look beyond the individual, or, more accurately, *around* the individual, in order to understand the numerous pressures and influences on behavior affecting the spread of HIV.

Similarly, there has been a great deal written recently about the feminization of AIDS in Africa and the reasons for this astonishingly rapid shift. Much of the writing centers on issues of gender inequality, both institutional and cultural. An example from the Women's eNews article "In Lesotho and Swaziland, AIDS Activates Women," is typical of this sharpening, passionate focus: "More and more African women fighting AIDS on the continent have come to the realization that women without political, financial and social rights are, in most cases, unable to resist demands for sex or even negotiate practices that would protect their health." In Lesotho, when a woman marries, she effectively becomes a legal minor, under the control of her husband -- unable to get a bank account, take out a loan or own property without his permission. There is also an implicit double standard in the culture in which men, regardless of their marital status or involvement, are assumed (and encouraged) to have multiple sex partners while women are forbidden the same freedom and bounty. "Banna ke mekopu; Basali ke likh'abeche" is a Sesotho saying which translates as "Men are pumpkins; women are cabbages." In other words, by their nature, men must roam around the vegetable patch, visiting all the cabbages, while the cabbages, again by their nature, must stay where they are, waiting to be visited.

I wondered what I would find if I looked at HIV-related behavior through Campbell's broadened socialized context, in connection to the ways in which young women in Lesotho were being put at a higher risk for infection? How would I even begin to approach these ideas in a country, and at a university, and in a culture where I was a stranger? I didn't know -- but I was counting on theatre to serve as my introduction.

VENUS AS A DOORWAY

Even before I boarded the plane for my journey to Africa, I was involved in an urgent theatre project in Lesotho. Two days prior to my departure, I'd received an email from the U.S. embassy's Public Affairs Officer in the capital city of Maseru (3). He wondered if I might be willing to give a talk on African-American theatre at an event the embassy was planning for Black History Month (just a few short weeks away). Because I'm more a theatre-maker than a theatre-lecturer, I proposed that I actually *present* some African-American theatre instead, using students at the National University and a few scenes from the intriguing, controversial play, *Venus*, by African-American playwright Suzan-Lori Parks.

The play is about Sarah Baartman, the so-called Hottentot Venus, an African woman who was lured away from her home on the Southern Cape by the British and, because of her prominent posterior and astonishing genitalia, put on display in a London freak show from 1810-1814. Baartman's story is well-known in Southern Africa, especially since her body was only returned to the post-apartheid government in Pretoria in 2003, after a highly publicized struggle with the government of France, which until the 1970s had kept her remains on display in the Museum of Man. Beyond that, the play was by an African-American woman, it addressed colonialism and misogyny and it was stylistically very different, so it would be challenging for the student actors.

**Thabo Mokotso as The Negro Resurrectionist
& Matumabole Phafane as Venus in *Venus***
Photo by Katt Lissard

I could never have imagined the tremendous impact of
Venus. Using a cast of 14 students (balancing class and study
schedules), an edited version of the script (70 of the 165 pages),
and in an agonizingly short three and a half weeks of rehearsal, we
put together a provocative and entertaining show. We opened just
under the wire, three days before the end of February, to an invited
audience of faculty, embassy and NGO personnel, and expatriates
from the capital, and performed a sold out second night to a rowdy,
appreciative throng of students. Lesotho Television was on hand
for the opening and scenes from the performance were shown the
following evening nationwide. Demand from students for more
performances was so intense we continued to stage the play on
campus at points throughout the semester. We even took the show to
the capital where we played to a standing room only crowd. Finally
-- and seemingly miraculously -- our production was picked up by
a professional house in South Africa, the Performing Arts Centre of
the Free State (PACOFS) in Bloemfontein, where we were housed,

Matumahole Phafane as Venus
Photo by Katt Lissard

fed and given a three night run at the Observatory Theatre for which the student actors were paid.

Venus struck a strong chord in Lesotho and in South Africa. But it wasn't until the show opened and I was finally able to turn my attention to the "real" work I thought I'd come to do that I realized two things: *Venus* was part of that work; and the show had opened a door for me into the very questions I wanted to examine about HIV and behavior and young women in a way that would never have been possible without it.

TALKING/NOT TALKING: THE SEVEN SILENT SIBYLS

Of the seventeen students working with me on the *Venus* show, seven were also in the Theatre for Development course I was teaching. This arrangement would prove to be a proverbial "marriage made in heaven." The seven were all women and because of the intensity of our *Venus* rehearsal schedule and the subject matter of the play, we were getting acquainted on a level that would not have been possible without the deep, collaborative dynamic creating an ensemble theatre piece requires.

The collaborative energy of these seven was going to be pushed even further. To fulfill the applied component of the Theatre for Development course, we were going to create a completely original piece of theatre around issues of HIV and AIDS. This piece of theatre would be performed publicly at the university's AIDS Day ceremony the end of April -- a performance I'd promised the organizers we'd be ready for. Time, once again, was short.

We started by improvising around something I'd noticed within the first 24 hours of my time in Lesotho -- the A, B, Cs of AIDS prevention. The "A, B, C's" is one of the most prominent and widely-promoted prevention programs in the sub-Saharan region, but with, obviously, little success. Everyone, it seems, knows the A, B, C's -- *Abstain from sex, Be faithful,* and *Condomize.* You can see the trio painted on the sides of buildings, displayed in shop windows, stapled to bulletin boards, and printed on t-shirts that are given out for free by NGOs. Not only are people tired of the litany, they're immune to three messages that, particularly for women, are often moot to begin with because of the realities women face in relation to safe sex:

Message: **Abstain from sex** Reality: Rape and forced sex; women don't choose

Message: **Be** faithful Reality: "Faithful" women are infected by their partners -- her *situation*, not behavior, is risky

Message: **Condomize** Reality: Coercion and forced sex -- women can't negotiate. ("Global Coalition on Women and AIDS Report")

We had a great time improvising constructive ways to make fun of the A, B, C's and to point out how impossible they were for young women to successfully adhere to, but regardless of how close we might get to issues of sexual abuse or sexual coercion or even basic questions of what it was like to be young women in a culture in such obvious transition -- they were, after all, as college students, living lives that many of their parents in the rural villages had no comprehension of -- still, I couldn't get them to go anywhere below the surface and actually talk about themselves. They would, however, tell me lots of things about everyone else: other students in the *Venus* cast, instructors on campus, siblings, aunts, uncles, people in their villages. They were also happy to repeat what I began to think of as "national bulletins" -- the rumors that were everywhere about things like why, for example, the Queen wasn't producing a male heir (Campbell 5).

I began to think of this as the Talking/Not Talking paradox – the seven young women were almost completely silent in reference to themselves, but had absolutely no problem talking voluminously and virulently about everybody else. There had to be a way to make this contradiction work for us -- and quickly! We were way behind and needed to generate some material (any material) for our approaching deadline. I decided to give them a written assignment, something I'd been reluctant to do because I wanted our work to stay physical and spontaneous.

"Do you know anyone with a skeleton in their closet?" I asked.

Silence. The women were looking at me in wide-eyed confusion. Another language issue, I thought to myself. Students accepted for admission to the National University have to be proficient in English, the language in which classes are conducted, tests are given, texts are written, and papers are submitted, but the language of Lesotho is Sesotho. My knowledge of Sesotho was still very rudimentary, but no matter how good their English was, it would have been impossible for them to know every idiom and aphorism.

"We bury our dead in the ground," one finally answered, with barely concealed contempt for my ignorance of Basotho custom.

"No, no – that's not what I mean!" Of course they'd never heard the expression. Not only that, it wasn't the best choice of words in a country increasingly overwhelmed with images of death. "I'm sorry," I said, "it's an expression in my country. What it means is a secret someone is keeping, a deeply buried secret that no one sees or knows about because it's so well hidden -- that's why we say 'a skeleton in the closet.'"

The mood in the room shifted. Deeply buried secrets, after all, especially someone else's were interesting.

"I want each of you to write a monologue," I told them. "The monologue can be written as if it's you who is speaking, or it can be written as if it's another character who is speaking. But who ever it is who is speaking, they are talking about a skeleton in their closet, or in someone else's closet. OK?"

It was a simple exercise, really, but it changed everything. Because not only was I giving them permission to put down on paper possibly some of the most egregious examples of behavior

Improvisation Esercise: TellingSecrets/Hiding Secrets
Photo by Lucy Winner

they'd ever witnessed, heard about, or been victims of, I was also giving them permission to pretend that whatever they wrote had nothing at all to do with them.

GOSSIP AND SILENCE

Exploring the devastating effects on individuals and their families who are publicly identified as having the virus, Campbell writes about the power of stigma to keep people silent and untreated:

> The experience of very many people living with HIV/AIDS in southern Africa appears to be one of deepening poverty, isolation and an inability to satisfy basic needs such as food and shelter. Given the stigma and terror that surrounds the disease in the public imagination, people live in fear of rejection by their communities and formal health services, and fear for their children. Because of a fear of rejection, people living with HIV/AIDS are often reluctant to seek out or access services, opting instead to live without support or treatment. Those who disclose their status often become victims of violence, either from partners or family members, or from communities where HIV is regarded with fear, denial and stigma. (5)

If anything was apparent in the "skeleton" monologues the seven women brought with them to the next class and eagerly read aloud, it was the specter of stigma, abandonment and ostracism that each spoke about, no matter what the deeply hidden secret – rape, incest, abortion (which is illegal in Lesotho), poverty, homosexuality. HIV and AIDS hovered in the background of each piece, but not as a featured villain. Instead, the virus was the unspoken, acknowledged in every village, every family, and every circle of friends.

Most of the women chose to either be someone else through the monologue or to talk about someone else, but the writing was so immediate and palpable that even if it wasn't direct experience they were sharing, they were, at best, one degree removed from the secrets they revealed. It was a profound exercise for them in letting themselves speak and a profound lesson for me in finding other avenues for tapping the unspoken.

After hearing the seven monologues, and in an effort to start at a point of commonality, I mentioned the ubiquitous presence of the virus in all the pieces and asked the group what would happen if the characters who were speaking in their monologues discovered they were HIV positive -- who might they tell about their status? "This isn't you answering," I told them, "it's the person whose story you just told us."

"Who would you tell?" I asked again.

"I wouldn't tell anyone," the first woman answered. "No one."

"No one?" I asked. "Not your sister?"

"Not a sister. Not my mother. No one," she answered.

"Not my husband. Not the priest. No one." Another chimed in.

"Not my best friend. Not my dearest cousin."

"No one."

"Not my brother. Not my lover. No one."

"Not a soul."

"No one."

It was obvious to all of us, at the moment this magical, powerful incantation ceased, that we had discovered something.

**Matumahole Phafane & Kekeletso Montayane
rehearse "whispering rumor"**
Photo by Lucy Winner

We started again, almost from scratch – working with a
new energy and excitement on creating the performance, which
we decided to call *Do You Want to Hear What I Heard?* By pulling
together bits and pieces from the harsh, revealing monologues the
seven women had written, we began to craft a spare, highly visual
piece of theatre that was reliant on accessing some of their most
basic fears in relation to HIV and presenting them in a context
that was provocative, funny, interactive and compelling. The virus
rendered young people silent, but we could turn that silence on
its head by making it into a call-and-response with the audience
about their own reluctance to face reality. None of this would have
worked, I'm convinced, if we had not had access to what I came
to think of as our secret weapon: seven brilliantly-colored Chinese
fans I'd brought along from New York, with which we created a
visual vocabulary of gossip and silence:

Telling a secret/gossip: fan covering mouth/eyes visible
– in pairs or trios

Shield: both hands on fan, held out in front of chest -- a protective barrier

Hidden: fan collapsed/hidden behind back

Lying: fan open and down -- sly and deceptive

Exposure/telling the truth: fan open and up – i.e. chorus line

Attack: fan closed, reverse hold, pointed toward someone, like a knife

Silly: fan down like skirt

Rehearsing the fan vocabulary
Photo by Lucy Winner

While many of the performances that result from the work of practitioners engaged in Theatre for Development can be tedious, didactic attempts at educating people about various issues, in *Do You Want to Hear What I Heard?* we struggled with questions of artistic form and aesthetics. I had a strong desire to bring both beauty and humor to the performance. The result was a startling theatre piece. It was both serious and funny, interesting and poignant, and unlike anything people on the campus of the National University of Lestho had seen before. The thousand-plus students who attended the AIDS Day ceremony kept referring to the play as "a film" because it was so completely outside their experience of the years of message-oriented theatre that had been crammed down their throats. For weeks after the performance, you could hear students bandying lines from the piece back and forth across campus.

"Do you want to hear what I heard?"

"Of course!"

"You can't tell anyone."

"Never!"

Makaoli Ramashamole
Photo by Lucy Winner

The exploration into the roles of gossip and silence in the spread of HIV and AIDS didn't stop with our performance at the National University's AIDS Day in April 2005. It was, in fact, only the beginning. Since then, and in partnership with three other schools (the University of Witswatersrand in Johannesburg, South Africa, the University of Sunderland in the U.K., and the State University of New York, Empire State College in New York City), the Winter/Summer Institute in Theatre for Development has been created (www.esc.edu/wsi-lesotho). Successfully launched in Lesotho in June of 2006, WSI will continue on a biennial basis to explore issues of HIV and AIDS using theatre as our laboratory.

NOTES

1. In Lesotho the people as a whole are referred to as the Basotho, an individual is a Mosotho, and the language is Sesotho. Pronounced: *Leh-sootu, Bah-sootu, Mo-sootu* and *Seh-sootu*

2. Theatre for Development is used to describe a wide range of theatre methods and techniques (originating with the work of Augusto Boal) that are usually participatory in nature, involving the audience in some way, either interactively during performance or in post-performance facilitation; and that are concerned with issues related to development in its many definitions.

3. Because there was no Fulbright agency in Lesotho, the Public Affairs Officer at the U.S. embassy in Maseru at the time of my Fulbright tenure, Jed Dornburg, served as a resource, guide, host, advisor and liaison between me and the ambassador.

WORKS CITED

Campbell, Catherine. "'Letting Them Die': Why HIV/AIDS Prevention Programmes Fail." *Population and Development Review.* Ed. Susan Cotts Watson. The Population Council, Inc. 1 Dec. 2003. (HTML).

Global Policy Network Report 2006. 16 Dec. 2006. <http://www.gpn.org/data/lsotho.html>.

The Global Coalition on Women and AIDS Report 2004: A UN AIDS Initiative. 16 Dec. 2006. <http://www.womenandaids.unaids.org>.

"In Lesotho and Swaziland, AIDS Activates Women" *Women's eNews,* 24 Oct. 2005. <http://womensenews.org/article.cfm/dyn/aid/2502>.

FINDING LIFE-GIVING WORDS IN THE LIFE-SHATTERED WORLD OF CANCER

Nancy Pierce Morgan, MA-TLA

• • •

"I hate sitting here so sick and seeing all these healthy people walk by," Fran trills in her operatic voice. "I can't stand it!" A moan follows that begins at middle C and crescendos to high C and back again. Others nearby in the radiology waiting room stare at their self-appointed spokesman. "Do you know Nancy?" she addresses an audience glancing up from newspapers and cell phones. "She's the art director. She'll teach you to write poetry. She's wonderful!"

Disarmed by Fran's impromptu promotion, I continue reading to her from Garrison Keillor's *Good Poems*, a reliable source of uplifting, sometimes humorous and always accessible poetry. When I read to Fran, she listens quietly, attentively. She forgets about cancer and relaxes. Fran's favorite is "Sometimes" by Sheenah Pugh. She always asks for it, or she recites Mary Oliver's "Wild Geese" by heart. When she is distressed about her illness, we talk about poetry, sing "Summertime" from Porgy and Bess, or discuss which of her own poems she would like to submit to *Lombardi Voices*, our anthology of writing by patients and caregivers. Her mood brightens as she sings her farewell to me. Fran is back in balance.

In the six years I have served as Director of Arts and Humanities and writing clinician at the Lombardi Comprehensive Cancer Center, Fran is one of the few patients I have worked with who has full command of the range of language needed to manage the intense emotions a cancer diagnosis and treatment evokes. She recognizes the scope of her health crisis and articulates hope, despair, humor, and anger, often to the surprise and dis-ease of the community caring for her. Public outbursts are not the norm at Lombardi. Perhaps they should be. I follow the lead of this articulate mentor, and search for ways to coax people with cancer, and those who care for them, into expressing what they need to say and giving their feelings the space and attention necessary to achieve a sense of peace, focus and direction.

I have observed patients who write their way out of depression, anxiety, anger, and desolation over lost connections with friends and loved ones. Cancer is a life-shattering force. Words are the pieces selected with care to reconstruct one's identity and the community devastated by cancer. For most people, finding words is neither easy nor quick. Aversion to writing imposed by teachers or career burden must be overcome.

"I'm not a writer." "I have no talent for writing." "I hate writing." "I write for work -I don't want to do more." The damage done by societal attitudes toward the arts and talent is pandemic. People are cut off from the very tools they need to transcend crises.

So we go back to the point of alienation and begin again. We talk about process, playing with words, (paint, music, movement). I offer simple writing exercises using themes people can relate to regardless of age, culture or socioeconomic status. Music and imagery evoke emotion, stimulate memory, affirm identity. We write about gratitude, traditions, turning points, mentors. We recall that back-to-school feeling when leaves and weather turn. At quarterly readings, participants begin with apologies: *It's not really finished. This is kind of personal. I'm not exactly a poet.* Yet each person's reading brings nods of recognition and the courage to read the poem about cancer tucked underneath. Readings generate animated conversations about deep-seated fears, anger over insensitive comments of friends, and frustration that cancer offers no exemptions from life's usual annoyances. Colds, unruly teenagers and parking tickets continue to torment. Exposing vulnerability through writing leads to deep bonding and emotional cleansing. At the close of the reading, faces are relaxed, friendships are formed, gratitude is expressed.

Anecdotal evidence supporting writing as an effective complement to traditional medicine abounds. I have as many stories as there is time to tell them, but I work at a renowned cancer center where research is the respected language and currency. With the encouragement of my supervisor Dr. David Irwin, I have ventured into the scientific culture, following the lead of Dr. James Pennebaker and others who for more than twenty years have reported promising evidence from controlled, randomized, clinical trials that writing about highly personal and emotional topics produces psychological and physiological benefit.

If writing enhances the health of people who are disease-free, why not people with cancer? People with chronic illnesses like asthma, arthritis and pelvic pain who participate in expressive writing studies experienced fewer symptoms (Norman 174, Smyth 174). But investigators who engage cancer patients in writing find mixed results, including some improvement in self-reported physical symptoms but little psychological benefit (see studies by Stanton, DeMoor, Walker for more information). People with cancer do not respond consistently to the traditional writing paradigm in a laboratory setting, but they respond very well at Lombardi. What have we learned in the clinical setting that may contribute to improved writing outcomes for people with cancer?

The original writing paradigm for research requires participants to delve into their past and write about their worst personal trauma in as much emotional detail as possible (Smyth 174). Participants write in isolation and turn the writing in after each twenty-minute session for three consecutive days. Subsequent studies by Pennebaker and others vary the number of days, length of writing, and span of intervention.

A study design for people with cancer needs to take into

account participants' extremely fragile emotional state. They should not be further traumatized by delving into the personal crises experienced in the past. Compounding the trauma may further jeopardize patient health and at the very least minimize compliance with research protocol. The traditional research design requires participants to write in isolation to rule out social interaction as a confounding factor. Isolation, especially for the Bone Marrow Transplant patients I work with who are confined to a hospital room for four to six weeks, may compound their distress. Writing with a facilitator has been shown to reduce post-writing anxiety, a temporary side effect that may impede a cancer patient's sense of well-being (Smyth 174-84). In previous studies, cancer patients have resisted instructions to write about the benefits of cancer (DeMoor 615-19). Assigned affect, whether positive or negative, may invalidate a patient's present emotional state. It seems appropriate to allow patients to fully express the feelings of the moment by offering appropriate prompts to elicit these feelings. When I approached Dr. Pennebaker about shifting from past to current issues as writing topics, he concurred, offering an amended writing prompt that suggests participants "write about thoughts and feelings about issues related to cancer" A research design that acknowledges the impact of the health crisis cancer patients face, demonstrates respect for the need to express a broad range of affect, and includes a writing facilitator to manage any post-writing distress, may improve compliance and outcomes of writing research for people with cancer.

Contributors to the book, *The Writing Cure*, point to the two decades of solid evidence of the benefits of expressive writing in laboratory settings and declare it is time to test writing in real world settings (Lepore 29). This is my intention. My collection of patient and caregiver poems and essays, and the transformations I have witnessed as a result of writing, compel me to learn the language of research and assemble a team of statisticians, psychologists, doctors and nurses. Together we will seek evidence to prove to my colleagues in the medical community what I hear, see, personally experience and know is true: Writing is a simple, noninvasive, accessible tool to manage emotions and transcend the psychological and physiological effects of cancer.

"They say I have little time."

"But you have all day to write."

Smiling, she takes the pen.

WORKS CITED

DeMoor, C. et al. "A Pilot Study of the Effects of Expressive Writing on Psychological and Behavioral Adjustment in Patients enrolled in a Phase II Trial of Vaccine Therapy for Metastatic Renal Cell Carcinoma." *Health Psychology* 21.6 (2002): 615-19.

Keillor, Garrison, ed. *Good Poems.* New York: Penguin Books, 2002.

Lepore, Stephen and Joshua Smyth. *The Writing Cure*, Washington, D.C.: American Psychological Association, 2002.

Norman, S.A., et al. "For Whom Does it Work? Moderators of the Effects of Written Emotional Disclosure in a Randomized Trial Among Women with Chronic Pelvic Pain." *Psychosomatic Medicine* 66 (2004): 174-8.

Pennebaker, James W., and Morgan, N.P. personal correspondence 28 Oct. 2004.

Pennebaker, James W. "Putting Stress into Words: Health, Linguistic, and Therapeutic Implications." *Behavioral Respiratory Therapy* 31.6 (2002): 539-48.

Smyth, Joshua. "Written Emotional Expression: Effect Sizes, Outcome Types, and Moderating Variables." *Journal of Consulting and Clinical Psychology* 66.1 (1998): 174-84.

Smyth, Joshua et al. "Effects of Writing About Stressful Experiences on Symptom Reduction in Patients with Asthma and Rheumatoid Arthritis: A Randomized Trial," *JAMA* 281.14 (1999): 1304-09.

Stanton, Annette, et al., (2002) "Randomized Controlled Trial of Written Emotional Expression and Benefit Finding in Breast Cancer Patients." *Journal of Clinical Psychology* 20.20 (2002): 4160-4168.

Walker, B. L., L. M. Nail, and R. T. Croyle. (1999) "Does Emotional Expression Make a Difference in Reactions to Breast Cancer?" *Oncology Nursing Forum* 26.9 (1999): 1025-32.

CAUGHT IN THE TENSION BETWEEN CHILD AND ADULT: STORY IN DRAMATHERAPY FOR TROUBLED TEENS

Mandy Carr

• • •

"Everyday language is not the natural language of feeling for children... It is that of image and metaphor," writes Margot Sunderland (2). It is this assertion that speaks for the potential of dramatherapy to help underserved or at-risk teens through their transition to adulthood, even in troubled situations.

The arts therapies can support children in expressing, exploring, processing, containing and working through issues, in an indirect way. Often through the enactment of a symbolic story, young people can acknowledge and accept feelings they experience, and find more positive ways of coping with them. I aim to examine why the arts therapies in general, and dramatherapy in particular, can be important interventions for adolescents and why this should take place in schools, rather than in an external clinic. I will then reflect on how dramatherapy can operate in a school, briefly examining two examples from my clinical practice, one which uses storymaking as the main focus and a second which uses text, namely Shakespeare's *Romeo and Juliet*. I will outline key features of working therapeutically in an educational context. Finally I will cite some of the reactions of young people and their teachers to the work.

Richard Frankel views adolescence as "a period of profound physical, psychological and cognitive change, creating uncertainty and instability" (108). Such uncertainty and instability is often magnified by poverty and the social challenges it catalyzes, particularly at UK inner city schools. There are often many aspects of deprivation, sometimes including profound social and economic need; early abandonment by parents; migration from war torn countries such as Somalia, Zaire or Iraq; sexual, physical or psychological abuse. I do not wish to paint an inaccurate picture of British cities in the early 21st century. There are, of course many young people from stable backgrounds. However, for a sizeable minority, the above needs are pressing, and resources to meet them are limited. Imagine an ideal world, where appropriate clinical support was available to all. Would it still be necessary to bring in therapists to work alongside teachers? The answer is yes. There are three main reasons for this. First, many parents or caregivers are not in a position to ensure their children attend therapy. Second, some parents view therapy as "pathologizing" their child and are more open to it taking place in school. Young people too, can easily feel labeled, singled out as having 'something wrong' with them. Therapeutic work in school can normalize therapy. Finally, teachers can be supported by therapists at school, in understanding the needs of their students and given help in processing their own reactions to behaviors that can seem challenging or overwhelming.

The British Association of Dramatherapy defines the main focus of the work as "the intentional use of the healing aspects of drama and theatre as the therapeutic process" ("British Association for Dramatherapy"). Teenagers often find it difficult to talk about their feelings. Dramatherapy, of course, provides a confidential space. I believe that the young people drawn to this intervention can discover in exploring their emotions and inner worlds a sense of safety that comes from working through an art form. If we ask adolescents how they are, they will probably say, "Okay." Ask them to express how they are through movement, an image or a sound, and a different story and sense of release often emerge. "If you want to speak to troubled children or have them speak to you, you are far more likely to be successful if you do it through their language – the language of image, metaphor or story" (Sunderland 3).

Setting up therapy in schools can be a delicate process. It is essential to have regular communication with all staff, explaining the purpose, focus and confidentiality of the work. Teachers often address children's emotional needs with great skill. However, their primary focus is educational. Therapists, working one to one or with small groups, have the emotional well being of the child as the primary focus. Dramatherapists work organically with what comes from the child, establishing boundaries but also treating children with respect and rewards rather than punishment or threats. Dramatherapists also work as part of teams when appropriate, and in consultation with parents and teachers, all in the service of the child.

The school needs to find an appropriate manager. Referral systems need to be set up, as well as a system for evaluating and reviewing the work. Regular supervision, preferably by a suitably qualified dramatherapist, is essential. This partly aims to help the therapist to separate his or her own emotional reactions and issues from that of the client, so that clear and healthy professional boundaries can be maintained. In the UK, dramatherapists are required to be members of the Health Professions Council, which provides a code of ethics for this kind of work.

When a young person is referred for dramatherapy, the therapist offers an assessment session. This gives the child the chance to have a taste of the work and make an informed choice as to whether he or she thinks it would be of benefit. The therapist can also see whether this is an appropriate intervention and make decisions about whether to offer one to one or groupwork, or to advise a different way of working. A child will only be offered a place if he or she and the therapist agree. Having assessed hundreds of young people, a small minority, around one in ten, have not wanted to proceed with the work. I have found dramatherapy inappropriate for a similar number, perhaps because the children have not been drawn to working imaginatively or because another intervention will probably better meet their needs.

In one session I facilitated, which used storymaking as the primary assessment tool, I saw clearly how powerful it is for young people to devise their own stories and work with them dramatherapeutically. G. was an eleven year old girl in a secondary school in Tottenham, North London. The area has recently been described as one of the most socially deprived in Western Europe. The school has over a thousand students, a significant number of refugees and 59 different languages are spoken. It is a well organized school, whose headteacher has created a special unit which houses Counseling, Drama and Music Therapy and Mentoring programs. "Geri" and her family had come from Brazil, when she was five years old. She had been referred by teachers because she had been fighting and verbally abusing teachers. She seemed visibly relieved when offered the chance to see if Dramatherapy might be helpful.

Children quite regularly make comments like "I've had counseling, but how can I *talk* about this stuff!" The arts therapies allow them to flag up issues in alternative ways, and to choose which issues to work with. One of Geri's initial activities for example, was to work with me using a process called "Image Dialogue," devised by Augusto Boal (also Brazilian, by coincidence). Therapist and client start by creating together a posture of two people shaking hands. The client steps out, while the therapist remains frozen in the posture. The client examines the image of the therapist with hand outstretched, and joins her to create a new image. The therapist then steps out and creates another image etc. Thus a spontaneous dialogue/dance is created wholly through movement. At the end of this activity, Geri discussed the images she had made and decided that they represented friendship, fighting and rejection.

I then offered her the chance to create a story using "The Six Piece Story Structure," a device developed by Mooli Lahad, an Israeli dramatherapist. Geri created a story through drawing pictures in response to series of questions I posed. She drew a woman in a café surrounded by people, yet all alone, looking down. The woman wishes for a railway ticket away from the people who bully her, and a genie appears and promises to offer these bullies -- who burgle her house when she's asleep -- a wish if they'll stop "picking on her." The genie then invites the woman to go in front of the faces of the people and say "Your wishes are broken."

In subsequent sessions, Geri started to explore the issues, from the perspectives of the different characters. She played the woman, the genie and the bullies, afterwards exploring her feelings in these roles and the differences in body and voice of the three roles. One significant moment came when she was playing the role of the woman, the victim, allowing herself in role to fully experience the feelings of fear and isolation, which were so overwhelming in her life. Perhaps she unconsciously dealt with them by projecting them onto others, behaving aggressively towards them.

There are many issues arising from this work, but the key point is that Geri was able to work with the safety of dramatic distance, and to do the following:

- Discuss for a long time the feelings and experiences of the characters, having created an authentic, trusting relationship with the therapist.
- Explore the differences between magical solutions and realistic strategies.
- Express some of her own anger and distress, putting it into the "container" of the role or story.

Renee Emunah points out that "Acting–out adolescents already posses keen dramatic abilities: acting out tends to be dramatic, expressive, energetic, focused, compelling and provocative" (154). She goes on to describe the process whereby a teenager can learn more controlled ways of expressing potentially overwhelming feelings, like anger: "Rather than complete immersion in the rage, in which nothing else but feeling exists, the actor is aware of him or herself. Strong feeling is not suppressed but mastered" (154).

I've also witnessed how the text can serve as this kind of container for strong feeling when working with people with learning difficulties in Swiss Cottage, a reasonably wealthy area in North London. This very well run school, with 120 children from the ages of two to 16, had an established history of teachers working alongside speech and language, occupational and music therapists.

"Jack" was a fourteen year old English boy. Despite severe autism, he was highly imaginative and loved performing. In the classroom he had become more and more anxious and withdrawn. Each lesson started with the six to eight students in a circle. Jack had become unable to join the circle. He would sit, trembling, leaning backwards and forwards, moaning or talking to himself. Eventually he worked in a quiet room on his own, with a support assistant.

Jack's home situation was complex. His father had walked out and his mother had married again. The stepfather found the challenge of a teenage boy with autism very difficult. In turn, he became more autocratic in his response to Jack, allowing him no personal space or freedom, eventually locking him in his bedroom with a video camera trained on him. Social Services were heavily involved in sorting out this abusive situation. Jack was terrified of his stepfather and, like so many abused children, he had been told by his family that he must not speak about it.

Jack was studying *Romeo and Juliet* in his English lessons. In dramatherapy, he chose to focus on the scene in which Juliet's father hits and insults her, because she will not do as he asks, namely marry Parris. Talking of his daughter, Capulet comments "I think she will be ruled in all respects by me" (Act 3 Scene 4, Line 13). It is clear why this had such a resonance for Jack. Juliet begs Capulet to listen to her point of view: "Good father. I beseech you on my knees/ Hear me with patience but to speak a word." He replies: "Hang thee, young baggage, disobedient wretch!" He goes on to hit her, Shakespeare alluding to this with the three words, "My fingers itch" (Act 3, Scene 5, Lines 160 and 164).

Jack created postures and delivered the lines I have cited. He alternated the roles of Juliet and the father, and with me playing the other role, he improvised his own lines. He then discussed the feelings of both characters. He also took on the role of an observer, commenting on the bullying behavior of the father and the victimization of his daughter. He worked with the posture of the father and of Juliet. He created a movement piece in which he started with the victim posture he had created for Juliet, and transformed it gradually to the bully posture of the father. He then located a posture in between with which he felt most comfortable. He explored the breathing patterns, physical posture and quality of voice elicited, and experimented with how he could use this in his own life to overcome anxiety. He was never asked to comment on the details of his own life situation, and his anxiety was the only aspect of his personal life mentioned. All other feelings and dilemmas were discussed in the context of the piece of drama he had chosen. This took six weekly sessions. Teachers noticed that during this period he was able to join his classes and contain his anxiety.

What do the young people themselves feel about their experience of Dramatherapy? I always invite my clients to complete a questionnaire, and to add their own comments. Although the questionnaire is an informal form of assessment, it has brought me intriguing evaluations: 100% said that they enjoyed acting out stories, 80% that they felt "listened to," 90% felt it helped them to understand other people and communicate more clearly, 70% that it helped them to manage their behavior and 40% that it helped them to feel good about themselves. Comments included, "When we're angry we can move the anger away from us and control it," and "I had fun and let out my feelings." A 12-year-old girl whose mother had been left behind in the war in Zaire said, "Dramatherapy helped me feel better about my mum. When I came to this school I used to get in trouble every time. Now I don't."

Teachers of children who had participated in dramatherapy also were asked to filled in a questionnaire, exploring to what extent dramatherapy had been an effective intervention. 80% noticed a slight or noticeable improvement in listening skills and empathy and social skills, 60% saw a noticeable improvement in working with others and 40% a significant improvement in behavior management.

Richard Frankel observes, "What is therapeutic for adolescents is to be granted the opportunity to reveal themselves in the context of a genuine relationship" (4). The confidential dramatherapy space can foster such a relationship. The blend of authenticity of relationship; a partnership between youngster, therapist, parents, the school and other professionals; good supervision and management; and the use of the arts as the metaphor/ container can offer a potentially transforming *experience* to young people. Adolescents, in particular, can feel invaded and inarticulate when asked to talk about their emotional lives, caught in the vivid tension between being children and being adults. Perhaps the therapeutic use of stories can support young people in learning to bear the tension.

WORKS CITED

British Association for Dramatherapy. 2 Feb. 2007. <http://www.badth.org.uk>.

Emunah, Renee. "From Adolescent Trauma to Adolescent Drama: Group Drama Therapy with Emotionally Disturbed Youth." *Dramatherapy with Children and Adolescents.* Ed. Sue Jennings. London: Routledge 1995.

Frankel, Richard. *Adolescent Psyche.* London: Brunner-Routledge, 1998.

Shakespeare, William. *Romeo and Juliet.* New York: Washington Square Press, 2004.

Sunderland, Margot. *Using Storytelling as a Therapeutic Tool with Children.* Sunderland, England: Winslow Press Ltd, 2000.

Note: In England, the term "dramatherapist" is used for what, in America, is called "drama therapist."

THE THREE CANDLES OF
HILDA STERN COHEN'S STORY:
AN INTERVIEW WITH GAIL ROSEN

Caryn Mirriam-Goldberg, Ph.D.

• • •

Gail Rosen is a professional storyteller, certified facilitator, hospice volunteer and workshop leader for women's groups, bereavement groups, schools and special populations. She tells stories to audiences in synagogues, churches, schools, hospice and hospital organizations, camps and conferences as a way to help audiences define and understand their own sense of meaning, and to see and feel connections in their own community and with those of other cultures and faiths. Gail is also the founder of the National Storytelling Network's Special Interest Group, the Healing Story Alliance.

One of Gail's powerful stories, "For Tomorrow," a living tribute to Holocaust Survivor Hilda Stern Cohen, has brought together Gail and others involved with the story around the world. This combination of oral history, the poetry of Hilda Stern Cohen, and Gail's own experience with finding and telling this story re-create the European world lost in the Holocaust while also captivating thousands who have heard this story with the miracle of Hilda Stern Cohen's spirit. The story also helps listeners learn how Jews have rebuilt their lives after the Holocaust, and it continues to serve as a gathering place for Jews, Poles, Germans and others seeking reconciliation and connection.

When Gail told "Choose Hope," a story about telling "For Tomorrow," at the Power of Words conference in October of 2006, all of us in the audience were amazed and awed by Gail's interweaving of Hilda's story with her own along with stories of how

Gail's telling of this story in Germany brought together Germans and Jews seeking reconciliation.

Gail spoke with me just days after returning to her home in Baltimore from Poland where she had told "For Tomorrow" in six cities during February of 2007. More can be found on Gail at www.gailrosen.com and "For Tomorrow" at www.hildastory.org.

CMG: Tell me about your recent trip, and what brought you there?

GR: I just got back from Poland where I had the opportunity to tell the story -- Hilda's story -- in some of the places where it happened. For the first performance, I found myself standing in the Cultural Center in Lodz, Poland where she spent almost four years in the ghetto, and saying the words of the introduction where I refer to Poland and then realizing that I didn't have to say it was Poland ... I had the opportunity to perform at the Auschwitz museum for over 150 of the guides who show people through that place every day (more than a million visitors come to Auschwitz each year). These are people who are immersed in the numbers and details and the dates of this place. As I was telling Hilda's story, I kept thinking, "What would she think?"

CMG: What would she think?

GR: I just don't know. I hope she would have some feeling of satisfaction. The closing words I use in the story are: "We won. Hitler is dead, and we are still here. I have three children and three Jewish grandchildren." I hope she would see it as a triumph that her story of suffering and surviving has been witnessed in the place where she suffered so much. We were in the town of Lodz -- and that ghetto was where Hilda's boyfriend died, her grandparents died, her mother died, her father died -- and we were exploring what we knew of the ghetto. We found the school building where her transport from Frankfurt arrived -- 1,300 people in a train, and she was the only one who survived. The transcripts I have from her say that her transport was taken to an old school building where each family sat in one place on the ground. Now it's an apartment building and a complete slum. There was graffiti, peeling paint, a rat in the window. I knocked on the door of an apartment, and the oldest resident answered and was willing to talk with us and light a candle with us.

We had the opportunity to talk to Polish people who were very concerned about the image they and their country have in the eyes of the world that people would refer to Auschwitz as a Polish death camp. That's inaccurate: It's a Nazi death camp. Yes, there were Poles who collaborated with the Nazis, but many Poles defended Jews at a tremendous cost to their families.

CMG: What else did you experience there?

GR: A lot of people in Poland were very interested in Jewish Culture. There's this flowering of Jewish culture that has nothing to do with Judaism, but has to do with Klezmer [music], and Jewish food, so it's odd…For the first time, I find myself thinking, "I'm begin to get how the Native Americans feel about white people telling their stories." There's something about Jewish cultural appropriation, and yet there is an appreciation for Jewish culture, and people who are Jews or have an affinity feel freer to gather as Jews.

CMG: Where has Hilda's story taken you?

GR: It has taken me to Germany (five times). The first time I went, I attended as part of the Compassionate Listening Project for German and Jewish Reconciliation. It was really invaluable to me because it helped me get past the stereotype that existed in my mind and heart about Germans, which comes from what I know of the Holocaust, and all the movies and TV shows. The emotional reaction I had to hearing the language and getting to know, deeply know, a number of German people, and form relationships and hear their stories about what happened, and their stereotypes of Jews was great in breaking through a lot of stuff so that I could be present there in a different way. So when I went back to the town where she was born to tell the story to people who knew her, who could point out her father's barn and house, I could take it in much more easily. On that trip, one of the young women I had met through the Compassionate Listening Project was Eve Rennebarth, who read the poems [Hilda's poems] in German, and I just treasure my friendship with this young woman.

CMG: You've told the story around the U.S., Germany, Poland, and where else?

GR: Canada, and in Israel.

CMG: What kind of responses have you gotten?

GR: Mostly, people who come are very appreciative that I'm telling the story for someone who is no longer here. I begin my stories by saying, "I'm not Hilda" [so that they know] I am just telling her story as she told it to me, but it is not my story. What's appreciated is her poetry, and also the prayers that frame the story. The prayers provide counterpoint to the story; the words of the liturgy support the vignettes in the story and also are counterpoint to the story. At one point, Hilda asks where God was in the camps, and she says, "God was with us, suffering and dying with us." When I told [the story] in Auschwitz, the director of education said many in the camps lost their faith or found their faith, but he had never heard of a survivor finding God in the camps [this way], and he was moved and had a lot of appreciation for how she was able to shape her life.

CMG: One thing you do very well is to deal with the ethical issues involved in telling someone else's story. How did you learn to navigate this with such compassion and wisdom?

GR: Thank you. Right from the beginning, Hilda said to me, "Do you tell stories of the Holocaust?" and I said, "No, I don't feel entitled to tell them, they're not my stories." I had not been drawn to tell stories of the Holocaust because I didn't feel I had any right to them, my life has been incredibly blessed, and to pretend I knew anything about what people suffered doesn't seem possible, and so when she asked me to tell her story, I felt blocked, even after she died. Sitting in a workshop with Doug Lipman [storyteller], trying to process my feelings, I found myself saying, "I've never known a day of hunger; she was an Orthodox Jew, and I'm barely observant," and I finally had an epiphany. I listened to myself, and realized that if I can put that [these thoughts] into the beginning, maybe I can tell her story. In the beginning, the story had more of me, and now I've dropped some of that out. Now I say that she went though this trauma and this pain and this struggle, and I'm not Hilda. She strived to live the life of *Kiddush Hashem* (honoring God), said all the prayers, observed dietary laws, and I'm not Hilda.

CMG: In some ways that phrase, "I'm not Hilda," works as an incantation for the story.

GR: Absolutely! It allows me to give myself permission to speak her words, and now I say, "I am not Hilda," in German and Polish.

CMG: What is it like to be a vessel for this story?

GR: I've met incredible people, and I have a different relationship to hope that I would have had because of telling this story. I would not have done the traveling that I've done, so it's lifted me out of my world. The connections that I made because of other people making connections with this story [are remarkable], like with Bill Gilcher from the Goethe Institute, the arm of the German government that promotes the German language and culture around the world. Bill was approached by Dr. Werner Cohen, Hilda's husband, and he [Bill] saw her poetry and immediately saw its brilliance, and helped get it published. He also set nine of her poems to music in the style of German art songs ... Then there was Rabbi Elizabeth Bolton of the local Reconstructionist congregation here, where I attend occasionally. I knew she was musical, but I didn't know the extent of her background, and I just happened to be listening to a NPR [National Public Radio] show where she was interviewed, and she said, "In my opera training," and it just so happened that she and I were getting together. I played her some of the music and asked if she was interested, and long story short, she ended up coming to Poland with me. Because Liz is singing the songs with me, and because of her spiritual knowledge, she could research the melody that might have been sung for the prayers, so it's much more integrated. In Poland, I had a translator, Michal Malinowksi, a storyteller, and he wanted to translate basically in tandem, phrase by phrase, sentence by sentence. He stood next to me, and we found a rhythm, and soon with him standing to my left, and Liz to my right, there was an energy between the three of us.

When I begin the story, I light three candles. In Judaism, we light candles for three reasons: One is to enhance the holiness of holy time, like [lighting candles for] Shabbat, and if you choose to hear this story, you're helping create holy time. The second reason is to honor in memory a person who is gone, and Hilda died in 1997. And the third is to celebrate a miracle, and a miracle happened: Hilda survived, the Jews survived. In the middle of the week of telling the story [around Poland], I had handed the matches to Liz and Michal to each light one candle with me.

CMG: In addition to founding the Healing Story Alliance and focusing so much on stories about or that speak to healing in some way, it seems that this healing story also speaks to cultural healing. Could you say something about the meeting ground this story creates for social transformation?

GR: People who have become involved in it are constantly astonished at the serendipity and blessings that come to each of us who has gotten involved in it. The series of events that led to Liz joining, or Bill joining -- they continue to happen. We were doing the last rehearsal/performance [in Baltimore] before we left for Poland ... and a man walked in whom neither Liz nor I knew, and he said, "You're going to be in Poland, you're going to perform in Krakow?" It turned out he lived in Krakow. The organizer [setting up the tour] hadn't found a venue yet in Krakow. He said, "Do you need a venue, and can I arrange it for you?" By 8 a.m. the next morning, we had a venue, at the High Synagogue in Krakow, built in 1570. Someone else is in charge!

For those of us involved, seeing that happen over and over again, sharing that with people as well as the story, it's amazing. I can't really speak of the impact it's had on audiences at large, but I do know that the people whom I'm intimate with in this story feel their lives have been enriched. Hilda's family has been wonderfully supportive. They want Hilda's story to be heard by as many people as possible. Their hope is that it brings people back to Judaism and Jewish practice in addition to letting people know the story happened, it's real, and this is what one person's life was like, and how she integrated this story, not only surviving but thriving and living a meaningful Jewish life.

...

RIGHT LIVELIHOOD THROUGH TRANSFORMATIVE LANGUAGE ARTS

...

ASKING ETHICAL QUESTIONS: A TLA ETHIC AS CONSCIOUS, CONNECTED, AND CREATIVE ACTION

James Sparrell, Ph.D.

• • •

There has been a pile of dirt in my driveway for about a year and a half. No, it's bigger than you're picturing – probably the size of a truck without wheels and covered by a huge luminescent blue tarp. It wouldn't pass as an art project and was probably more of a monument to good intentions in the garden. But through two complete gardening seasons I had not had time to distribute it in all the good places I wanted new rich loam. I suppose somewhere inside it was my protest against the inflated housing market in town, which would preclude my moving here, if I tried to today. I used to live next to people who fished for a living; people who had only been out of the state once (and the Maine border is only a five-minute walk away); and people who worked their whole lives at the nearby Naval Shipyard. Now I live next to a physician, a retired physicist, and well-to-do business officers and owners. My cold frame, for starting vegetables in spring, was once a springboard for all sorts of gardening conversation with the neighbors and mail carrier. Now it is a sort of blight of embarrassment in the yard.

Yet I must say that not one person has complained about the big blue pile of dirt in the driveway. The physician, who recently moved in, did stop by and chat about the critical importance of "keeping property values up," but I could easily ignore that. What got me stuck on my relationship to that big blue pile was contemplating writing an essay on ethical practice. I began to think about what it means to be a good neighbor, and the physicist who is trying to sell his home and needs to move to a retirement community, whose windows look right on that pile of dirt. I no longer felt comfortable in making my gardening and deflationary statement in his face. So on the second day of fall I spent a day pushing a wheelbarrow and dodging wasps, and the pile is gone. The tarps are folded and stored in the shed.

What struck me is that I began to see the dirt pile in a way I hadn't seen it before. If I believed in affordable housing in my community, my big blue pile was not serving for much more than a rationalization for being too busy to do the work, and there were infinitely better ways that I could work toward a more socially equitable community, better ways to make a political statement. In the process of this shift in my relationship to the dirt, there was a change in my consciousness of it, a challenging of my own assumptions and beliefs, and a possibility of new and creative ways of participating in community. It is often the way in which we pose the questions that limits our thinking and reasoning about what are ethical answers, and keeps our social reasoning vacillating between the false dichotomies of parallel ruts in a well-worn road.

It is my opinion that we are animals first, and animals with big brains second, and that much of the time our big brains are spent in rationalizing what our more animal aspects have guided us to do. The spirit of ethical thinking is to use those big brains like a flashlight in the dark, directing our actions, directing our thought in conscious ways as to how we want to relate to others and to the natural world.

It is not possible to ask questions that we have not been able to form. As professions develop ethical codes, they function to suggest common questions that practitioners ought to be thinking about; to raise consciousness regarding the consequences of practicing in a particular way. Codes are constantly in a state of flux and evolution, which is an exciting thing. Unfortunately as *ethical thinking* moves into *ethical codes* there is sometimes a tendency to discard the reasoning aspect and focus on a sort of legalistic adherence to the code.

In the world of Western psychology ethics have had a good hundred-year history of debate and development and at times are bewilderingly complex. For example, the APA (American Psychological Association) guidelines at this time may deem it acceptable for a psychologist to assist in the development of strategies to aid US forces in psychological torture of "detainees," while it might be considered unethical, as a violation of confidentiality, for a clinician to greet a client in a grocery store (Mayer 60-71). I don't say this to imply that ethical guidelines are without merit or so confusing that they are not worth attending to, but to suggest that they deal with complicated life situations, reflect social, political, and religious beliefs and values, and are constantly in a state of flux and development.

For the world of TLA, a relatively new area of study and practice, the ethical questions and development of ethical guidelines are in their early stages. And there is much to glean from the work of other disciplines and practices including education, journalism, social activism, expressive arts, and psychology, as well as other disciplines and practices. A preliminary code of ethics for TLA has been developed by Mirriam-Goldberg and is presented in Table 1 on the following page.

Table One: CODE OF ETHICS FOR TLA

Transformative Language Arts students and alumni may refer to themselves as TLA educators, artists, activists, facilitators, coaches, writers, storytellers, and workers or by other terms that connote their work in the community. We offer these guidelines for all people engaged in TLA in their communities.

1.	Continually improve their artistic practice, services, publications and research through relevant continuing education as a TLA artist and facilitator.
2.	Do all that's within their realm to assist the respective agency, organization, business or institution they're affiliated with in providing competent and ethical professional services.
3.	Work intentionally within the realm of TLA, and not practice therapy or present themselves as therapists in any way. When therapy or psychological intervention is needed, make appropriate referrals. Be knowledgeable about other appropriate alternatives relevant to the populations with whom they work.
4.	Respect and protect the confidentiality of what individuals reveal in individual sessions or in workshops, sessions or classes, which also means maintaining an atmosphere of confidentiality and mutual respect.
5.	Do not engage in activities that seek to meet their personal or professional needs at the expense of the people they serve.
6.	Do not engage in any sexual, physical or romantic intimacy with those they serve.
7.	Do not condone or engage in sexual harassment, which is defined as unwelcome comments, gestures or physical contact of a sexual nature.
8.	Guard the individual rights and personal dignity of all through an awareness of the impact of stereotyping and unwarranted discrimination (i.e. biases based on age, disability, ethnicity, gender, race, religion, or sexual orientation).
9.	Respect the integrity of and promote the welfare of those with whom they work. In group settings, take reasonable precautions to create the kind of atmosphere that fosters creativity and personal growth.
10.	Secure written permission in the form of an informed consent form before using any information from workshops for research or any kind of publication or public talk, including but not limited to interviews, client writing samples, narratives of workshops, etc. Make special arrangements with workshop participants for the exact scope of research and/or the use of pseudonyms or other ways to protect participants.

Several major ethical themes can be seen to emerge from these principles. A number of items focus on the general theme of *competence*, either by developing or improving areas of expertise or creative practice (writing, artistic practice, research), or practicing within areas of competence, doing what you know, and also seeking to provide evidence that TLA practices are effective in meeting their purported goals and objectives. In this sense, there is also comfort with the idea of not-knowing, and not having all the answers, but being open to learn and listen from clients or participants. Competence also implies a knowledge of how and when to refer an individual for other forms of education, medical care, psychotherapy or other potentially necessary or beneficial services. This touches on a related theme of *doing no harm* which acknowledges both the powerful benefits and the limits of a TLA practice in providing help and fostering social or personal change, again necessitating the likelihood of referring participants to other kinds of community care when needed. *Doing no harm* also involves non-exploitation of individuals, nondiscrimination, and providing a context that seeks to ensure that participants will be respected and able to work in a climate of safety and trust.

The principal of respecting *individual autonomy* is evoked in the process of obtaining informed consent for activities, obtaining permission for the use of client materials in other contexts or for participation in research activities. Individuals are viewed as being competent to make wise judgments regarding what they choose to do or not do, but need truthful, accurate information on which to base their decisions.

An underlying value implicit in the ethical code for TLA is that TLA is reflected in a practice of *connection* and *community*. In this regard, practitioners of TLA seek to remain related to a wider community of those engaged in TLA work to hone their skills, provide support, critique process, evaluate methodology, share techniques and ideas, and to provide consultation on ethical dilemmas that will arise. Community engagement is also evident in the TLA practitioner seeking to know other kinds of therapists, educators, spiritual advisors, artists, writers, activists, and professionals in their geographical area so that referrals can be made in an informed, supportive way, not just from a phonebook. TLA practice works to resist community fragmentation.

Implicit in these guidelines are also the principles of *beneficence* and *justice*. The spirit of this work is tied closely to principles of progressive, democratic education which seek to acknowledge injustice and work toward positive social change. In that sense the work is not neutral with respect to social values. And TLA ethics are not just about not doing "bad" things, but to be affirmatively and actively engaged in work that challenges violence, injustice, ignorance, exploitation, oppression, and other societal ills.

Consciousness and *self-knowledge* are essential to the implementation of ethical principles in actual practice. It is vital that practitioners be able to identify themselves within the TLA work, in terms of their own potential capacity to hurt or harm, even unintentionally, and also to identify themselves with respect to their power in the TLA work, and potentially harmful consequences of that. Power dynamics cannot be eliminated even if attempts are made to minimize them. Bird does a wonderful job of discussing the political dynamic present in narrative therapy, which like TLA, seeks to acknowledge and challenge dominant cultural paradigms. She describes the importance of exposing and negotiating elements of power within the work, and acknowledging that the practitioner almost by definition comes from a position of the insider or one reflecting power in the relationship, e.g. teacher-student. It is vital to recognize that any attempts to address this inherently have costs and benefits. For example, some people use self-disclosure as a strategy for minimizing power over another person and to reflect a commonality. I recall in my own psychotherapy, my wonderfully supportive, infinitely patient and wise therapist telling me about traveling to her son's graduation from Stanford with a Ph.D. in literature, just as I was finally completing my Ph.D. and deciding that I would not attend, knowing also that none of my family would be able to attend either. My experience involved both an enjoyable sense of her pride and a shift toward equalization of power, as well as one of irritation and abandonment. Self-disclosure is a useful but complex tool, not unlike a shotgun.

Ultimately, ethical practice in a TLA context will likely result in coming into relationship with the community and the local world in new and unexpected ways. Rather than simply imparting (or bestowing) knowledge, TLA practice seeks to pursue understanding and discovery so that both the TLA practitioner and the relevant community will experience change and construct new understanding. The flashlight shines on the blue tarp and the pile of the dirt that lies underneath, and calls for a different vision, a creative understanding of relationship that may involve some difficult work, a shift in perspective or even heavy lifting.

It has been some months, but I did notice that the physicist's condo sold within days of my having moved the dirt pile. The doctor doesn't come by or speak anymore, and I noticed that the city counseling is considering several proposals to provide more affordable housing in town. Consciousness comes with a price; ethical questions resist complacency and acknowledge the complexity of life and the emptiness of simple answers. In the words of Greg Brown,

> ...Life is a thump-ripe melon,
>
> so sweet and such a mess.

WORKS CITED

Bird, J. To Do No Harm: Keynote Address. Pan-Pacific Family Therapy Conference. Melbourne, Australia. 6 Nov. 2006.

Brown, Greg. "Rexroth's Daughter" *Covenant*. Red House Records, 2000.

Mayer, Jane. "The Experiment." *The New Yorker* 11 July, and 18 July 2005: 60-71.

Mirriam-Goldberg, Caryn. *Transformative Language Arts Handbook: Social and Personal Transformation Through the Spoken and Written Word*. Goddard College: Plainfield, Vermont, 2006.

FINE LINES: QUESTIONS EVERY WRITER OF SELF MUST ASK

Karen L. Campbell, MA and
Jeanne Hewell Chambers, MA-TLA

Confession is good for the soul.
Find and use your authentic voice.
Tell your truth.
The truth will set you free.
The pen is mightier than the sword.

As writers, storytellers, performers we've heard all these axioms ... and more. And we know they're true. Words can change individual lives, legions of people, even the history of the world. Because our words have such power – especially when we use our clear, authentic voice, speaking from our lives, and because it's impossible to write about ourselves without writing about others as well – we writers have a tremendous responsibility. As Martha Montello points out in her excellent essay about ethics and life writing, "Our shared sense that the stories of others, inextricably part of our own, represent privileged communications raises the question of whether life writing is always a form of trespass. At the very least there's a constant tension between the need to reveal and the wish to conceal" (46).

Writing from our personal, lived experience can offer various rewards for ourselves and others, but in so-called life writing we must constantly navigate the fine line between confession and concealment, between claiming our truth and trespassing. With so much at stake, it's vitally important that we recognize and address what we're doing.

Ethics – as we use the term – is the philosophical discussion of the moral principles governing the rightness and wrongness of certain actions and the likely outcome of our actions.

While it's important to discuss ethics, let's face it: it's not always interesting, and it's not always cut and dried. In an effort to be more engaging, we've taken several case studies – real life case stories since we're dealing with writing from real life. We've condensed the scenarios and split them into two parts. First we present the basics of the case, followed by some fine lines: questions we, as writers, need to ask ourselves whenever writing from real life. After the questions, we reveal how each writer searched for and eventually found resolution to the difficult but necessary questions. Then when you're warmed-up and comfortable, we conclude with discussion of possible implications and still more chewy questions.

Let's begin:

1

Being a good daughter and a responsible writer, Patricia Hampl let her mother read the poem before the book went to press. Because the poem revealed something her mother had steadfastly kept secret, Patricia's mother initially objected to this particular poem's inclusion in the book. Knowing it was some of her best work, Patricia assured her mother that epilepsy was nothing to be ashamed of, that it certainly didn't require privacy. Furthermore, there were no harmful consequences to follow the exposure: her mother wasn't going to be fired, she said, since we all know that "no one" reads poetry (208-210).

FINE LINES TO PONDER:

- Is it our legal and moral duty to let others read what we have written about them, or is it merely good manners?
- Should we let those we've written about read the work?

(a) after it's written, regardless of future venues in which the work might be seen;

(b) when there's a good likelihood that others -- be it friends, relatives, teachers, or strangers -- will read the work;

(c) only when the work is to be published?

- If we let them read the piece and if they say "no", should we shift into persuasion mode and try to change their minds?

- Can we, as writers, liberate others with or without their consent? Who are we really liberating and why?

- Is such intended liberation an act of responsibility, nobility or self-advancement/aggrandizement?

2

Wanting his son to know his paternal grandfather, 50-year-old Richard Freadman decided to pen a book about his dad who'd died four years before the six-year-old son was born. Having an eager, energetic writing muse, Freadman got a sudden picture of how the book might go and wrote the first 80,000-word draft in about two months. Interest and excitement built as his memories flooded the pages. As is not at all unusual, once written, these stories became "powerful and revealing" (123). Freadman seemed to know himself and his father better. Dedicating time to this project -- and the mere act of ordering words one before the other -- helped Freadman work through some of the memories and attach meaning to frequently told family stories. Not only would his son know his grandfather, future generations would know their ancestors. Yes, there were both sociological and psychological value to the project, and this growing sense of purpose and benefit stoked Freadman's writing fires.

In the inevitable editing phase, however, Freadman began to give more consideration to the other people mentioned in his writings and the people who would likely read the finished book. How would they react to being included? He and his dad remembered certain events differently; how would friends and family members react if their memories differed?

FINE LINES TO PONDER:

- How much of a responsibility do we, as writers, have to protect the privacy of others? Does any right of privacy extend to those deceased?
- At what point does our writing of others become an invasion? Where's the line between telling our own life stories and invading the privacy of others?
- When we are writing our own life stories from our memory banks, how sure can we be that we are telling the truth, the whole truth, and nothing but the truth?
- What if we show our writing to others mentioned in or affected by the writing and their account differs? How do we address that?
- What's the difference between trust and truth?

3

In his book *Vulnerable Subjects*, G. Thomas Couser writes of the book and consequent movie *Iris*, which depicted John Bayley's memories of his life with the late philosopher and writer Iris Murdoch. Iris Murdoch, Couser says, is doubly vulnerable because Alzheimer's (a) leaves her subject to abuse and exploitation, and (b) it renders her a possible target for misrepresentation since she is, at the time of the writing, incapable of editing Bayley's work, of having final say over how she is portrayed. "She is clearly unaware that Bayley is writing about her," Couser writes, "and she is without competence to consent to having her dementia so publicly portrayed. (The feature film based on the book was produced after Murdoch's death.) Since Murdoch would likely never have wanted to be represented as incompetent, there is some question as to the ethicality of such representation" (x).

FINE LINES TO PONDER:

- Why do we tell and write our stories? Is it to clarify the meaning of our life? To establish identity? To gain sympathy? To raise money?
- If informed consent cannot be obtained, who has the right to tell the story? Parents? Spouses? Best friends? Offspring?

4

In what amounts to a very candid process paper, Alice Wexler writes of mapping lives for those affected by Huntington's Disease (163-173). Her mother developed Huntington's Disease, and her sister, Nancy, ultimately became one of those responsible for developing the predictive genetic testing for Huntington's. Wexler struggled to decide what to include in the book and what to leave out: her lesbianism, her father's affair, disclosure of her mother's disease, and even discussion of whether she and Nancy took the predictive genetic test themselves.

FINE LINES TO PONDER:

- Do we have the right to tell another's story even when it's an integral part of our own? Even when there are health issues and information that might help others suffering the same illness?
- Is it okay to disclose information about others while shielding ourselves from public display?

Now that you've had a chance to think about the four situations presented here and grapple with the questions each raises, read on and see how the writers resolved the issues at hand.

1

When unable to convince her mother to allow publication of the poem, Patricia Hampl reluctantly offered to delete it -- if it would make her mother happy.

(Even though it was the best poem in the book.)

(Even though it was the first poem in the book.)

(Even though she felt it was some of her best work.)

In other words, Patricia played on her mother's desire to see her daughter succeed. In the end, Patricia was victorious -- her mother eventually said "Okay, leave it in." As she writes of the incident:

> *I didn't pause to think she was doing me a favor, that she might be making a terrible sacrifice. This was good for her, I told myself ... The wicked witch of secrecy had been vanquished. I hadn't simply won (though that was delicious). I had liberated my mother, unlocked her from the prison of the dark secret where she had been cruelly chained for so long.*
>
> *I felt heroic in a low-grade literary sort of way. I understood that poetry -- my poem! -- had performed this liberating deed. My mother had been unable to speak. I had spoken for her. It had been hard for both of us. But this was the whole point of literature, its deepest good, this voicing of the unspoken, the forbidden. And look at the prize we won with our struggle -- for doesn't the truth, as John, the beloved apostle promised, set you free?* (208-210)

Memory being what it is, Hampl revisited these conversations with her mother several years later and was shocked to find that her mother had always hated the poem and had only agreed to leave it in the book out of love for her talented daughter. After much consideration, Hampl came to see the sacrifice in her mother's consent. She came to see -- and encouraged others to see -- what a fine line it is, this suiting up as a liberator for someone else, and how on the other side of that incredibly thin line is exploitation that can destroy relationships and create harm that has the potential to destroy lives.

2

As enthusiastically dedicated as he was to this project, Freadman moved it aside to give time to some questions and concerns. The last section of his book became a sort of coda in the form of an essay on the ethical complexities of this particular project. In his essay Freadman first decides on a genre name he's comfortable with, in this case "relational auto/biography" (128). Then he satisfies himself about trust and truth and how a life writer (or in this case relational auto/biographer) can never really tell the truth, the whole truth, and nothing but the truth since other family members are involved and one must be concerned with their comfort levels, too. Finally he brings into play the topic of what he calls relativized trust, a blanket of trust we bestow on others or have bestowed on us as though we assume such bestowal when we say things like "Yes, I'm going on the trip anyway. He would have wanted me to go" (131).

As part of this writing project, Freadman gave serious consideration to his motives for wanting to write a book about his dad and giving ethical thought-time to whether his dad would have really wanted him to write a book about him or not. In the end, Freadman conceded that there's no way to be absolutely sure to what degree a deceased relative would be willing to have his or her life exposed in a book. Weighing his desire to create something for his son and future generations, his loyalty to self, his love of reading and writing, possible benefit to others outside the family, the effect it might have on other family members who would be mentioned in the book, and the consequences of self-revelations, Freadman ultimately decided to write and publish the book *Shadow of Doubt: My Father and Myself.*

3

In considering *Iris*, Mr. Couser's primary concern is "the ethics of representing vulnerable subjects -- persons who are liable to exposure by someone with whom they are involved in an intimate or trust-based relationship, but are unable to represent themselves in writing or to offer meaningful consent to their representation by someone else" (xii). He goes on to say that of primary importance is life writing done within families, that the closer the relationship between writer and subject, the higher the ethical stakes.

Mr. Couser calls it "autonomy," this acknowledgment of "the other" while writing one's life stories (22). "The agreement of a subject to confide in a collaborator or life writer, then, is not carte blanche, not a waiver of privacy rights, but rather a willing sacrifice of privacy with the goal and expectation of some compensatory benefit" (22-23). He's especially concerned with the question: Whose duty is it to respect the integrity and the rights of those considered to be vulnerable subjects?

4

After spending considerable time wrestling with questions of what to include in the book and what to leave out, Wexler ultimately decided to leave out any indication of whether or not she and her sister even took the test, even though it met with swells of complaints. The deciding factor, writes Alice, in whether to include this information in a book she intended to be a view of one family's struggle with Huntington's Disease -- a view from the inside out – was the possible discrimination against herself and her family members in areas of insurance and employment (170).

FURTHER CONSIDERATIONS AND APPLICATIONS

We have offered the challenge of some hard questions: questions we continue to grapple with and anxiously debate. These questions can paralyze us, stop us in guilt-gripping tracks, send us slashing through our writing to protect all – including ourselves – from harm. We tread lightly those fine, supposedly visible lines between what is *ethical, reliable,* and/or *scientific* -- concepts sometimes conflated (if only in unquestioning acceptance of established methods). So to encourage ourselves in the rigorous self-interrogation the above stories surely demand, we turn to a story of other cases, of research intended directly to produce knowledge that will improve the (now analyzed, labeled, distorted) lives of those exposed through making that knowledge public. In this text, the scientist/artist/cultural worker/researcher drags the three together, only to wrench their shapes into yet other, dishevelled but grinning questions.

In his article "Desire and Betrayal in Community-Based Research," Francisco Ibáñez-Carrasco offers a guiding metaphor that may apply in some measure to the enterprise of personal storytelling as it does to his work of community-based (usually collaborative) research (CBR), though possibly not as aptly as to the cases he discusses. Still, the metaphor is evocative beyond its most obvious appeal, reminding us of power dynamics, still in play, and of the hegemony of desire: *La Malinche* was "the enslaved daughter of a noble Aztec family," given to conquistador Cortez, who became his "translator and confidante and is said to have betrayed the trust of her own people by helping him in his invasion of the Aztec world" (37, 39).

The settings of Ibáñez-Carrasco's community-based research projects might well be settings in which TLAers operate and from which we create knowledge, for he, too, works with "vulnerable populations"[1] such as homeless queer and questioning inner city youth in Vancouver, Canada. In pulling threads from the densely-woven con/text of these particular CBR projects, we intend not to claim sameness, but rather the chance to recognize solidarity in difference, for in his carefully blunt, deeply nuanced discussion of the challenges in his work, Ibáñez-Carrasco challenges us all to re-examine our desires, consider our betrayals, and perhaps become driven to design methods that would bring our "subjects" and ourselves to more level ground.

But we expressly do not advocate that all readers imitate what amounts (in this necessarily brief introduction) to our (typical!) white North American/European appropriation of *La Malinchismo* which, Ibáñez-Carrasco informs us, "Latin American workers in fields as diverse as political economy and psychology have employed ... to denote not only weakness for what is foreign but also seduction" (39).

The metaphor, though, does offer TLAers the chance to reassess and claim our respective ethno-specific and other hybridities, and therefore all of our membership in communities (imagined[2] or otherwise!) -- rather than assume the right to name and describe various populations as Other to some EuroAmerican academic norm.

As with CBR, the people with whom TLAers work are supposed to be at the center, the work "driven by its 'owners'," yet because we, too, sometimes share the "vulnerable" identities of those whose work we are facilitating, we're not sure if we're in the center (of the margins!) *with* them, or should be. We, too, face the question of self-disclosure -- if, when, how much? How much might block the discovery and expression of an individual participant's different experience?

The same question trips the wish to share learning discoveries of, for instance, a workshop process, especially if the "successful" conclusion of a culminating thesis or research proposal rests on disclosing what was said and what was implied for both us and our subjects. For example, if I disclose my experience, do I become unreliable, because my invested interest makes me unable to be scientific, objective? But share we must if our effectiveness is to be evaluated as it must often be for us to obtain the needed funding for workshops or grades for passing.

But then again, who am I speaking *for*? With what goals in view?

To earn a living is surely the first inescapable answer. And to counter-balance that primary and practical desire we have to ask: Is it okay to ventriloquize workshop participants, be the star of the show, the one who'll directly benefit from *my* analysis and presentation of the work? (Wouldn't they write it very differently than I, especially that translated "I" cowering back in my ambivalent membership in the academy and its curiously baffling tongues?)

Ibáñez-Carrasco identifies himself and his colleagues as "cultural workers who inhabit ... intimate borderlines" between different educational institutions, communities and Non Governmental Organizations because their work "spills over the institutional boundaries of research to popular pedagogy and activism" (38-39).

So, too, does the work of many TLAers.

What we suggest in recommending a close reading of this text is that many of us in TLA, especially those dedicated to progressive education, to individual and collective liberation, to contributing through our individual language arts to social justice, are also easily weakened, and seduced by that which was "foreign" -- the jargon, exotic methods, madness of academy we've studied so hard -- as well as by a desire to market our CVs. The very title "handbook" and the scores of papers we've ploughed through on Qualitative or Quantitative Research invite complacency in which we might tell ourselves, "I've studied, scrupulously followed Informed Review Board guidelines, gotten over those hurdles, so surely all the "issues" have been addressed -- right?"

Yet ethical issues push and pull us -- if we honestly engage with them -- into deeper, wider and more enduring considerations. TLAers, whatever the specifics of our individual ethnic/scholarly hybridity, are often in a further "hybrid role" as "translators/ facilitators" and interpreters of others' stories (Ibáñez-Carrasco 39). We, too, are often facilitating expressions of experiences among people who may not have the dubious privilege of our border and language crossing, our academic dunking; though they are most certainly co-creators of the field we call TLA. We, too, when we produce our public knowledge, are sometimes "climbing mountains" on others' backs.[3] To frame and articulate the questions with which we might continually interrogate our individual desires, and the extent of our betrayals is crucial. It is one of the most exciting and potentially helpful aspects of our privilege. Ibáñez-Carrasco offers some key questions:

> Does advancing knowledge need to be intimate, perilous, and ambivalent in order to be productive? Or, conversely, do conventional forms of making knowledge public, such as basic science research, take care of the "subjects" by *not reciprocating*, by looking without ever *seeing* what is really there? (36; first emphasis ours)

We know that being both insider and outsider to a particular identity, or sub/culture, brings curiously vexed privilege, the possibility of insight probably corrupted by our ambivalent insider/ outsider desires.

As with the case studies and questions we present above, Ibáñez-Carrasco concludes his highly nuanced readings of his research case studies "by betraying *you*, my own reader, and not offering answers at all, but *an invitation to* thrive *in the uncertainty, anxiety, and ambivalence of research projects that include our biases, love, desire and betrayal"* (36; our emphasis).

In conclusion, there are never one-size-fits-all answers to the fine lines of writing about another's -- or even just our own -- experiences. There are no easy-to-follow formulas for determining what to include and what to leave out. Yet by acknowledging and communicating that "uncertainty, anxiety and ambivalence" of our research, and by continuing to use the questions we ask as doorways into other essential questions, we stand a better chance of finding an ethical entry to honoring the living stories around us.

NOTES

[1] A polite, sanitized ducking of the many different experiential realities this umbrella term homogenizes. And, by its coy movie censorship wording, it implicitly places hosts of people outside the [speakable?] norm. Not much wrong with politeness, certainly. Unless it herds those so named into corrals at the outer edges and then silences the questions that ask how the very different and often violent behaviors that created "vulnerability" are so delicately disappeared under the name, while those now vulnerable are viewed askance.

[2] Benedict Anderson's thought, though dated and contested, still deserve consideration as to membership in our now transnational, globalized, interdependent, and virtual "communities." See: *Imagined Communities: Reflections on the Origin and Spread of Nationalism.* (London & New York: Verso, 1991 [1983]).

[3] For further challenging discussions that expose the desire and betrayal in academe, see Ann duCille's deeply provoking essay "The Occult of True Black Womanhood: Critical Demeanor and Black Feminist Studies" (*Signs* V.19, N.3, Spring 1994) and Chela Sandoval. *Methodology of the Oppressed.* Theory Out of Bounds Series, V.18 (Minneapolis & London: University of Minnesota Press, 2000).

[4] We offer deep thanks to our revered colleague Francisco Ibáñez-Carrasco, but deeper for paying insufficient attention to the far more complex questions he raises in his work.

WORKS CITED

Anderson, Benedict. *Imagined ComMunities: Reflections on the Origin and Spread of Nationalism*. London & New York: Verso, 1991 [1983].

Couser, G. Thomas. *Vulnerable Subjects: Ethics and Life Writing*. Ithaca, NY: Cornell University Press, 2004.

duCille, Ann. "The Occult of True Black Womanhood: Critical Demeanor and Black Feminist Studies" in *Signs* 19.3 (Spring 1994).

Eakin, Paul John, ed. *The Ethics of Life Writing*. Ithaca, NY: Cornell University Press, 2004.

Freadman, Richard. "Decent and Indecent: "Writing My Father's Life." *The Ethics of Life Writing*. Ed. Paul John Eakin. Ithaca, NY: Cornell University Press, 2004.

Hampl, Patricia. "Other People's Secrets." *I Could Tell You Stories*. New York: Norton, 1999.

Ibáñez-Carrasco, Francisco. "Desire and Betrayal in Community-Based Research." Eds. Suzanne De Castelle, Francisco Ibáñez-Carrasco & Erica R. Meiners. *Public Acts: Disruptive Readings on Making Curriculum Public*. New York & London: Routledge Falmer, 2004. 35 -56.

Montello, Martha. "Confessions and Transgressions: Ethics and Life Writing." *Hastings Center Report*, V. 36, N. 2, 1 March 2006.

Wexler, Alice. "Mapping Lives: Truth, Life Writing, and DNA." *The Ethics of Life Writing*. Ed. Paul John Eakin. Ithaca, NY: Cornell University Press, 2004.

THE GOOD AMBUSH:
A TWO-VOICE ESSAY ON IDENTITY, EXPERIENCE AND STORYMAKING

Patricia Fontaine, MA, and Karen Campbell, MA

• • •

PART ONE: REACHING OUT TO
FACILITATE CHANGE

By Patricia Fontaine

The ring of participants begins to settle as Karen Campbell, a faculty member at Goddard College, and I, a student in Goddard's TLA concentration, do the paper-shuffle, slight cough, eye contact preamble that means we're ready to begin. I steal a glance around the room to gauge the mood, get a sense of who showed up. There are floor starers, and those with notebook open, expectant. A few nervous ticks: the leg jiggle, the hair twirl. My heart swells a bit, as it always does with this opening round of silent vulnerability. I do not underestimate the willingness and courage it took to arrive at this workshop. I am pleased there is color variegating the whiteness of most of our skins, and I see I am not the only one who looks older than she is.

Suddenly, it is quiet. *Too quiet,* as the rough faced cowpokes say to each other in those predictable Westerns, riding into the slot canyon, right into the ambush. I sigh, and take a breath. Teaching this workshop, I know an ambush is coming, and I hope I have the mettle to meet it.

It is like this with every workshop I pilot, the pause to prepare for what I ruefully call the *good ambush:* the moment of humility, of getting my britches yanked, of realizing no matter how well I prepare and how well I surf the unexpected, there will come a moment (or six) when I will be challenged to stay in the saddle, and admit, to myself and the participants in some way that sustains the group, that my privilege ambushed me.

It wasn't always so. When I knew less, but was inflamed more by earnest activism, I thought there was much I had to teach. Now, I find there is more I have to learn. Certainly, I provide the framework, the definitions and terms, the exercises, and closure. I work hard to facilitate well the emotional weather that kicks up when we prod privilege out of its hiding places. But the more I facilitate, the more I am humbled by what lays in wait in any workshop, and particularly so when we take on the hard-wired, deeply imbedded nature of privilege and its unlearning.

I'd like to tell two stories of ambush; one that helped me cut my teeth as a teacher of *Race, Class, and Gender;* and one that went down in the recent TLA Diversity and Social Justice workshop I co-facilitated with Karen Campbell.

I've encountered two basic kinds of ambush: the one where the cowpoke is jumped on from overhead; and the one that comes right out of the scrub brush on either side. One has to do with the often-unconscious arrogance of the well-meant facilitator (hence the height -- a kind of self-ambush); and the other has to do with the often-appropriate resistance or defence of participants (hence the sideways offensive). Both are excellent learning devices, and often happen in tandem.

CLEOPATRA

The setting of the first story is a small community college in Vermont, early nineties. Our cowpoke is lathered up about a first time gig teaching Sociology 201: *Race, Class, and Gender.* I have prepared assiduously, creating a tidy, and to my mind, thorough exploration of the complex internal and external nature of oppression. We will investigate each "ism" from Institutional,

Cultural, and Individual perspectives, thanks to my customizing of the work of Joseph Barndt's *Dismantling Racism* (20).

The first day of class goes quite well. I passionately introduce them to the subject. There is a mini-rebellion when I pronounce that we are *all* racist, sexist, and classist. This is quelled with assurances that I am too, of course, and that we learn 'isms from those we trust and love. Bolstered, I decide to riff off some of the outrageous things we've been denied knowing: George Washington was a slave owner! (Loewen 42); Helen Keller was a radical socialist who marched for women's suffrage! (Barndt 20) ; and Cleopatra was actually a coffee-skinned African, not Elizabeth Taylor with heavy eye make-up![1]

A young man's hand shoots up -- he challenges me on the spot. Cleopatra was a *Greek*, he asserts. Where did I get my information? I am rattled, panicked. *Ambush!* I mumble something about not getting the facts straight, and limp on, but the young man persists, launches into a rant about teachers who don't know the facts, the nature of conjecture, why don't you acknowledge the contributions of anthropology? "How can I be a racist if I've never even met a black person?!" He glances around the classroom of 20 to 40 year olds -- some trying a different academic setting, some trying to break out of dead-end jobs. "I assumed we'd be studying *about* these differences, not looking at our own stuff." Some nod. Others look away or fiddle with notebooks, find shoes to tie.

I do not remember exactly how I made it out of this canyon. Perhaps I accept his comments, agree to check my research, and move the class along.

During the following week I pluck out the prickers of hubris. I meet with more seasoned teachers, hatch a plan that acknowledges my mistake and hopefully engages the student.

Next class, I ask the young man to talk during break. I apologize for my inaccuracy, note that this is not an anthropology class, but one based more on liberation theory. To me, anthropology investigates culture and society from the position of an observer regarding "other." Liberation theory works to create awareness about the nature of "other," and the "systematic, institutionalized, ...day-to-day imbalance of power" implied (Creighton and Kivel 13). He stands, arms folded, silent. I realize he isn't the first and won't be the last student who challenges what I'm saying.

I mentally revisit the principles of "teaching from the heart" that I've taken pains to design this course around, particularly the notions of learning cooperatively, teacher openness, and owning our power as teachers (Thompson and Disch 5). I straddle that uncomfortable place between abject humility and professionalism. Perhaps, I offer, we can use the semester to collaborate in the classroom. I ask him to keep a keen ear and pass on whatever knowledge he's gleaned from his own studies. He nods, and tells me his mother, the psychiatrist, was often at odds with his father, the anthropologist. We ride warily into the next classes, and although he continues to challenge some of my statements, I come to see him as an ally, one who helped unsaddle my unexamined privilege early on.

This is what I meant earlier by the difference between teachers who teach exclusively, and teachers who learn. In my eagerness to display my chops in the anti-oppression department, I disregarded my privilege as a white, upper middle-class, would-be academic. There was a small but powerful ambush brewing in my head – the kind that says, offhandedly, *I'm going to whip these kids into shape.* Lord, what I didn't know. What comes to mind is Audre Lorde's notion of "unaddressed privilege" (132). My unaddressed privilege was a depthful analysis of my identity, how I came to teach that class, and why. I wanted the glory of giving these folks their light bulbs, but I learned that I needed mine unscrewed by the real life deal so many of them brought to that first class: the Vietnam Vet trying to tamp down his anguish, the EMT worker who was ashamed that he cried at accident scenes, the single mother belittled by the agency she hoped would make sense of food stamps, the rural Vermonter who was scared of people of color, the young woman angry that people sniggered at her deaf father's atonal voice.

In this story, there was another less visible ambush from overhead. Although I gave room in our exercises and discussions for addressing disability, it did not make an easy fit with my tidy, three-tiered lesson plan focusing on the big 'isms (gender, race, and class). I see now how resistant I was to meet my own appearance disability and engage my students, and myself, in unlearning what activist and scholar Simi Linton terms *ableism:* the nondisabled-centric oppression of disability (9). It took immersion in TLA's insistence on personal identity work, and lucky connections to colleagues who are disability activists to integrate the implications of living able bodied with a distinct, birthmarked face.

Postscript: A few years later, my lover hit black ice, flipped her car. Her battered body dangled in midair on a remote road. When the rescue outfit arrived, she deliriously called my name; worried I would be frantic she didn't show for our date (I was). When the young man attending her heard my name, he told her he had been my student. He told her he has never forgotten what he learned in that old class about oppression.

STEPPING IN

The second story begins with a complaint: my recent grumble to TLA faculty that there wasn't enough attention paid to diversity awareness. I was told that the Goddard community was smack in the process of defining and refining its work on Diversity and Social Justice. Perhaps I'd like to lead a workshop? Once again, alongside the true urgency I have for justice flits that tiny fairy of arrogance with the covert message: *let's whip everybody into shape.*

Working with Karen Campbell on some of the hottest days on record refreshed my humility. We crafted a workshop we felt would introduce, enable practice of, and inspire anti-oppression/

liberation awareness, while honoring the folks who were already living social justice in their work and experience. Our wrestling with the challenge of facilitating with integrity as sweat dripped into our sushi brought to mind the principle of "courageous self-inventory" artfully described by Amber Kinser.[2] For me it's more a process that resembles washing a floor: Drip. Revise. Acknowledge privilege. Mop brow with napkin. Admit 'failings, struggle, doubts.' Revise. Mop.

It was our decision to try and give an overview of definitions and models (particularly on privilege and power), an opportunity to try out methods for interrupting oppression, and spend the lion's share of our time together engaging an exercise called *Step Out.* Also known as "The Power Shuffle," this exercise asks folks to literally step out of line if they meet any of the criteria we read out, e.g.: "You are of Arab descent"; "You were raised in an isolated or farming community"; "You have a visible or hidden disability" (Criegton and Kivel 14-16). The goal: to have participants reflect on their responses as both individuals and part of a sundry group.

We agreed to include in our introductions what poked us into this work. I found myself telling the airport story: oppression first witnessed, and the ensuing paralysis of helplessness and shame. I learn later in my social justice education this is common hazard for the earnest yet uneducated liberal.

Midwestern airport, early eighties, late at night. My plane has been delayed, and I case the place for something to eat. Loud hoots from the only open bar. Asian man behind the counter is trying to close. A posse of white men in business suits harasses him mercilessly. I can smell the liquor from where I stand, a good ten feet away, anguishing what to do. I am alone, and a woman. The men are drunk and belligerent. You can guess the ending. I walk away, go cry in a bathroom stall, shaking with fear and frustration. It is a memory that never grows stale and still.

We carry on with the workshop, and as I've learned to

do over the years, ditch what seems superfluous on the fly so we can have deep time with *Step Out*. As I suspected from comments leading up to the exercise, engaging with it has profound impact – especially the point at which we ask folks to look around once they have stepped out of line, or pause to feel what it was like to choose not to be so visible and stay put.

The pairs are abuzz, and the energy of the room soars once we open the discussion. Perceptions pop like those tiny sponges immersed in water. We squeeze in a small tour of a model for interrupting oppression, and again, the room buzzes: everyone is eager to apply their shiny awareness. By now you might be wondering: where is the ambush? Just ahead.

In closing, I thank folks for helping me re-think my inaction at the airport. Immediately there is a clamor of advice about what I could have done and sympathy for my ignorance. I am uneasy at this stage of the workshop -- I sense that the eagerness to *do something, use something* to begin the process of change is spilling into our closing. We need to find a way to return the focus to their own reflections. As Karen and I work to still the room, a quiet, direct voice from one of the women of color extends like a lariat: "What if he didn't want or need your intervention?"

Ambush! I sit stunned for just a few seconds (to a facilitator, this seems like time without end). I acknowledge, once again, my ignored and well-meant privilege. Intervention without permission in the experience of someone being oppressed (commensurate with speaking *for* an oppressed group without firsthand knowledge) is another hallmark of the unconscious liberal. The handout we included on *Interrupting Oppression* encourages us to consider the risks and benefits of any interruption, and to build in support, but confronting racist police officers with swat gear requires different skills than interrupting Uncle Mac's annual anti-Semitic holiday diatribe. Still, my friends on the other side of oppression often note that uninvited intervention is more difficult for them than overt racism or ableism.[3]

Karen and I exchange looks. We are both sweating profusely. The group begins to quiet, and we prepare to ride off into the August noon. But one more ambush awaits.

REACH OUT

In some rare workshop endings, there is the ambush that presents as a gift: the unsolicited, completely spontaneous hearts-cracked closing-ritual ambush.

Our time up, we need a quick and significant closing -- and we decide to have everyone simply name one thing they were taking out of the workshop, one thing they would pack in to their little take-out container, to savor later. I did not think, going last, what I would say -- but inspired by the stretching of us, something sent my hand out, fingers spread. "Reach Out!" I said. And suddenly everyone thrusts his or her hand out, open, reaching in along the edges. This is an ambush of goose bumps, the kind of magic that no facilitator can conjure or contrive. This was the good people of this workshop, turning vulnerability into gesture. And it is gesture, says writer, healer, and activist Deena Metzger, conscious, determined gesture, that will be a vital part of what heals, what helps us remember what to do, and how to take what we discover into what we must live and create (15).

The woman who tossed the lariat? She began to sing, in a deep honey voice, "Reach out and touch, somebody's hand. Make this world a better place, if you can." Those good workshop participants: they rode out singing.

PART TWO: DIGGING DEEP TO ADDRESS DIVERSITY AND SOCIAL JUSTICE

By Karen L. Campbell

TLA is all about social justice for people whose color, shape, economic status, sexual orientation, gender expression, mobility, or abilities (among vast numbers of quite human attributes) are designated either strange or a threat to safety of the norm. Yet "Diversity" and "Social Justice" are difficult terms for they are already becoming homogenizing euphemisms for the almost hidden labelling of Others, making it difficult to speak of what it means to address privilege and oppression. At Goddard College, the current scholarly home of TLA, the Board of Trustees and the college, as represented by its Diversity and Social Justice Committee, have outlined clear goals, and definitions of diversity and social justice[4] to frame the core values that ground the work we do. Nonetheless, important as it is to identify goals, I think we would all admit it is rather easier to set goals reach them.

In the Individualized MA program, where Caryn Mirriam-Goldberg initiated TLA, the faculty and generations of students have long struggled to find ways to "walk" our social justice "talk," both in our educational approaches and in our degree requirements. Along the way, we've experimented with workshops, keynote addresses, small group exercises and many other prompts to make visible the assumptions about who we are and how we see others. The workshop Patricia Fontaine and I offered (as she explains above) was one such means of exploring diversity in a meaningful way at the college. We also hoped that the participants might help us to see what we cannot see -- messy bits of our individual and communal imaginations that prevent us from doing the work we want to do. This workshop was also intended to help students begin writing their identity essays, a requirement that asks students to reflect upon their personal motivations in their research and practice. Put another way, this requirement nudges us to identify and grapple with "biases"[5] that corrupt or distort our research and our practice, and probably fool us into cooperating with the normalizing forces of our respective cultures in ways we do not notice; and absolutely would not approve if we did.

Let me rush to assure that, despite the title "Identity Essay," we do not see identity as an uncontested or singular concept. I do not "have" one identity but rather both consciously and (unfortunately) unconsciously *identify with* different "ideas, experiences, purposes, emotions ... on many grounds, including gender, age, region, profession, and ethnicity" (Essed 129). So what I confront are unconscious identifications with and/or benefits from (for instance) white privilege, nationality, and perceived or felt abilities and states of "health." Another challenge is sometimes flagging energy. I don't just need ambushing by students and colleagues to keep on widening my vision of how I see myself and am seen -- I need inspiration. And in TLA words are our inspiration -- our words are the tools we use to make empowering change.

Many TLA facilitators engage with what are often labelled "vulnerable populations." By this, I think we mean people (often including ourselves) who acknowledge experiences that caused them damage -- damage that the *professed* values of their culture[6] would deem unacceptable. Such populations include what are often called "underserved" or "at-risk" teenagers, abandoned or traumatized children, communities struggling with poverty, individuals in recovery from, or trying to survive, forms of violence such as rape, incarceration, life-threatening illness, and other phenomena or ways of being that incur social stigma. Another way to look at these populations is to see the common societal silencing within them: Their individual stories are often marginalized to the point of invisibility within culture-at-large.

TLAers facilitate[7] self-expression in the spoken, written

or sung word (possibly also accompanied by visual expressions such as fine arts, dance or acting), or what we might call the telling of untold stories. These expressions are -- in powerful ways -- expressions of "different" identities, *interpretations of experiences* (and their e/affects) that have been hidden, suppressed, ignored and therefore set outside what Audre Lorde called the "mythical norm" (116).[8]

Experience, then, is one of TLA's core values since TLA, no matter the population in which it's practiced, is very much about helping individuals and communities express experiences often not recognizable, for example, in mainstream media and culture. I was pondering the relation between "difference" and experience, and the risks people had taken in sharing their experiences during our workshops, when suddenly I was hurtling back to an old "ambush" found, of all places, in theory. But theory is story, too, I reminded myself, and scuttled to dig up historian Joan Scott's 1991 essay "The Evidence of Experience" in which she examined the elusive, unstable meanings and power accruing to the word experience, in history and in literature, its (then) growing use in countering supposedly "objective" representations of different groups of people by historians who were *not* those people. Scott also raised an essential question that relates to TLA, diversity and social change: the role the evidence of experience might have in effecting change – or *acting merely to affirm dominant cultural norms.*

Scott noted efforts by historians of difference to bring suppressed experience to light -- make visible experiences that might challenge or counter previously established versions of normative history; telling those untold stories. Back in the '80s, for those who'd been left out of history this was empowering. The ambush, though, came when Scott pointed out that this strategy, though within "the [orthodox historical] rules that permit calling old narratives into question when new evidence is discovered" (776), is in danger of affirming the forces that defined such differences.

When experience is taken as the origin of knowledge, the vision of the individual subject (the person who had the experience or the historian who recounts it) becomes the bedrock of evidence on which explanation is built. Questions about the constructed nature of experience, about *how subjects are constituted as different in the first place, about how one's vision is structured -- about language (or discourse) and history -- are left aside.* The evidence of experience then becomes the evidence for the *fact* of difference, rather than a way of exploring how difference is established, how it operates, how and in what ways it constitutes subjects who see and act in the world. (Scott 777; my emphasis)

Scott asked tough questions about the relationship between language and experience: how humans come into aspects of being through language or discourses they experience but whose definitions they do not necessarily accept (culture doesn't always "take"!); and how experience "can both confirm what is already known (we see what we have learned to see) and upset what has been taken for granted" (793).[9] My point here is to ask -- as Nadine Gordimer did in a somewhat different context (another ambush!)[10] -- if justice is the same as, or if it necessarily results from, empowerment? As we facilitate the telling of stories -- experiences -- tell our own, or present those of others, are we utilizing our chance to analyze how social structures *shape our stories and our experiences*?

As any new field begins to establish itself, so its methods, approaches, styles of practice become established, which presents us with both an opportunity and a risk. TLAers at Goddard want to avoid the very real bind of establishing methods, approaches and styles of practice that are exclusionary, and instead continue to collaborate, co-create our own epistemologies. TLA has already recorded some exhilarating personal transformations through the telling of stories -- and we celebrate them. But as the numbers using the word to empower and liberate ourselves grow, we need also to be sure that our presentation of stories will not effectively affirm the validity of our/some being marginalized, nor how we live our lives in ways that marginalize -- and silence -- others, but that they expose how excludable identities come into being and then are suppressed.

For me, a major challenge comes from my experiences doing theatre with people with developmental disabilities[11] and in disability studies as theory. I keep having to ask myself why it is that although I'm constantly concerned about my responsibility for racism, classism, and sexism, etc., in my work at Goddard ableism tends to be an afterthought -- as if I am not sure how, *or whether*, I might be colluding in its continuation. In theatre work with people with disabilities we constantly struggle against the pressure from sponsors and even advocates to ensure the actors will not burst out with lines (observations, experiences!) that might shock the audience, and to "showcase" those whose talents will not challenge conventional notions of public performance. In other words, the content of (improvised) performances the actors wish to present so that audience notions of "normal" are left firmly in tact – associated with venues where only the mainstream gather.

European colonial and postcolonial history shows me that race & racism, sex/gender & sexism & heterosexism, class & classism were constructed[12] by humans, and often held in place through unspeakable cruelty. Whoever in the past effected the constructions I have inherited, I'm now responsible for their continuation. *Dis*-ability & ableism, though, I think I've sometimes allowed myself to believe (falling into that old nature v. culture trap), are not constructed. But Simi Linton and (more personally) Sunaura Taylor[13] ambushed me when they demanded to know why "disability" is so rarely situated among our concerns: not only right up there with the (recent) tussle between racism and classism, and not only in applied fields such as medicine, special education, behavioral psychology or rehabilitation (where disabled people rarely conduct but are the *site* of studies), but in all of academe (Linton, 77-80, 132-136). Linton demonstrates again and again that disability *is* present everywhere -- though, as with Toni Morrison's demonstration of the defining yet unrecognized black presence in white literature[14] disability is haphazardly used as (*now* I see) insufferably arrogant metaphor for lack (127) confirming the normalcy of the power-holders. Disability is central throughout different social histories, sciences, and arts, though rarely from the perspectives of people with disabilities, and Linton makes it resoundingly clear that it is high time we did something about it.

Linton is not suggesting we pretend human capacity for social survival ranges along a pleasant continuum. On the contrary, she calls for a "recognition of disabled and nondisabled people as distinct groups" (121). As with other marginalized groups, though, we should not conclude that "nature" has created the oppression because nature authored "difference," but that social, economic, political and cultural structures discriminate against and oppress people by constructing acceptable and unacceptable differences. Linton shows how absolutely imperative it is to ensure disability studies permeates liberal arts attention, with humanities *and* sciences equally in need of her and other scholars' findings on the meanings human societies have attached to particular "impairments," and how these meanings rationalize practices that disenfranchise and marginalize people with such impairments.[15]

To underline the urgent need for those in language and liberal arts to engage in critical analysis of the marginalization of disability, race, class, gender and other outlawed categories, I consider another form of ambush, an example of presenting experience in a way that challenges the supposed "truth" of authoritative discourses that separate disability into spaces "where it is primarily stated in terms of deficit or pathology" (Linton 86).

Philosopher Ladelle McWhorter's *Bodies and Pleasures: Foucault and the Politics of Sexual Normalization* is in itself a powerful demonstration of liberation through personal story. This autobiographical work records how McWhorter's deep engagement with Michel Foucault's efforts to expose the construction and contingency of norms, saved her own marginalized life, and helped her shape personal actions to destabilize the politics of normalization.

Amidst her impressive analysis of much of Foucault's work, McWhorter offers a canny reading of a practice Foucault called counter-memory. In this now mostly ignored case, there was a publication juxtapositioning the personal memoir (ignored at the time) of 19th century "hermaphrodite,"[16] Herculine Barbin, with public authoritative pronouncements about Barbin.[17]

Barbin was believed female at birth, and had become a convent teacher, though apparently did not develop "typical" female bodily characteristics. Barbin and another convent teacher developed a relationship that was interrupted by exposure of Barbin's indeterminate gender through an emergency health issue. When Barbin successfully achieved a change of legal sex status after medical examinations and hearings, the partner's parents forbade further contact, Barbin lost the convent living, and committed suicide in 1868 (McWhorter 201-204).

McWhorter's assessment of Foucault's work in presenting *Herculine Barbin*[18] seems to me an example worthy of TLA attention. Foucault does not tell Barbin's story. Instead he brings ignored experience -- Barbin's own memoir -- into public view but alongside the 19th century public knowledge about Barbin that effectively destroyed Barbin's life: medical records (including autopsy), other papers documenting education, newspaper reports, the birth certificate amending Barbin's sex, and a novella, *Scandal in the Convent*, published some years after Barbin's death

(McWhorter 200, 202).

Through this strategy of counter memory – Barbin's memory countering the voices of authorities that defined Barbin's person – Foucault makes it possible for Barbin to speak to us, and implicitly warn us to be diligent in questioning the right of authorities who name and define us because he also exposes the contingency of authoritative knowledge.

Barbin was not served by Foucault's efforts. But perhaps I now stand readier to work toward social justice because I am better equipped to resist and encourage others to do so: To begin, for example, by asking why people with disabilities, their perspectives and experiences are absent in my workplaces and in public theatre; by recognizing the only justification for my work in theatre with people with disabilities is in supporting the actor's desire to perform counter memories, not the audience desire for familiarity; and by chanting that ambushing statement: *disability is a state of being socially marginalized and discriminated against.*[19]

At this historical time, when media stories protect us from knowing how we hand economic greed-lords the right to distort the significance of *our* stories by using them to define the edges of *their* profit, their normalcy, our greatest strength is that TLAers operate not only in the isolation of academe (notoriously slow to change), but in several different communities. The stories we create or facilitate are not just healthy local knowledge, a solace to those who recognize in them aspects of their own hitherto "exceptional" experience. Like *The Vagina Monologues*, a book and performance that uses language to speak for an often-silenced part of the female anatomy as well as to speak out against violence toward women, perhaps, our stories have a chance to harness and mobilize global dissent, and resistance to those above-mentioned norms. If we then join our communities in studying identities and how they are brought into being, expose what makes anyone's stories ignorable in the first place, we could make a very real contribution to creating healthy communal resistance, dismantling oppressive discourses and structures, and changing social inequities.

NOTES

[1] Overheard at an Association for Women in Psychology conference. 1993.

[2] Feminist teaching and mentoring requires first and foremost courageous self-inventory. This is at once its most important and most complicated component. In my work, this inventory takes the form of three questions: First, am I focusing on where my students are right now and am I maintaining the patience it will probably take to get them somewhere else? Second, am I finding teachable moments beyond the classroom? Am I extending my work to the broader campus community and then extending it beyond that? Finally, am I presenting myself as the feminist who has it all together and who now has a wisdom and understanding that make feminist living easy, thus flattening the will of my students because the goal feels beyond their reach? Or am I demonstrating the courage I'm asking them to muster by being bold enough to admit my failings, my struggle, my own doubts, thus exemplifying the complexity, and more importantly the humanity of feminist living?"

[3] Of course, there are moments when permission is impractical, e.g. if a woman is being beaten or a child molested.

[4] (Excerpted) Working Definition of Diversity

Diversity is "otherness," or those human qualities that are different from our own and outside the groups to which we belong, yet are present in other individuals and groups. It is important to distinguish between the primary and secondary dimensions of diversity.

Primary dimensions are the following: age, ethnicity, gender or gender identity, physical abilities/qualities, race and sexual orientation. Secondary dimensions of diversity are those that can be changed, and include, but are not limited to: educational background, career path, geographic location, income, marital status, military experience, parental status, life and work experiences, and religious, political and philosophical beliefs, perspectives, social standing, and opinions.

Working Definition of Social Justice

Social justice is defined generally as the equality of human rights for all which includes access to the freedom of speech, employment, pay and benefits, resources, information, economics, power, and voice within an institution and society ... (Goddard College Diversity Plan, Diversity and Social Justice Team, September 2006).

[5] Or motives, which, as Ibáñez-Carrasco notes, "are grouped under one dubious classification" as if by identifying, naming, we regain innocence; pack away and so negate all other veins of self-other treason. See: Ibáñez-Carrasco, Francisco. "Desire and Betrayal in Community-Based Research" in Ibáñez-Carrasco & Meiners, eds. *Public Acts: Disruptive Readings on Making Curriculum Public.* (New York & London: RoutledgeFalmer, 2004: 35 - 56).

[6] I think we have to retain space for perceiving experience in culture-specific contexts.

[7] Most students engaged in simultaneously studying and creating the developing field of TLA undertake a practicum, internship, or other practical application or testing of theoretical knowledge that will produce not simply useful experience as a TLA facilitator/ performer but insights they will make into public knowledge -- knowledge that they hope will contribute to social justice.

[8] Lorde actually said, "In america, this norm is usually defined as white, thin, male, young, heterosexual, christian, and financially secure. It is with this mythical norm that the trappings of power reside within this society" (116). In western academe, too, norms are enforced and these include methodologies inherited from the EuroAmerican beliefs and practices of the past -- as Linda Tuhawai Smith in *Decolonizing Methodologies: Research and Indigenous Peoples* (London & New York: Zed, 1999) so clearly explains.

One mythical norm is that of producing "objective" knowledge. The practices of different "disciplines" are often, as Scott notes of history, "foundational discourse[s]." And she is worth quoting here at some length: "These foundations ... are unquestioned and unquestionable; they are considered permanent and transcendent. As such they create a common ground for historians and their objects of study in the past and do authorize and legitimize analysis; indeed analysis seems not to be able to proceed without them. In the minds of the foundationalists, in fact, nihilism, anarchy, and moral confusion are the sure alternatives to these givens, which have the status (if not the philosophical definition) of eternal truths" (780).

[9] I should note that I am revisiting only a kernel of Scott's article (much oversimplifying). Many have answered her in subsequent years but controversies over experiences that define "identity" and "difference" have not gone away. In fact, they have intensified for many "different" people here in the USA.

[10] In her 1994 post apartheid novel, *None to Accompany Me*, a character asks somewhat impatiently: "Empowerment ... What is this new thing? What happened to what we used to call justice?" (285).

[11] In Japan and in the USA -- different cultural milieu with different theatrical conventions, but similar in at least some of the expectations of audiences.

[12] This statement should not be taken literally. Clearly not all human phenomena are cultural constructions – the story is far more complex – but I think it's fair to say that many more people now accept the notion of culture's constructions than did when Beauvoir told us women are not born but made.

[13] Artist, disability activist, elegantly biting theorist, and (at the time) Goddard student, Sunaura Taylor made a start on my denseness in her extensive undergraduate project examining disability in (though often hidden from) histories, arts, artists, environmental,

social and political sciences. This work provides a crucial political and personal distinction between "disability" *as a state of being socially marginalized and discriminated against* and "impairment" – the differences that are seen as placing certain individuals outside the normalized standards of behavior specific to any one culture. See: Sunaura Taylor. "Walk on your Head, sing with your Sinuses: A History and Memoir of the Scandalous Nonconforming Body" (BA Senior Study/book in progress, Fall 2005) and her website: http://www.sunnytaylor.org/.

[14] Toni Morrison. *Playing in the Dark: Whiteness and the Literary Imagination.* (New York: Vintage, 1992).

[15] See especially chapters 4, 5, and 6. Although I have horribly simplified some of the most astounding ambushes I have read in a long time in this brief introduction to Simi Linton's book, I (not humbly) advise it is core reading for everyone, whatever our field.

[16] "Intersex" is a more accepted label today, and "hermaphrodite" considered insulting.

[17] Barbin, Herculine. *Herculine Barbin: Being the Recently Discovered Memoirs of a Nineteenth Century French Hermaphrodite.* Introduced by Michel Foucault. Trans. Richard McDougall. (New York: Pantheon Books, 1980).

[18] She counters other scholarly appraisals and presents characteristically nuanced arguments (therefore well worth equally careful reading). See for contrast: Rousseau, G.S. "Review of *Herculine Barbin. Being the recently discovered memoirs of a nineteenth-century hermaphrodite*" *Medical History* 25(2). April, 1981: 211–212.

[19] See note xii above.

WORKS CITED

Barndt, Joseph. *Dismantling Racism: The Continuing Challenge to White America.* Minneapolis: Augsburg Fortress Publishers, 1991.

Barbin, Herculine. *Herculine Barbin: Being the Recently Discovered Memoirs of a Nineteenth Century French Hermaphrodite.* Introduced by Michel Foucault. Trans. Richard McDougall. New York: Pantheon Books, 1980.

Creighton, Allan and Paul Kivel. *Helping Teens Stop Violence: A Practical Guide for Counselors.* Alameda, CA: Hunter House Inc., 1990.

Essed, Philomena. *Diversity: Gender, Color and Culture.* Trans. Rita Gircour. Amherst, MA: University of Massachusetts Press, 1996.

Ensler, Eve. *The Vagina Monologues.* The V-Day Edition. New York: Villard, 2001.

Gearheart, Sally Miller. *Wanderground: Stories of the Hill Women.* Denver: Spinsters Ink Books, 1979.

Gordimer, Nadine. *None to Accompany Me.* London: Penguin, 1994.

Kinser, Amber E. *Philosophy of Feminist Teaching and Mentoring.* 11 Jan. 2007. <http://www.osclg.org/membership/kinserfemte achermentorphilosophy.pdf>.

Linton, Simi. *Claiming Disability: Knowledge and Identity.* New York: New York University Press, 1998.

Loewen, James. *Lies My Teacher Told Me: Everything Your American History Textbook Got Wrong.* New York: Simon and Schuster, 1995.

Lorde, Audre. "The Uses of Anger: Women Responding to Racism." *Sister Outsider.* Trumansburg, New York: Crossing Press, 1984. 124-133.

----. "Age, Race, Class, and Sex: Women Redefining Difference." *Sister Outsider.* New York: Crossing Press, 1984.114-123.

Morrison, Toni. *Playing in the Dark: Whiteness and the Literary Imagination.* New York: Vintage, 1992.

Metzger, Deena. *Entering the Ghost River: Meditations on the Theory and Practice of Healing.* Topanga, CA.: Hand to Hand, 2002.

Thompson, Becky and Estelle Disch. "Feminist, Anti-racist, Anti-oppression Teaching: Two White Women's Experience." *Radical Teacher* 41: 1992.

McWhorter, Ladelle. *Bodies and Pleasure: Foucault and the Politics of Sexual Normalization.* Bloomington and Indianapolis: Indiana University Press, 1999.

Scott, Joan W. "The Evidence of Experience" in *Critical Inquiry,* V17, N.1, Summer (1991): 773-797.

RESTORATIVE JUSTICE AS STORYTELLING

Lana S. Leonard

• • •

Restorative justice is an ancient, healing art with storytelling at its core. It is experiencing a renaissance today as a response to high recidivism rates among juvenile offenders, overcrowded, expensive prisons, victim's rights and community policing movements. In restorative justice, crime is viewed as an offense against a person, not against the state. Accountability amounts to repairing the harm to the relationship. Personal storytelling opens minds and hearts and makes it possible.

Picture a circle of people, all in some way impacted by the same crime, coming together to allow offenders and victims alike to tell their stories in a place of safety and respect, to define the harm and create an agreement together on how to repair it. There are dozens of small, community based restorative justice programs in the United States. It is pervasive in the juvenile justice systems of Canada, Wales, England, New Zealand and Australia.

The circle often includes elders and community members with special experience or expertise. Circle participants have been "pre-conferenced" and understand the guidelines of safety and respect, truth telling, spirit of cooperation and skill of deep listening required for a successful conference. They understand that accountability comes with the responsibility of repairing harm. Circles tend to last two to three hours and end with an agreement that repairs harm to victim, community and self (something that helps the offender make better choices). Agreements must be completed in a designated time frame. If not completed, the case is referred back to the traditional court system.

Criminal cases where there is a likelihood of re-victimizing the victim -- domestic violence, incest, and child abuse, for example, are not appropriate for restorative circles. Restorative justice is not a quick fix or a good fit for chronic, repeat offenders who have no other frame of reference but criminality. Restorative justice is not therapy; it is conflict resolution, although it is not uncommon to find a certain number of therapy sessions as an item in an offender's agreement.

Restorative justice practitioners often hear from their juvenile offenders, "I had no idea so many people cared about me." Resilience is tapped when offenders recognize the power to see themselves and victims in a new way -- someone valuable who made an unwise choice. They are encouraged to see themselves as separate from their behavior. The behavior is disdainful, but not the person.

Offenders' assets are surveyed and circle participants search for ways offenders' talents can benefit the community in some way. A stolen item was returned in one circle but the damage to the reputation of teens was tarnished. The offender, an unusually good artist, created two colorful, artistic posters for the local library, which was badly in need of art. The art, album covers for rock bands, was a hit and served to polish up teens' reputation as well.

In restorative justice circles, victims, previously "invisible," now have a face and a story. Not having given their victims a single thought before or during the crime, upon hearing victims' stories, offenders can become caring and empathic. They can, for the first time, actually feel the wider impact of their wrongdoing on their victims and community. Juvenile offenders often say, "I had no idea that my actions affected so many people -- people who care about me." They experience remorse and an internal desire to make it right. Ninety-two percent of the time the cause and effect experience stops offenders who complete agreements from re-offending.

They are asked to "self-sentence" after hearing the harm and hearing some suggestions from the circle. "I am so sorry", one teen said in a circle, "I had no idea me and my friends were causing you such stress by trespassing. We'll make new signs and post them where the kids get in and tell everyone to stay off that vacant land." When they complete their agreements, offenders have the satisfaction of cleaning up their own mess and being welcomed back to the community as a valuable person. They build bonds and relationships that help sustain pro-social behavior.

In a restorative justice circle I conducted with Dr. Beverly Title in Colorado, the offender looked like a school bully who had slammed a smaller kid on his head "pile driver style" on the playground and broken the child's neck. The child had to wear a "halo" for months to stabilize his head. Imagine how the father of this 10-year-old victim felt about the "bully" who hurt his child. Yet the father agreed to come to the conference -- the only way he could legally have a say in what happened to the offender.

When the offender told his story, the father's face visibly showed the shift of consciousness that lies at the heart of how stories transform lives. As he heard the story, the father's face was transformed from furious and vengeful to compassionate and wanting to help. The offender said, "I am fat because of my kidney disease, I'm home alone a lot. I never had a dad and mom is a cocktail waitress so I don't see her much. We don't have money for sports teams or after school stuff. I love to watch pro wrestling on TV and that's where I got the "pile driver" move I tried out on Danny. I didn't think I could really hurt him. I feel bad and I'm sorry. I don't have any friends to play with."

The father was touched to the core by the offender's story and offered to pay for and coach the offender on his local football team. He said, "Son, you come to my house on Saturday and I'll suit you up and we'll go to the field together." The circle agreed on of 50 hours of community service. The offender would help the young victim with the broken neck both at school and at home. They developed a relationship. The offender got a family and the family got an energetic helper while their son was physically limited by his neck brace.

The storytelling that takes place in restorative justice circles transforms listeners and tellers alike. By telling their story from the frame of reference of a healthy survivor of crime, victims, previously in fear, can re-mythologize themselves. The person who offended them is now just a scared kid who is willing to hear the harm and make it right as much as possible. Offenders' stories can convey another side of themselves which will be listened to with respect. These stories of harm and healing mend and weave relationships back together -- often stronger than before.

Storytelling plays another important role in restorative circles. Archetypal or personal wisdom stories told by elders or community members can paint a picture of desired behavior, possibilities of how things can be, and a template for pro-social behavior. These stories carry a sense of the mystery and wonder of life and evoke a sense of timelessness and reverence. The stories, told as openings or closings to restorative circles, can offer courage and benefits of values such as patience and kindness. Animals are often the characters whose experiences we share and whose lessons we learn in these tales.

"The Devoted Son" is a story of ancient peacemaking found in many tribal archives. It is reminiscent of the "bully" with the kidney disease who found friendship instead of rage in a restorative justice circle. In this story, there was a terrible murder of one friend by another in the same tribe. Everyone shouted, "Kill him!" The grandfather spoke softly. "Will killing him return our boy to us?Will killing him help feed our people?"

When they called the young man to his fate they said, "See that tepee?" he said, pointing to the tepee of the young man he had killed. "It is yours now." "See those horses?" they said, pointing to the dead man's horses. He nodded again. "They are yours now. You are our son. You will take the place of the one you have killed."

He looked up slowly to the faces surrounding him. His new life had begun and so had theirs. The young man became a devoted son. By the time he died, he was known in all the tribes as the model of a loving son.

Restorative justice and the powerful healing effect of its storytelling component is a natural fit for juveniles who commit misdemeanor crimes and are not habitual, hardened criminals. It can nip early criminal behavior in the bud, turn lives around and save the justice system millions in the future.

Restorative justice measures are effective in solving much bigger problems of crime and violence on a national as well as individual level. Successful programs 5 to 10 years old in Colorado, Oregon and Minnesota hold conferences for felons and adults. South Africa, after suffering from years of apartheid and beginning its new democracy, initiated the Truth and Reconciliation Commission -- a restorative body designed to offer opportunities for victims to tell their horrific stories and be heard. The commission also offered offenders a chance to listen to these stories, verbally admit wrongdoing, and ask for amnesty. The success of this commission is proof positive that storytelling by victims of crime is healing in itself.

I believe restorative justice "as storytelling" holds answers for nations struggling with warlords, religious zealots and terrorism across the globe. Telling and listening to each other's stories hold the clues and seeds for understanding, increased compassion and, ultimately, peace. Combatants would come to realize that we are all ultimately responsible to each other -- we are all related.

"IT UNFOLDS BEFORE WHOEVER WALKS ALONG IT": MAKING A LIVING THROUGH TLA

Caryn Mirriam-Goldberg, Ph.D., CPT

• • •

It unfolds itself before whoever walks along it.
- Tao-te Ching

FALLING IN LOVE WITH YOURSELF AND LEAPS OF FAITH

Deciding to do TLA as your work is not just one leap of faith, but a continual series of tiny jumps over occasional puddles and paradigm-wide hurdles along the path we find by walking it. While there are no maps about how to create for ourselves the work we will best love and that will best interface with our community's needs and dreams, there are some lanterns along the way to illuminate what signs our lives are showing us. The advice of Idene Goldman of VisionWorks, who specializes in helping people develop their livelihood, that calls us to fall in love with ourselves is surely one of those lights:

> My job is to get people to fall in love with themselves. I call it 'inner education.' First, people need to take the time to be quiet and discriminate between shoulds versus urges. Second, care about yourself enough to listen to yourself. Third, embrace your present job. It's the backdrop and stage setting for your growth as an individual. Choose to get all you can out of a situation. And if you need help listening to yourself, get help. We need a mirror to see ourselves inside too. ("On the Path to Right Livelihood")

Goldman calls on us to use our ability to discern our motives in our work, listen to our intuition, and use the material at hand (like the present job) as the starting ground for where we want to go. Such advice is not only valuable for what it tells us, but for how it can help us keep from tripping into the grand freak-out question that just about anyone dives into when considering a life's work in TLA: *Can I make a living at this?*

I hear this question often from prospective and current students in Goddard's TLA concentration as well as from people I encounter during airport layovers in Cinncinnati or at family Thanksgivings in Orlando (although then, it's usually worded, "You can make a living at *that?*"). Given the visible and invisible forces of community opportunities, regional biases and limitations, individual talent and daring, our socio-economic system, and probably karma, luck, the magnetic pull of the earth, the variabilities of ecosystems, I usually begin with this phrase: "It depends."

It depends on whether you feel called to do this work, whether it's something you've always known, even before you had the words for it, was part of your life's work.

It depends how willing you are to put yourself out there in your community, offer what you have and see what doors open.

It depends on how committed you are to truly getting to know the needs of your community while simultaneously listening closely to the resonance (or not) in your own soul.

It depends on looking at your own motives and biases, limitations and fears honestly, and facing what you need to face to become more present for yourself and for others.

It depends on having enough education (whether formal, information, or a combination of the two) to learn your craft and also learn what you don't know so that you don't cause damage out of ignorance.

Most of all, it depends on doing excellent work.

Is this the work that's right for you? Perhaps it depends on this question most of all.

Goldman's invitation to fall in love with ourselves as a way to find out seems to me to be the most sensible approach: such attention to our own best thinking and feeling not only helps us inhabit more of our own minds and hearts, but it helps us see the path. If we can't see the path, I suggest taking a line from Mary Chapin Carpenter: "By toeing the track I knew" ("John Doe #24"). Sometimes just a sense of feeling (what we feel in our bodies, what our intuition tells us) can help us find the way. As the *Tao-te Ching* says, the path unfolds before whoever is walking it. It's not something we need machetes, shovels, cement and teams of hired hands to create: it's there, just like there are paths in the woods all around my house made by the deer, coyote and other critters; paths I can't see until I'm walking them.

COBBLING, LUCKING INTO AND INVENTING OUR WORK

You would find your vocation where your talents meet opportunity.
 - Aristotle ("On the Path to Right Livelihood")

Those of us doing TLA as our work are walking parallel paths born of shared histories, traditions, practices and values. The expression of how TLA plays out in terms of having a job is obviously as varied as TLA, however. In some cases, people land a job that's beyond their wildest dreams. I know a woman who, after leading a community writing workshop that was attended by the wife of the local hospital's president, was invited to be that hospital's full-time resident writer. Nancy Morgan, whose marvelous essay appears in this book, studied psycho-oncology as her MA in TLA from Goddard before being hired as Arts and Humanities Director of the Lombardi Cancer Center.

The more common way people make a living through TLA is through cobbling together this and that -- freelance writing work with storytelling performances, workshops for the elderly with writing grants on the side, organic gardening while facilitating eco-poetics retreats. In the past decade, I've facilitated intergenerational workshops for teenage girls and local elderly women; retreats with a singer-songwriter; an all-men's (except for me) writing workshop; and storytelling and writing sessions at hospitals for people living with cancer. I've also written grants with collaborators in four states, made mandalas with junior high kids in a small western town, rehearsed my poetry with dancers and singers, and led urban, low-income children of color on a poetry treasure hunts at rural retreat center. If nothing else, this work is always fresh, new, alive.

Yet this work also needs to be balanced with doing our own language arts, whether that means finishing the novel, polishing the story to be presented, connecting with others in the community to create a new theatre offering, or singing to the moon on a still night. We do this work because this work is us, and that daily dance -- both marvelous and challenging, kind of like staring into the eyes of a newborn while trying to wash the dishes – is just part of making our own livelihoods.

The variety of jobs we do are ones so newly invented that many of us probably couldn't imagine this work when we were asked as kids, "What do you want to be when you grow up?" Whether we have a tenure-track job at a university and create spoken word performances in between grading essays, or whether we get to nap at 2 p.m. but then wake at 2 a.m. wondering if the check for the freelance work will arrive in time for the rent, we're part of the collective inventing of this new profession. Is it risky? Of course, but then again, what profession isn't in a time of corporate down-sizing, college and university budget cuts, and massive publishing industry changes? If this is the work that calls to us, nothing else will satisfy us. And we can bring the tools and values of TLA to the invention of our profession, including: the ability to respond to what comes out of the blue; innovation in designing our own careers; an ethics born of being immersed in our communities; imagination that lets us see how often juxtaposing things (like making a living and making art) create their own pattern; patience and presence in listening deeply to ourselves and others; and a hunger for truth, connection, and expression.

Finding opportunities is often like finding the path: we don't necessarily have to build them, but we sure need to be aware enough to see them when they appear. I once spotted a small ad in for a mini-grant to do a writing workshop, and so I applied to the National Association for Poetry Therapy Foundation to do workshops for Native American women at the local Native American center. The grant was funded, but the center sent the grant to a local housing authority, something I never would have expected. Eight years later, I'm still doing writing workshops for local income women of color -- one of the richest experiences of my life -- at the housing authority, which was impressed enough with the work of the initial mini-grant to now direct federal funds for drug and alcohol prevention to the workshops. This is not a scenario I could have imagined, but because I walked through each door as it opened, the opportunity unfolded itself on my path.

Creating, lucking into and unearthing such opportunities also require us to learn about our communities. Simply following our natural curiosity about what's happening to the people in our town or city can bring to light ways to make a living close to home, whether it's doing a storytelling gig at the neighborhood school or collaborating with other artists to mirror the stories of the community back to itself. This curiosity pulls us out of our heads and houses to openings of community centers, school plays, neighborhood block parties, business anniversary parties, and hospital open houses where we can meet people, get to know what they do, share what we do, and then see where the seeds find fertile ground.

Of course this also takes a certain amount of guts, and a belief that what we have to offer is of value, or if the faith isn't yet there, enough gumption to act as if it is until it is. This kind of trust is nothing to sniffle at while worrying about not enough income to pay the utility bills, poise to present our work to people, and confidence to believe we are good enough.

A student of mine once decided she wanted to do writing workshops for people facing terminal illness, so she prepared a little portfolio of her writing, a workshop proposal, and her nerves to visit with the director of the local hospice. As soon as she told her story – of losing her brother and understanding the role of art in such a loss – the doors swung open, and she got to do that workshop, and many others. She's now training in palliative care to broaden her work in her home city. In her case, the experience of her own story of loss led her to her TLA work, but it also gave her a way to talk with prospective employers about her deepest motivations, and a way to reach these employers, too.

In so many cases, the stories that brought us here show us the courage, language, and inspiration to go forth and make the work that fulfills us.

THE SPACE THAT HOLDS THE WITNESSING

When I was a teenager, living through what I was sure was one of the worst divorces in the history of New Jersey with both my parents barricading themselves in different parts of our house, I found that one man outside my family made all the difference in my life. He was my youth group leader, a large guy losing his hair but in full possession of a high-pitched voice and a wicked sense of humor. Each week, he and I would huddle together on the floor of our local synagogue before youth group, and I would tell him what was happening at home. Because I had a good witness -- someone who continually told me that I wasn't crazy, I was just caught in a living hell – I found the strength to turn to writing, to reach out to others, to find my way. All my good witness really had to do was listen: give me a mirror to see myself through his eyes.

If TLA workshops are about any one thing, they're about creating environments -- both in how we set up the physical space of the workshop and the "internal space" that holds the group -- where we can serve as witnesses to each other's lives. Whether it's an art center auditorium where local teenagers are reading their poetry to their peers, a small bookstore back room where elderly men and women tell stories of their youth, a retreat center where traumatized children create a collaborative play, or a circle of mats in the woods where adults listen closely to the forest sounds to inform their writing, space and witnessing are twined elements of a successful TLA experience.

As far as the physical space goes, we need to arrange chairs in a way that we can all see each other in a room small enough that the group can have necessary closeness and yet large enough to avoid claustrophobia. Having hot coffee or cold tea, cookies and pretzels and little chocolates can also enhance a space as well as enough light and good seating.

When it comes to where to meet, it's good to use our connections and imaginations, and also to think carefully about where this particular group or client would feel most at home in this work. Spaces to rent -- and sometimes to barter use of -- include community centers and other public-owned buildings (which often rent out meeting spaces), hospitals, libraries, schools, bookstores (if they have some uninhabited -- except for the books -- spaces), churches or synagogues or mosques or temples, retreat centers, not-for-profit centers, colleges and universities (not to mention having outdoor meeting spaces where and when appropriate in parks, campgrounds, and other settings).

The topic of whether to ever hold workshops at home is one widely debated by people in this field -- some believing that it crosses a personal boundary to invite people into your home for a process that might be a tad therapeutic, and others believing it helps builds community, and besides, it gets the house clean.

Maybe all of the above is true, and as someone who occasionally holds workshops in my home, when I decide to host something at home, I take some time to turn my home over in a sense: clean up, set up chairs, bake something fragrant, light a candle, ask my husband and kids to temporarily relocate (although I have to admit my dog throws herself -- and she is large -- on the laps of people occasionally when they write). I cannot emphasize enough the importance of having any particularly distracting persons you live with out of sight for the workshop; kids running into the middle of someone reading a passage about being sexually abused tend to ruin everyone's day, and it shatters the safe space that's needed to create. I also set boundaries as to what's open for people to wander into and what's not. Closing doors to bedrooms, laundry rooms, etc. can work wonders in this regard, and also it helps to tell people, "We're in the living room, and you're welcome to sit outside on the deck and write, or even in the yard. The bathroom is behind me, and refreshments are over there" -- just a little statement that clearly communicates what's workshop and what's not.

But much of setting and holding the space has to do with how we facilitate the inner space of a place to allow for people to witness each other and themselves: the way we help the group co-create whatever unnamable thing it is that makes it safe and welcoming for people to take artistic leaps into the wilds of their hearts. Repeatedly, I find this comes down to having clear and strong ground rules: guidelines for how the group will work together and how individuals can work on their own that will, ideally, enhance community and free individuals to create through making and sustaining a safe, creative space in which we all dwell when we're here.

The ground rules I use (in the appendix of this article) come out of my experience facilitating writing workshops for pissed-off teenagers, bored elders, intergenerational Latinos, low income Native American women, middle-aged white people going through big transitions in their lives and other groups. Sometimes I play with the wording a little, or boil these down to just five or six items, but generally, I'm trying to communicate one strong message: All that we do here supports people taking ownership of their writing and their artistic process, their time here. When that message gets across, I find that people naturally land in the place where they can fully respect each other's artistic process, each other's writing, and each other's time much more deeply. From there, true listening -- to ourselves and to each other -- happens.

There are many other ways to construct ground rules, such as the work of Patricia Fontaine, and Vanita Leatherwood, who share their excellent sets of agreements in the appendix to this article. There are many manners of ground rules or agreements in a good many writing guides (see web.goddard.edu/~tla for more resources), and the group itself -- if appropriate -- can construct its own agreements.

These agreements or ground rules are a community contract that helps us self-govern. If, for example, one of the agreements is confidentiality, and then someone breaks that confidentiality, there's something to refer back to in making a decision (whether it's made by the facilitator or by the group itself) as to what to do in this case. If someone tends to talk too much, a community agreement to have time for everyone to share their stories -- plus some active facilitation -- can help keep the group from being swallowed up by one person's voice. Just about every time I've read my ground rules to a group (and lightly discussed them), I've heard some sighs of relief because ground rules have a great tendency to turn down the volume of fear for many people. They're basically a way to say, "hey, you're safe here, and we're really going to listen to you and let you do what you need to do in this context, and now you go, girl (or boy)."

It's also important to draw out necessary ground rules for specific situations: If I'm facilitating a group where I notice that a member has a tendency to insult other members, I might stop and ask if we can agree to no insults, sarcasm or jibes (if this wasn't already clear in my ground rules). If I have a person who tends to bring up personal therapy issues in an inappropriate way (e.g. "Can we skip this next writing exercise so everyone can help me figure out what to say to my step-mother about how she never loved me?"), I can refer back to the ground rules, or to the basic implicit or explicit understanding about the purpose of this group.

Both the ground rules and attention to setting up the meeting place up help us to set the space. Good facilitation helps us to keep that space.

BE HERE NOW: FACILITATING IN THE PRESENT

The most important thing I know about facilitating a workshop is being present. And the most important thing I know about being present is that it's a life time practice, and it has everything to do with dropping my luggage at the door, paying attention, getting up the courage to act when I need to act, and holding down the impulse to act when I need to listen. Here's more detail on how we can cultivate greater presence in our facilitation.

- *Drop the luggage at the door*: All of us have found ourselves in charge of something -- like facilitating a group, directing a performance, teaching a class -- at a moment when we would much rather be at home wearing flannel and sipping tea while reading a stack of old magazines. Yet when it's time to facilitate, it's time to drop that luggage at the door -- the fight we may have just had with a spouse, the worry over the bank account, the exhaustion the coffee hasn't yet quelled. This is a kind of surrender (that I talk more about in the final essay in this book), but it's a necessary surrender. When it's time to show up for work, it's time to show up -- and the best we can do is be there, but also be tender with ourselves in the process.

- *Pay attention*: What is intuition but close attention we pay to the sensations in our bodies, the voice in our heads, the strange, small feeling that we can't ignore? If we aim our eyes and ears toward what's happening in a group or coaching session -- toward the body language and faces around us, what's being said and not said -- we naturally will have a stronger sense of what we need to do as facilitators.

- *Act when needed*: Sometimes we see something in a group that needs interruption. Maybe a member has started to talk about a story she's working on, and she's been talking for over five minutes already with no sign of taking a breath. Maybe someone is talking on his cell phone while someone else is preparing to read her poem, or a person said something that insulted all the gay Latinos of the world. While it's easier to do nothing, nothing is the last thing we want to do in such cases because otherwise, we're not doing our job in serving the group. Interrupting bad behavior takes constant grace and courage, and most of all, a quick letting go of whatever anger we might feel at the behavior. If, in my nicest voice, I say, "Please, no cell phones in group," but I'm still pissed off as hell, the whole group is going to know it, and the person I addressed will be hurt; in short, the situation will escalate, and good facilitation is about de-escalating potentially dangerous situations for a group so that the group can tune into its best work. What helps me drop the anger is to tell myself that the bad behavior in 99.999% of the cases has nothing to do with me, take a deep breath, open my heart, and say something as calmly as I can. If I don't know what to say, I have options: I can ask the group to take a break, and then talk with the offender privately; I can name for the group what's happening ("I'm feeling uneasy about Susie's comment about gay Latinos") and ask the group for help -- including Susie herself -- on how to move forward; I can even say that I don't know what to do. Easy to say these things? No. Any clear way to know exactly the right thing to say? Of course not. But this is part of the exhilarating, scary and ultimately satisfying life-long education in facilitation.

- *Listen carefully and sit on your hands*: There are also the reverse situations. When we might feel compelled to say something, but we really need to listen. If someone accidentally insults someone else, and now the two of them are working it out, while I want to side with the offended, the best thing for me to do is to give them my attention, be quiet, and then help move the group along. If someone starts crying after reading something, it's often more effective and more sensitive to give a moment of silent witnessing to the situation, and then move along rather than gallop across the circle and gather the crying person in my arms. Part of good facilitation is being mindful of my motivations for action, and sitting on my hands if I realize those motivations are at odds with what's best for the group.

- *Know and don't know what to do*: This is where we circle back to paying attention. It's up to each facilitator, in each moment, to give the situation his/her best and cleanest attention, and then do or not do what's called for. Anyone who does this work knows well that we don't always do what we wished we had done, but those moments are called "learning opportunities," and we have to be tender and forgiving of ourselves as we are of others to do this for the long run.

Being present also means learning from the group -- what to say, what not to say, how to say it with our body language, our ways of sitting in silence and breathing with the group. For me, the wake-up call came about eleven years ago when I was teaching a literature class at a Native American university. I was in a bad mood one day because I had just realized the job I loved doing here was being eliminated. I loved my students, but when I walked into that classroom, I was so pissed off that I really should have been locked up in a therapy closet somewhere.

Yet I adjusted my voice, spoke to them in a kind tone, made eye contact, acted like a calm and okay-feeling person when I asked them to pull out their writing to share. The whole class crossed their arms across their chests and looked down or away from me. I tried to coax them with my words, but they wouldn't acknowledge me or what I was saying. I tried to make a joke. No one laughed. Finally I sat on my desk, and said, "Look, I'm in a really bad mood, but it's not because of you. Hey, I'm sorry." They looked up, threw back their heads, and started laughing, and soon I was laughing with them. It turned out to be a great class.

At that moment, I realized that teaching – and this obviously goes for facilitation too (which is a way of teaching, I believe) -- is about our whole self, and no amount of words said the right way will work if other vital ingredients are missing. There's also so much of what we do as facilitators that goes beyond words. Someone shares something painful for him, and we pause, exhale slowly, make eye contact, let the group have a moment of silence to honor what was shared. Someone starts to interrupt, and we gently gesture to them to wait, and keep our eyes on the speaker. Sometimes I sit quietly while people write, imagining golden light encircling the group, or in a really tough group, pray fervently.

While I'm not addressing book-length considerations of facilitation regarding working with different populations, dealing with difference (whether differences in learning styles or physical ability differences), or many aspects of facilitation here, I want to at least touch on one vital facilitation tool we need to always use: assessment. We can learn how we're doing and how to do better through evaluation forms for participants to fill out, having an outside observer sit in and watch a session (with permission of the group of course), writing our own assessment, or just standing up -- our back to the group as we face a big piece of paper -- and have them brainstorm on what worked and what needs work. What's important is that we earnestly seek feedback on how to do this work better, and that means not making the group feel beholden to only say good things because it might massage our egos a little more. If the feedback is mean-spirited, we can shake the anger off and see if there's anything left of value. And we can use the helpful feedback, comment by comment, to learn how to be here more and to serve the work better.

Marketing Without Selling Your Soul to the Devil

A business man meets the devil, who turns out not just to wear Prada but to be a marketing whiz. "Sell me your soul, and I'll give you unimaginable profits," the business man, or in some cases, Rumpelstilskin, says. Unfortunately, in just about every movie, fairy tale or reality show where the protagonist needs to choose between his soul and fame and riches, it turns out that not having a soul is a lot more important than paying a hefty mortgage, or in the case of Darth Vader, ruling the universe.

Marketing, which pits making profit against being a decent person -- along with industrial and corporate practices that destroy the earth and rip apart communities -- is not a life-affirming business practice. It's obvious, from the mess that we're in these days, that too much emphasis is placed on buying useless things we don't need made by people who had their local economics destroyed in the process.

What's a TLAer to do? Well, since we are people of the word, we need to fetch that word, "marketing," and reclaim it as both an ethical and sustainable business practice that helps bring greater balance to our communities and culture. This means redefining marketing as a way to do the work we feel alive doing, and conducting our marketing in ways that further strengthen community.

Marketing is about putting ourselves out there, come what may, to see what comes. It's a way of saying, "Here I am, world." This means also believing in our work and ourselves enough to put it out there, or at least acting as if we do. And it helps tremendously to go into marketing with the attitude that whether people respond or not is usually nothing personal. It may just be a signal to retool our marketing, or the focus of our workshops or coaching or consulting, or it simply may have nothing to do with our work at all but forces well beyond us.

Developing sustainable business practices also means putting together marketing tools that help us keep on keeping on in livelihoods that don't swallow up too much of our energy, health and sanity. It means doing marketing in a way that's above-board, clear, and connected to our values. For example, because I value ecological restoration, I tend to look for recycled paper for flyers. Mostly, though, it means giving the same kind of consideration to how we put ourselves out there as how we facilitate the work with people in here.

Here's my quick summary of marketing tools and considerations:

- *Go where your audience is:* If you're doing a workshop for people with HIV/AIDS, you can put out flyers at various health clinics, transgender centers, other places where you believe people interested in this workshop may go regularly. If you want to attract middle-aged women going through menopause and other changes, put up flyers wherever they hang out in your town: bookstores, gallery openings, coffee shops, health and women's centers. If you're after teens in an urban area, try to get material distributed by teachers at local schools and be sure to get flyers up at whatever restaurants, surf shops or other places they're likely to feed and water. If you believe what you offer is a good adjunct for people in therapy, send your brochures to all the local psychologists and psychotherapists in your community. If you want to do a storytelling weekend for couples, get in touch with marriage therapists in the region.

- *Develop marketing tools that reach your audience:* Think about what kinds of marketing tools -- flyers, postcards, emails, ads, articles in newsletters, newspapers, webzines, weblinks, and other ways of posting your work -- reach the audience you're trying to draw. Think about what images and phrases and explanations would best reach your audience (e.g. I wouldn't use an image of an ecstatic child for trying to get teenagers to a drama workshop, but I might use that image for inviting middle-age women to reclaim their creativity).

- *Marketing need not be outrageously expensive:* Many people have the mistaken idea that two main mediums will get people to workshops or services: Having a website and placing ads in magazines and newspapers. I have watched too many people place ads at great expense with limited results. Website design and ads are probably the more expensive marketing tools out there, and they may not have the kind of draw or shelf life (how long information will hang out with your audience) as lesser-expensive options, such as flyers you make yourself, bookmarks (talk about a good shelf life!), postcards, emails, and other options.

- *Word of mouth rules:* No matter what your TLA work is, there's nothing like word of mouth to enhance that work. People are more apt to attend the performance, the workshop, the retreat, the consulting session if someone they know and trust recommends it. That's because most of us trust and listen to our friends, family and acquaintances more than we trust and listen to ads for new services or websites we come across.

- *Get moving:* The most helpful way I know to do marketing at the community level is through posting a decent flyer at every appropriate venue in town to get inquiring minds to inquire, especially people who believe enough in their own intuition to say to themselves, "Hey, I've seen that flyer six times today, and every time I see it, I want to find out more and do that workshop, so maybe I should."

- *Do it yourself:* Flyers are low-cost to produce -- and most of our computers come up with programs that make flyer-making (and font-choosing -- remember decades ago when we would use rub-on lettering?) a breeze. It's also fairly easy in our age of digital cameras and friendly computers to take your own photos, or use clip art (most word processing programs, such as Microsoft Word, have this art easily available) to come up with stirring and thrilling images to illustrate your words. Flyers are fairly inexpensive to copy, and you can also buy your paper in bulk through sources in your community or through the internet. Leftover flyers can be recycled, or you can print on their backs if need be.

- *Or get help:* It's sometimes very possible and also immensely helpful, especially for the graphically-challenged, to barter design services with a designer. I got a whole website out of trading workshops for life with a great web designer, who was just getting started at the time and wanted to learn more design techniques. I've also delighted in using businesses such as vistaprint.com and other on-the-web printing services -- as well as Microsoft Office and other software -- that have ample templates (and sometimes access to fantastic images) to create a flyer, postcard, bookmark, poster, tri-fold brochure, business card, etc.

- *Use email:* One of the most effective ways to publicize coaching, consulting, performances or workshops is through emails. Put together an email list (carefully typing all the emails in, a comma and space between each), and then you can cut and paste your list into an email, but make sure you send it out blind-copy so that you won't be giving out everyone's email addresses (which could cause confidentiality problems). Include a paragraph about the event, information about getting more information, and be considerate about not sending out the announcement too often as one person's gold is another's spam.

- *Learn from "Branding":* "Branding," a term that used to be designated for brands of products but now is used for everything from a college's image to the Dixie Chicks, makes me think of a hot iron symbol heading toward the flanks of a defenseless animal or some fast food business's logo. Yet it has a useful connotation for us when it comes to marketing: By cultivating a similar look or logo or tagline (second line usually after a heading that says what you do, such as the "Writing and Singing for Your Life," the tag line Kelley Hunt and I use for our business, Brave Voice), you make your work more recognizable.

- *The rule of three....or five....or...:* Depending on who I've spoken to about this over the years, I've heard anything from 3-7 times as the average number we need to show someone something we're marketing to get them to respond. Just sending someone one postcard or one email usually won't do it: Find ways to show prospective clients the possibilities of your work for them from different angles over several times.

- *Say who you are and what you do:* Written material gives you a way to get inside people's pocket or purse, ride in their car or sit at their table with them and explain what you do and why and how you do it. A few tips: always use your name – it helps you build your livelihood, and it also gives credibility to the workshop (would you enroll in a workshop if you didn't know who the leader was?). Tell a little about you -- a few sentences about what you've done related to this work (publishing, performance, storytelling, awards, writing, facilitation). If you don't have enough to write an impressive blurb, write one from the heart, letting people know that it's your greatest passion to help people find their voice or sing their own songs. Tell what the workshop or service is, including the workshop title, when it is, where it is, what the workshop is about, who would benefit from attending, cost, payment information (including payment plans accepted or partial bartering possible if you wish), and then have a number and/or email people can contact for more information.

A note about competition: Many of us cannot help but have a territorial twinge when we see someone posting flyers for a workshop or performance similar to what we do. I remember that when I started doing community writing and healing workshops, my thought, when encountering flyers from "the competition" was, "This town ain't big enough for the two of us." What I realized over the years was that: 1) The more people who do TLA in my community, the more a need for TLA will grow, providing me with more opportunities; 2) The people who don't do TLA well, or ethically, or kindly won't and don't last; and 3) There's way more to be gained by pooling our resources than competing against each other.

So when you see a competing flyer, don't cover it with your own (for one thing, you don't want to invite that kind of karma in your life). Instead, make sure that you never do anything (including talking behind your competition's back) to hurt others in the market. If those doing similar work as you are really good at what they do, you might be able to learn a lot from them about how to do better outreach yourself. You might take this all a step further by calling together people doing arts-based workshops to run ads together, hang each other's flyers, share mailing lists, refer people to each other.

One of the great joys in my TLA life came when I realized I could no longer do all the workshops coming my way, and I needed to train someone else to do those workshops. Luckily, there was a great facilitator-in-waiting, whom I met for coffee over the next year or so, and now she's doing the workshops I used to do. It's outrageously satisfying to find that my work not only supports me, but creates opportunities for others, and at the same time, I know that I'm indebted to the people who did writing workshops here and there over the last 20 years in my town, who helped create the market for what I do.

By marketing with our mind and heart in gear, we can change business as we know it, and create the kinds of community connections that will help our own cups runneth over.

MONEY, MONEY, MONEY

How do we make making a living a holy thing? The entire program of spirituality is to make our life one thing, and not a group of pieces working against each other. There is nothing wrong with money; there is something wrong with greed, since it negatively separates us from each other. There is nothing wrong with charging for services one does professionally; there is something wrong with using professionalism to put oneself above human need or to objectify others.
- Betsy Robinson (52)

One of the challenges for just about everyone I know who does TLA is what to charge, in part because it's just confusing to know what's appropriate, and in part because many of us just happen to have issues with money and/or the lack of it in this culture. In workshops I've facilitated on class issues, I was amazed to discover that many others feel scared, nervous or unsure when discussing what they make, what they want to make, what seems like too much, what is surely too little. In the supposedly classless U.S.A., I've heard estimates of middle-class as being defined as making $25,000 each year to making $250,000 each year. Money is just hard to talk about for so many of us because we don't want to seem greedy, needy, or seedy.

Money is also tricky because it's so entwined with power in this culture. The politicians who get elected, more often than not, have hefty bank accounts fueled by donors and/or investments. The shiny, happy people on so many television shows and movies obviously are not worrying about whether they can afford the four-pack or 12-pack of toilet paper at the grocery store. Many of us (myself included) grew up believing that at least some of our self-worth was tied to what we made in the workplace.

How this translates into doing TLA for a living is that, most of all, any of us (I'm raising my hand here) with money issues need to continually look at those issues and learn from them: Are we feeling entitled to make a living without much effort because of our history? Are we sabotaging ourselves when it comes to marketing because we feel awkward making money doing what we love? The questions are vast, and the answers are individual. Yet there are also life rafts in the great sea of money to grab onto when it comes to how to determine what to charge for TLA work.

Whether we're planning private workshops that we do all the marketing for, or whether we're bringing a proposal to do consulting with a business or not-for-profit group, one of the keys around us is simply what other people charge who live in our region and do this kind of work. For private work, look carefully at your market -- who you're pitching your workshops toward, and what their needs, limitations, and possibilities are. I suggest that you start collecting information in your community about similar workshops: what does the local arts center charge for classes? What do people offering painting therapy workshops, or spiritual guidance sessions, or movement and dance classes charge? If you can find someone, or several, who do workshops similar to what you're planning, look at the average charges. Keep a note pad on you, and pause at entries to super markets, art center bulletin board, or book store windows or ledges. Particularly aim your gaze toward workshops, coaching sessions, and other venues for healing or the arts offered by people who have been doing this for a while and seem to be making a living from it.

You also may want to offer a sample class -- a taste of what you're ready to launch as a workshop series or coaching service -- through a community center, library, food cooperative, health clinic or other venue. Do it for free or charge a very nominal fee (like $6-$10 for an evening), and make the event shine -- serve cookies and iced tea, bring in a bouquet of flowers or light a candle; do whatever you think will create an inviting atmosphere for the people you want to reach that makes them want to return. Give freely of yourself, and hand out flyers for future workshops and services at the end of the session.

When planning a workshop series or coaching service or other TLA service through a business, not-for-profit organization, or institution, again, you can research what others charge who do similar work. If you're planning on writing workshops for people with cancer, contact people in your area or around the country who do similar workshops -- you can probably get names of who to contact through the National Association for Poetry Therapy, or the Amherst Writers and Artists Institute or even by doing a web search. Call up or email your colleagues in the field, and find out what they do, what experience they have, and what they charge (trying to be as courteous as possible in using their time, of course).

You can also speak directly with the organization or business about what it has in the budget for such services, asking your contact person, "What kind of funding do you have available for this kind of service?" or "Could you give me an idea of what you usually pay for someone to do what I'm offering?" While there's the danger of getting into a cat-and-mouse game of trying to outwit the other on money, I've found that a frank and earnest approach can sometimes cut through that danger, especially if you know already what you need to make from the workshop. If they offer more, you can nod slowly, tell them it's acceptable. If they offer less, you can respectfully ask if more funding can be found (and if you're willing, if there's anything you can do to help).

In my experience, I've often found that sometimes a business, hospital, school or clinic contacts me with great enthusiasm about offering writing workshops to its students, patients, clients, or consumers, but then after a meeting and a flurry of emails, that interest may go underground for a while ... six months or even a year or longer, and then one day, it may well surface again. Sometimes I'll just get an impulse to check in with them, and other times, I'll run into the person I spoke with at a coffeehouse, or she or he will call me out of the blue, and kazam! They have the funding and are ready to roll.

So even if something doesn't come of presenting your wares to a prospective venue, keep in mind that timing is everything, and in many cases, if not now, later. Later might turn out to be better for you too.

In all cases -- whether private workshops or public ones, whether workshops or sessions held in an office or home or meeting place -- it's important to pay enough attention to the money end of things to do appropriate follow-through without getting worn down by it. Many hospitals, schools, or centers that hire you will want you to send them a bill, and you should do this promptly, not just because it gets you your money faster but because it also communicates your credibility in this work, and your seriousness about Right Livelihood through TLA. In some cases, if the check isn't forthcoming, send a polite email or call to make sure it's in the works. Don't take it personally if the check is delayed or if someone forgot to process the order. Even if it is a personal affront, which is unlikely, why give it any energy?

With private workshops, it's important to have a clearly-communicated payment and refund policy, telling people in writing when the payment, or payments, are due, and letting people know how soon in advance they need to cancel to get a full or partial refund. There's nothing wrong with charging someone a nominal fee for your time if he or she cancels a week before the class, and there's nothing wrong with not giving a refund to someone who didn't turn up for class, especially since you might have sold that spot to another participant. Treat your workshops or coaching as your business; don't apologize or agonize over asking for payment or refusing full refunds, but also set your policies fairly in concert with what other places and people in your area do.

At the same time, no matter where you do your work, there's always the possibility of extenuating circumstances. If someone's child dies a day before class, of course I would give a full refund along with a sympathy card and some prayers. If an agency I've worked with for five years suddenly loses a major grant, of course I would offer to do a free session to close an ongoing group I've been doing (as well as help them craft another grant to continue to hire me). I do these things because I would feel all wrong not to, and incidentally, it's good for sustaining my work all around. People remember kindnesses and moments of flexibility, all of which are a way to help that path unfold by walking it.

THE GIFT MUST ALWAYS MOVE

Over two decades ago, I chanced upon the article in the now defunct *Co-Evolution Quarterly* by the very much alive Lewis Hyde called "The Gift Must Always Move." As soon as I read the first line, "I would like to write an economy of the imagination" (10), I was hooked, and by the time I finished this article, I knew its words would be landing in me for years, maybe (and obviously) decades, changing my life. Hyde, a poet who went on to write one of the most important books of our time, *The Gift: Imagination and the Erotic Life of Property*, asks the question, "What would be the form of an economy that took the imagination as its model, that was an emanation of the creative spirit?" (10).

Hyde studies market-based economies of the Western world (where we are what we own) in contrast to the gift-based economies of many traditional and indigenous cultures (where we are what we give). Living according to the market economy, where we invest in only what would bring greater material wealth, is at the heart of many of the world's ills according to Hyde, who explains:

> At that point commerce becomes correctly associated with the fragmentation of community and the suppression of liveliness, fertility, and social feeling. For where we maintain no institutions of positive reciprocity, we find ourselves unable to participation in those "wider spirits" ... unable to enter gracefully into nature, unable to draw community out of the mass, and finally, unable to receive, contribute toward, and pass along the collective treasures we refer to as culture and tradition. Only when the increase of gifts move with the gift may the accumulated wealth of our spirit continue to grow among us, so that each of us may enter, and be revived by, a vitality beyond his or her solitary powers. ("The Gift Must Always Move" 30)

Hyde looks for answers of how to receive and give – for the collective treasures -- in international folk tales as a way of unearthing more of Western culture's traditional ways. What he found in many tales, but particularly in one Scottish tale called "The Girl and the Dead Man" is that, "The gift not only moves, it moves in a circle" ("The Gift Must Move On" 16).

I think of this -- how what we give moves in a circle, eventually coming back to us, and then eventually going on from us to others -- as the best explanation of TLA as a profession. The gifts we give to our community, to our art, to our families, to the earth enable us to enter into a more reciprocal relationship with the world and the earth. Being involved over our lives in this kind of exchange is liberating for us and those we share ourselves with along the way. As Hyde explains,

> I speak of the inner gift that we accept as the object of our labor, and the outer gift that has become a vehicle of culture. I am not concerned with gifts given in spite or fear, nor those gifts we accept out of servility or obligation; my concern is the gift we long for, the gift that, when it comes, speaks commandingly to the soul and irresistibly moves us. (*The Gift*)

Such an understanding not only dissolves the barriers between giving and receiving, but it gives us a way to feed our souls and our communities through the work we do in the language arts. We serve and are served by the art, our communities, and the earth that gives us the ground under our feet on which to walk and to take those leaps into our life's work.

Such an attitude of generosity cannot help but bring us, sometimes in small and surprising ways, guidance in turning what we love into how we support ourselves, phone call by email by rehearsal by meeting by workshop by discussion by solitary reflection on it all. Seeing the sudden and small miracles around us is a way to receive our gifts, whether in the form of a dying woman saying how this writing workshop was the most important thing she did for herself in her last year, or a child standing up before his community to read a poem of his soul.

It doesn't take a rocket scientist to figure this out, but then again, maybe it does:

There are two ways to live: you can live as if nothing is a miracle; you can live as if everything is a miracle.
- Albert Einstein

WORKS CITED

Chapin Carpenter, Mary. "John Doe #24." *Stones in the Road.* Columbia, 1994.

"Albert Einstein Quotes." *Think Exist.* 26 Feb. 2007. <www3.thinkexist.com/quotation/it_is_a_miracle_ that_curiosity_survives_formal/145949.html>.

Hyde, Lewis. *The Gift: Imagination and the Erotic Life of Property.* New York: Vintage Books, 1983.

----. "The Gift Must Always Move." *Co-Evoluation Quarterly* 35 (Fall 1992): 10-30.

Middendorf, Bobbye." On the Path to Right Livelihood." *Conscious Choice.* 14 Feb 2007. <http://www.consciouschoice.com/ 1995-98/cc095/rightlivelihood.html>.

Robinson, Betsy. "Finding Peace in the Spiritual Marketplace." *Spirituality and Health* (Nov/Dec 2005): 52.

TLA Resource Pages. 26 Feb. 2007. <http://web.goddard.edu/ ~tla>.

APPENDIX A:

GROUND RULES FOR WORKSHOPS

Caryn Mirriam-Goldberg, Ph.D.

• • •

1. Don't worry about spelling, grammar, and most of all, making sense.

2. Write what you know as well as what you don't know.

3. Follow your writing, not the suggested exercise, the facilitator or what you think you should write. Write what wakes you up the most.

4. Feel free to experiment with poems, stories, dialogues, essays, letters, and whatever other form the writing wants to be.

5. Practice trust. Trust yourself to write what you need to write, how you need to write it.

6. Remember that all revealed in this workshop is confidential.

7. Treat all newborn writing with great respect and tenderness so that it can grow.

8. Reading your writing aloud is always optional.

9. No self-deprecating remarks allowed (especially when preparing to read your work).

10. Strive, as much as possible, not to compare your writing with the writing of others, and not to critique, interpret or analyze away what your writing is trying to show you.

11. Witness others. Listen carefully with your full attention. It will enhance your ability to listen to your own words.

12. Please share your responses to one another's work -- what moves you, what stands out for you -- but please refrain from critiquing or analyzing the work.

13. Treat all you do as a delicious and invigorating experiment. Play. Take chances. See what way leads to way, and what words

lead to words.

APPENDIX B:

TLA WORKSHOP AGREEMENTS AND GUIDELINES

Patricia Fontaine, MA

• • •

This is challenging work in the best of circumstances. So that we can feel safe enough to be honest and true to our experience, we agree on the following:

- *Confidentiality* – We agree to share what we learn but to not repeat anything said by anyone in the workshop without his/her permission. Same applies for talking outside the workshop to someone about what he/she said without their permission.

- *Amnesty* – The companion to confidentiality. We agree not to treat others differently, blame them, or hold what they said against them after the workshop.

- *No Put-downs* – We agree not to put down, make fun of, minimize, or attack others in the workshop -- or ourselves (i.e. "this may sound stupid, but …)

- *Right to Pass* – Each person has the right to pass if he/she doesn't want to talk.

- *Please Speak from your own experience.*
    o *Use "I-statements"*- we agree to speak for ourselves and our own experience and not speak for others unless asked to. This means using "I" instead of

"You," "We," or "They."

o *No Cross-talk or Piggy-backing.* Each person has the chance to say what he/she wants without having it debated, denied, or attacked, OR agreed with or supported. The statement gets to stand on it's own without being taken over by someone.

- *Feelings* – Each of us will experience feelings about something said or done in this workshop -- it's part of the healing process. Each of us agrees to respect and allow expression of those feelings, *including our own.*

- *Respect / Listening* – Each of us agrees to listen to others and be listened to. One of us talks at a time. We are resources for each other.

- *Practice Compassion* for self and others -- we're all learning.

- *Check Assumptions*: Privilege and differences are not always visible.

Customized from *Helping Teens Stop Violence: A Practical Guide for Counselors, Educators, and Parents.* Allan Creighton and Paul Kivel. Alameda, CA: Hunter House Inc., 1990.

APPENDIX C:

TLA WORKSHOP AGREEMENTS

Vanita Leatherwood

• • •

It is important that each of us participate in creating a safe space to explore, share and create. In that effort, we agree to:

Confidentiality
"What happens here stays here." We agree not to repeat or describe anything that is said here by anyone without their permission.

Safety & Grace
We agree not to hold what others have said against them, not to blame or treat others differently after the workshop.

Respect & Compassion
We agree to listen and honor our own and others' experiences, stories, perspectives and work. We agree not to put down, laugh at or minimize ourselves or others.

Honor
"Whatever you write is right." We agree to honor the emotional and creative expression of ourselves and others. We agree not to judge or critique. No one has to justify his/her feelings. We agree that each person has the right to "pass" when he/she does not want to speak.

Speak from our own experience
We agree to speak from our own experience, to speak from a place of "I," not "you," "they," or "we." We agree to let each person have his/her say, not to debate, put-down or argue.

ON STARTING A WRITER'S WORKSHOP

Irene Borger

• • •

Praise Allah, but tether your camel to its post.

- Sufi saying

How-to manuals may be useful for learning to poach a salmon, put on a condom, or wrap a sarong in fifty fetching ways. But, as with writing, creating a workshop isn't a matter of following someone else's recipe. The workshop that *you* organize (or organize *and* lead) will be a reflection of your particular constellation of beliefs, goals, education, worldview, passions, quirks, limitations, aesthetics, teaching and learning style (as well, of course, as the needs, desires, aesthetics, limitations, etc., of the people with whom you work). Given that, there are many things to consider and sources on which to draw.

I began developing a "Questions to Think About" list when I led a "How to Start a Writing Workshop" workshop at the 1994 *AIDS, Medicine and Miracle* conference, then sent it to readers who contacted me after an article on the Workshop by Louise Steinman appeared in the September/October 1994 issue of *Poets and Writers*. This is a revised and expanded version of those questions as they appeared in the Appendix in *From a Burning House*, Washington Square Press, 1996.

I went on to lead two year-long "Teaching the Teachers" courses to writers who were committed to starting pilot workshops in other AIDS service agencies in Los Angeles County. We saw these questions as areas of inquiry rather than as an agenda. There are implications, ramifications, even stories, inside the questions. There's a lot to discuss.

To work with someone who cares to write (or *is* writing)

is a gift and a responsibility. To work with someone facing a life-threatening illness demands clear attention, and a willingness to be astonished, disturbed, responsive, in short, to serve as a witness. Some people assume that such work requires fearlessness. (What's *that?*) Such work does offer the opportunity to develop the skill, or practice, of working with difficult emotions, one's own and those of others, as they arise.

The point of these questions: To enable you to shape an inspiring workshop that feels safe *and* challenging, that honors the participants *and* writing *and* the writing process. These questions are meant to encourage you to create an experience that matters. What do you need, to develop, so that you can be a skillful teacher, a sensitive group leader, and, maybe, even a muse?

These questions are meant to whisper in your ear, *"Pssst,* you might think about this and *this* in organizing, teaching, assessing and funding your workshop." At best, the questions will encourage you to articulate your own visions and draw your attention toward matters you haven't considered. There are no "right" answers. While some of the questions were directed specifically to working with people living with HIV/ AIDS, most are as useful in setting up a private workshop as they are in creating one for battered women, runaway teenagers, cancer patients, etc.

When I started the Workshop in 1990, I had taught dance history at the University of California, Riverside, for six years, had been in writing workshops, had been a published writer for seven years, and had been a teaching assistant in graduate school before that, but I'd only taught a handful of daylong writing workshops. If you had asked me then, "How do you keep the focus on the writing and not on AIDS?" or ""How do you work simultaneously with people who have varying levels of education and writing experience?" or "What issues may arise in a group in which people are both asymptomatic and close to death?" or "What's the difference between a writing workshop that may be 'therapeutic' and a therapy group?" -- I wouldn't have had any answers. So don't be daunted by the mass of questions. They are tools -- not an inquisition -- to allow you to take stock of what you already know. Much of what you bring to the table will be intuitive. It might be useful to pull out a notebook, or your laptop, and make this an interactive process.

While planning is essential, so is being open and fully present to the moments that arise, drawing on things you've developed for years, and *not holding anything back*. (It's as Annie Dillard wrote about writing: "Spend it all, shoot it, play it, lose it, all, right away, every time … Anything you do not give freely and abundantly becomes lost to you. You open your safe and find ashes.") If you are called to do this work -- I'm not sure how one could do it conscientiously or for long, otherwise -- and you're patient, and don't need to become rich, you will find a way to do it well.

BEFORE

- What is your motivation in wanting to start a workshop?
- Do you have an agenda? political, spiritual, emotional, literary, other? Will it guide you? Focus you? Limit you?
- Have you worked with, lived with, cared for, or lost people living with HIV/AIDS? What emotional issues are you presently dealing with in regard to HIV/AIDS and is this a good time for you to start writers' workshop? How emotionally, creatively, intellectually, physically, spiritually available are you to do this work right now?
- Do you love writing? Do you read a lot? How do you feel about listening to other people's work? To work that isn't polished? Work that may be written by "nonwriters?" Work that may never be revised?
- How good are your listening skills? How can you improve them? What other skill(s) do you think you will need to

develop? Can you learn them on the job?

- Have you taught before? Would you say you have an insider's knowledge of the creative process? Do you like sharing what you know? Have you ever led a group?
- Do you hope to act as the organizer for the workshop and find a skillful teacher or do you want to lead it yourself? If you are looking for someone to lead the workshop, how will you find them? Try them out?
- Are your strengths literary or social? What do you think you'll need to work on to prepare to teach well?
- Are you interested in encouraging the development of both psyche *and* techne (spirit *and* craft)? What, then, is needed?
- Do you have writing outlet, a writers' community for yourself? Are you writing?
- Do you have a support system composed of professionals and/or peers or tools to enable you to stay clearheaded and openhearted in the face of strong emotions and suffering? (Meditation teacher Yvonne Rand talks about the *necessity* for people sitting in the teacher's seat to be in a feedback loop.)
- Do you know other people working with people with HIV/ AIDS? Are they available to speak with and think through issues or problems with you?
- What makes you feel most nervous about starting a writing workshop? About working with people with HIV/AIDS? Are these realistic concerns? How can you address them? Are you familiar with some of the physical and psychosocial problems common to people living with AIDS? Would it be useful for you to take an "AIDS 101" course offered at many clinics and AIDS service agencies?

RESEARCH AND LOGISTICS

- What local AIDS organization, or community group, could be a good sponsor? (With potential clients? Outreach capacity? A newsletter? Ability/willingness to publicize? Convenient location? Available space?)

- Are you interested in working with a special population? Women? Teenagers? People of color? Spanish-speaking people with HIV/AIDS? Gay men? Lesbians? IV-drug users? People in recovery or in the hospital? Caregivers or professionals working with people with HIV/AIDs? What would be an appropriate agency for you to work with?

- If you do not already have a relationship with a local organization, how can you find out more information on the services in your area? How will you research their agendas?

- What do you need to do *before* you propose starting a workshop? (For yourself? In regard to others?) What *information* do you need to acquire and think through to write a solid proposal?

- What will you do if the agency people you contact are overworked, busy with providing health and legal services, counselling, food and meals, home health care, public policy, funding, having too many clients, etc. -- and don't understand or even have time to think about "creative writing" or "art?" What do you need to do in order to write a proposal that vividly conveys the usefulness of such a workshop, in the context of the agency's mission? And convinces them that you are an ideal person to do the work? What practical ways can you make it easy for them to say yes? How will your workshop support *their* goals?

- Once you have made arrangements with an agency to offer a pilot workshop, would it be useful to ask for an informal letter of agreement detailing your respective obligations and concerns?

- What kind of space is available? Where can you find a room that is quiet, private, comfortable, and accessible to people who may not drive or be able to walk up stairs? Are there tables and chairs? Do they need to be set up? (By whom?) Is there a couch in case someone needs to lie down? Adequate lighting? A nearby bathroom? How's the air circulation and temperature control? Is there a hot plate for boiling water for tea?
- What materials will you need? Pens and notebooks? Boxes of herbal teas and cups? How will you cover the cost of copying handouts and printing initial leaflets? Could a local merchant supply these things in exchange for publicity?

IMAGINING THE WORKSHOP

- Before you go further, imagine the first meeting. If someone were only able to make only one session, what would you want them to get out of it? With that in mind, how will that shape what you do? (I read that ball player Joe DiMaggio said he always tried to play his best because at every game there was always one kid who would only see him that once).
- Why do a pilot workshop and not jump into an ongoing project? You can test the waters, examine what works and doesn't, see just how much interest there is, how committed you actually are, begin a relationship with a host organization, and gain some experience should you wish to apply for funding.
- Imagine a pilot workshop: How many weeks would it be? Six? Eight? Ten? How long would each meeting be? I've found three hours to be ideal for groups of between eight and twelve people; this permits sustained writing and interaction and is not too taxing for most people. It can include a warm-

up, then a longer exercise with thirty minutes for writing, a short in-room break, and a chance for everyone to read and get feedback.

- When are you available? How much time do you have for preparation and teaching? If this workshop will be free, how much time can you spend doing it without getting paid? Or do you need to receive an honorarium or, at the least, coverage for the cost of materials?

- What time of day will sessions take place? How will you balance the needs of people who are sick and may find it difficult to get up early and/or to go out at night with the needs of people who are HIV-positive, healthy, and working a full Monday-to-Friday schedule? Could you offer the class on a weekend?

- What do you propose to do? A workshop that focuses on process and generating writing? A workshop focused on poetry? Short stories? Autobiography? A place to bring finished work for guidance and critique?

- Who is the group for? Anyone with the desire to write? Any requirements?

- What's the best way for you to learn the creative needs of the people who enroll? An informal conversation? A short form with simple questions?

- Number of people who can join? Limited enrollment is necessary for everyone is to have the chance to write, read aloud, and get feedback. Since people may not be able to attend consistently, it's important that everyone be given the opportunity to read work aloud at each session.

- Do you want to lead a drop-in group or a workshop with ongoing members? How will this decision affect the group dynamics? The nature and quality of the work and the feedback? In my experience, a real and sustained dialogue and a deeper level of trust are possible only in an ongoing group.

- How will people find out about the workshop? In an agency publication sent to clients? A flyer posted on a clinic bulletin board? A local newspaper or bookstore? On the radio?
- Regarding the flyer or advance publicity: How would you describe the workshop and its goals in one sentence? Is there a quote that sums up the spirit of what you imagine? What about a contact number or email address for registration and more information?
- Have you made sure that the flyer or article will be published and/or distributed in plenty of time for potential participants to respond and make plans to come?
- Do you want to speak with everyone individually before the first meeting? Are you going to give out your home or office phone number? When will you be available to talk on the phone? How will you make these things clear? From the start, what kind of boundaries do you wish to set?
- Do you have everyone's address, phone number and email? Are you going to do a contact list? Does anyone wish to attend meetings anonymously? How will you handle this?
- As you've proceeded in your planning, has your purpose become clearer? Are you primarily interested in the development of craft? Of expression? Release? Healing? Community? The growth of bold, individual work? Can you imagine having high standards without expectations?

EXERCISES, PROGRAM PLANNING, AND FEEDBACK

- How will the materials you bring support your goals?
- Given that health problems and other commitments may prevent people from attending every week, how will you structure the format so that each meeting is self-contained and not dependent (like a university course) on sequential meetings?

- Source material is essential. If you don't already have a file cabinet, or notebook or another system for saving great writing, writing about writing, newspaper clippings, as well as quotes, passages, lists of poems, short stories, to build exercises around, what can you create?
- Who are your favorite authors? Who would you enjoy reading aloud to other people? Which books, stories, poems, do you find yourself remembering, or quoting from? What sentences, pictures are tacked up on your refrigerator and bulletin board? Is there any writing you are afraid of? Won't read?
- How catholic is your taste? Do you read work by both women *and* men, people of color, gay, lesbian, and straight writers? Stylistically varied work?
- What have you learned about becoming a wilder, more articulate, risk-taking, writer? How can these skills be conveyed or taught?
- How will you model your responses to people so that they can begin to trust their own instincts, so they can feel challenged but not *judged?* How will you allow the *unknown* and the *unconscious* to be alive in room? How will you make sure that no writing or writer is sabotaged? *The ability to develop skills in this area will "make or break" a workshop.*
- Given your intentions and group members' goals, what do you consider useful and appropriate feedback? I continue to learn a lot from the concept of "Right Speech," one tenet of the Buddhist Eightfold Path, which asks "is what you are about to say both true *and* useful?"
- Do you want to be the only person to give feedback? If group response is part of your plan, how will you keep it on track? How will you model feedback to prevent destructive comments? Reading more about the creative process might

be useful in your thinking about this.

Clearly, there are as many styles of response as there are personalities. It seems to me that the best way to decide what feels useful and authentic is to re-examine the function of the workshop and the subliminal, as well as the professed, desires of the writers. New Mexican writer and artist-in-community Joan Logghe responds to in-session writing by repeating the vivid images and phrases. Novelist Jane Smiley, teaching at the university level, critiques manuscripts and forbids the use of the words "like" and "dislike." There needs to be a difference in the way one responds to a just-written first draft and an almost finished work. One technique I use to give feedback developed naturally over time: while someone is reading their work, I jot down particularly strong words, ideas and images -- their exact words -- and shifts in the text (with paragraph marks), on the left side of the page, with quick hunches about underlying issues and the gist of the piece on the right. Most of the members of the "Teaching the Teachers" Workshop tried this and found that it increased their ability to pay attention and give precise feedback; several others said it interrupted their ability to listen. If you practice you can learn to do both at once.

It is essential to figure out how to encourage writers to develop their own, yes, authority. Choreographer Liz Lerman has developed a feedback process for dance that addresses this which can be useful in literary matters, too. Her article "Toward a Process for Critical Response" is published in the booklet *Are Miracles Enough*. Peter Elbow's book *Writing Without Teachers,* (Oxford University Press, 1973), could also be useful reading. Poet Rachel Hadas worked with people at Gay Men's Health Crisis; her book *Unending Dialogue: Voices from an AIDS Poetry Workshop* (Faber and Faber, 1991) is also illuminating.

- How can you see to it that, from the very first meeting, the focus of the workshop is *writing*? How can people introduce themselves through their work?

- How will you keep the focus on *writing* when working with people who may be in crisis? Remember: people have a choice whether to go to a writer's workshop or a support group, and some may be attending both. What's the difference, in your mind, between "therapy" and "art?"
- When people experience writing as "healing," what do you think is happening?
- Can you imagine creating a "safe space" without being New Age-y or cloying?
- How can you create exercises that heighten awareness of craft while inviting substantive content? That permit a focus or touchstone yet need not be exactingly followed? How might you craft an exercise so that it triggers invention or memory (or whatever it is you're trying to elicit), but also makes it clear that exercises are simply meant to be like sand in an oyster, (a) that there's no "right way" to do them, and (b) that the best thing a writer can do is listen for the voices and images that arise in his or her own head?

When I began the Workshop, I asked my friend Deena Metzger (who, by that point, had led workshops for more than twenty-five years) how she thought up exercises. "I don't know," she said, "they just come to me." After a few months of doing the work, transforming exercises I had learned from Deena, from books, and from other workshops I'd taken, I began to notice that ideas for exercises, like ideas for writing, *did* begin to arise out of the air: from a newspaper article, from a remark in a radio interview, from a stack of photographic postcards, or the first line of a poem.

There are numerous books with stimulating exercises: Deena Metzger's *Writing for Your Life* (Harper San Francisco, 1992), Robin Behn and Chase Twichell's *The Practice of Poetry* (Harper Perennial, 1992), Anne Lamott's *Bird by Bird* (Pantheon Books, 1994), Natalie Goldberg's *Writing Down the Bones* (Shambhala,

1986) and *Wild Mind* (Bantam Books, 1990), and Steve Kowit's *In the Palm of Your Hand: The Poet's Portable Workshop* (Tilbury House Publishers, 1995) as well as the thousands of great books of poetry, short fiction, collections of essays, and interviews with writers. The journals *Poets and Writers, BOMB, Threepenny Review* and *The American Poetry Review* are rich resources. A member of the "Teaching the Teachers" Workshop suggested that I list particular books and poems here, but I'm not convinced that would be of use to *you*. I urge you to try out all exercises before you teach them so you can clarify your instructions and see how they might work, and as you proceed, to invent your own exercises and fit the needs of the people you are working with like a perfect shoe.

While I primarily work with the notion of "story" in prose, rather than with the craft of poetry, I find the work of many narrative poets to be ravishing and useful in inspiring attention to language, form, the workings of mind, and intensity. Plus, it's possible to read several poems aloud in one session and still have time to write. (It's not realistic to assume people will read the short stories and essays you may hand out.) The poems of Claribel Alegria, Raymond Carver, Michelle T. Clinton, Mark Doty, Carolyn Forche, Tess Gallagher, Yusef Komunyakaa, Dorianne Laux, Audre Lorde, Susan Mitchell, Paul Monette, Frank O'Hara, Sharon Olds, Michael Ondaatje, Robert Pinsky, Adrienne Rich, Rainer Maria Rilke (as translated by Stephen Mitchell), and many others have lived with us in our rooms. So has the prose of numerous writers including Bernard Cooper, Joan Didion, Gretel Ehrlich, Eduardo Galeano, Susan Griffin, Jamaica Kincaid, Milan Kundera, Carole Maso, Tim O'Brien, Grace Paley, Susan Sontag, Trinh T. Minh-ha, Alice Walker, and David Wojnarowicz.

There are endless sources for writing exercises – visual, auditory, and tactile as well as written; keep your attention tuned and you'll never run dry.

THE FIRST SESSION

- Imagine yourself in the workshop. Are you "teaching," "leading," "directing," or "facilitating" it? How does your verb choice reveal your role and intention?
- What would be a stimulating, pleasurable first exercise? (Make sure to try it out first yourself.) What pieces of writing will you bring? Do you want to inspire? Challenge? Soothe? Fire up? Open consciousness? Astonish with sound and rhythm, and linguistic possibility? Induce wit?
- How will you establish the parameters regarding process, schedule, and privacy? How will you introduce yourself? In what ways will you encourage people to take personal and creative risks?
- How early do you need to arrive to make sure that the room has been set up? Do you need keys to enter? Are you giving out notebooks? Copies of material? A roster or simple questionnaire to fill out?
- How will you proceed if only one or two people, or no one, show up? What will you do if people arrive late? Or leave early? Fall asleep? Get sick?

MONITORING THE PROCESS

It can be useful for you to keep a journal to evaluate what did, and didn't, work, to remember what people said and to think about:

- How did you respond to people and their writing?
- What were the social dynamics like?
- What made you uncomfortable? What was difficult? What questions arose that you felt ill equipped to answer?
- Did you have enough time? Did you try to do too much? Were you rushed?
- If the feedback petered into chat or medical issues, were you able to guide the group back toward writing?
- Were you able to include everyone? What can you do if

someone consistently hogs time? If someone doesn't feel comfortable speaking up?

- How did you end the session? Were you able to start and stop at the agreed-upon time?

- Was there something you didn't really want to pay attention to? (What do you remember from the corner of your eye?)

- What writing issues came up? Is there a way you could incorporate them into subsequent sessions? How are you responding to all manner of content, form, and language? Have you cut off anyone's creative impulses? Is the Censor or the Critic active in the room?

- If someone was blocked or hypercritical of his or her own work, what methods can you devise to encourage freer writing, experimentation, or playfulness? How can you work with this through writing itself and not veer into psychological analysis?

- How can you encourage personal expression without having the workshop turn into a therapy group?

- Are there some people who didn't come back? Will you call them? Are they ill? Or, did something make them feel this wasn't the group for them?

- How can you best serve the people who are *actually there* and not your original agenda?

- Given that members of the group may be at very different stages of health, how can you acknowledge, support, and incorporate the realities of what's going on with group members while keeping the focus on writing? Ask yourself again: *What is writing for?*

- Are any group members in the hospital? If they'd like to see you, are you available to make visits?

- Consider consulting with someone on an ongoing basis (as therapists do with supervisors) in regard to the effectiveness of your teaching and the group process. How can you do this in a professional manner without violating the confidentiality of what goes on in the group?

NEARING THE END OF YOUR PILOT PROJECT

In measuring the effectiveness of your workshop, you might ask:

- What worked? What could work better?
- Has the writing grown? Is it more daring, truthful, inventive, vibrant, lucid?
- Do the group members exhibit or report pleasure in writing? More confidence in their process? In their work?
- What sort of documentation will enable you to demonstrate to others that this was a useful experience for the participants? If you are planning to apply for a grant to start an ongoing workshop, what sort of documentation would be useful to have? Your own diary? Examples of the work? Again, consider the matters of confidentiality, privacy, and anonymity.
- Will you work with the writers to polish and present their work? Will you self-publish group work? Do you plan to record it? Is everyone involved comfortable with that? And if not? At AIDS Project Los Angeles, we planned to have the first public reading at the end of nine months. The first journal, *Witness*, wasn't published until the Workshop had been information for two and a half years. This kept the concentration on the writing, on investigation and risk-taking, not performance; it also created a close-knit group. Be aware that if you attempt to document or present the group to others too early, you will interfere with the writing process as well as with the group dynamics. Still, you may want to find a method to celebrate work and, if you are doing a short-term workshop, a way to create closure.
- Could you plan a small reading at the end of a two-to-three month session in the space where you meet and limit

the invitations to friends of those in the workshop? How would members feel about having someone from your host organization in the audience? If the proposal to do a reading elicits mixed response, what will you do?

- If you do a second series, or want to start an ongoing workshop, will you open the group to new people? How will you incorporate them into the process?
- Do you wish to organize "sessions" -- e.g. eight meetings, a fall series -- or do you want to create an ongoing weekly workshop?

ON FUNDING

While the rewards of service or "right livelihood" cannot be measured in economic terms, and while many people enjoy volunteering, if you are highly qualified and there is a need for what you can do, there is no reason that you should not be paid for your work. A terrific book to read on the function of art and the giving of gifts in a market society: Lewis Hyde's *The Gift: Imagination and the Erotic Life of Property*. Given the present state of AIDS funding, the demands on existing services, and the growing population of clients, it is highly unlikely that you will walk into an already-funded arts position in an AIDS service agency. The arts, if they are thought of at all, may be viewed as recreation, entertainment, the icing on the cake. This is not meant to discourage you or to intimate that people who work in AIDS care are philistines -- of course not; it is to suggest that you probably will need to initiate research by yourself.

While federal, and so, state, funding for the arts is in disarray, there are still "artist-in-community" grants with applications reviewed by peer panels. In my experience in California, these grants are given to individuals who are sponsored by a host institution; monies are paid directly to the artist; some grants stipulate that a matching portion must be paid by the agency.

In other cases, the agency need only provide the space to work and a strong letter of support. You do not have to hire a grant writer to fill out these forms; most public agencies publish clearly written guidelines and offer free sessions to assist applicants in reviewing the criteria and submission process. I have worked on the other side of the table, too, as a funder, and know that panelists -- who are real people! -- prefer reading honest, clear prose, not grant speak.

While thousands of private foundations in the United States fund arts and literary programs, AIDS and other regional services, the bylaws of most foundations prohibit them from giving grants to individuals. In other words, you need either to find those foundations that *can* offer direct grants or to discover sources from the AIDS-service agency you are affiliated with hasn't yet tapped. In the latter instance, you will need a legal relationship with the agency, either as an independent contractor or as a staff member, to receive foundation founding. What is known as "AIDS funding" falls under many categories; it is not just a health issue. Be creative in your search.

The Foundation Center in New York has up-to-date, cross-reference foundation directories, and many sister libraries at foundations throughout the country; these centers can provide you with funding literature and offer short workshops on how to apply for grants. See http://foundationcenter.org.

Throughout the years I was the artist-in-residence at AIDS Project Los Angeles, I had the words of a Thai meditation teacher, the Venerable Achaan Chah Subato, on the wall next to my desk. A good lesson in perspective.

> *One day some people came to the master and asked, "How can you be happy in a world of such impermanence, where you cannot protect your loved ones from hard, illness, and death?" The master held up a glass and said, "Someone gave me this glass, and I really like this glass. It holds my water*

admirably and it glistens in the sunlight. I touch it and it rings! One day the wind may blow it off the shelf, or my elbow may knock it from the table. I know this glass is already broken, so I enjoy it incredibly."

...

SNAPSHOTS:
A DAY IN THE LIFE OF
TRANSFORMATIVE
LANGUAGE ARTS

...

YOU ARE ALREADY A WRITER

Pat Schneider

• • •

I was educated, as most of us were educated, to believe that writing is something very special. That it's not the same as talking. That it's what published authors do. That it is done by people who understand an esoteric language of literature. I was given an education by a local church in St. Louis. I worked hard to learn that esoteric language; I worked hard to hide the fact that I grew up poor, so I could sound like T. S. Eliot and other poets with privileged education.

To a certain extent, I succeeded. I had plays published; I had a libretto performed in Carnegie Hall. But eventually, while in an MFA program, another student, Margaret, changed my writing life by insisting that I write about my absent father. He left us when I was four; I had been taught to hate him, and I did. Truly, I had no desire to write about him; I felt I didn't know anything about him. One night Margaret was particularly insistent. She talked about her own father, and urged me to write about mine. After she went home, I sat on my couch for several hours, unable to sleep. Finally in the middle of the night a little rhyme began to sing itself in my mind. This is how it came, with never a word changed:

> Daddy was a bad man
> He made Mama cry
> I loved him, Mama said,
> but love can die.

> Daddy was a weak man
> He told a lie
> I loved him, Mama said,
> but love can die.

You look like your daddy,
green, green of eye
I love you, Mama said ...

In that nursery rhyme, I learned the deepest terror of my childhood. Even in the poem, the fear is unspeakable, and so the last line only comes as an echo in the silence of the omitted line: *but love can die.* It was the simplest of verses, coming no doubt straight from the four-year old child that I had been. I thought I was writing about my father, but what the poem revealed to me was the fear I held even at four that my mother would stop loving me like she stopped loving my daddy. I've never offered that verse for publication, but it opened a door through which, later, a whole book came, my memoir, *Wake Up Laughing.*

Deep, honest writing comes with our most intimate voice, the voice that comes from our subconscious, the voice that gives us memory and imagination. It's the voice we use with best friends and lovers, with siblings and parents. Most people don't understand the treasure they carry in their own subconscious minds. I didn't understand it myself until one day in my 30s, when my only sibling, my brother, came to my door. He told me one time that he'd been an alcoholic since the day he took his first drink, right after he was dismissed from a second orphanage at age 17. On that day when he came to my door, he was homeless, frequently in jail for being what was then called "a drifter." My brother was my best friend, and he was desperately lost.

He took a piece of paper out of his billfold and handed it to me. It was old and creased, and it had his handwriting on it – handwriting that I believed only I, in all the world, could read. It was about "motorcyclists from hell" who were chasing him, a brilliant metaphor for alcoholism. In that moment, I realized that my brother was as much an artist as I would ever be, but no one would ever know it, because he couldn't spell, he couldn't write legibly, he couldn't type, and he didn't have a formal education. The shock of recognition I experienced that day – that being an artist is about being brave and telling the truth in your own voice -- is the origin of my workshop method, the Amherst Writers and Artists model; the origin of my books on writing, and the film that has been made about my work with low-income writers. Everyone is already an artist with words.

Not being able to write is a learned disability. If you can talk to your best friend or lover, if you can make your brother or sister laugh, move them to anger or to sadness with your stories, you can write. If you can daydream, you can write. If you can cuss, pray, joke, tell what happened in the hospital cafeteria to a friend -- you can write. So don't tell me you can't write. I know better!

We are all artists. That's what the ancient Judeo/Christian/ Moslem texts mean when they say we are *created in the image of God*. We are *created* creators, artists, with a vast reservoir of possibility in our subconscious minds. There is no such thing as "talent," if by that we mean that some have it and some don't. Listen to this poem by Bobby Hastings, 10 years old, living in a housing project near my home. He wrote this poem about his father in one of our workshops for under-served children:

Weed

It is life.
It grows from the ground.
It is ground up like meat.
It gives him a sharp and good feeling,
that gives me a sharp and painful anger.
He rolls it like a red carpet
and licks it like a lollipop.
My anger gets deeper
as the smell gets worse.

As he smokes me
I get hotter and hotter.

That is a very good poem! "He rolls it like a red carpet/ and licks it like a lollipop." Those are great similes – did anyone teach that ten-year-old about similes? Did he sit down and think, *I believe I'll use a simile now*? "My anger gets deeper/as the smell gets worse./As he smokes me/I get hotter and hotter." How subtle, how excellent a reversal, how effective a metaphor for anger! How did Bobby do that? Where did he learn all that craft? Grace Paley said, " ... if you say what's on your mind in the language that comes to you from your parents and your street and friends you'll probably say something beautiful."

Here's a little poem in the language that comes to me from my original home:

Old Goat

This body, old goat,
old ornery, familiar friend
and enemy,
stays tethered to the pasture
it was born to
and to the farmer
it calls God.

Some days when rain
on the tin roof of the barn
is music, and sunlight
trembles on the wild pokeberry leaves,
this old goat, body,
mistakes a thunder-clap for revelation
or orgasm, and twitches in ecstasy.
Some nights in winter, corralled

in a stall, this old goat
remembers distant thunder
and almost understands
that body itself is holy,
then eats its sweet domesticated oats
and beds down in its ordinary hay

at the ending of an ordinary
day.

Whether you are a famous poet with a background of great privilege, or a 10-year-old living in the projects, there is a craft in your subconscious mind that is so wide and so deep it may in fact be infinite. Some believe that it is: That when we create, we tap into an intelligence beyond our own. That may be, no one knows for certain. But I prefer to just stand in awe of the human mind itself -- believing that everything we have seen and heard, everything we have read or watched on TV, every sensory impression that has come to us, even every dream we have dreamed, are all recorded in the mystery of our minds -- and as we now know, some memories at least are stored in the cells of our bodies. We have been practicing the art of using language all our lives -- all day, every day, in our thinking and in our speaking -- even in the night in our dreaming. If we will only trust our own voices, tell our own deepest truth or our own imaginings, we will have exactly the right voice. We are, each one of us, geniuses -- that's what it means to be created in the image of God -- or if you prefer, that's what it means to be human.

I have worked with thousands of writers, and I can tell you this: Most of what I do is help people to unlearn the lesson they were taught in school: "I can't write." Everyone can write. Everyone is already a writer.

THE WONDER OF PARADOX

Nancy G. Shapiro

• • •

Paradox is my favorite word. Buried within its meaning are the volatile words *conflict, contradiction, absurdity* and *truth.*

My first conscious awareness of the presence of paradox in my life was when I moved to Mexico right after my son Ben's 11th birthday. New love -- in the persona of charming, handsome Barry -- was the instigator of change. I sold my car, my furniture, and arranged for Ben to stay with his dad until the end of the school year. I was leaving my son and at the same time my soul was chanting incessantly,

This is the right thing to do.

I was numb with sadness, yet ridiculously hopeful, as we began the drive to San Miguel. On Christmas night near the west coast Mexican town of Culiacan, Barry and I were kidnapped by four armed bandits.

I'd left my son, job, community, and life as I'd known it for more than 17 years, and there I was, a *gringa*, in a new culture, robbed and scared. I wrote an article for the local English-language newspaper to warn others of the dangers of traveling in that area.

Putting it down on paper, I discovered the aftershock of the robbery—an extreme nervousness and a hot deep rumbling in the pit of my stomach. I was calmer after the article was finished; I slept better, without bad dreams. The sense of being violated, common after being robbed, diminished weekly until it disappeared.

I also stumbled upon the surprising miracles of that night: the keys left in the car door, the fact we were physically unharmed, the backpack untouched with cash, passports and credit cards intact.

That paradoxical article started me writing. Poems poured

out like snowmelt. Poetry's form and rhythm enabled countless words to appear, words I had swallowed, hidden, forgotten, never known I possessed.

There in Mexico writing found me, grabbed hold and never let go. That first year I didn't understand my sudden, almost constant urge to write. Now I know I was saving my own life. Flannery O'Connor wrote, "I write because I don't know what I think until I read what I say." Like O'Connor, I, too, don't know what I think until I read what I write. So I write -- poems, essays, articles, fleeting thoughts and phrases on scraps of paper.

So much has changed since that tumultuous time. Poetry and writing still save me, over and over. Paradox keeps appearing too, on a fairly regular basis. I came across these words during a recent seminar:

… I too have heard the dead singing.

And they tell me that
This life is good
They tell me to live it gently
With fire, and always with hope.
There is wonder here

And there is surprise
In everything the unseen moves…

This is an excerpt from the poem *An African Elegy*, by Ben Okri. Born in Nigeria, he now lives in England. He began writing at age 14 when, in his words:

"On this particular day, it rained," he says, "and this day changed my life. Everybody was out and I was in, alone. I was sitting in the living room and I took out a piece of paper and drew what was on the mantelpiece. That took me about an hour. Then I took another piece of paper and wrote a poem. That must have taken me ten minutes. I looked at the drawing and I looked at the poem. The drawing was dreadful and the poem was ... tolerable, bearable. And it became clear to me that this was more my natural area."

His was an awakening out of pure happenstance. So too was my own awakening as I read his words:

> *They tell me to live it gently*
> *With fire, and always with hope...*

Gently. With fire. These are paradoxical words. They speak of opposites, of contradiction, exactly the stuff of life. Who has not experienced those moments when events around us are speaking in tongues of flames, the heat of the situation threatening to burn us and everything around us into small crispy pieces of insignificance?

Yet if we are true to the voices inside us, the heat brings light also, it forces us to see to the other side of things ... *always with hope*...to sudden realizations of kindness, empathy, the occasional necessity of being singed by flame, the wonder of miracles large and small.

I constantly listen for the voices that move me to the other side of things; this is my own "natural area." Perhaps I hear the dead singing. Or my own words, finally brave enough to hum their unique sound. Or maybe it's a larger voice heard above the persistence of every day noise.

Hope is the space between gentle and fire. It is a space I call Paradox, with a capital P, as if it were its own country, vast enough to contain all seeming opposites, all glaring contradictions. The fiery, gentle truth is that both fire and gentleness are essential to life here on earth; sometimes they appear in the same breath, at the exact same moment. I am in continual awe of this phenomenon.

This was my awakening as I read Ben Okri's words -- *Hope* is where I live. *In everything the unseen moves*...and always, always, I am surprised.

WORKS CITED

Okri, Ben. *An African Elegy.* London: Jonathan Cape, 1994.

"Talking with Ben Okri." *Emeagwali.* 27 Feb. 2007. <http://emeagwali.com/nigeria/biography/ben-okri-19jul92.html>.

YOU DON'T WANT TO BE A MEMBER

Carol Henderson

• • •

I returned recently from leading a weekend writing retreat on Emerald Isle, North Carolina. Sounds delightful, right? Imagine lying on the sand, letting your thoughts meander across the page, taking long beach walks, swimming. You sit in a circle with others, sharing newly minted words. A breeze wafts off the Intracoastal Waterway. The perfect weekend.

Yes.

And no.

Yes, the weekend is beautiful. But it's a writing group we all wish we'd never needed to join. We're all bereaved mothers -- mothers who have lost children.

The group started as a day-long workshop in Winston-Salem in 2002. A local hospice, a church and a college sponsored the event. I had taught a lot of writing classes but never an all-day workshop devoted exclusively to dealing with grief over the death of a child. I planned the day carefully, working with a psychologist on the schedule and content. I knew that the material we were dealing with was volatile and hard.

The workshop met in a board room, around a long table. The 14 women participants ranged in age from mid-20s to mid-60s. Some were religious; others had lost their faith when their children died. Some were never believers. Most of the women had done little writing. For introductions, each woman wrote briefly about the death of her child and then read what she had written.

One woman had lost a baby to SIDS; another, one of her twin sons soon after birth. There were mothers of adult children who had died by suicide. A woman lost both of her children in a car accident -- and the driver of the car was her best friend's older son. The friend was also there, having lost her own younger son in the same accident. There were cancer deaths, sudden deadly infections. My son had died in open-heart surgery.

The room was freezing cold, but the women began to thaw and open up. They wrote about their lives before and after their losses, about funerals, about their children's legacies. They wrote about grief craziness, about the hideous trauma mothers should never have to endure. No subject was off-limits. We had all "been there."

At the end of the day, the women wanted to meet again.

We met for a morning writing session six months later, at a hospice center. Six months after that we met for a weekend in the mountains, at a cabin somebody lent us. Ever since, we've been meeting every six months. We stay in touch, between meetings, by Instant Messaging and e-mail, and in-person visits when we can. We're scattered across North Carolina and Virginia.

We'd give anything to have our children back -- we'll always be full of regret and grief. But there is a special solace in this group that comes off the pens of these women. Writing helps to shift perspectives, increase understanding, give fresh meaning to what we all know is a life-long struggle, a life-long gash in our hearts. Now, when we get together, we are comfortable enough to tease each other. At times we're irreverent. We laugh heartily, cry heartily, and share hearty meals.

This last weekend we had a new member -- Katie Gray, age three months, the daughter of our youngest mother. She's a tough, happy baby and she was our centerpiece. We all held her, shared in her care. She brought so much joy and healing. Soon, we'll have another baby girl. Her parents, who lost both of her older brothers, haven't met their baby yet; she's being adopted from China. But she already has a name.

Her name is Hope.

LOSING CONTROL, FINDING VOICE

Rhonda Patzia, MA-TLA

• • •

Because fear of suffering and of losing bodily control are so deeply embedded in our culture ... the disabled usually are debarred from communicating their experience effectively.

\- Anita Silvers

When we six women with multiple sclerosis circled up to tell one another our stories of living with chronic disease, I had no idea of the fun we'd all have in releasing our experiences to one another. We were out of control. It was messy. It was incontinence without shame.

I wonder if perhaps the most debilitating aspect about having MS is suffering the silence that creeps into our experience of it, potentially cutting us off from family, friends, society as a whole, and even ourselves. In our case, silence is not imposed from the outside. Granted, the fears of society become our fears as well, but ultimately we're responsible for how we respond to them. And often we choose silence.

How safe, we might think, not to face our fears, not to speak honestly of our experience. Maybe we believe that silence will make the "hard stuff" go away. It can't. Our silence will only give the "hard stuff" power to keep us weak and scared. Audre Lorde says it perfectly: "Your silence will not protect you." Silence only leads to illusory control.

With my convictions about the harmfulness of self-imposed silence, I vowed as I began to facilitate daylong workshops for women with MS that my ultimate goal in coming together would be communal expression. Even if nobody else is asking us point blank about our experiences, our stories, we must share them with one another, I thought, as practice for sharing them with the world.

I wanted to create an atmosphere of acute listening and telling, and so I decided to set aside an hour and a half of our time for a story circle. First off I laid down my "rules" for storytelling: "Contextualize it." "When did it happen?" "Give us details." "How did it make you feel?" "Please listen attentively." "Only talk when it's your turn, when you have the chicken" -- our talking stick. "Respond to other stories with your own similar story, or tell a completely different one." "Yes, of course you may laugh."

After discussing the above guidelines during the first workshop, I proceeded to tell a story, which was followed by a smooth circling of expression by the other women. When it was my turn to tell another, I felt a story, a socially taboo one, demanding to surface from hiding. Although I had already shared it with another community, I felt impelled toward silence with these strangers. But I chose expression. After all, I thought, most people with MS share my same taboo condition.

I told of my first major incident of urinary incontinence, of being stranded and having to sit down in a lonely football field and pee my shorts, of having to cover up the mess by drenching myself with a full bottle of water.

The women responded with hesitant laughter but no comments. Then as we began to go through the circle again, I found myself in the middle of a great communal release. Tami half-smiled as she told us of having to, in front of her family, sit on a towel and pee in a canoe, because if she had jumped in the water, she would have tipped the boat over. Carol, while attending to clients, had to excuse herself and rush to the bathroom. Even though she didn't quite make it, she returned to the room with wet pants and an air of confidence, pretending that nothing had happened. "I really don't know whether to laugh or cry," she said.

Lynn chose not to tell a story, but offered that black pants are the best cover-up for accidents. The final incontinence story of the circle was one that burst us all open: On a recent trip with her boyfriend in his 18-wheeler, in the cab, Holly, built a makeshift toilet, consisting of a large flowerpot filled with kitty litter. "If you find one big enough," she said," you can just sit there comfortably. Clean-up is simple."

After we were finished I felt the tone of the room lighten. We all seemed to move around with new ease, smiles, and trust. Maybe they felt like I did: relaxed and happy for having released to this small community, in the form of a story, such a weighty silence. The sharing validated my experience and, consequently, validated me. Did the other women feel the same? Did they accept their experience differently, with new confidence, for being given permission to communicate and not to hide? We were all out of control, and that was okay.

Idealistically, I hope that together we have begun something: that we have freed our stories from both our bodies and our circle to let fly through the world. As a result, might others be more apt to circle up and also communicate their "taboo" experiences, whether they arise from illness or from the general work of living?

THE CUTTING EDGE:
NARRATIVE THERAPY, NARRATIVE, AND
RECONSTRUCTING EXPERIENCE

James Sparrell, Ph.D.

• • •

It was a dark and stormy *day*, as I drove north to Freeport, Maine, home of L.L. Bean, the store with no locks on its doors because it is open every day, all the time. I was rushing out of a hectic day of work in a public school and trying to catch the opening evening of a Narrative Therapists' Retreat. This title was a little odd in that I had never been to a professional development workshop or conference that had been identified as a *retreat* -- somehow I was leery of the idea, expecting that a retreat essentially involved sitting around at night, drinking cocoa, and of course holding hands and singing songs. I associated this concept with church camps rather than continuing education in psychology.

After several hours, I found myself driving off onto a dirt road and down a narrow strip of land that led down to the Maine coast. It seemed even darker than I might have expected for 4 o'clock in the afternoon when I came on the magnificent, looming stone estate house that had been secured for the retreat. As I walked through a heavy wood door, I heard an odd humming in the distance. I was standing in a grand entryway with a set of elegant curving stairs to my right, and to my left I could see a dimly lit room where the conference -- no, retreat -- seemed to be taking place. There were about 40 people packed into an elegant sitting room. A fire was laid in the grand, open stone fireplace, and the room was illuminated by two or three incandescent bulbs. I eventually realized that the power was out from the storm and the humming I had heard in the distance was a generator.

Lynn Hoffman was introduced as the next speaker, clearly

a grand dame of Narrative therapy and beloved of this group. She started by talking about the awkwardness of introductions and how one time she had been at a loss for an opening exercise and did something where she went around and felt everyone's knees. Okay. So I'm thinking, "Well, I haven't checked into the motel yet, but I could stay in Freeport tonight, do some shopping in the morning and then head home if we are going to be feeling each other's knees all weekend." But she didn't do that, and instead came around to everyone in the room took our hands in turn, looked each of us in the eye, learned our names and thanked us for coming. Now that was different and not nearly as bad as grabbing knees.

The weekend proceeded from there, often running counter to traditional professionalized expectations. One workshop on ethics emphasized the importance of an ethic of *disclosure* of a client's efforts and successes to help build a story of success and community support, rather than an ethic of confidentiality, which while it is a valuable tool, can also reinforce shame and isolation. Another ethics workshop was centered on the community of therapists sharing, if they felt comfortable, an instance in which they felt their professional ethical code conflict with a personal ethical stance and how they handled the situation. It turned into a sort of confession of care that would be unheard of at a "professional" conference, where rules are sometimes emphasized to the exclusion of conscious decision-making.

One of the most profound moments of the weekend, besides watching the cows graze right outside our dining room windows with the ocean glittering beyond the pasture, was a presentation on adolescent cutting. It was odd that I chose to attend this session, since I usually just go the other way when the topic comes up because of my own anxiety about how to respond to someone who deliberately cuts. But a number of guidance counselors had come to me with concerns about adolescent cutting and how they might respond in addition to their traditional responses which they felt were inadequate, and I felt a sense of responsibility to see if there were some new ideas here.

Two of the presenters had conducted a bit of qualitative *co-research* as it is termed in Narrative therapy. Rather than assuming a sense of knowing on the part of the investigator, he or she starts with a stance of *not-knowing* and wanting to hear and learn but not in the context of an authoritative relationship. So they recruited several adolescents who engaged in cutting and were interested in the project, obtained consent to proceed from their parents, and then filmed them discussing their past experiences of cutting and related thoughts. They talked about feelings in their body, social aspects of cutting and peer relationships, reactions from others, and what might contribute to cutting or not cutting. But the goal of the conversations was not on how to make them stop, it was on understanding the experience more carefully.

Some things that the teens said sounded like echoes of what therapists had told them, and may or may not reflect their actual experience, such as "I cut because I am feeling empty," or "I cut because I just want to feel something," and I wasn't sure how spontaneous those descriptions were or whether those responses had been suggested to them.

Apart from what felt to me like those canned explanations, other themes emerged that I felt were extraordinarily enlightening. One of the teens talked about cutting as a sort of hobby, where she would plan ahead, look forward to it, set some time aside, and discuss it with her friends. When actually doing it, she would feel her "adrenalin pumping" and feel herself "getting lost in it." Another girl talked about how she started by rubbing her skin with an eraser which was seen as more acceptable, but was also much more painful than cutting herself superficially with a knife. There was also discussion that unlike physical and sexual abuse that many of them had experienced, there was a sense that cutting was not "abuse" in that it was a consensual act. Cutting was also asserted as something real and tangible in a world where their conscious reality was often disputed or questioned. One teen spoke of it as a way of trusting herself, "I know that I can control it." There also was an emphasis on wanting to clarify that cutting does not always or often reflect a suicidal intent, that it is its own thing, "cutting."

What opened up for me in listening to them simply talk on film was how I felt like I might begin to find a way to have a dialogue about what cutting is, and that I could begin to know something because I had heard from the people who knew the phenomenon the best. And it was clear that cutting meant different things to different people at different times. I was also able to form my own associations to sanctioned injury in pursuing my own hobbies. I had recently cut myself chopping vegetables to make soup, burned myself while making jelly, and experienced fairly intense physical pain (along with elation) when completing a hundred-mile bike ride, pedaling into the wind for the last 15 miles. This Narrative therapy approach had given me a way of being able to begin to have a dialogue about something that had seemed so unfamiliar.

This exercise in watching the teens speak their experience on film and tell their story of cutting helped me to realize that I had my own implicit, automatic narrative that was unconscious, poorly articulated, and was really a dead end story that went something like "cutting -- bad -- stop it." There were no characters, no plot, no movement, no sensory connection, just a very knee-jerk authoritarian reaction.

As I took a walk down to the shore, on a muddy path stepping over many floppy branches downed by the storm, I thought about the inevitability of narrative that neuropsychologists such as Gazzaniga and Cozolino have written about – that the left hemisphere is irresistibly involved in weaving sensory experience into some form of meaningful story – and yet how this opens up the possibility of personal or social change that is the intent of a TLA approach. As Cozolino puts it, "Because we can write and rewrite the stories of ourselves, new stories hold the potential for new ways of experiencing ourselves and our lives. In editing our narratives, we change the organization and nature of our memories and, hence, reorganize our brains as well as our minds" (103). This is precisely what had happened for me, by listening to the stories of others and then retelling my own relationship to pain and the meaning of injury.

As I walked back to the big old stone house slowly warming in the damp morning sun, I was excited to think of the democratic nature of stories; everyone can (and does) participate in creating narrative meaning. It is not the domain of psychotherapists alone, just as anyone can dream and think about the meaning of their dreams. Here was an intersection of many traditions: storytelling, psychotherapy, neuropsychology, social change, and documentary film, at the very least. Without realizing it, I was locked in an authoritarian disease model of cutting. And such a model resists being informed or changed through experience. As the Narrative therapists at the retreat noted, power resists dialogue and it is significant and meaningful work to seek to engage "power" in dialogue. And yet, by simply allowing these teens to tell their story, that is exactly what happened, so that my understanding become richer, more complex, or with a "thicker" plot, in Narrative therapy terms. New knowledge could be constructed, and that knowledge was held in a community, in this case the circle of investigators, teens, and those of us who witnessed the film, rather than being held by an expert or an authority.

Predictably, I suppose, we did end up outside on the last day of the retreat on a huge outcrop overlooking the shimmering Atlantic, in a large circle with joined hands, singing together. But by then I was ready for it, for a new story about that, too.

WORKS CITED

Cozolino, Louis. *The Neuroscience of Psychotherapy: Building and Rebuilding the Human Brain.* New York: W. W. Norton and Company, 2003.

Gazzaniga, Michael S. *The Ethical Brain.* New York: Dana Press, 2005.

A FIRST-TIME FACILITATION EXPERIENCE: HORMONES, MOODS AND FOOD

Becci Noblit Goodall

• • •

Teens. Writing. Teens.

Think about that. Think about hormones and moods.

That's what I am thinking as I drive to the Juniata College library to meet the group of kids who'd agreed to meet me for a writing workshop, the one such workshop I would facilitate. Wearing my "Mom sweatpants" and "not particularly cool running sneaks," I suddenly feel as if I was actually 13 heading into unknown territory. My daughter is with me in the car; she's 16 and definitely the cool kid I never was. By cool I mean she's already on her own path. Self assured, intelligent, and independent. All the things that scared me when I was a teen because I didn't have them.

A thought enters my head. It is something deep and insightful I wrote down from one of my professor's workshops on facilitation: she said to bring food. I cut a U-turn and head down Highway 22. Now I'm going to be late but at least I'll have snacks. I run into the dollar store where I buy a bag of tootsie pops, glitter pens, and Chubbs fat notebooks ... Perhaps I can bribe them to like me. To listen. To write out their hearts.

Three weeks ago I had this master plan that I'd mapped out over the summer. It involved working with incarcerated teens. So I knew many of the variables: A. they were troubled; B. they all had drug problems; C. they would never be there if they hadn't been arrested at some point. I'd be in the same room every Saturday with a counselor for assistance. But that workshop possibility unraveled, leaving me to pull this thing together in two weeks, and now it feels helter-skelter, which is basically how I live my life.

I drive on, thinking of the glossy magazine pictures that speak to the evils of commercialism, pictures I plan to use as a writing exercise.

"Erin, will this work?"

"Mom, yeah sure, yes." She's fiddling with her iPod and has called ahead to her friends to warn that I'll be five minutes late.

"It's ok, Mom, they know you're late for everything." That's great. The only thing they know about me is that I'm always late.

I start to panic. If this were a movie it would sound like one of those old WWII flicks -- the ones where everyone's in a submarine playing poker to the sounds of swing music before the horrible sirens start. It's hard to breathe. So I babble mindlessly. "But is it cool? Will they think it's cool?"

"Mom why are you asking me … this is your thing. You're a writer. Do your thing."

"Rrrright." I was sorta looking for an answer here. Some kind of guidance.

At a red light an insight comes to me. There are some basic things I've learned so far from raising a teen. And though I don't know everything, there does seem to be a certain constancy. For one thing they act as if they don't want structure or rules of any kind, yet they function best within guidelines. As I think of Erin's peers I realize that the most troubled kids either have no parental guidance or are overwhelmed by oppressive rules. And I realize that I've been burned by both ends of this spectrum myself.

The other constant is boredom and creativity. Most of Erin's peers who are bored with school and life are simply not being challenged by the adults in their lives.

So my job today is to challenge their innate creativity while providing a loose yet visible structure. They're looking to me as writer. I can't waffle on this or I'm gonna lose them.

We pull into the parking lot, and I lug the food, magazines and other supplies to the room where a small huddle of kids waits. A soft spoken boy, Robert, with long brown hair hangs at the periphery. Another boy, Lloyd, listens to headphones and has this look of such sheer boredom. Shit. I continue to introduce myself and shake hands with each. Ted is self-assured and looks ready to go. Erin is there but somehow looks different as she mills with her friends. Randy mentions that no one could get Kara by phone, but she was planning to come. This is such a tiny group, and this worries me because it lends an immediate intimacy which may or may not work.

We sit at a round table in the Juniata College library basement. They aren't saying much. I'm pretty much talking. And they're just looking at me to explain the writing exercises, and what it is I want them to do. In a strange and crazy way, I feel excited. I tell them that within the structure of the workshop. I stipulate that they be passionate about what they're writing and that they should write about something they've wanted to write in school but couldn't because of school policy.

That was the magic word.

A hand jabs into the air, and one of the kids says, "I'd like to work on some short stories about the history of Marijuana." The bored kid is suddenly interested.

Me: "Sure, but you'll probably want to use a pseudonym to protect yourself. I'll see what I can find you to read."

Next kid says: "Hey, can we go around the circle."

Me: "Sure. Go."

"Well I've done some work on hell houses.(1) Is that something you can do? And some peace protests in DC. I've actually filmed a documentary on hell houses which is screening here at the college in two weeks," Ted says. He's already taking classes at the college. His parents are professors. This is what he tells me as he holds eye contact with every single word. "This is me" he says with his eyes.

Erin wants to write about media images, maybe something to do with the idea of Barbie dolls. I feel odd having my own daughter in the group. But she is the reason I've been thinking about this magazine in the first place as she often chafes within the school writing classes. Then we finally get to Robert, who is painfully shy. He looks so uncomfortable as he squirms and rubs his hands over his face as if he needs to crawl under the table.

So I say: "It's cool if you don't want to share with the group. You can email me your ideas or maybe bring some writing to next meeting."

"No."

Then this torrent of words jumbles out in disjointed sentences, but with such passion. One kid insults his school.

"So do you all hate school?" There I go … making one of my classic generalizations.

This upsets Robert a little. "I never said I hated school. There's things I like about school. What I said was that there's this thing about it that I hate. That I think doesn't get talked about."

Ok. Clearly I need to listen to exactly what they are saying.

Lloyd: "I don't hate school so much as wish it didn't bore me."

Erin: "Me too."

Ted: "Yeah. I don't hate it."

Ok. Now one major assumption of mine has been shredded.

Now that we've introduced ourselves around the table I explain what I have in mind for the magazine we'll publish of our writing. I tell them that this is totally their thing and ask them to kick around some name ideas. I say that nothing is taboo but that those who feel the need to write about drugs/alcohol/sex should probably use a pseudonym. I explain that this isn't a class but a place where they can write from their own power. I'm not requiring anything other than free-writes and discussions during workshop time and some media imagery work which we'll talk about during class. They'll bring media images that speak to them in positive or negative ways.

So I figure now might be a good time for a free-write. *Please let this work.* I pray to the god of pizzas and lollipops. I explain the idea of free-write and that this is not really a thinking exercise but a letting-out type thing. "Start with one idea and then whatever words are in your head just throw them onto the page as fast as you can."

"Sort of like vomiting onto the page?"

I don't know who said that, but yeah, I guess that's one way of looking at it.

"What should we write about?" The red-head again.

"What do you want to write about?"

"Pot." Again.

"Ok, make that your first word but keep going."

Everyone else is ready and looking at me.

"On your mark ... get set ... go."

I hadn't planned to write ... but I don't want to stare at them as they write, so I start scribbling stuff ... mostly nonsense ... anything to make it appear as if I'm not watching them.

I'd planned to stop them at two minutes, but they are still frantically writing as if there will never be another moment to write in their lives. So I add a minute. Scribble some more words -- mostly connecting, beginning or ending words. And. But. If. Perhaps. It. Done.

Four minutes and still they scrabble and hunch over the fat little notebooks.

Ok, five. Five. Stop!

They look up and they look different. Something has changed in their eyes.

Lloyd doesn't look bored. Erin is deep in thought and

smiling. Ted looks as if he's going to jump out of his skin. Robert is smiling.

Obviously Ted has something to get out so I ask him if he wants to read, which he does. He practically starts reading before the end of my sentence. It is this beautiful abstract free-write that flows out and wraps me in silver. He finishes reading, then says that this is what happened to him last night doing a certain thing. He smiles. His whole group smiles. They are friends. They know what he did last night. I don't and I don't need to.

We talk about a possible essay that might come out of that piece.

After that we go around the table and Erin reads her piece on body images and Barbies. This is a new side that she's decided to entrust to me. I notice that Robert has closed his notebook and placed clasped hands on top.

Lloyd reads his bit next and he doesn't have nearly as much as the others but his lines are fluid and stream of consciousness. His work reminds me of some beat poetry. He mentions that he can't write under the pressure of a timed thing, that it sort of stressed him out. I notice Robert is still sitting there looking extremely uncomfortable. His smiling face has gone nervous and sweaty. He's actually wringing his hands.

I say, "I've got some other stuff to talk about, Robert, so if you'd rather communicate with me by email we can do that later or you can work off of that free-write to begin an essay or short story."

"Yes. No. No. I don't want to read mine in group. I'll email you." He's so relieved. It's like letting a bit of air out of a taut balloon.

We wrap up the meeting as I ask them to bring outlines and media images from magazines, which we'll talk about. We all agree that we don't want to meet in a library again as it feels too schoolish. So we'll meet in front of the library next week but everyone will come with ideas for a better meeting place, which we'll go to from the library.

Driving home I realize that although I made many missteps I was right on with the most crucial of my generalizations. These kids have so much to say. They have long days and nights floating inside that are literally begging to be freed. Lightning bugs in jars, I think. And the food worked too, most of it gone as they wrote and listened to words that can only be whispered or thought at school. Words that parents may not wish to hear. Wonderful beautiful words.

I am again amazed at the awesome transformative power of writing.

NOTES

1. Hell Houses, also know as Doom Houses, are haunted house-style attractions typically run by North American fundamentalist Christian churches or parachurch groups.

BATTLE PAY: STORYTELLING ON A DIME

Jackson Gillman

• • •

There is a certain piece in my repertoire of which I am very protective. It is an hour-long story called "Hard Knocks" which portrays a feisty adolescent and his deaf sister as they try to cope with their father's increasing alcoholism. Due to the sensitive nature of the program, when I perform it in high school assemblies, I am very particular about lights, sound, staging, and most especially preventing any potential distractions.

Because of experiences like the one I will describe, I now always assign a staff "watchdog" so that I won't have to break out of the mood of the story to deal with any disturbance. Very rarely do I ever have any kind of problem because as the drama unfolds, the audience usually becomes very protective of the story as well.

I had occasion to perform this piece at a special school which serves as a kind of a last resort for troubled youths, from elementary age on up. I am reluctant to present this program for younger children, but the administration had previewed it and insisted. The students were a relatively wired group, but as they became invested in the story, they became respectfully attentive. In the delicate parts of the story, you could literally hear a pin drop, but in this case it was a dime which rolled from the front row. It was a minor distraction, but I was glad when the dime finally stopped, far from its young owner.

The boy, perhaps eleven years old, got up to retrieve his dime. That was the end of it, or so I thought. To my chagrin, he dropped it again a few minutes later, shattering a dead quiet. It was too much to hope that he'd let it lie: again the retrieval, a bit more distracting than the first.

This occurred several more times during the course of my

presentation, which was intense enough, thank you. At each drop, roll, and stop he would stop, drop, and crawl after it. The kid wanted his dime, but not badly enough to put it in his damn pocket and leave it there. I quietly prayed each skirmish would be the last. Why did this butter-fingered boor have to land a place in the front row?

This story generally requires all of my concentration, but this time a massive number of my brain cells are working overtime, as I think about what to do the next time this dime-bomb explodes on the floor. Try a quick, icy Don't-even-think-about-it glare at him? Casually stop, drop and crawl, and pocket it myself? No, mostly what I'm thinking about is how NOT to think about the loose cannon on maneuvers in front of me with his semi-automatic which he fires off at random. This is just one of those supreme tests of professional mettle which I must pass in order to receive my storytelling medal of honor despite the concentration-piercing metal shrapnel. Then, after I've displayed my steely cool under fire and it's finally all over, I can take the kid backstage and execute him.

No, but as hard as it might be for me to do, I do need to say something to him afterward. This is a lot to think about while delivering an emotionally grueling drama. I actually do manage to override the flak, both external and internal, and the otherwise quiet focus I receive from these youngsters with so-called clinically deficient attention spans, and their ovation, is the badge of valor that I am awarded. Yet the hardest part of my job still lies ahead.

I owe it to the performers who follow me, to the boy who was simply unaware of the distraction his behavior caused, and to myself, to speak to him, though the backstage execution idea still has its appeal. The easiest thing of course would be just to forget about it and not say anything. It was over after all, and it went very well, considering. As gentle as I would try to be, it can't help but be a squirmy encounter. Why bother? Because I know I'd kick myself soundly on the way home if I didn't.

I hate this but I am going to make myself do it. I am going to approach him. No, he's approaching me. He's smiling. He tells me he really enjoyed the show and he takes my hand -- to shake it, I assume. No, to give me something. It is a dime. It *is the* dime. I try refusing it but he is insistent, he wants me to have it. Not to accept it at this point would be ungracious. My rehearsed words of reproach have no place here, as it all sinks in. He was probably holding it, or trying to, the whole time to give to me afterwards. This is not a Purple Heart for injuries received in the line of fire. It is a boy's dime, made of some silver alloy, but to me, it is my battle-pay and it is pure gold.

What can I say? Words fail. All I can muster now is a most sincere "Thank you."

A NATIONAL TEASURE HIDDEN IN VERMONT: A TRIBUTE TO THE BREAD AND PUPPET THEATER

Katherine Towler, MFA

• • •

No more chairs. No more flowerpots. No more shoes. No more windows. One by one, they stepped forward in their loose white shirts and white pants, setting the papier-mâché objects on the gymnasium floor. *No more frying pans. No more trees.* There was a slow, sure rhythm to the way they crossed the floor and placed the brightly painted representations of the objects before us. Their voices rang out at set intervals, like the tolling of a bell. Each pronouncement was a stab to the heart. *No more birds* ...

The year was 1981, and I was a member of the audience in Burlington, Vermont. I had heard of the Bread and Puppet Theater, but had never seen them before. Their performance that night in the gym of a local school -- if you could call it a performance, for really it was as much a sacred ritual as it was a performance – has stayed with me all these years, indelibly stamped in my mind. When I think of the threat of nuclear war, I inevitably recall those men and women dressed in white, with their homemade sculptures, setting them in front of us like gifts. With searing simplicity they made me feel, as no political speech or tract could, what it would mean to unleash a nuclear weapon in the world again. They made me know in my bones the utter devastation and folly and cruelty of war, and they did so with the crudest of props, with no amplification, with the most ordinary words, the most basic images, and the sparest of gestures. This is the genius of Bread and Puppet. This is what makes them a national treasure.

I did not encounter Bread and Puppet again until ten years later, when I met my husband and began spending summers in the Northeast Kingdom in Vermont. The farm in Glover where Bread and Puppet makes its home is just half an hour from the cabin my husband inherited from his grandfather. Throughout the 1990s, a central ritual of our summers was attending Bread and Puppet's Domestic Resurrection Circus, a two-day free performance held on the farm. First there was the circus, a rollicking collection of skits, many on political themes, interspersed with "animal acts" featuring people dressed in gorilla and tiger suits, and stilt dancers, and huge puppets. The stage was a field, with the audience of ten to twenty thousand seated on blankets up the slopes of a natural amphitheater. The Bread and Puppet ragtag Dixieland band played; the puppeteers in their floppy white shirts and pants circled the field carrying flags emblazoned with *Sister Moon* and *Brother Wind*; and the circus ended with "When the Saints Go Marching In" and Peter Schumann, founder and director of Bread and Puppet, dancing in an Uncle Sam suit atop twenty-foot high stilts, blowing a trumpet.

In the evening, there was the pageant, a sort of morality play in which good engaged evil every year, and good always won in the end, but not before a price had been paid. The pageant relied on hundreds of people, many taken from the audience an hour before the performance ("We need sixty people to carry flags," someone would shout, and volunteers would spill down the hillside). Beginning just before dusk, the pageant was conducted almost entirely in silence, with the bands of performers and mammoth puppets coming down the hillsides, enacting a symbolic drama pitting the little man and woman against the system -- though in its many layers of symbol and meaning, the pageant was "about" much more than this. The particulars of the story were different each year, but the ending was the same: the great Earth Mother puppet would appear at the top of the hill, as though rising from the darkening sky, and with her huge hand maneuvered by countless unseen puppeteers, she would set fire to a towering figure of evil, vanquishing the "mammon" once again.

The scale and drama and beauty of what Bread and Puppet does defies description. This is an art that must be experienced. The simplest way to define Bread and Puppet is to say that they are a political street theater group, and yet their work encompasses the political while drawing on myth and religious tradition and symbolism in a potent mix that transcends any one of these strands -- and becomes that much more powerful and rich because it cannot be reduced to one element or another. One of their recent shows, titled "The Insurrection Mass with Funeral March for a Rotten Idea," was billed as "a nonreligious service in the presence of several papier-mâché gods."

The complete lack of artifice, perhaps more than anything else, is what makes the work of Bread and Puppet so startling and moving. How difficult it is to achieve such clarity and purity in any art form. Like a Zen master or Christian mystic, Peter Schumann understands what it means to be human at the most simple level and never loses sight of this understanding. His work holds up a mirror: this is who we are and who we might become, for better or worse. This is the human drama in which we have been engaged for centuries and in which we will go on being engaged if we are lucky.

In 1998, the twenty-seventh and last Domestic Resurrection Circus was held. The crowds had become too large and unmanageable, and in the makeshift campgrounds around the farm where thousands stayed, a man was accidentally killed in a fight. Bread and Puppet made the decision that the free performance could not go on. In the years since, Bread and Puppet has presented a somewhat scaled-down version of the circus and pageant on the farm on Sunday afternoons throughout the summer. They continue to travel as well, performing at colleges and theaters around the country, and sometimes abroad. Describing themselves, they write:

Bread and Puppet, one of the oldest noncommercial, self-supporting theaters in the country, has created politically and socially aware shows with a commitment to community participation since 1963. At present, our shows are antiwar, anti-Capitalism, anti-Globalization and pro-Vermont independence.

In a rare interview in 1980 (he prefers puppeteering to talking), Peter Schumann said, "Puppetry and all the arts are for the Gods, are wild, are raw material, are bread and sourdough ... are for life and death, births, weddings, exaltation and sorrow, not for professionals and specialists of culture." In a more recent interview, he amplified these comments:

> But the real gist of the thing is art as practice, as common practice. Acrobatism in art is something that is disgusting to me and has nothing to do with community and community-building ... I am proposing a cultural insurrection ... an insurrection of scavengers against a system that is not about scavenging and not about preserving and not about taking things as they should be.

My husband and I have brought many people to the Bread and Puppet farm over the years, to tour the museum (two stories of giant puppets and other wonderful stuff in an old barn) and to see their performances. One friend on a first visit wept through the entire circus. To find this in America today -- a gathering of people that has nothing to do with the making of money and everything to do with an experience of community and humanity -- struck her as a miracle. And it is a miracle. The puppeteers live communally on their farm, growing their own food. They regularly recruit local people to participate in their performances (our Vermont paper features an ad the week before the July 4th parade: "Anyone who wants to march with Bread and Puppet wear white and arrive ten minutes before parade time."). They fund their work entirely from donations and the sale of their posters and banners. They make their sets and props from cardboard and papier-mâché and junk salvaged from the dump.

It was Juvenal, the Roman satirist, who wrote: "Two things only the people anxiously desire – bread and circuses." Bread and Puppet ends performances by distributing slices of their homemade sourdough rye bread, baked in outdoor wood-fired ovens, slathered with garlic aioli. This basic food is so good, so satisfying, so filling, so rich. Maybe it's the Vermont air, or the views of the hills on all sides, but bread has never tasted better. The same art that is found in everything Bread and Puppet does is at work here. There is nothing fancy or complicated about that bread with its few ingredients, about the beauty of garlic and oil and salt. This is the stuff of life. Bread and Puppet reminds us that, most of all, we must feed and be fed, that in the face of world-wide suffering and injustice, we must protest and, in the midst of protest, celebrate.

BEARING WITNESS TO LIFE, DEATH & EVERYTHING IN BETWEEN AS A PERSONAL HISTORIAN

Jeanne Hewell Chambers, MA-TLA

• • •

Sometimes people aren't as afraid of dying as they are afraid that their life has been devoid of meaning. As a personal historian, I interview people, record their memories, scan their photos and documents, shape their memories into narrative, do enough outside research to give context to their milestones and important decisions made. I preserve their memories and memorabilia both digitally and in the form of books, and while it takes a long time and a variety of skills, perhaps the most important thing I do is to bear witness, giving clients an opportunity, a reason, and the assistance needed to bring order to the stories that swirl inside. Simply providing this mirror often helps folks realize that even if they haven't discovered a cure for diabetes or male baldness or forgetfulness, even if they haven't built the world's tallest skyscraper or made more money than Bill Gates or invented a car that gets 95.3 miles to the gallon, their life has still been significant. As you will see in these four vignettes, significance isn't always big and flashy and limelight-able -- sometimes significance shines in the simplest acts: drawing pictures, baking a cake, writing letters, sitting close, or washing the dishes.

"Do you *really* think you can do something with all this mess?" Lucile asks rather sheepishly as she hands me an old wooden apple crate filled with four years' worth of handwritten notes, photographs curled with age, lacy-looking greeting cards, and yellowed recipes textured with drippings. "I'm just an old farm wife and mother," she says, looking down at the spotlessly clean floor.

I reassure her, then we talk a bit about binding options for the finished book. "Oh, just bind it like this notebook" she adds and points to a spiral-bound composition notebook on a nearby table.

"Miss Lucile, are you sure you want it bound like that? I think your stories are worthy of a much more substantial binding."

She looks pleased, but unconvinced. "I'm sure nobody's gonna' want a copy except my children," she says, "and they might not even be all that interested."

"Well, then, your homework assignment is to make a list of everybody you want to give a copy of your book to," I say as I hand her that spiral-bound composition book. "Keep your list in here."

A few weeks later, I'm back at Miss Lucile's kitchen table, eating a piece of warm pound cake and showing her how to mark any changes she wants me to make in the first draft of her book. "Are you making your list?" I ask between bites. She chuckles and says yes, but she still thinks she'll just need a few -- maybe one for each of her children – and spiral binding will still do quite nicely.

Miss Lucile, like many of my clients, doesn't own a computer or do email, so I drive back to her house two weeks later to pick up the first draft with the changes she wants made, and she announces that she's considering ordering 25 paperback books. When I pick up the second draft with her final approval, she tells me, "Go ahead and order me 50 hardbacks."

The books come in, and she's downright delighted with the rose on the cover, so glad she opted to go with hardback books. One month after I delivered the 50 books to her, she calls to order 50 more copies. "You won't believe all the notes and cards and letters and phone calls I've gotten about my book," she says. "People have even called to ask if they can have a copy. Imagine wanting a copy of my stories -- I'm just a farm wife and mother."

Six months later my phone rings. It's Lucile inviting me over for supper. As I clean my plate, she shows me the old wooden apple crate, filled with notes, photos, and recipes that will soon become her second book -- and she pulls out the tattered spiral-bound composition book to show me the already-long list of friends and family members who've requested a copy.

***

Mr. Vicks, 91-year-old, wants to write a book about his father, an electrical contractor in Persia around the time of World War I. My information-gathering turns up various paintings done by Mr. Vicks and his father -- pastel renderings of various family residences. When interviewing one of Mr. Vick's sisters, I discover that she paints, as does Mr. Vick's son and granddaughter., Surprisingly, none of them knew of the artistic talent preceding them, only that they were related to engineers. All told, seven of Mr. Vick's eight siblings were artists, numerous nieces and nephews are artists, as are many of their children. In the end, family members hold a book filled not just with stories, but with beautiful art created by generations of a family that had long since drifted apart due to geographical and age differences.

***

Mr. Hughes, a blind 90-year-old man whose health is fading noticeably, sits on the love seat with his wife whose memories have long since been erased or overgrown by Alzheimer's. Mrs. Hughes' quiet, easygoing, agreeable nature hinges in large part on her physical environment remaining dependably the same from day to day. She sits in her favorite spot: tucked right up next to Mr. Hughes. The caregiver sits with us, and we spend a good bit of each interview session letting Mrs. Hughes get acclimated to me, allowing her all the time she needs to get comfortable with my presence.

We're past the nice, introductory chit-chat, about ready to start telling stories. Mrs. Hughes pats her impeccably done hair and runs her hand down her freshly-laundered skirt, straightening out wrinkles only she can see, slips her arm through her husband's arm, and we begin.

Mr. Hughes tells stories about coming to America as a little boy, about teaching himself chemistry, about having to stay out of school when he was 14 years old to support the family while his father recovered from a work-related injury. During the story about starting a new school and being put back a grade, Mrs. Hughes -- who doesn't recognize her own children any more -- corrects something Mr. Hughes says, then asks him a question and fills in the details he neglects to mention. She asks another question and another, and before long, Mrs. Hughes slides her arm from her husband's arm and moves just far enough away from him to allow her to turn and face him. She continues asking him questions and begins sharing her memories with us -- memories that we all thought had disappeared forever in the folds of her brain. Then all too quickly, she's once again tucked up next to Mr. Hughes, silently smiling, patting her hair, handpressing wrinkles in her skirt, and quietly humming a tune none of us recognize.

***

Ruth grew up in poverty-stricken West Virginia. The third of four children, Ruth had one younger sister and two older brothers. Times weren't the only things that were hard -- people were hard, too. Fighting was a routine means of communication, and family feuds were passed on from generation to generation to generation. Ruth wanted to preserve her stories -- she was absolutely sure about that – but she wasn't at all sure she could handle the travel back in time. She had no desire to relive the hardships and hurts that filled her childhood.

At the end of the first two-hour session, Ruth said, with tears streaming down her cheeks and dropping off into her lap, "I can't believe the difference this has made. I thought I felt only hatred for my childhood days and for my brothers and sisters, but I've remembered nothing but GOOD things about them." And so it was at the end of every one of the next five sessions -- Ruth declaring how surprised she was that she remembered so many good things and saying oh, how she would've hated to die thinking she had only bad memories.

At the end of our last interview, she announced that she'd written a letter to the adult children of her eldest brother Bill, telling them stories about him and the kind things he'd done for her and for others. Recognizing that he was an alcoholic, Bill had run away from his parents' home during his late teenage years. He married, had children, then, finding it impossible to give up the bottle, he ran away from his family when his children were small. Ruth hadn't seen these nieces and nephews in four decades or more, but she found an address for them, and filled their mailbox with wonderful stories about their dad. She showed me the letter she'd received in response to those stories, thanking her for acquainting them with a father and relatives they had never known. Years later the correspondence continues, punctuated by a family covered-dish reunion every now and then.

Story -- both the telling and the listening -- is a search, and when shared with intention and received with intention, story has the power to reveal something important to us all. We are connected through story, we are changed through story, we are saved through story.

Note: Names were changed to protect the privacy of my clients and their families as per my signed agreement with them.

MAKING JOURNALS, MAKING LIVES

Nina Ricker, MA-TLA

• • •

By providing a small group of at-risk adolescent girls with the materials to make journals with hidden compartments and fold-out pages, I was trying to offer them a way to combine art and writing to address identity issues. It seemed to be a fairly straightforward exercise -- the hidden compartment, a pouch between glued-together pages -- would become a place for storing fragments about their deepest selves, and the fold-out pages would spill open with the parts of themselves they wanted to reveal most. I told them they weren't expected to share anything they chose to write in the hidden compartments or even write in that part of their journals during our workshop time. "And there are no rules for what you choose to tuck inside the hidden part of your journal," I said. "You can write a favorite song lyric or a line from a poem." I was pretty excited about showing them how to make a special place for themselves, even though I never expected to know what any of them chose to write and place inside these private spaces.

Only they didn't seem to need privacy. Right before my eyes they began work on filling the hidden compartment. We hadn't even begun our writing exercise yet, and they were reaching for paintbrushes and gel pens to write and embellish the notes they would place inside. And the size of what they wrote was huge and bold and always colorful. Not one of them looked to see what another was writing, yet they all wrote the same thing – their names. One or two of them added hearts or flowers, but none of them wrote anything more than that one word. And their names also became the subject of the fold-out pages of their journals, spilling across the pages in splashes of color.

At first I thought I'd failed them somehow, that I hadn't

explained the exercise the way it should've been explained, that it was *supposed* to be about a lot of words. Then I remembered all those moments I spent writing my name when I was younger. I remembered what an important word it was to me. Our name is the first word we learn to write and the one we spend the rest of our lives trying to define.

GOD BEHIND BARS:
FACILITATING A MEN'S SPIRITUAL
WRITING GROUP AT A STATE HOSPITAL

Scott Youmans, MA-TLA

• • •

One of the degree requirements of the Transformative Language Arts program at Goddard College is to complete a community-based practicum. Some students seem very clear about the population they want to work with from the moment they set foot on campus. I was not one of those students and I found myself struggling to create a practicum in my final semester.

Considering all of my resources, I turned to Reverend Ben Hall, a community minister at my church in Cranston, R.I.. He was leading a spiritual discussion group as part of his role as Director of Pastoral Care at the nearby Eleanor Slater Hospital. Each week he met with a group of men and offered them the opportunity to share in meditation, reflection, and discussion around readings from various religious and spiritual texts. My vision for a poetry group fit with this format, and he liked the idea of having me come in for six hour-long sessions over the course of the winter. It would be my first experience working with men in a state corrections hospital, a population not often heard from or listened to.

Constructing the program, I envisioned a series of sessions that progressively built on each other, starting with listening to and discussing poetry, and culminating in having men write and share their own work. However, before starting the series I learned that the men would not be allowed to use pens or other writing instruments. There had recently been a stabbing with a pen on the unit, and the unit's director asked that we not even hand out crayons.

The thought of leading a poetry session with incarcerated men was already uncomfortable for me to consider, and the stabbing heightened this anxiety. When thinking about leading this group, I imagined being challenged or ignored or threatened, and worried that I lacked the experience necessary to handle such events. Would I be "man enough" or professional enough to sit in a circle of men behind bars? Would we be able to connect on some level? And at the center of these questions: What would we learn from each other?

The men in the spiritual discussion group had been on the unit for varying lengths of time and their ages ranged form late teens to over 60. Each had been convicted of a crime and had later been diagnosed with a mental illness or had been found not guilty by reason of insanity. Most were medicated, which for some men made it hard for them to read, concentrate, or even see. Some men couldn't read, and one man didn't understand English.

Nine men chose to come to my first group. We began with introductions and a period of silent meditation. This would be the format for all the sessions: meditation and an opening reading, a check-in, and the reading or activity for the session. For the first day's introductory check-in, I asked men to tell me their names and their favorite flavor of ice cream. This combination helped me to remember each individual throughout the series. Even if I forgot a man's name, I could remember his flavor. I still remember the man who liked coffee – he would often fall asleep during the group.

The first discussion poem was "Breath" by Kabir. It was directly related to the spiritual nature of the group and the process of meditation that introduced each group. Each man had a copy of the poem to look at as I read it twice and then asked for responses: Which lines caught your attention? Did something in the poem stand out to you? Their responses were wonderful. Unlike my fear-filled visions of how the group might go, each man commented on something in the poem. The poem leads the reader on a journey looking for god, ending with the line, "Student, tell me, what is God? / He is the breath inside the breath." This prompted one man to respond, "God is inside of me ... us ... he's not outside, but within."

The second poem I offered was "Guardian Angel" by Rolf Jacobsen. It gave voice to the feelings and sensations that someone is always with us, looking out for us in some way. I wasn't sure what the men's responses would be to the idea of a guardian angel. I asked them, "Do you have a guardian angel?" And nearly every man reflected back on friends and family members either who were far away or who had died. The tangible presence of these memories helped many of the men get through their days and "be good," as one of them remarked. Then I asked, "Imagine that your angel is beside you right now. What would you say to him or her?" Many men took this opportunity to beautifully offer thanks and gratitude to their angels.

This first session gave me the opportunity to learn about setting my expectations, reacting to the group's response to the poems, and about just letting the process be and unfold. Sometimes, the expectations I brought to the group would interfere with my ability to lead the group. For example, the one man who I had been told was a Muslim left the circle while I read the Kabir poem. This caused me to skip a beat. In that moment, I was both angry that he had left and worried that I had offended him; both feelings distracted me. Later, in talking with Rev. Hall, he reminded me that most men come into and leave the group whenever they want and I shouldn't take any of it personally.

While I was mindful of the content of the poems I presented, I couldn't protect participants from their own associations, from possibly connecting with troubling or stressful memories. For example, when men responded to the "Guardian Angel," they began remembering friends and family who had passed away. I hadn't anticipated this response from them and I was afraid that this would bring the group down or cause participants to get upset as they remembered past losses. However, as the men continued to respond to the poem and to each other, they gained strength and connection from their memories.

Breathing in to my own fear and not controlling the discussion, I was able to allow these wonderful responses to happen. Rev. Hall later reminded me that these men don't often participate at all in the discussion, and he saw that the majority of the men were participating and clearly connecting with themselves, the group, and the material. The important thing was for me to listen to these men who often aren't listened to, giving and receiving as both a facilitator and a member of the circle. So much of what I learned during the entire six-week series was present in this first session.

One of the most precious gifts I received during the whole series was being able to facilitate the men's creation of their own poems. Using markers and an easel, I had the men call out nouns, verbs, and adjectives around particular topics and then assembled the words into a poem. The group chose the theme of "Home" and I prompted them with, "What do you think of when you think of home?" Words and associations began flowing, and I could barely keep up! The enthusiasm I saw in the men as they called out words and responded to each other's words – with laughter and thoughtful consideration – was beautiful. I did have to manage their playfulness, ensuring that all the men were heard and that the loudest and most talkative didn't monopolize the group. After we filled a page with words, we began putting them into a poem filled with the memories of home – luxuries that they hadn't experienced in a long time.

As the weeks passed, I realized that these men were isolated, not only from their friends and family outside, but even from each other and even from themselves due to their conditions and medication. Different social, cultural, and faith backgrounds separated them; some may not have even liked each other. Despite their diverse backgrounds, the process of their creating a prayer together amazed me. The men may have called out different prophets and phrases from their personal faith traditions; however, the culminating result was non-denominational and seemed to touch each man. It became the closing reading for the remaining sessions. At the beginning of the group, I brought in a closing reading from someone else, now they were listening to and reciting their own words at the close of each group.

By the end of the group, they wrote a prayer poem together that echoes the common theme calling each of them to the group. The poem was named, "God Be With Us."

GOD BE WITH US

Whether in weakness or in strength
Please keep my family peacefully
    and humbly in mind
    And give me patience like a white dove
    Give me the health I need to soar
        in this world
    Helping the sick and ourselves
    God helps those who help themselves
    God smiles on us because
    God is everywhere
    World Peace

MORE THAN JUST OUR STORIES

Pam Roberts

• • •

It was a cold December night when I sat in Genie Zeiger's writing workshop and tried to listen to my fellow participants. With sweaty palms and a quickening heart, I tracked the progression of readers, as, one by one, the members read what they had just written.

I felt the circle closing in. It was now time for the man on my left to read. I would be next. As he picked up his yellow lined pad and began a story about his cousin's wedding, I could barely listen as he described a joyous occasion, blessed with family from both sides and a sunny day. The bride, of course was beautiful, wearing a flowing white dress and a radiant smile beneath her bald head.

Bald head? He had my full attention now. Apparently the bride, his cousin, was undergoing chemotherapy for breast cancer. In the midst of the bride and groom's hopeful decision to go ahead with the wedding despite uncertainty about her health, she had made the brave decision to wed bald-headed, without wig or veil.

As was the custom of this workshop, when he finished reading, others responded with comments about the writing, its strengths, particulars of the language, the rhythm of the piece. I was mute. I could not bring myself to speak, I did not even know if I still had a voice.

Then "Thank you," the man said, and he turned to me. My head spun. I wanted to pass. I wanted to run, I wanted to do anything but sit here in this living room and read my words. I can't do this! I thought.

I tried to take a deep breath, tried to quell the wavering in my voice, tried to stem the tears that blocked my vision, tried to keep my hands from trembling as I picked up my notebook. How ironic to be the next reader, because what I had written about was how, just days before I had heard a surgeon say, "You have breast cancer."

My reading had a rocky start. I stumbled, I paused to collect myself, but I made it all the way to the end. And when I finished the room was completely still. Except for my heart thundering in my ears, there was silence.

Then someone spoke. "That was a powerful piece. The narrator's description of being on the phone with the surgeon was very vivid and real."

And another said, "The short sentences and repetitive language built tension and made us feel the fear."

And another added, "What brave and honest writing. This is so needed, it helps us address our own fears."

I felt the heat rise in my cheeks. I had done it! I had written about something so scary, my very new breast cancer diagnosis, and had shared it with my fellow writers. They, in turn, had given me feedback on my writing and helped me to feel safe and supported. In this process I had found a moment of respite from my fear. In fact, more than that, my fears had been transformed.

That was 13 years ago, the first time that I experienced the healing power of writing. I have since come to believe strongly in it, to believe that everyone has a story and that the telling and the hearing of our stories is healing. And in this healing lies the realization that we are more than just our stories.

After that night I continued to write in Genie's workshop about my experiences with breast cancer. It was as if once the dam was broken the force was too powerful to stop. Every week, on a Tuesday night, I gulped down my dinner, kissed my kids goodbye, and drove up the winding hill to Genie's house. Every week I wrote about my journey in the land of breast cancer, and then I read it to the group. Sometimes what I wrote was funny and sometimes it made all of us cry. While I lost my breast, underwent chemotherapy, joined a support group, and tried numerous forms of complementary healing, from acupuncture to nutrition to psychic surgery, I wrote.

This went on for about five years. Sometimes I wrote playful little ditties, but for the most part, no matter what Genie suggested, I wrote about my experiences with breast cancer.

"Write about a dream," she might say, and I would start, "In the time before I was diagnosed, I had a dream about a possum who clung to me no matter how often I flung him away. When I awoke I just knew."

"Write about a photograph," she might suggest, and I would write, "In this photo, I have two breasts and now I have one and everything is both different and the same."

What I found during this time was that my writing was healing me even more than the therapies I was trying. It was healing to express my fears and grief and then write myself into a place of stillness. Very gradually, over time I wrote my heart open and found peace and acceptance.

I believe that healing is not the same as cure. There is no cure for breast cancer – you can have a recurrence at any time, but there is healing, which to me means finding clarity and harmony in body, mind, spirit and feeling. Healing is feeling whole.

A couple of years ago I concluded four years at the IM School of Healing Arts in NYC where we learned wholeness healing. We learned that we are born whole but get fragmented by life, so healing is connecting with that memory of wholeness. We do it within ourselves and in relationships with others, by bringing our loving attention.

For me, a way of connecting to that memory of wholeness is through writing. Because of my healing experience as a member of the writing workshop I became a leader of writing workshops for people touched by cancer, and I have seen time and time again how we are moved to tears as we read the words that express our deep truths. Writing like this, within the intimate community of a workshop, is an act of courage, connection and ultimately transformation. As we share our stories, we find that we are more than just our stories.

PERVASIVE CARETAKING IRONY

Debbie Harris, MA-TLA

• • •

The first night of my caretakers workshops I tried to keep my nerves in check. My biggest fear at that point was that no one would show up. Caretakers are some of the busiest people, so finding some who had a free evening could be the biggest challenge of my practicum experience.

Five minutes into my explanation of the Goddard Transformative Language Arts graduate program, my participation in it, and my need for a workshop practicum experience as a requirement of the degree, a hurried lady entered the room. She seemed to know the other attendees, as she greeted them while taking the consent form I handed her.

I wasn't surprised that these workshop participants knew each other. My husband, an elementary school teacher and vice-principal, assisted me in gaining use of the school library for the meetings and in publicizing the workshops. All of the people who came were associated with the school in some way -- teachers, teacher's aides, parents of a student at the school. When we went around the circle introducing ourselves and telling our favorite nickname, the hurried lady introduced herself meekly as Kathy. The first session focused on defining what and who caretakers are. Kathy participated very little. When the meeting was over, she was the first one out the door.

Despite my nerves, I felt that the first session went well, though I was a bit distressed about Kathy's apparent lack of interest and wondered if she would return the following week. She did return, complete with lists and graphs of how much time she spent on caretaking responsibilities, how much time she spent on herself, and to what degree she would like to shift these calculations. I was impressed but wary. She appeared to be an overanxious participant. Still, I shared her work with the other workshop members and verbally marveled at how well she grasped the concept of the "pervasive caretaker," a person who feels she must care for others everywhere she goes.

As news of the workshops spread around the campus, two additional women joined the group. After having set up the workshop sessions, I discovered that the amount of time required for the practicum portion of my degree had been increased and that I would need to add an additional four sessions. Though under other circumstances, I might be reluctant to change the dynamics of the group once it had been formed, I welcomed new people as a way to keep the group going for the desired length.

A few days after the arrival of the new people, Kathy sent me an e-mail stating that she had wanted to share something with the group at the previous meeting, but had held back due to the presence of one of the new people. It seems that Kathy had a history with the woman's not being discreet in keeping to herself personal information shared with her in confidence. In my return e-mail, I told Kathy that I was sorry she felt unable to share her story because of the newcomer. I expressed my hope that she had been able to share her news with someone, but hoped that she would feel free to share it with the group if she so desired. I concluded my e-mail by assuring her that at the next group meeting I would verbally reiterate the written workshop "guidelines," one of which was the need for complete confidentiality of information shared by group members. The following Wednesday, I opened the group as I had promised Kathy I would, with a review of the guidelines. By the end of the session, Kathy had shared her story.

As the meetings continued, Kathy participated more freely and shared more actively. We shared our first memories as receivers of care, our first experiences as providers of care, and even discussed caretaking and its connection to grief, after a 5th grade student of the school died in a tragic car accident. The group was bonding in a wonderful way. As the facilitator, at times I felt almost unnecessary. Then I started to see the workshop setting more as a cake -- the participants were the ingredients and I was the spoon, stirring and allowing the members to mingle in a new way, a way that helped provide insight and transformation.

At the last session I asked each participant what s/he had expected when first coming to the group and what each person felt s/he would take away. We laughed when the parents of two of my husband's students stated that they had worried when he gave them the flyers for the workshop, because they feared that he was singling them out as being in need of parenting skills help and thus in need of the workshop. Knowing I worked for a medical group, Kathy said she wondered if her blood pressure would be taken at the meeting. She continued that she wasn't really sure what the workshops would be about, but that she came because she felt she should support me by attending. The irony was not lost on me: She came to the workshops to help take care of me -- she was a pervasive caretaker. Throughout the weeks of the workshops, Kathy re-evaluated her caretaking priorities and drastically changed the number and arrangement of those priorities. She even began to include herself among those for whom she should care. Still, I could not forget that Kathy only began attending the workshops because she was exhibiting a behavior pattern that I was attempting to change -- in myself and others. So it appears that when it comes to trying to get the busy caretaker to attend a workshop on caretaking and pervasive caretaking, one method is to be that caretaker's object of care.

A LEGACY OF MEANING:
WRITING WITH ELDERS

Anna Viadero

• • •

I do not want to sound biblical, but they *did* march into the senior center that day in 1998 two by two. I think that's a reflection on the culture people age 70 and older come from, bound by World War Two and the coming together of a country. It's much deeper than friendship. It has to do with survival.

They were mostly women, because after a certain age there are more women statistically than men. In that first group of twelve who had signed on for memoir writing there were ten women and two men. The youngest was 69 (a woman) and the oldest was ninety (also a woman). They came in grumbling things like, "I'm only here because my daughter/son MADE me come." "I'm not a writer." "I'm not sure why I'm here." Three were college educated. Three had written before and had been published. All had come from a time when writing brought images to their minds of red pencils that shaped their early self-expression and sometimes cut them off at the knees. All were more closed than open.

"Write about what happened around your kitchen table when you were young," I said.

Heads bent and pencils and pens scratched on school notebooks filled with lined paper. I don't remember anyone hesitating or asking any kind of clarifying question. I asked them to write for twenty minutes, but they wouldn't stop.

"Just five more minutes," I said. Twice. Finally after more than half an hour they stopped under duress and read what they had written.

Joe remembered his family stuffing feather pillows around their kitchen table in rural Western Massachusetts. It was the only time his mother would open up to them and tell them her stories. It was where he first heard about her return to Poland from the US just before WWI broke out. She was homesick and needed to show her family her first born -- a daughter. This writing was the beginning of a longer piece Joe would write on his mother's return from Poland to the US during WWI.

Eileen remembered the political discussions that went on around her kitchen table. Her home in Queens, NY was a lively place. Her father, a newspaper editor, kept them all current. I imagined Eileen's outspoken nature being shaped there.

Warren remembered struggling with homework around his kitchen table in upstate New York. He remembered how his parents told him at the kitchen table that he'd have to go to Catholic school to try and right his academic wrongs (which were much bigger than any of them could imagine.) The piece ended with Warren leaving the Catholic school and enlisting in the Army, which would become more of a family to him than he ever dreamed. "But that's another story all together," he said.

That day a door swung open for these people who "weren't writers" and had been "forced to come" to this writing group. When I look back I can see they found their voice and its power that first day, but if you asked any of them they'd say it took a while. They saw themselves in other people's experiences and they found hope and compassion for parts of their life that had been hidden for years. As they listened many took notes. "I thought I didn't have anything to write about and now I have too much," said Charlotte.

At first I thought that what they felt most comfortable writing was based on concrete prompts, but as they trusted the support of others and their own voice, magic seemed to happen. They began to write about feelings and emotions, too.

Joe wrote about his youngest daughter who was born severely disabled. Just minutes after her birth doctors told him and his wife to just let her die. He wrote about how he fought for her life and grew to love her part in his life. He sobbed when he said, perhaps for the first time to anyone at all, that trusting his love for her and her love for him was the single most valuable thing he had done in his life. People in the group sobbed too, and some said "It's really good to see a man cry," and Joe was perfectly OK with that.

Wilma, who married in 1918, wrote about a time she wanted to leave her husband, something frowned upon back then. She wrote about how tough it was to work for something you're not sure you quite believe in anymore, how exhausting it was to make it back to baseline and how lonely she felt not being able to share that with friends who might not understand her wish to leave and not "work at it."

Charlotte wrote pining for a time when imagination was king. A retired teacher, she mourned the loss of imaginative play for today's kids. Writing about a ledge in her neighborhood that could become any number of places to play -- ship, house, treacherous cliff -- she said she couldn't go back even to see that ledge one more time because the power of imagination that had made that ledge come to life was no longer alive.

Since 1998 a few have died, but those who are still around write, whether or not they come to our monthly ongoing group. Some supplement their income with their writing. Some have become radio commentators. Some have created family newsletters. Some are going through boxes of family memorabilia and writing stories about bracelets and rations coupons and vintage clothing they've saved, "just so the next generation has an appreciation for what went before." They all complain that there is far too much to write about and there is never enough time. They are proud to be recognized as writers now when their work is published in local papers and neighbors and friends acknowledge their stories. They all have been emboldened by their writing

When elders write it works against the invisibility and isolation that they feel. It helps them find a voice that many have never had. It lets them say what they've never felt brave enough to say. It makes them remember. It helps them leave a legacy. It lets them share in meaningful ways not just with younger audiences, but also with their peers. It helps them put their life in perspective at a time when many are hungry to do just that.

THE SURPRISE OF ENDINGS:
TLA IN A CANCER WRITING GROUP

Linda Garrett

• • •

I usually can figure out how to snag an "A" in an academic class. But now that I have enrolled in this TLA writing group for cancer survivors, it's a little different. No grades, of course, but still I'm an over-achiever, primed to please and ready to give the teacher what she wants. So what does this teacher want? Never mind that I'm living with advanced stage ovarian cancer, most likely facing some form of chemotherapy for the rest of my days.

The facilitator gives us a handout: "Ground Rules for Writing Workshops." Good. I love handouts. What's this? Number One is "Don't worry about spelling, grammar and most of all making sense." Huh?

I'm used to playing by the rules, but this one mystifies me. Why bother to write anything unless it makes sense?

I'm afraid it took me awhile to understand this. At first I still tried to make pretty-looking sentences and paragraphs. But eventually I did loosen up and look at writing for this class differently. It didn't have to be all neat and clean -- with an introduction and summary -- tied up with a bright red bow for the teacher. It just had to be honest and direct and nothing more. It could be tattered and a little smelly, but this teacher would still like it. I even began to suspect that the smellier the better, at least for this writing class.

The faster and more unselfconsciously I wrote, the more the raw emotions tumbled out. Writing like this began to free those things that were not previously allowed to come out and play: whether that was the child within, the beast within, or the squirrel within, I don't know. But I do know that it accessed parts of me that were surprising.

Perhaps most surprising were the endings. All of us in the class usually had endings for our writing exercises: a sudden insight, a firm statement, a question, an ending that was funny or rhymed or just plain fit well, or perhaps a strong emotion or a simple realization, such as "I'm content to leave things as they are now." I don't think we did this consciously. I don't believe we were writing toward specific endings. They just happened serendipitously and wonderfully.

Some of my ending lines included:

"You do not have to die with everything on your To Do list crossed off."

"Congratulations, you made it."

"Can you love things you've never seen?"

"I'm through being nice. Up against the wall, motherfucker."

"I can see the circle close now."

"It was time to howl at the moon and run with my own pack."

"I want my life to be razor-sharp and not well-rounded."

"Every fiber of me begs to wake up -- to wake up, electric, stunned, and newly alive."

It seemed a little amazing that, given perhaps only ten minutes to write each piece, we all would usually end our writings so definitely. Very few times did I hear someone's writing just disappear into thin air, floating free and flimsy, without some kind of ending to it. We often ended with a type of "I see" or "I am" statement.

As a cancer patient, I am concerned with endings. Especially my own personal ending. So perhaps I should not have been surprised when, for the last line for the writing exercise "I Used to Be, But Now ..." I wrote "I used to be a person with a future; but now I am waiting to die." My unhappy bluntness surprised even myself. We cancer patients are not really supposed to think things like "I'm waiting to die." It's not good for the immune system, we are told. It's not the optimism or mature resilience we are supposed to have. Shame on me for writing, then saying that, out loud. I had said something forbidden.

But this is how TLA writing works. The smelly and the hidden (or occasionally the pleasant and the lovely) tumble out into the light of day. Fearful emotions that may have been suppressed and discouraged can find their way to the page, and then are read out loud to others in the group. Witnessed in this way, the writings are embraced by their authors and become undeniable truths. They become real.

Sometimes our endings surprise us. Sometimes they can delight or depress us. Sometimes they are nothing but more questions. But the writer must remain open to all the possibilities within, for any of them may become her truth at a given moment.

EPILOGUE:

THE ART OF SELF-CARE IN TLA

Caryn Mirriam-Goldberg, Ph.D.

• • •

Nobody told me there'd be days like these
Strange days indeed -- most peculiar, mama
- John Lennon

When we imagine facilitating a writing and ecology workshop, consulting with a business on storytelling for a more just workplace, or coaching an at-risk teen on developing a local theater project, we probably see our work glowing with meaning, ourselves alive with purpose. Yet there are and surely will continue to be those times when we're fighting a cold, driving to our work in a car in bad need of a major repair, just hanging up the phone from a teenage son who's freaking out over his physics exam, and worrying about whether we actually paid the electric bill. Strange days -- and sometimes nights -- indeed.

We have stories in many traditions to illustrate the need for the sustainers to sustain themselves -- such as "The Shoemaker's Children" who go without shoes while their good father shods the whole town. Yet we still face the challenge of cobbling together a living as a workshop facilitatior, consultant, educator, Transformative Language artist, and in many of our lives, mediator between arguing teens, chauffer for younger children, night watch woman for older ones, dishwasher, laundress, constant student in accounting 101, and always-behind-the-season gardener.

This essay is not meant in any way to suggest that there are fits-all solutions for any of us reading this, or for any one of us over the changes that life brings us, often point blank and on the afternoon you would be least prepared to deal. Instead, I offer up the notion of pondering -- along with the ethical dimensions, purpose and logistics of our work -- how to be students of self-care so that TLA will serve those who serve their communities.

Like many of you, I sometimes find that the very things that bring me such joy and freedom, such liveliness and meaning, are also the things that keep me from joy and freedom, liveliness and meaning. As a workshop facilitator, educator, and writer, not to mention a mother of three (did I mention two are teenagers?), I've done phone conferences while prowling grocery aisles for the pizza sauce; facilitated a heated debate -- while driving up to a hospital to lead a writing group for people with cancer -- with the kids over who gets to watch his or her video; and loaded dishwashers while poetry readings, conference budgets and student melt-downs danced in my head. I've also journeyed through serious illnesses, some having to do with whatever mystery of the cosmos lands bad news on us with no clear reason why, some coming from the toll persistent multi-tasking can take on a gal ... or a guy for that matter.

Taking care of ourselves over the long haul in whatever work we do is essential to being able to lead a life where we actually have time to read the poem, write the novel, hold the kitten, walk the woods, inhabit the bath and generally feel our own pulse again -- as individuals, as part of the larger world, and as people who come alive in the afterglow of language. The balance between work and play and doing nothing at all and doing all we're passionate about is a precarious one, shifting from moment to moment. It's a little like holding a very full glass of water while walking quickly ... up a hill ... in high winds ... with a dog chasing you ... a too-heavy and ill-fitting backpack ... a thunderstorm approach ... and did I mention our shoes are too tight?

Yet I believe that one of the most crucial things we can do for ourselves and for each other is to foster a continuous education about the art of self care. This encompasses everything from the dilemma of watching your computer screen download 59 emails at just the hour you were going to work on your own writing, to that moment you're facilitating a storytelling session for teens, and you're panicking just a tiny bit on the inside because you're worried that your own child is going to fail math, lose his direction for his life and blame you. It includes the feast and famine swings of being a writer, workshop facilitator, storyteller, educator, counselor, healer, and/or artist (e.g. "has the check come yet?") as well as the quiet moments when you realize your body is trying to tell you something, and it's time to listen.

Growing into our work in balance with growing our work in the world means breathing into the inexplicable understanding of living in this body, this time, this place while also trying to book enough work to balance the check book without having to do special breathing exercises. The moment-to-moment answers of what to do (read the book, answer the phone messages, lie in the hammock or, if you're like me, stare at the wall wasting your time wondering what to do with time) are extremely individualized and mutable. Since the answers are so individual, even for each person at any given moment, and since the answers are mostly known best by the ones asking, I wouldn't presume to offer you any one-size-fits-all solutions. What I do offer instead are the things I tell myself -- everyday -- as my cup runneth over with questions and blessings while I'm thirsting for health or answers.

- In general, treat yourself with utter tenderness, as if you are your own best beloved ... until you realize you are. Treat yourself like you would treat your best friend (provided your best friend isn't a masochist).
- Spend some time every day, even if it's only 15 minutes, alone. Breathe. Do whatever relaxes you (walk, sip tea, lie on the couch, stare at tree). Ask yourself how you feel, and listen carefully to whatever comes. (Key tip for people like

me: buy a hammock, hang it up, lie there, and don't bring the cell phone or a notebook along for the ride.)

- Before facilitating a workshop or beginning a performance, take a moment to connect with your heart beat. Place your hand over your heart. Or take your own pulse. This will remind you that you're in a body. If you're carrying anxiety or heaviness or pain, imagine placing it in a beautifully furnished room, and tell it, "I'm going to go to work now, but I promise to come back to you, Sweetheart. Watch a favorite movie or just rest, and I'll see you in 90 minutes."

- If you take a glass jar and fill it all the way up with rocks, you'll get to the point where you can't put in any more rocks … but you can pour in sand to the top … and then you can pour in water. Don't treat self-care as the water you pour in at the end of the day, filling in small spaces. Instead, treat it like the rocks that go in first. This means doing the walk that refreshes you, the yoga that relaxes you, the lying under a tree that replenishes you before turning the computer on.

- Do all you can to get a good night's sleep. Avoid the computer screen before bed, if possible most of the evening (I struggle with this mightily!). Try aromatherapy baths or lotions, quiet music, walks, old magazines, hot cocoa – whatever helps you slow down.

- Treat the work you're most passionate about with enough respect to give it its own time and space, and then don't miss your appointment with it. I strive to keep write-and-wander Wednesdays each week (where I don't allow myself to do anything but my own writing … or wandering) because I know that if I wait until Friday to do my own writing, it won't happen. Find what works for you, and treat it like an appointment that absolutely can't be broken.

- Reach out to friends and colleagues facing similar challenges. Meet for breakfast or afternoon tea or evening decaf to talk about what you're facing and how to take loving care of yourself in the process. Perhaps you might want to form a talking circle, in which each person gets to say whatever she/he wants without anyone interrupting to try to fix what ails the speaker. The general rules for such circles are that each person gets an allotted amount of time to speak, no cross-talking is allowed, and deep listening is encouraged.

- Tell yourself that the work-work will still be there tomorrow, and there will always be more to do tomorrow. So you couldn't finish it all anyway! Think of your self-care as the ongoing foundation of all else you want to do in this life.
- Speaking of this life, try to remind yourself as often as possible what's most important to you. The more you can de-escalate the little things (the snitty email from your sister-in-law, the extra charge on your phone bill, your spouse fighting with your teenager), the more easily you can deal with those little things without causing yourself extra stress. Save your freak-outs for the freak-out-worthy whenever and however possible.
- When facing health issues, bring TLA along to treat yourself. I once helped heal a foot wound by singing to my foot (when I was safely alone of course). Write your questions, and then write or sing your body's reply (a great exercise is to let a part of your body tell its story). Seek out metaphors to help you reflect on yourself. Bring in the tools that help – colored pencils or gel pens, sturdy notebooks, great CDs.
- Treat the things you do to connect with yourself with as much respect as you would official therapy sessions (including anything from psychotherapy to massage therapy). Sometimes I tell myself I'm doing hammock therapy, movie therapy, ice cream therapy, nap therapy (great way to boost the immune system by the way – and so

is sex), walking therapy, friend therapy.

- If that word "therapy" isn't one that brings you a sense of health, don't use it – tell yourself you have an appointment with a shamanic flick, or a well-being walk. Or say what my kids say (although they often say it sarcastically): I'm going to my happy place now.

- When life becomes too stressful, first chance you get, declare it "spa day." Isolate yourself in a room in your home or a beautiful place you can set up a blanket outside without being disturbed. Play your favorite music, take a bath with eucalyptus or lavender, prepare yourself (or buy something already prepared) healthy and delicious food, read a book you enjoy, and if possible, get a massage or pedicure or whatever is a great physical treat for you. There's no need to travel to those high-priced spas in the Sonoran desert.

- Take vacations (even to the Sonoran desert if that's what you want). Real vacations. Not ones to visit family members so stressful to be around that you have to pack extra antacid. Not ones to work or pitch your work. Even if you only have enough time and gas money to get to your own backyard, declare yourself on a vacation (and don't bring your computer or cell phone along). Pitch a tent, sit in it with a cup of tea and good book, high quality organic chocolate within arm's reach and lot of pillows. If anyone or anything calls you (barring real emergencies), simply say, "I'll get to that when I get back from vacation. Wish you were here."

- There are inexpensive retreat centers all over the U.S., many of which are run by religious organizations. There are also camps everywhere, and off-season, they tend to be quiet, picturesque and quite affordable. Look into what's near you, and make it a habit to regularly visit a place where you feel renewed. If money is tight, see what work-study arrangements you can make (could you do a storytelling workshop with the staff or present something on writing and social change to the board?).

- Do what you love as often as you can.
- Live the poems, stories and songs you love.

...

CONTRIBUTORS
and
EDITORS

...

CONTRIBUTORS

· · ·

David Abram, Ph.D. is the author of *Spell of the Sensuous* (winner of the 1997 Lannan Award for non-fiction) and the author of numerous articles and essays. A magician, philosopher, father, storyteller, and bioregionalist, David has been named by the *Utne Magazine* as one of a hundred visionaries currently transforming the world. He is presently at work on a book exploring our animal nature. He makes his home in Santa Fe.

Sharon Bray, EdD is the author of *When Words Heal: Writing Through Cancer* and *A Healing Journey: Writing Together Through Breast Cancer.* She is an adjunct faculty member of the Pacific School of Religion in Berkeley, CA and leads expressive writing groups at Stanford and Scripps Cancer Centers in Palo Alto and San Diego, CA. Sharon holds a doctorate in Applied Psychology from the University of Toronto and studied transformative language arts at Goddard College and creative writing/literary fiction at the Humber School for Writers and University of Washington Writers' Program. She is a member of the American Psychological Association, Society for Arts in Healthcare, Amherst Writers & Artists, and the National Poetry Therapy Association. www.wellspringwriters.org

Irene Borger, MA, founded the Writing Program at APLA, the nation's second largest AIDS service agency, and served as artist-in-residence there for ten years. Editor of *From a Burning House* and *The Force of Curiosity*, Borger, a former UC Riverside faculty member, teaches at wellness institutes throughout the country. Her articles have appeared in numerous publications including *O, BOMB*, and on the *Wall Street Journal's* art page. A longtime meditation student, she is working on a book on listening. She serves as director of the Alpert Award in the Arts. www.alpertawards.org

Karen Campbell, MA has much experience facilitating drama & art workshops with various groups in Japan (where she resided for over two decades) and for the ARC of Arkansas (supporting adults with developmental disabilities), including their annual performing arts camp. She is on the faculty for the Individualized BA Program and the Individualized MA Program at Goddard College, where she specializes in colonial/postcolonial cultural studies, translation studies, gender issues and sexual politics and, more recently, the struggle to create and present authentic research through autoethnography/scholarly personal narrative, and what she would like to call embodied research. www.goddard.edu

Mandy Carr, B.A. (Hons) is a state registered dramatherapist, supervisor of arts therapists, and teacher who has set up dramatherapy in five inner city schools in the U.K. An elected member of the executive of the British Association of Dramatherapists for four years, she currently convenes its Equal Opportunities Subcommittee.

Francis X. Charet, Ph.D. has a background in psychology and religion with a particular focus on Jungian Psychology. He has taught at a number of universities as well as lectured before various Jungian groups and at the Jung Institutes in Zurich and in New York. He is a faculty member in the BA and MA programs at Goddard College and is the Coordinator of the Consciousness Studies Concentration there. www.goddard.edu

Jeanne Hewell Chambers, MA-TLA, is the CEO (Cavorting Evolutionary One) of herowntrueself, be that her professional self or her personal self. On any given day, whether she's writing, acting, or stitching, Jeanne has about as much fun as she can stand plowing her life to expose (in no particular order) twisted roots, rutilant rocks, and downright sumptuous relics. www.keepsakebiog raphicalservices.com and www.lifeinthealong.com

Patricia Fontaine, MCAP, MA-TLA has been teaching about difference for 20 years. She is a published poet, an adjunct faculty member at the University of Vermont, and a breast cancer survivor. She is in the process of earning a Master's degree in Transformative Language Arts at Goddard College and making quiet mischief next to Lake Champlain in Shelburne, Vermont.

Linda Garrett is a photographer and writer who has participated in many cancer writing workshops. She is currently writing about her experiences living with terminal cancer.

Jackson Gillman is a storyteller, songsmith, comic and movement artist. He has been dubbed "the Stand-up Chameleon" and has performed for the whole gamut -- nursery schools and nursing homes, incarcerated and intoxicated, blind and deaf. He has been Teller-in-Residence at the International Storytelling Center and featured at the National Storytelling Festival. www.jacksongillman.com

Greg Greenway has performed throughout the U.S., including at Carnegie Hall in the New York Singer/Songwriter Festival which was rebroadcast on NPR's World Cafe, an appearance on nationally syndicated Mountain Stage, and a show at the Rock and Roll Hall of Fame honoring Phil Ochs. Greenway now has six critically acclaimed solo releases: *A Road Worth Walking Down* (nominated for two Boston Music Awards), *Singing For the Landlord* (top five CDs for 1995 on the Internet Folk DJ list), *Mussolini's Head* (1998), *Something Worth Doing* (2001), *Greg Greenway: Live* (2003), and *Weightless* (2006). www.greggreenway.com

Deborah Harris, MA-TLA is a Goddard graduate and an adjunct faculty member of Hartnell Community College in Salinas, California. She focuses on English language development and literacy for Latino students, emphasizing language as a tool for life enhancement. She reads poetry to her students and requires journals each semester.

Allison Adelle Hedge Coke, MFA is Huron; Eastern Tsalagi; French Canadian; Portuguese. She grew up in North Carolina, Canada, and on the Great Plains. Her books include: *Blood Run* (poetry, Salt Publishing); *Off-Season City Pipe* (poetry, Coffee House Press); *Rock, Ghost, Willow, Deer* (memoir, University of Nebraska Bison Books); *Dog Road Woman* (poetry, Coffee House Press, winner of the American Book Award); *From the Fields* (editor, California Poets in the Schools); *They Wanted Children* and *Coming to Life* (editor, Sioux Falls School District Press); *Ahani: Indigenous American Poetry/To Topos International Journal* (guest editor, Oregon State University), and four other collections. She performs readings, workshops, seminars, talks, and she has created and organized many transformative language arts programs for many populations. She serves as a professor at the University of Nebraska. She is also an accomplished artist who has shown her work throughout the U.S. www.hedgecoke.net and www.hedgecoke.org

Carol Henderson is a writer and writing teacher, and also author of *Surviving Malcolm: A Mother's Journey Through Grief.* Her articles and personal essays appear regularly in many regional and national publications. She regularly facilitates workshops for parents living through the loss of a child.

Yvette A. Hyater-Adams, MA-TLA is a poet, essayist and transformative language arts practitioner. She works with people to express themselves in words to help care for emotional wellness, personal growth, and creative voice. Her research and narrative practice focus on the needs of women, with emphasis on African American women. The core of her work for 20 years has been developing innovative methods to support personal and organizational change. www.renaissancemuse.com

Kelley Hunt is a rhythm and blues singer who has three CDs to her credit, including the recent award-winning *New Shade of Blue.* She regularly tours the U.S. and Canada with her band, performing at blues and jazz festivals, on television and radio shows, and at concerts in a variety of venues. She has been featured six times on National Public Radio's "Prairie Home Campanion" as well as on "Austin City Limits." She also regularly leads workshops on jazz piano, songwriting, and singing. www.kelleyhunt.com and www.bravevoice.com

Lana Leonard, MA is program director of Sedona's first restorative justice program, the Sedona-Oak Creek Restorative Justice Partnership (SORJ). She and Dr. Beverly Title co-founded the private, not-for-profit agency Teaching Peace; helped create and develop the Longmont community Justice Partnership in Longmont, Colo.; and co-authored *Victim or Hero? Writing Your Own Life Story* and *Civility Rules* as well as *Restorative Justice in Action*, an implementation manual for community-based, restorative justice programs. With her husband Tracy, Leonard lives in Sedona, Ariz., where she also has served as youth commissioner and "Artist in the Classroom."

Katt Lissard, MFA, is a writer, activist and teacher. She is Project Director of the Winter/Summer Institute in Theatre for Development (WSI) (www.esc.edu/wsi-lesotho), which was launched this past summer in Lesotho, southern Africa (where she spent most of 2005

on a Fulbright). Katt is a Mabou Mines Theatre Resident Artist alum, an Affiliate Artist of the New Georges Theatre Company and a MacDowell Colony Fellow. She teaches at the State University of New York, Empire State College in Manhattan and is a visiting writer at Long Island University's MFA program in downtown Brooklyn.

Perie Longo, Ph.D., is past President of the National Association for Poetry therapy, a Marriage and Family Therapist in private practice, a Registered Poetry Therapist and Mentor/Supervisor for those in training. She directs the poetry therapy program at Sanctuary Psychiatric Centers of Santa Barbara and is an adjunct instructor for poetry therapy at Antioch University. She is the author of several volumes of poetry, the last titled *With Nothing Behind but Sky: a journey through grief* (Santa Barbara: Artamo Press, 2006). www.perielongo.com

Denise Low, Ph.D., is a professor at Haskell Indian Nations University where she has served as chair of the Humanities Dept. She was appointed in 2006 the Poet Laureate of the state of Kansas. She is author of over a dozen books, including many volumes of poetry, a biography of Langston Hughes, a collection of personal ecological essays, and several anthologies, including a celebration of the work of Leslie Marmo Silko. Her awards include grants from the National Endowment for the Humanities, a Kansas Arts Commission Fellowship in poetry, and numerous poetry prizes. www.deniselow.blogspot.com

Christopher Maier is a playwright and story-maker with studies in psychology, spirituality, and systems theory who specializes in creating and telling healing stories. He holds an M.A. in Communication Studies from Northwestern University, doctoral research in Performance Studies at University of Texas, and another

M.A. in Transpersonal Counseling Psychology from Naropa University in Boulder. His unique approach to re-visioning life stories has been presented in trainings for staffs of drug and alcohol-abuse, hospice and suicide-intervention programs, and storyteller conferences around the U.S. www.moving-stories.com

Shaun McNiff, Ph.D. is the Dean of Lesley College and University Professor at Lesley University in Cambridge, Massachusetts, an internationally recognized figure in the areas of the arts and healing and creativity enhancement, and the author of many books that include *Art Heals: How Creativity Cures the Soul*; *Trust the Process: An Artist's Guide to Letting Go*; *Art as Medicine: Creating a Therapy of the Imagination*; *Creating with Others: The Practice of Imagination in Life, Art and the Workplace*; *Art-Based Research*; *Depth Psychology of Art*, and *The Arts and Psychotherapy*. Dr. McNiff is a past president of the American Art Therapy Association and an Honorary Life Member. He teaches and lectures throughout the United States, Canada, Europe, Israel, and is considered by many to be the founder of integrated expressive arts therapy, having founded the first graduate program in this area and then supported the development of other programs throughout the world.

Deidre McCalla is an award-winning singer-songwriter, modern-day troubadour and preeminent performer in both folk and women's music circles, having performed with notables such as Tracy Chapman, Suzanne Vega, Odetta, Cris Williamson, and Sweet Honey In the Rock. An African-American lesbian feminist with five albums to her credit, Deidre's words and music traverse the inner and outer landscapes of our lives, chronicling our strengths and weaknesses and celebrating the power and diversity of the human spirit. www.deidremccalla.com

Caryn Mirriam-Goldberg, Ph.D. is founder and coordinator of the Transformative Language Arts concentration at Goddard College where she teaches. She is author of six books, including three volumes of poetry – *Animals in the House, Reading the Body* and *Lot's Wife* – and the award-winning *Write Where You Are*. She facilitates writing workshops for many populations, including the cancer community, women in low-income housing, and adults in transitions. She also co-writes songs with rhythm and blues singer-songwriter Kelley Hunt, with whom she co-facilitates Brave Voice writing and singing workshops and retreats. www.writewhereyou are.org, www.bravevoice.com, and www.goddard.edu

Nancy Morgan has a Masters in Transformative Language Arts, and is the Director of the Arts and Humanities Program at the Lombardi Comprehensive Cancer Center at Georgetown University Hospital in Washington, D.C. She is the writing clinician for weekly expressive writing sessions for patients and caregivers at Lombardi.

Caren Schnur Neile, **MFA, Ph.D**. is founding director of the South Florida Storytelling Project in the School of Communication and Multimedia Studies at Florida Atlantic University. Dr. Neile is founding managing editor of *Storytelling, Self, Society: An Interdisciplinary Journal of Storytelling Studies* and a recipient of an Oracle Award from the National Storytelling Network for leadership and service. A frequent contributor to books and magazines, she is also a Fulbright Senior Specialist and teaches and performs throughout the country and abroad.

Rebecca Noblit Goodall is a writer and facilitator of Transformative Language Arts, primarily for children and teens. She is currently completing her master's degree in Transformative Language Arts at Goddard College.

Rhonda Patzia, MA-TLA facilitates Transformative Language Arts workshops, primarily for women with multiple sclerosis. A writer and professional photographer, her work has appeared in publications such as *The Sun*, and she has had numerous gallery shows. She received her MA in TLA with a focus in Embodiment Studies from Goddard College.

Nina Ricker, MA-TLA is a freelance writer and artist living in Vermont. Her reviews and essays have been published in regional and national publications. She is currently developing illustrated writing workshops for kids with autism spectrum disorders.

Pamela Roberts is a writer, artist and healer who leads writing workshops for people touched by cancer, loss or addiction. Pam found writing to be an important part of her healing process when she was diagnosed with breast cancer in 1993. Her course of recovery led her to end her 20-year career as partner in a television production company and become an ordained graduate of the IM School of Healing Arts, NYC. She has two children and lives in western Massachusetts.

Gail Rosen is a consultant, educator, storyteller, writer, bereavement facilitator and hospice volunteer. Her work serves people in grief support groups and retreats, staff and volunteer trainings, memorial services, and workshops. She has presented at conferences including the Association for Death Education and Counseling, Compassionate Friends, the National Conference on Loss and Transition, and the World Bereavement Conference. Her story tapes include *Listening After the Music Stops: Stories of Loss and Comfort* and *Darkness and Dawn: One Woman's Mythology of Loss and Healing*. With Kathy McGregor, she presents "Healing the Healer," a burnout prevention workshop for hospice staff. Gail founded the Healing Story Alliance (www.healingstory.org), a Special Interest Group of the National Storytelling Network. www.gailrosen.com and www.hildastory.com

Nancy G. Shapiro is presently in the Health Arts and Sciences B.A. program at Goddard, and the NAPT training program for certification as a poetry therapist. She has published articles on wellness and the arts in several international magazines. Fascinated by the mysteries of the poetic world, she continues to use poetry and prose as guides toward insight and innovation.

Pat Schneider is the founder/Director Emeritus of Amherst Writers and Artists, a poet and author of nine books including *Writing Alone & With Others* (Oxford University Press), *Wake Up Laughing: A Spiritual Autobiography*, and five volumes of poems. Pat Schneider's libretti have been performed and recorded at Tanglewood and in Carnegie Hall by Robert Shaw & the Atlanta Symphony. Her work has been featured on NPR, on National Public Television, and four times on Garrison Keillor's "Writers Almanac." Pat is an adjunct faculty member of the Graduate Theological Union in Berkeley, California. Her new book is *Another River: New and Selected Poems* (Amherst Writers & Artists Press). www.patschneider.com

Jim Sparrell, Ph.D. has a doctorate in Clinical/Community Psychology from the State University of New York at Buffalo. He sees his work in clinical psychology as helping people to tell their stories, and to tell them in new ways, with new metaphors, new words, and sometimes new characters. He completed an internship at McLean Hospital/Harvard Medical School, worked in an inner city community mental health center in East Boston, and currently works with children and their families at a local school district and is in private practice. As a former contributing editor of *Mars Hill Review*, he has written and edited personal essays and critical reviews of music, literature, religion, and contemporary culture.

Janet Tallman, Ph.D., M.L.I.S. is director of the BA Completion Program at Antioch University in Seattle, WA. She previously taught at several alternative education institutions, including John F. Kennedy University, New College of California, and Hampshire College. Her publications and presentations include dozens of articles on adult learning, ethnographic novels, language and consciousness, ethnolinguistics, right livelihood, conversational styles, children's literature, feminism, and anthropology at home. She's done anthropological fieldwork in North America, Japan, and Yugoslavia. Her current interest is in the relationship between the writer and the anthropologist.

Katherine Towler, MA is author of the novels *Snow Island* and *Evening Ferry.* She teaches in the low residency MFA program in writing at Southern New Hampshire University and has received fellowships from the NH State Council on the Arts, Phillips Exeter Academy, and the Bread Loaf Writers Conference. www.katherinetowler.com

Shelley Vermilya, Ed.D. serves on the faculty of Goddard College and the University of Vermont, bringing progressive and traditional pedagogy into emancipatory praxis. She insists on passionate and persistent inquiry regarding power, race, class, ableism, gender, sexual identity and culture, and her writing has focused on identity development and pedagogy in these contexts. She is constantly curiosity to understand the complexities of prejudice and oppression, and resistance to liberation from these things. This curiosity informs and is informed by her two children, her lover and her gardens. www.goddard.edu

Anna Viadero is a writer who has been teaching memoir writing to seniors since 1998. She collects their stories and publishes a yearly collection called *Local Color* every June. Haley's Publishing published *Local Color: The First Five Years* which is available on amazon.com or at www.localcolormemoirs.com. www.annaviadero writes.com

Scott Youmans, MA-TLA facilitates writing workshops for men at festivals, conferences, treatment centers and hospitals as well as workshops for adults on myth and writing. A website designer and business man, Youmans also consults with TLA facilitators designing websites and other projects.

EDITORS

• • •

Caryn Mirriam-Goldberg, Ph.D. is founder and coordinator of the Transformative Language Arts concentration at Goddard College where she teaches. She is author of six books, including three volumes of poetry – *Animals in the House, Reading the Body* and *Lot's Wife* – and the award-winning *Write Where You Are.* She facilitates writing workshops for many populations, including the cancer community, women in low-income housing, and adults in transitions. She also co-writes songs with rhythm and blues singer-songwriter Kelley Hunt, with whom she co-facilitates Brave Voice writing and singing workshops and retreats. www.bravevoice.com, www.writewhereyouare.org, and www.goddard.edu

Janet Tallman, Ph.D., M.L.I.S. is director of the BA Completion Program at Antioch University in Seattle, WA. She previously taught at several alternative education institutions, including John F. Kennedy University, New College of California, and Hampshire College. Her publications and presentations include dozens of articles on adult learning, ethnographic novels, language and consciousness, ethnolinguistics, right livelihood, conversational styles, children's literature, feminism, and anthropology at home. She's done anthropological fieldwork in North America, Japan, and Yugoslavia. Her current interest is in the relationship between the writer and the anthropologist.

···

TLA RESOURCES

···

TRANSFORMATIVE LANGUAGE ARTS RESOURCES

• • •

TRANSFORMATIVE LANGUAGE ARTS NETWORK

The TLAN is a professional organization dedicated to networking, resource-sharing, and Right Livelihood through TLA. TLAN is governed by a council, and is currently in the process of incorporating as a not-for-profit organization that will provide networking, Right Livelihood, and other supports for transformative language artists and their communities. TLAN is also developing a comprehensive web-based resource center with resources on networking, Right Livelihood, TLA and diversity, outreach and marketing, the art of self-care for transformative language artists, grant-writing and fund-raising, ethics, and facilitation, coaching and consulting. Additionally, TLAN has just started a press with this publication as its inaugural book, and TLAN members are involved in growing TLA in the world through a variety of initiatives. Join TLAN and the TLA listsesrv at our website. www.tlanetwork.org

TRANSFORMATIVE LANGUAGE ARTS RESOURCES PAGE

This expansive collection of weblinks and bibliographies is sponsored by Goddard College's Transformative Langauge Arts concentration, and offers extensive information on Creative and Expressive Writing; Drama and Drama Therapy; Education and Development; Facilitation, Leadership & Community Building; Journal-Writing; Literacy, Linguistics and Language; Memoir, Life Stories and Autobiography; Mythology; Oral History; Organizations and Networks; Poetry Therapy and Bibliotherapy; Psychology, Expressive Arts, and Narrative Therapy; Right Livelihood; Social Transformation; Spoken Word; Storytelling. If you have additional resources to add, please send an email to TLAconference@godd ard.edu. The website can be accessed through www.goddard.edu/ academic/TLA.html or at web.goddard.edu/~tla.

THE POWER OF WORDS CONFERENCE

This annual conference, sponsored by Goddard College and the TLA Network, is focused on developing and expanding the reach of TLA in the world. Held each fall, the conference features keynote performers and workshop presenters who represent a wide variety of TLA genres including: memoir, poetry, storytelling, spoken word performance, singing-songwriting, fiction, expressive arts, and also ways to further develop and understand the mythological, historical, anthropological, and cultural aspects and implications of TLA. The conference also features specific sessions devoted to right livelihood through TLA. Partial scholarships are available, including scholarships for people of color through the Roxanne-Florence fund. For more information on the conference, please see www.goddard.edu.

TRANSFORMATIVE LANGUAGE ARTS CONCENTRATION AT GODDARD COLLEGE

This master's level concentration, part of Goddard College's Individualized MA program, is a 48-hour (four-semester) degree that features self-designed, low-residency study in social and personal transformation through the spoken, written and/or sung word. All students have five Concentration requirements to fulfill for the TLA concentration: 1) Ongoing Reflection & Integration; 2) Individual TLA Practice Development; 3) Theoretical Groundwork Exploration; 4) A Community Practicum; and 5) A Final Product/ Thesis. Core values of the Transformative Language Arts Concentration encourage students to explore empowerment and change as both individual and communal processes, and to foster greater perspective on their place in the world as transformative language artists and community facilitators, coaches and/or consultants. www.goddard.edu

CPSIA information can be obtained
at www.ICGtesting.com
Printed in the USA
BVHW030030200721
612093BV00001B/5